AMERICAN FOLKTALES

down." Jane Muncy Fugate's favorite family tale belongs to a vast and varied narrative family that also includes the enormously popular storybook tales "Hansel and Gretel" (AT 327A) and "Petit Poucet" (AT 327B). In all of these tales, children strike out on their own through the woods and come to the house of a cannibalistic witch or ogre. But "Merrywise" generally resembles versions of "Petit Poucet" more closely than versions of "Hansel and Gretel." For instance, unlike "Hansel and Gretel," "Merrywise" and "Petit Poucet" both contain the episode of the substituted nightcaps, through which the tiny hero and his brothers escape the villain by deceiving him into killing his own children.

Stith Thompson reports that "Hansel and Gretel" is far more popular than "Petit Poucet" in Europe, but U.S. versions of AT 327 and the closely related AT 328 tend to contain the episode of the substituted caps (see, for example, Lee Wallins's telling of "Little Nippy," story 191 in this collection). Indeed, the motif of the substituted caps is so popular in the United States that it sometimes appears—as in Randolph's Ozark's version (1958: 116–17; AT 1119, *The Ogre Kills His Own Children*)—as an independent tale. For another version of the substituted caps episode (attached to another tale type), see story 181 in this book.

After Merrywise and his brothers escape the witch's house, the tale follows a pattern not often found in U.S. versions of AT 327 and 328. As the witch pursues in her seven-mile-a-step boots, the children throw down small objects that become giant obstacles that temporarily restrain the pursuer. This "Magic Flight" motif often appears as an episode in American versions of another tale type, AT 313, *The Girl as Helper in the Hero's Flight*. Similarly, the closing episode, in which the villain lures the children into his bag and chases the hero up and down the tree, is quite rare in the United States. The only other American version of the tree-and-sack scene that I have found appears in the Cajun tale "Catafo" (Claudel 1943; Jimmy Neil Smith 1993: 53–56).

This is one of three Jane Muncy tales in which the hero is named "Merrywise"; the other two are stories 79 and 80 in this book. I have been unable to identify any other American or international tale in which the hero bears this name.

78. *One-My-Darling* [AFC 2003/001]. AT 123, *The Wolf and the Kids*. George Shannon (1992) presents thirty-five worldwide variants of this plot, demonstrating that the tale of a group of kids left alone at home who mistake the voice of a murderous beast for their mother's is well known throughout the world. Yet the great majority of versions are animal tales in which the young victims are baby goats (as in the Grimms' version [1987: no. 5] and story 183 in this volume, told by Caroline Ancelet) or some other vegetarian animal, for example an antelope (Dorson 1975: 400–404). One of the rare U.S. versions in with human victims is a Louisiana tale in which an alligator is the villain (Lindahl, Owens, and Harvison 1997: no. 56). The flesh-eating villain tends to be a wolf, although in a few cases, as in Jane Muncy Fugate's tale and the Dorson text just cited, he appears as a supernatural being. Baughman could find no U.S. versions, and Halpert and Widdowson include none in their massive Newfoundland collection, but I have collected two in Louisiana (Lindahl, Owens, and Harvison 1997: no. 56; and story number 183 in this volume). Although he has not published a text, folklorist John Shaw reports the tale in the Scottish Gaelic-language tradition of Nova Scotia, where it is often told to children as an informal exercise to help them remember stories. AT 123 has obviously thrived in North American oral tradition despite folklorists' neglect.

Yet "One-My-Darling" is distinctly different from the other North American versions that I have found. In the great majority of tellings, the eaten children are finally rescued alive from the ogre's belly, but in Jane Muncy Fugate's the villain succeeds in killing the children, and the mother goes mad and wanders through the world. The only other version of this plot that I have been able to locate is from Haiti (Wolkstein 1978: 166–70). Other, less-related texts were collected in the Caribbean by Herskovits and Herskovits (1936) and Parsons (1933); Parsons's text is reprinted and the Herskovits's summarized in Shannon (1992). See also motif G412, "Ogre disguises voice to lure victim."

79. *Old Greasybeard* [AFC 2003/001]. AT 301A, *Quest for a Vanished Princess.* Jane first recorded this tale for Leonard Roberts in 1955, and her performance was published fourteen years later as the title tale of Roberts's second major collection (1969: no.11). The version in this book, the first that Jane had recorded in forty-six years, took place less than two months after the September 11 (2001) terrorist attacks on the United States. Jane nuanced this later version to make the villain resemble Osama bin Laden, the assumed mastermind of the attacks.

Quest for a Vanished Princess is one of the most popular märchen in the United States. Among the four versions of the tale type found in this book (the others are stories 21, 42, and 43), three, including Jane's, make special note of the villain's beard: Maud Long's Fire Dragaman has a "big long blue beard . . . dragging the ground," and the title character of Sara Cleveland's "Old Graybeard" is a "little old man with a gray beard" who, like Jane's Greasybeard, gives his name to the tale. Like Jane's, other Appalachian versions of the story—notably Don Saylors's "Dirtybeard" (Leonard Roberts 1955: no. 2) and Jim Couch's "Little Black Hunchety-Hunch" (Roberts 1974: no. 104)—associate the hero with dirt, grease, or filth.

80. *The King's Well* [AFC 2003/001]. AT 577, *The King's Tasks*; AT 1050, *Felling Trees*; AT 1052, *Deceptive Contest in Carrying a Tree—Riding*; AT 1088, *Eating Contest*; AT 1115, *Attempted Murder with a Hatchet.* Jane first performed a version of this tale for folklorist Leonard Roberts in 1955 (Roberts 1969: no. 25); the tale transcribed in the present volume was Jane's second recorded version, performed forty-six years after her first. The opening section, in which Merrywise solves the king's tasks after his brothers fail, is little known in the United States. Baughman lists only one version, also collected by Roberts in eastern Kentucky (1955: no. 24); the closest published North American text is a fragmentary telling from Nova Scotia (Fauset 1931: no. 9; see also two texts published by Fauset under no. 18). Leonard Roberts found the tale so rare that he concluded that it derived from print rather than from oral tradition (1969: 194). Yet the story's second half, in which the hero repeatedly deceives the giant, possesses many close relatives in American oral tradition. For example, the episode of the hero's riding the tree pulled by the giant is found in New World locales as diverse as Kentucky (Roberts 1955: no. 62b) and Newfoundland (Halpert and Widdowson 1996: no. 114), and the giant's foiled attempt to kill Merrywise with a club possesses close parallels in North Carolina (Chase 1943: no. 1), Kentucky (Roberts 1974: no. 140), and Arkansas (Randolph 1955: 53–55). As with most of the American tales involving a boy's wit overcoming a giant's brawn, the largest number of oral versions have been found in the Appalachians, and their closest foreign parallels come from England, Scotland, and Ireland.

81. *Rawhead and Bloodybones* [AFC 2003/001]. AT 403, *The Black and the White Bride*; AT 480, *The Kind and Unkind Girls.* Folklorists have varied in their designation for tales following the plot of "Rawhead and Bloodybones": Baughman, for example, types this tale AT 403, yet he classifies a nearly identically plotted English tale as AT 480; in the following discussion, I will use 480. H1321.2, "Quest for Healing Water"; H1321.1.1*, "Quest for well at world's end"; D1381, "Child divides last loaf with fairy (dwarf)"; E341.4*, "Heads of the well grateful for bath"; D1454.1.1, "Gold and silver combed from hair." This is one of the most popular international tales, known in thousands of versions (see Roberts 1958). Jane first recorded this tale at age 11 (see Roberts 1955: no. 13). Leonard Roberts, who collected the tale from Jane, remarks that he heard another, nearly identical version of the tale in Jane's home county, and he expressed his belief that the two tales possessed a common source (1955: 223). I have collected two Leslie County versions of the tale, one (reproduced here) from Jane and one from Jane's aunt Glen

AMERICAN FOLKTALES

FROM THE COLLECTIONS OF THE LIBRARY OF CONGRESS

FOREWORD BY
PEGGY A. BULGER

EDITED BY
CARL LINDAHL

BASED ON THE COLLECTIONS
OF THE AMERICAN FOLKLIFE CENTER

M.E.Sharpe, Armonk, New York; London, England
IN ASSOCIATION WITH THE LIBRARY OF CONGRESS, WASHINGTON, D.C.

In memory of
Annie H. Lindahl (1890–1976), Lorene Rucker Wright (1894–1987),
Robert Josua Lindahl (1914–1994), Constance Wright Lindahl (1917–2001),
Agnes Vena Miller (1918–1998), and Vories Moreau (1925–2001)
My favorite storytellers

Grateful acknowledgment is made to the following for permission to reprint previously
published material: Estate of Lloyd Chandler, "Conversation with Death," by Lloyd Chandler.
Copyright © 2003 by Estate of Lloyd Chandler, Garrett Chandler, Administrator. All rights reserved.
International copyright secured. Reprinted by permission of Estate of Lloyd Chandler.

Library of Congress Cataloging-in-Publication Data

American folktales : from the collections of the Library of Congress / Carl Lindahl, editor.
    p. cm.
  Includes indexes.
  ISBN 0-7656-8062-9 (set: alk. paper)
    1. Tales—United States. 2. Storytellers—United States. 3. American Folklife Center. I. Title:
American folk tales : from the collections of the Library of Congress. II. Lindahl, Carl, 1947–

GR105.5A44 2003
398.2′0973—dc21

                                                                                    2003041557

Printed in the United States of America

The paper used in this publication meets the minimum requirements of
American National Standard for Information Sciences
Permanence of Paper for Printed Library Materials,
ANSI Z 39.48-1984.

∞

BM (c)   10   9   8   7   6   5   4   3   2   1

CONTENTS

VOLUME 1

3. J.D. SUGGS: ITINERANT MASTER   183

4. JOSHUA ALLEY: DOWN-EAST TALES FROM JONESPORT, MAINE   219

8. LEGENDARY AMERICA

9. TALL TALE AMERICA

11. PASSING IT ON: STORIES FOR CHILDREN

12. VOICING THE PAST: TALES TRACING THE PATHS OF AMERICAN HISTORY

Native American Visions

FOREWORD

The American Folklife Center's Archive of Folk Culture traces its origin to 1928, when the Archive of American Folk Song was established in the Music Division of the Library of Congress. For over seventy-five years our great national library has sought actively to gather in, preserve, and share with the American people the traditional songs and stories from our nation's diverse cultural communities and from around the world. Since its creation in 1976, the American Folklife Center has continued this important work as an essential part of its mission "to preserve and present American folklife."

The collections of traditional poetry and music in the Archive of Folk Culture are legendary, their reputation enlarged and spread in part by the series of long-playing recordings, published by the Library of Congress in the 1940s and 1950s, called "Folk Music of the United States." Many of the songs that became popular during the folk music revival of the 1960s were available to researchers, folk revival performers, and folk music aficionados because of these albums and because of the work done by folklorists and ethnomusicologists throughout the twentieth century seeking out and recording songs and stories that now reside in the Library of Congress.

Over the years the Folk Archive has broadened its purview to embrace a wide range of cultural traditions: occupational and regional culture; folk art and craftsmanship; and storytelling and oral history. Today, the archive houses over 3 million items, in the form of sound recordings, photographs, film and video, manuscript materials, and ephemera that document our cultural heritage and folklife. Thousands of people visit the American Folklife Center each year, or call or write, with questions about traditional cultural life and requests to use archive materials. With the recent addition to the collections of documentation from the International Storytelling Foundation; the September 11 Project;

the Veterans History Project; and StoryCorps, the archive is now as rich in the area of storytelling and oral history as it is in traditional music.

In light of this development, Carl Lindahl's book *American Folktales from the Library of Congress* is particularly welcome as a major contemporary publication that draws upon the spoken word traditions found in the Archive of Folk Culture. Here you will find Jack tales as told by traditional storyteller Ray Hicks; stories from the South as collected by John and Alan Lomax; as well as tall tales, jokes, children's stories, and personal experience narratives from contemporary American life.

In 1941, the Librarian of Congress, Archibald MacLeish, wrote that American folksong "tells us more about the American people than all the miles of their quadruple-lane express highways and all the acres of their bill-board plastered cities." MacLeish was a great advocate for using Library of Congress collections to educate the American people about their historical and cultural traditions. The Archive of Folk Culture's priceless documentation of our infinitely various heritage and the traditions of our many regional, ethnic, and occupational communities are contributing to this effort. Like the Library's folk music albums and other programs and publications of the last century, *American Folktales* helps to make our heritage of storytelling and oral history widely known and accessible to all, both for the present and for future generations.

Peggy A. Bulger
Director, American Folklife Center

ACKNOWLEDGMENTS

In Washington, D.C., too many titles are prefaced with "The People's": The White House and the Capitol are both "The People's House," though too many of their corners and workings are off limits to all but the most powerful. Yet, if any of our national institutions merits the title, "The People's Library," it is the American Folklife Center (AFC) at the Library of Congress, which strives both to serve and to preserve the traditional arts and skills of all the nation's people, no matter how otherwise underprivileged and underrepresented they might be.

In the early years of the twentieth century, the leadership of the Library of Congress sought to shape the institution into "a university of the people with the staff as its faculty" (G.B. Anderson 1989: 120). My experience at the American Folklife Center leads me to believe that this high ideal has been attained. Any person seeking information on the nation's folk culture is welcome to communicate, by phone or e-mail, with the American Folklife Center, or to obtain a research pass and visit in person to receive the serious and impartial attention of the Center's highly professional staff. Visitors come to the American Folklife Center to hear and research the voices of everyday people. The vast collections curated by the Center are thus also, powerfully and tellingly, *of* the people.

Over the past six and one half years, I have visited the American Folklife Center at every available opportunity in order to listen to, research, and transcribe the tales that appear in this book. During my visits, hundreds of other visitors also appeared to satisfy their curiosity and research needs. We were all well served. With a staff disproportionately small for the scope and importance of its responsibilities, the Center is always in need of more time, space, and positions than funding allots it. But the sheer weight and number of their obligations never compromised the generosity of the AFC specialists or the quality of the work they devoted to my research.

Alan Jabbour, former Director of the American Folklife Center, lent his support and enthusiasm as the project was conceived; the germ idea of creating this book was as much his as mine. He worked closely with Library of Congress legal counsels in drawing up the initial publishing contract for the book and offered my research continual encouragement. Peggy A. Bulger, who became AFC Director in 1999, generously supported this work in innumerable ways, notably by securing me work space in a crowded environment and by making it possible for me to duplicate otherwise inaccessible recordings for transcription. She has also shown extraordinary patience as the work dragged on past its first deadline.

The staff of the American Folklife Center kept its doors open for me as often and as long as they legally could, allowing me to spend as long as 8½ hours a day glued to headphones, playing and replaying masterful words captured by the primitive equipment of the 1930s and 1940s as well as by current state-of-the-art technologies. Public Events Coordinator Thea Austen duplicated numerous tapes to aid my research and leant her expertise to interpreting the materials collected by Benjamin Botkin. Administrative Assistant Doris Craig made time for even my most unreasonable spur-of-the-moment requests. Folklife Specialist Jennifer Cutting shepherded me through my research as a Parsons Fellow, tracked down photo permissions, and provided help in innumerable other ways. Judith Gray, Coordinator of Reference, duplicated essential recordings and shortened my work by hundreds of hours with advice on the various strengths and weaknesses of, and restrictions upon, the specific recordings that I sought. Robin Fanslow good-humoredly assisted me in audio and computer matters. Stephanie Hall offered technological advice, and her knowledge of the American Dialect Society collection, which she accessioned, led me to many of the finest stories in this book. Publications Specialist James Hardin provided crucial advice and expertise on publishing issues. Folklife Specialist Todd Harvey guided me through the intricacies of the massive International Storytelling Collection, which he has catalogued. Joseph Hickerson, former Head of the Archive of Folk Culture, who, though retired, continues to donate enormous time and energy to the Center, gave me tips and advice unavailable in any book, but secure in his memory, which constitutes a library in itself. Folklife Specialist Ann Hoog made available copious time, space, and equipment for my endless questions and research requests, and she guided me to the narratives from the September 11 Project (which she directs) that appear in this book. Rachel Howard offered invaluable information on the narratives collected by Zora Neale Hurston, and on the Florida Folklife Online Project, which she helped develop. Folklife Specialist Catherine Kerst provided me with lexical advice, sample permissions forms, and a good deal of other help. Folklife Specialist David Taylor supplied me with information on some of the AFC's more recent collections, and Processing Archivist Nora Yeh provided invaluable technical and reference help.

There are many others to thank. My initial visits to the American Folklife Center were made possible through a resident fellowship from the Virginia Foundation for the Humanities (spring 1997) for the purpose of studying Appalachian folk narrative. Further funding was provided by an award by the Gerald E. Parsons Fund for Ethnography (1998), administered through the AFC, for which Jennifer Cutting graciously served as my sponsor. Chairs Wyman Herendeen and John McNamara of the English Department of the University of Houston furnished at least as much support as the department could afford; Department Business Administrator Lynn Dale and Office Supervisor Andrea Short made sure that I obtained those resources; the generosity and vision of these four continually buoyed my morale. Former Dean W. Andrew Achenbaum of the University of Houston's College of Liberal Arts and Social Sciences secured funds purchase two transcribing machines to facilitate transcription. A University of Houston Research Development leave for the spring of 2002 allowed me to complete the manuscript. The University of Houston's University Scholars programs made it possible for students Sam Castello, Jean Norris, Able Windham, and Jennifer Williams to assist in the logging and transcription of research tapes. Folklore students Eleanor Dahlin, Melody Kelderhouse, Jenna Terry, and Stephen Tsui provided back-up transcriptions of the tales. Publishing agent Todd Hallman secured funds to allow folklore student Able Windham to accompany me to the American Folklife Center to research and duplicate essential recordings.

Martha Ellen Davis transcribed and translated the three Spanish-language folktales that appear in the book. Professor Barry Jean Ancelet of the University of Louisiana corrected my transcription of Cajun French. Professor Andrea Tinnemeyer of Utah State University offered early help with translation. Folklorists Tina Bucuvalas, Bill Ferris, Jim Leary, Stetson Kennedy, Chuck Perdue, and Nancy-Jean Siegel offered me advice, leads, and transcriptions to further this work. Jimmy Neil Smith, director of the International Storytelling Center, generously allowed me access to the International Storytelling Collection now on deposit at the American Folklife Center. Folklore professors Jim Leary and Joan Radner read the manuscript meticulously and offered inspired suggestions for its improvement, all of which I have tried to apply.

Family and special friends sustained me through difficult research times and through overlapping, and immeasurably more difficult, family crises. Barry and

Caroline et la famille Ancelet, Jimmy Bernard, Bessie Brown, Garrett and Bobbi and Dot Chandler, Cece Conway, Dana David, Dana Everts-Boehm, Jane and Bob Fugate, the late Judith Gilbert, Diane Goldstein, Leo Hackl, Elissa Henken, Mary Howell, Kris and Joel Klass, Sunni Lindahl, Anya Litovkina, Margaret Mackay, Sorrel and Mike and the McCarthy family, John and Cynthia McNamara, Joyce Moreau, Kim Moreau, Helena Putnam, Tony Santamaria, Jeannie Thomas, Veronika Toth, John Wahlund, and Carolyn Ware were always there, as they always will be, even if through most of this long journey I've been too far from all of them.

For my most immediate thanks, I return to the incorporeal voices and the ever-tangible staff that inhabit the American Folklife Center. There was something haunting about spending stretches of hours listening to dead people, many of whose voices have been stilled for decades in every other earthly form, but who still speak powerfully on disk, tape, and compact disk. The liveliness of their voices, trapped in the blurring grit of old-time technology, made their stories often seem to issue not only from the dead, but also from the land of the dead. The staff worked so efficiently at finding the recorded voices and at leaving me be, that every day in the reading room, I spent much more time listening to the tales of the departed than to the words of my living colleagues. In many respects, this book belongs as much the AFC's staff as it does to me; I hope they will not be disappointed.

But the greatest measure of my gratitude goes to the storytellers—the too many who are gone and the too few whom I have actually known—and to the family members of the departed storytellers who helped me bring their living words to this book.

I am honored by the graciousness of the living storytellers who have shared their arts with me and permitted me to share them with you: Barry Jean and Mary Caroline Spurlock Ancelet, Debra Anderson, Glen Muncy Anderson, Garrett Chandler, Daron Douglas, Janet Freeman, Jane Muncy Fugate, Lillie Haws, Doc McConnell, Joan Moser, and Lee Winniford.

The family members of departed storytellers have graced this book by allowing the voices of their kin to speak here, and often also by sharing with me their memories of these remarkable narrators: Phyllis Cleveland and Angela Folmer (daughter-in-law and great-granddaughter of Sara Cleveland), S. Ruth Ellen Doane (daughter of Lillian Doane), Walter Fithian (nephew of Newton Downey), Roy L. Hammons Sr. (nephew of Burl Hammons and Maggie Hammons Parker), Nora Guthrie (daughter of Woody Guthrie), Rosa Hicks (wife of Ray Hicks), Mary Holecheck and Ethel Smith (daughters of Quincy Higgins),

Lee F. Jackson (son of John and Cora Jackson), Jane Long Douglas (daughter of Maud Long), Jo Lunsford Herron (daughter of Bascom Lamar Lunsford), Kim Moreau (son of Vories Moreau), Leozie S. Broadnax (granddaughter of E.L. and Leozie Smith), Martha Ann Suggs Spenser and Toka Suggs Saunders (daughters of J.D. Suggs), and Bertha Wallin McDevitt (daughter of Lee Wallin).

Finally, to all those eloquent speakers, living and dead, whom I've know only through your disembodied voices: I listened to you so long that I feel I've gotten to know you some, if never quite enough: Perry Allen, Vernon Allen, Joshua Alley, Evelia Andux, Ziomara Andux, Ernest Arnold, Mary Eva Baker, Michael Bruick, Tillman Cadle, Arthur L. Campa, Charles Carter, W.D. Casey, Margaret Chase, Sara Cleveland, Levette Jay Davidson, John Davis, Lula Davis, Lillian Doane, J. Frank Dobie, Newton Downey, Uncle Alec Dunford, Janet Freeman, Dr. and Mrs. Norman Freestone, Dominick Gallagher, Will Gilchrist, Archer Gilfillan, Joseph Graham, George Griffith, Woody Guthrie, Burl Hammons, Laurie Hance, Alberta Harmon, Samuel Harmon, Lillie Hawes, Buna Hicks, Ray Hicks, Roby Hicks, Quincy Higgins, Sam Hill, Son House, James L. Huskey, Cora Jackson, John Jackson, Aunt Molly Jackson, "Buck Asa" Jefferson, Gaines Kilgore, Annie Agnes Kingston, L.A. Ledford, Hector Lee, Maud Long, "Lucky Jake," Bascom Lamar Lunsford, Frank Mahaffey, Sloan Matthews, Bill McBride, Doc McConnell, Joan Moser, Martin Noriega, Father Sarsfield O'Sullivan, Ellis Ogle, M.C. Orr, Maggie Hammons Parker, Mary Celestia Parler, John Persons, Jerry Philips, "Clear Rock" Platt, Wilbur Roberts, Flora Robertson, Bill Robinson, Amooneta Sequoia, Laura Smalley, E.L. Smith, Leozie Smith, J.D. Suggs, Margaret Sullivan, Jake Sutton, Roy Turner, Lee Wallin, Lee Webb, Eartha M.M. White, George Young, and Paul E. Young. I live with every word you shared with me.

INTRODUCTION

Perhaps the most important mission of the Library of Congress is to cultivate and sustain an American Memory. Numerous Library offices devote themselves to chronicling the public lives and acts of the official leaders of this country, the presidents, senators, Supreme Court justices, as well as the major legal and institutional developments that we have come to regard as the highlights of our history. For all the importance of these institutional memories, the Library of Congress is made inestimably richer by the enormous collection of sound recordings housed in American Folklife Center (AFC), which was established in 1976 to "preserve and present" the songs, tunes, and tales, the sung and spoken treasures of our unofficial culture. It is not too great an exaggeration to state that the American Folklife Center and its historic Archive of Folk Culture constitute, in effect, the most important repository for the folkloric memory of the nation.

The tellers of most of the remarkable tales assembled here are long dead, but their voices still sound inside the walls of the American Folklife Center, where they have been kept alive on aluminum and acetate disks, reel-to-reel and cassette tapes, CDs, and other media. In the past, the only means of knowing these stories was to journey to Washington, obtain a Library of Congress research pass, and visit the AFC reading room, where, one by one, the separate reference tapes holding the individual tales would be secured, and the visitor would then replay each on the machines provided for that purpose by the American Folklife Center. Now, and finally, some seventy years after the earliest of the stories were recorded, many of them can now be shared, anytime, anywhere, with anyone who reads this book.

The history of the Archive of Folk Culture stretches back seventy-five years to 1928, when it was established under the name Archive of American Folk Song (AAFS). True to that name, the organization specialized in the collection and curation of American traditional music, primarily song, but with a substantial representation of instrumental folk music. In its remarkable history, the Folk Archive has captured and preserved some of the great creations of American traditional music, including the country blues of Leadbelly, the Dust Bowl ballads of Woody Guthrie, the coal miners' laments of Aunt Molly Jackson, and the driving banjo tunes of Samuel Harmon. As often as not, these great performers are remembered, and still heard even today, largely because the Folk Archive researchers recorded them. Once housed at the Library of Congress, the recordings became, in effect, the property of the American people.

Yet this priceless property, afforded a security proportionate to its worth, has been carefully guarded. Although many recordings were released commercially and others aired on radio programs and, more recently, on Library of Congress Web sites, most of the music has been confined within the walls of the Library, to be heard only by visiting researchers, and usually to be duplicated only in certain special cases, for scholarly purposes. Nevertheless, zealous musicians and music lovers have traveled thousands of miles to visit the Folklife Reading Room, listen to the tapes, and absorb masterpieces of traditional musical art that they would otherwise have had to search years to find, when indeed these folk creations could still be found on living lips. Largely through the efforts of the folklorists who ran and staffed the Folk Archive, Leadbelly's "Goodnight, Irene," Woody Guthrie's "This Land Is Your Land," Aunt Molly Jackson's "Ragged, Hungry Blues," and Samuel Harmon's "Wild Boar" have been heard by millions.

The importance and success of what are now the American Folklife Center's music collections are so well recognized that many forget, if indeed they ever knew, that the Center is also a great storehouse of folktales. Many of the same musicians whose songs were painstakingly preserved until "rediscovered" and transformed into national and international hits were also storytellers. Leadbelly, Woody Guthrie, Aunt Molly Jackson, and Samuel Harmon were just a few of the great musical artists who were also substantial storytellers, and the folklorists of the AAFS collected their tales in addition to their tunes. These unpublished works of oral art are arguably comparable in importance to the musical arts of their legendary creators.

The voices translated into writing in this book belong, for the most part, to some of the nation's most important and accomplished, yet least recognized individuals. Some of the greatest storytellers recorded here were poor and little known beyond the borders of their folk communities. When he was recorded at age 91, Joshua Alley was still working nine-hour days in a fish cannery in Jonesport, Maine, and he wasn't working simply because he needed the exercise. Recorded at age 69, Samuel Harmon was a displaced person, having been driven out of his home community of Cades Cove, Tennessee, when the federal government appropriated his family's home to create the Great Smoky Mountains National Park. Neither of these men may be said to have exerted even a minimal effect on the economy or the politics of this country, but both—with the help of the visionary fieldworkers who sought them out and recorded their voices— have vastly expanded not only the record of our national traditional artistry but also our cultural memory.

As they told their tales into the fieldworkers' microphones, these exceptional if little-known folk would, as often as not, share not only their stories but also stories *about* their stories: accounts of where they were when they first heard their tales, who told the tales, and why the tales were important to their families and their neighbors, as well as to them personally. Thus, the folktales presented here not only embed the values and cultures of the tellers but also serve as springboards for the tellers' memories of former times. The finest of these narrators provide not only great entertainment but also a substantial education in the lifestyles and values of the communities in which the tales were shared.

Joshua Alley's nonagenarian voice, recorded in 1934, carries his readers and listeners back to a wintry afternoon in the late 1840s, when he learned one of his first folktales.

When I was a little fellow, about so high, I lived down on the Head Harbor Island. . . . [A]nd there was an old fella come down there to buy some fish, of my father. I remember all these things. And he told the story, and it was a bitter cold day, and we sat outdoor. We walked down to the shore with him because he had paid his visit and bought the fish and was going to leave and said that he'd forgot to tell the old man, my father, this story before he left the house.

So we sat down on the bank where the wind raked right on to us. Oh, a bitter cold day. And he told the story. And father learned it, hearing him tell it. And I set there as quiet as could be and never said a word.

And when we got up to the house, my father says to me, "You didn't learn that story, did you?"

And I said, "I think I did."

"Well," he says, "Go ahead and tell it."

I told the story. Says he, "You got it all right."

Now, I was but a little fellow about so high, but I've always remembered it.

The story turned out to be very long: it ran to more than thirty-five minutes when Joshua Alley retold it in 1934. No wonder he remembered so vividly the circumstances in which he had learned it. Because the memory of how he first heard the tale seems to have been almost as important to Alley as the tale itself, his memories and evaluation of the tale are included in this book. This anthology contains, for the first time in print, Alley's full-blown description of how he came to learn this tale, his reflections on which parts of the tale are true and which false, and, of course, the tale itself ("The Bear's Tale," story 62 in this collection); to my knowledge, no other version of this elaborate and haunting story has ever been collected from any other storyteller.

For Joshua Alley, any good story is an act of both art and memory. From him we learn not only about the entertainments of his time but also about its daily life and local history. When Alley was a boy, coastal Maine was filled with all manner of dangers: hostilities between Europeans and Native Americans were still part of the cultural landscape, and wolves still roamed the seaside forests. So, in addition to such artful fictions as "The Bear's Tale," this book presents Alley's historical legends about the conflicts between the earliest settlers and the Indians ("Man Warren Beal and the Indians," "Wrestling the Chief," and "Chute's WedgeTrick," stories 63–65) and the ongoing struggle between his tiny settlement and the natural forces that threatened to overwhelm it ("Dodging the Wolves," story 66). Like most memories that have been shaped into story form, these tales may not be entirely factual accounts of the lives and times of his ancestors and older contemporaries, but there is no doubt that they carry a significant measure of social truth, reflecting as they do the values and lifestyles of the fishing and farming families of coastal Maine in the mid-nineteenth century.

Samuel Harmon is another of the little-known, yet very important curators and shapers of America's folkloric memory. A virtual pauper with only one year left to live when fieldworker Herbert Halpert visited him in the Great Smoky Mountains in the spring of 1939, Samuel Harmon nevertheless possessed great riches of art and memory. The exceptional nature of his ballad repertoire was already known among scholars in 1939, but none of the academics were yet aware that Samuel Harmon was also a master teller of tales. His stories hold a special place in American folklore history, for they are the earliest sound recordings of the famous Hicks-Harmon Jack Tales, a body of oral fiction immortalized in the retellings of Richard Chase and made even better known by the performances of America's most famous traditional narrator, Harmon's great-great-nephew, Ray Hicks. The Jack Tales of the Hicks-Harmon family constitute a special treasury of Appalachian narrative; when told by a master like Samuel Harmon or Ray Hicks, they are permeated with the natural and cultural landscape of the mountain families that nurtured and reshaped them over many generations.

From Sam Harmon, as from Joshua Alley, we learn of the intimate details of how these stories were passed on in the circumstances of daily life. Sam was the grandson of Samuel ("Little Sammy") Hicks II, and it was from "Granddaddy Hicks" that Harmon learned his folktales. Granddaddy Hicks died before Sam reached his teenage years. We also hear Sam, now a grandfather himself, describe how his own grandchildren, as hungry for his stories as he once was for his grandfather's, drive him to exhaustion by begging him to tell his tales over and over again:

> I stayed with my son and he had a house dug in the ground. And through the summertime, why, me and [his] kids would lay in that house down in the ground there—it's called a storm house. And they just weared the life out of me to tell em tales. And I told em tales and tales and tales and told em all I did know, and then I just had to go to making em up some and telling em to get shet of em, to get rid of em. "Why," they'd say, "Grandpa, *do* tell us another tale. Grandpa, do *please* tell us one more tale and we'll let you alone." Well, I'd get so sleepy that it appeared to me like I just couldn't keep my eyes open.

In the Harmon family, folktales tended to follow a grandparent-grandchild line of transmission, through which the oldest members of the household taught and entertained the youngest. Sam's tales were a big part of his childhood learning, and he in turn shaped them into a major teaching tool for his son's children.

Like Joshua Alley, Sam Harmon was a master of both local history and fictional narrative. He told such wildly imaginative Jack Tales as "The Marriage of the King's Daughter" (story 6), but also related, as in his account of "How I Bought and Stole My Wife" (story 1), some finely etched personal experience narratives depicting the daily life of his neighbors and the special moments of his youth.

Whether presented as true or false, as fact or as fiction, these tales, created by ordinary people in everyday situations, all combine extraordinary acts of memory with uncommon imagination. No matter how fanciful the tales that follow, each is true in certain ways. It is a true record of the teller's imagination, it is true to the teller's remarkable memory, and it truly expresses the philosophy,

Ray Hicks performing at the first National Storytelling Festival, 1973. The recorded performances of the National Storytelling Festival were acquired by the American Folklife Center in 2001. (International Storytelling Center)

esthetic, and value system of the teller and of the teller's community. It is my hope that this book will convey to its readers a strong measure of the social and artistic truths of the extraordinary speakers whose words are captured here.

THE PLAN OF THIS BOOK

This book, then, takes its shape from the conviction that even the best stories only grow better as we get to know their tellers. I hope that readers will agree with my assessment that each of the tales gathered here possesses sufficient entertainment, esthetic, or cultural value to stand by itself and be enjoyed for itself. Yet if I were to break up the repertoire of one gifted teller and distribute the stories into various thematic niches—tall tales, ghost stories, jokes—readers would be denied a deeper sense of the sources, uses, and power of that speaker's art.

Therefore, this anthology is organized to focus primarily on the tellers, rather than the genres, of the tales. The first thirty-two stories represent a sizeable chunk of the recorded repertoire of America's best-known family of traditional storytellers. Then follow fifty-three tales representing the art of five individuals. Wherever possible, I have added recorded autobiographical comments from the storytellers and provided information about the speakers and their lives that will, I hope, bring the reader closer both to the stories and to the storytellers.

The second half of the book is, indeed, broken mostly into generic and thematic units: legends, tall tales, jokes, children's stories, narratives concerning local and national history. But even in these sections, the tales are subcategorized by individual storytellers: whenever feasible, I've placed together two or more tales from the same teller and prefaced the sequence with a headnote providing information on the narrator, the collector, and the performances. Thus, the section on jokes contains five tales from Son House, four tales each from Arthur Campa and Cora Jackson; three each from Levette Jay Davidson and John Davis, and two each from Archer Gilfillan, Gaines Kilgore, and Joan Moser.

In choosing to emphasize the teller over the tale, I have no doubt sacrificed a certain measure of variety and diversity, but I have done so with the conviction that the reader will feel compensated by a fuller knowledge of the narrators resulting from exposure to not just one, but several of their stories.

Wherever feasible, I preface each cluster of two or more tales with the teller's own accounts of her or his experiences as a listener to and teller of stories. As a rule, the story or stories beginning each cluster are those that convey the most information about and atmosphere of the communities and environments in which the tellers learned their tales. Thus, by following the stories in the order presented, readers will experience something of the personal and social contexts from which the stories emerge, contexts that make their marks on even the most fanciful fictions, most of which are found toward the end of each section.

Despite its storyteller-centered approach, this book is also intended to serve as a useful, if partial, guide to *American* storytelling traditions and to represent insofar as possible the cultural wealth and diversity of the nation's narrative store. Readers will find here the arts of storytellers of African, Appalachian, Bahamian, Cajun, Cherokee, Cornish, Cuban, English, French, German, Irish, Mexican, Nisqually, Osage, Ozark, Scottish, and Welsh descent. Presented here are the occupational storytelling traditions of bar owners, barbers, convicts, cowboys, craftspeople, doctors, dog drivers, ex-slaves, factory workers, farmers, fishers, folklorists, innkeepers, linguists, lumberjacks, migrant workers, miners, ministers, minstrels, musicians, office workers, railroaders, sailors, social workers, sheep ranchers, singers, soldiers, and teachers. And the tales of this collection were learned, told, or set in some forty of the fifty United States as well as in the District of Columbia.

The comparative notes on the tales (pages 335–56 and 663–86) emphasize personal, community, regional, ethnic, and national dimensions of each story for which I have been able to find significant parallels, sources, and analogs. These notes guide readers to other published and archival versions of the tales found here and provide a sense of the popularity and distribution of each tale type within the United States. Thus, the notes for Maud Long's telling of "Jack and the Heifer Hide" (story 23) direct readers first to the other versions of the tale recorded and published from the tellings of Maud Long, and next to versions told by other members of her family and residents of her region. The notes further refer to tales told or collected by the other storytellers and folklorists represented in this book. For example, many folklorists think of the heifer hide story as peculiarly Appalachian, but the notes to this tale reveal that Zora Neale Hurston collected a well-told African American version from a 14-year-old boy in her hometown of Eatonville, Florida.

The notes go on to direct the reader to other published and archived American versions of the tales. I hope that they will be of service to readers interested in finding how particular individuals, communities, regions, and ethnicities shape similar, but significantly different stories from shared plots and themes.

This book is also a record, however slight, of the women and men who recorded the taletellers. Folklorists have long known the truth of the dictum, "It's not just your word, but who you give it *to*." Great storytellers always tailor their tales to suit the particular needs, expectations, and esthetics of their audiences. The more powerful the tellers' art, the greater their sensitivity to the storytelling environments. The collectors of these tales played major roles in shaping the performances; thus, we simply cannot know certain crucial aspects of the stories without knowing something of the folklorists who collected them. This is especially true for those performances collected before 1950 (the great majority in this book), when the technological constraints of sound recording were so great that they effect considerable alterations in the tellers' styles. The early collectors were working uphill against dauntingly artificial environments. In American storytelling traditions, tales are most typically told in intimacy, in relaxed settings, and as outgrowths of normal conversation. When a collector (often a personal stranger and a cultural outsider) enters a home in the company of a technician, lugging a 300-pound tape recorder onto the front porch or into the parlor, the normal storytelling context instantaneously vanishes. The technology demands that conversation stop and that the storyteller cut herself off from the others in the room and stand on cue to perform into a giant sound-trapping funnel. Not only the reciprocal quality but also the pace of the performances is affected. The early machines could capture no more than five minutes of speech before the disk was full and had to be discarded or replaced. This required a speaker to stop in the middle of a tale and wait for a minute or more to resume it. When Joshua Alley told "The Bear's Tale" (story 62), the longest narrative in this book, he was interrupted six times for record changes in the course of just one performance.

Two factors, above all, can help compensate for such an otherwise hostile storytelling environment: an absolutely composed and unflappable narrator, and a supportive and sensitive collector. The relationship established between the storyteller and the folklorist is essential for a strong performance. In many ways, this book as much about the relationships between storytellers and collectors as it is about stories. If it were not for the special, reciprocal bonds formed between Joshua Alley and Marguerite Chapallaz, Sara Cleveland and Kenneth Goldstein, Will Gilchrist and Sterling Brown, Sam Harmon and Herbert Halpert, Son House and Harry Oster, J.D. Suggs and Richard Dorson—these tales would not exist as we know them today, and many would no longer exist in any form at all. Even the troubled relationship between Aunt Molly Jackson and Alan Lomax was a special and fruitful one. To ignore the collectors would be to neglect an essential part of the performance.

Therefore, this anthology discusses the collectors' effects, wherever measurable, on the performances transcribed here. One of the book's sections is organized around two of the nation's most influential collectors: John A. and Alan Lomax. Sketches of many other collectors appear in the introductory discussions of the various narrators and tales, and an index of the collectors and the American Folklife Center's major narrative collections is found at the back of this book.

For readers interested in particular types of tales (ghost stories, for example, or jokes), I have provided an introductory discussion—"American Folktales: Their Stuff and Styles"—that addresses their interests and guides them to the stories they seek.

THE SCOPE OF THE AFC COLLECTIONS AND THE SCOPE OF THIS BOOK

As of 2002, the collections of the American Folklife Center comprised more than 75,000 hours of sound recordings, many, not yet fully accessioned or catalogued. Thousands of folk narratives of all varieties are embedded within these collections, but even with the help of the Center's exceptional staff, finding them is not always easy.

Even once found, some of the finest narratives in the archive were not available for presentation here. The AFC has substantial holdings from North America's oldest storytelling traditions: the myths, legends, historical accounts, and ceremonial tales of the Aleut, Cherokee, Haida, Hopi, Karuk, Lakota, Navajo, Nez Perce, Onondaga, Puyallup, Seneca, Seminole, Tlingit, Tuscarora, and Zuni cultures, to name a few of the groups that have contributed stories in their native languages. For example, twenty-two cylinders recorded in 1931 by Benjamin Paul and Delphine Ducloux contain many tales of the Chitimacha people (catalogued as AFS 18472 and 18473 in the AFC collections); thirteen wire spools recorded by Fred Lukoff in 1948 and 1950 feature Onondaga narratives (catalogued AFS 14345-57); these priceless tales are told, respectively, in Chitimacha and Onondaga. It was beyond my learning to translate them and beyond my budget to have them translated. Other stories (for example, the hundreds collected by Professor George Carey and his students in Maryland) were deposited with restrictions; they are available for listening but not for publication purposes.

The American Folklife Center has never claimed its collections to be a complete or fully representative survey of American traditional culture. Even if such a survey were possible, the financial and staffing constraints under which the Center has labored could not have created it. Nevertheless, the Center's holdings are remarkably rich, and this cultural wealth is directly attributable to the extraordinary drive and dedication of its collectors and researchers. For example, more than 2,000 of the Center's first 3,000 catalogued recordings were made by just two men—John A. Lomax and Alan Lomax—over a five-year period (1934–1939) during which John received twelve dollars a year for his efforts and Alan was the only salaried staff member of the Archive of American Folk Song. During much of this time only one, technologically troubled recording machine was available to both collectors.

The interest and expertise of the early collectors, combined with the cultural currents of their times, led them to concentrate on certain regions, genres, and ethnicities more than others. Folk music collectors favored African American blues, field hollers, and prison work songs; Appalachian ballads and instrumental tunes; and the European-derived musical traditions of the East Coast. The great majority of the early recordings were the result of collecting expeditions to the southern states. Since folktales emerged largely incidentally from music-collecting sessions, this book leans heavily toward southern storytelling, in particular the narratives of African Americans and residents of Appalachia.

Since 1976, the American Folklife Center has done much to compensate for the biases of the early collectors by progressively sending its researchers to explore previously underrepresented regions, groups, and genres. Among the most notable recent fieldwork projects have been multiethnic and multioccupational surveys of the folklife of rural Montana and the urban East (Lowell, Massachusetts and Paterson, New Jersey), as well as an extensive study of Italian Americans in the West. These collections did not consist primarily of folk narrative, but all include substantial numbers of stories, a few of which appear in this book.

Since 1980, the American Folklife Center has increasingly turned its attention to folktales. In 1983, University of Pennsylvania folklorist Kenneth S. Goldstein collaborated with AFC interns Holly Cutting Baker and Amanda Dargan to generate the institution's first comprehensive index of spoken-word recordings. Portions of that 211-page manuscript have recently been corrected and updated by intern Jacob Steelman. In 1987, AFC director Alan Jabbour oversaw the acquisition of the first massive collection consisting exclusively of spoken-word material in English, the recordings of the American Dialect Society. In 1995, Joseph Hickerson directed the publication of a finder's list detailing the extensive and varied "Tales of the Supernatural" to be found among AFC holdings (Delcambre et al. 1995). In 2001, the current director, Peggy Bulger, acquired the

Maggie Hammons Parker, teller of "Dream No More" (story 200), sharing stories with future AFC Director Alan Jabbour. (Photo by Carl Fleischhauer)

Center's largest narrative collection to date: the sound recordings, printed materials, and ephemera of the International Storytelling Center, including all the performances recorded at the National Storytelling Festival held annually in Jonesborough, Tennessee. Folklife specialist Todd Harvey is currently cataloguing this massive collection.

If the collections of the American Folklife Center suffer certain limitations in representing the depth and diversity of America's storytelling traditions, this anthology suffers considerably more. Although I have spent six years researching the Center's recorded folktales, I have had to neglect some of the greatest narrators and best collections. In addition to my (previously noted) ignorance of Native American languages, I lack the linguistic skills required to translate thousands of other narratives recorded by American speakers of Armenian, Czech, Danish, Dutch, Finnish, Plattdeutsch, Russian, Swedish, and Yiddish, among many other tongues.

Furthermore, my own research interests and areas of knowledge have played a role in narrowing the scope of this anthology. Like most of the early collectors, I have confined my collection and study of stories largely to Appalachian, African American, and generally southern traditions; specifically, my work has led me to storytellers in the Arkansas Ozarks, southern Indiana, eastern Kentucky, Cajun Louisiana, and the eastern extremes of Tennessee and Texas. Broadening my base of knowledge in order to make this anthology more representative of the true range of the American Folklife Center's holdings has provided me with a welcome, but far from complete educational experience.

A NOTE ON THE RECORDINGS AND HOW THEY ARE TRANSCRIBED

The folktales rendered here in written form are all transcriptions from audio recordings of spoken performances. The type and quality of the recordings have varied enormously over the years. The oldest recordings (1933–1940s) were made on massive record-cutting machines, most of which weighed two hundred pounds or more. As the performer spoke into the sound trumpet, a metal needle, vibrating with the pitch, tone, and volume of the speaker's voice, dug grooves into a disk (generally twelve inches in diameter) made from acetate or aluminum. The recording time for each side of a disk was about four minutes. Thus, the longer earlier tales that appear in this book cover four or more sides—meaning that the performer was interrupted three or more times in the course of the tale and had to drop the thread of the tale and wait for the technicians to change the disk in order to resume recording.

The size of these machines, the four-minute capacity of the disks, the presence of sound technicians, the awareness that recording time was precious and not to be wasted (an awareness sometimes unconsciously communicated by the collectors)—these were all factors that worked against the composure of the tellers and the natural rhythms of their stories.

Some of the narrators, like Woody Guthrie, Aunt Molly Jackson, and Maud Long, were supremely confident speakers who could not be shaken by any number of stranger-listeners or technological mishaps and intrusions. Yet the great majority of the tellers, even those with extensive previous experience recording their songs and instrumental pieces on the same machines, showed at least some

The cumbersome sound technology of the 1930s: Recording equipment in the trunk of John Lomax's car. (American Folklife Center, Library of Congress)

measure of hesitation when asked to perform their tales. Commonly, these artists were familiar with staged musical events, but they were accustomed to telling stories in much more relaxed and intimate settings. Most of their narratives, especially the historical legends and accounts of supernatural experiences, typically emerged from a fabric of conversation; they had rarely, if ever, before been delivered as set pieces, on cue. True, some of the stories (including jokes and märchen, or fairy tales) were closely cognate with the musical performance pieces: these pieces were set inside performances frames (for example, beginning with "Once upon a time" and ending with "And when I left there, Jack was doing awfully well"), often requested by a specific title ("tell us the Heifer Hide tale"), and performed on demand. But even many of these were typically told by older people to their very small children and grandchildren, and some tellers understandably balked at repeating them for adult strangers in the presence of a sound recorder.

Developing technology solved many of these performance problems. The reel-to-reel tape recorder, first used in studio recordings and widely available in portable models after 1950, allowed the collectors the time to help create more relaxed storytelling contexts and took significant pressure off the narrators.

The varied styles of the tellers, together with the various media on which their voices are preserved, make the transcriptions in this book appear nearly as varied as the tales themselves sound. Sara Cleveland, Jane Muncy Fugate, Son House, and Maud Long are among the great storytellers whose tales are relatively easy to transcribe. These narrators tend to speak slowly, clearly, and evenly. Their syntax and grammar conform so closely to standard written English that the stories move from the spoken to the written word with little difficulty (at least in those cases where their voices have been cleanly recorded).

But some of the greatest storytellers featured here are among the hardest to translate to the page. Four of the masters—Joshua Alley, John Davis, Sam Harmon, and J.D. Suggs—presented enormous difficulties. The recordings of all four were technologically flawed: Davis's stories, in particular, were so poorly miked that I found it almost impossible to transcribe them. Equally daunting, all four of these performers communicated in language and styles profoundly different from those of standard written English. The vocabulary, rhythms, and intonations that make these narrators so enjoyable to hear also make them extremely difficult to read. Each of the four sticks to his community's traditional narrative esthetics and seldom if ever attempts to "translate" for the benefit of outsiders. As a rule, the more valued such performances were within their now-vanished traditional communities, the less likely they will be readily understood by casual readers in the twenty-first century.

In the transcribing the tales in this book, I have attempted to follow faithfully two fundamental principles. First, there is no fully satisfactory way to translate a work of spoken art to the printed page. Many deeply learned and intensely dedicated folklorists—including Elizabeth Fine (1984), Zora Neale Hurston (1935), Dennis Tedlock (1971), and J.D.A. Widdowson (Halpert and Widdowson 1995: liv–lxix)—have labored to create transcription systems to make written version of oral tales *look* the way they *sound*. In their efforts to convey the unique accents, rhythms, pitches, and stresses of a speaker's voice, scholars have employed a great range of visual tools, including eye dialect, special orthographic conventions (including italics, boldface, caps, and poetic line-breaks), and the international phonetic alphabet. My experience has led me to the conviction that such efforts have lost more in readership than they have gained in accuracy.

The more faithful to the spoken voice transcribers try to be, the more complex their systems are likely to become. The more complex the transcription, the more likely it is to clutter the page with symbols and spellings unfamiliar to the nonspecialist reader, the more the sense of the tale becomes lost in the web of artifice designed to capture its sound, and the more readers are likely to be turned away. Yet, for all the efforts to convey the spoken voice in written form, I know of no system yet devised, no matter how complex, that can successfully communicate a particular person's voice to a reader who has never actually heard that person speak.

My avoidance of dialect spellings is based on convictions best expressed in the work of Dennis Preston (1982; 1983). Preston offers strong evidence to support his contention that such spellings (which, he demonstrates, have been used disproportionately and inaccurately by folklorists in rendering the speech of African Americans and southern whites) represent a condescending professional bias.

The transcriptions in this book therefore render the spoken word in standard written English with very few exceptions. Even when the speaker drops the first syllable of *because* or the final "g" of *grinning*, I typically employ the dictionary spellings rather than *'cause* or *grinnin'*. I have employed a few nonstandard forms (for example, *gonna* for *going to*) that have become so familiar they have taken on near-standard status for readers. I particularly favor *wanna* over the standard forms *want to* or *want a*, because in such phrases as *wanna* fight, the nonstandard form could substitute for either *want to* or *want a* and hence is actually more likely to reflect the narrator's intent.

I have deviated from the Standard English rule only when, in my judgment, the speaker uses variant pronunciations to convey a special meaning or effect. For example, within the same tale, a certain narrator will pronounce the word *them* in two distinct ways, sometimes sounding and sometimes dropping the initial *th* sound; in such cases, the transcription will sometimes spell the word *them* and at other times *em*. Similarly, some speakers will use as many as three pronunciations for *fellow* and on rare occasions, when these variations seem to me to carry some semantic weight, I will render the word *fellow*, *fella*, or *feller* to reflect the speaker's choice. In certain cases, the narrator seems to be using variant pronunciation for purposes of effect or characterization. For example, in her performance of "Merrywise" (story 77), Jane Muncy Fugate alters her pronunciation toward the end of the tale, particularly when describing the witch and rendering the witch's speech: although Jane typically uses the standard "get," "them," and "running" elsewhere in her tale, she changes her pronunciation to say "git," "em," and "runnin" toward the end.

The second major guiding principle informing these transcriptions, I regard as at least as important as the first: The speaker's words are the speaker's words, and they cannot be shuffled around without the loss of something essential to the story. Therefore, I have not intentionally changed any of the storyteller's words, nor have I changed the order in which those words were spoken, in any of the tales printed here. There were, however, cases in which I was forced to omit certain words and phrases. When, for example, the speaker's words were unintelligible to me, I had to leave them out. Furthermore, there were certain cases in which the speaker shared socially sensitive information that, in my opinion, should be deleted: for example, when a speaker named a neighbor or family member and identified that person as a witch or a criminal, I left out that person's name. There were also a few instances in which storytellers broke away from their tales to mention persons or events irrelevant to their stories, for example, in answering a telephone that rang as the tale was being recorded. In other cases, when a speaker made a mistake (for example, saying "him" for a character who is everywhere else described as a female) and then corrected it, I have omitted the words spoken in error; in such cases I am confident that had I been able to find the storytellers and ask them to review the transcripts, they would have urged me to drop those misspoken words. Finally, in a very few instances, I omitted a substantial number of words from tales that, in my opinion, readers would have found too difficult to follow had I preserved all the speaker's verbiage. Two tellers repeatedly used certain phrases (for example, "you know"), in my opinion, not because they were trying to stress certain points, but because they were more or less unconsciously buying time while searching for the right phrase; it is my belief that like most readers of this book, these tellers would find that to include all these repetitions would detract from their tales.

In my efforts to be faithful to the speakers' words, I employ the following five spelling and punctuation rules:

1. Like Dennis Preston (1982), I have tried to transcribe faithfully all morphological variations from Standard English. These are not merely variations in pronunciation but, rather, unique aspects of the teller's vocabulary. Thus, these transcriptions record the use of such common variations as *come* (past tense) instead of *came* and *ain't* instead of *isn't*.

2. I have used ellipses (. . .) exclusively to indicate that one or more of the speaker's words have been deleted from the transcription. (Some folklorists employ ellipses to indicate a long pause on the speaker's part, but I never use them for that purpose in this book.)

3. Em-dashes (—) indicate pauses and false starts, as well as grammatical shifts that present little problem in oral communication but may prove confusing to a reader without a marker to indicate that the narrator's syntax is changing course.

4. Within a tale, square brackets ([ ]) surround any words not spoken by the teller. Bracketed words supply information that cannot be gleaned merely from reading the teller's words. A phrase in brackets may be used to indicate a gesture made by the speaker that is important to the sense of the story (for example, "She stabbed herself here [speaker thumps his chest with his fist]"), describe significant audience reactions (for example, [loud laughter]), translate a foreign word or phrase (for example, *padroncito* ["little godfather," or, here, "boss's son"]), or correct an inconsistency (if, for example, the teller uses "she" in describing a male character, the word will be replaced by [he]).

5. *Italics* indicate vocal emphasis; I have tried to use these sparingly, and most often when emphasis seems to me to alter, rather than merely to intensify, the narrator's meaning.

As this book goes to press, thirteen of its 215 tales are available, through the American Folklife Center, in audio form on the Internet. Five tales are from Florida: "Antonio the Woodcutter" (story 187), "The Girl Who Didn't Mind Her Mother" (story 178), "Jack and the Beanstalk" (story 190), "Miss Martina Cockroach and Mr. Perez Mouse" (story 186), and "The Fig Tree" (story 185). Readers wishing to hear these tales may access the home page of "Florida Folklife from the WPA Collections, 1937–1942," click on "Audio Titles," and search for any of the six titles as just listed (three of the tales can be heard in Spanish, three in English; none is transcribed on the Web). The eight remaining tales are from California (136–139 and 209) and Texas (99–101). I urge readers to listen to these tales online and to check the transcriptions in this book against what they hear on the Web.

Two of the Florida tales serve as rough gauges of how I have handled all the transcriptions in this book. In "The Girl Who Didn't Mind Her Mother" (story 178), Eartha White's voice emerges more distinctly than do most of those recorded in 1940, largely because she speaks slowly and precisely and enunciates clearly. I believe that I have captured the entire performance as she delivered it, with the exception of one sentence (the seventh paragraph of the transcribed tale), from which I have deleted four words. The sentence as heard on audio goes:

"I'm in my father watermelon patch—and cane field, rather."

I have omitted the four words and replaced them with ellipses to render the following sentence: "I'm in my father's . . . cane field. . . ."

Eartha White was obviously correcting herself during her performance, and in my judgment she would have chosen to omit the same four words that I deleted in my transcription. Elsewhere in her tale, her speech is notable for its precision and clarity, and it is my belief that she would have taken offense had I preserved in writing an error that she corrected in her speech.

A second audio tale, "Jack and the Beanstalk" (story 189), was far more difficult for me to transcribe, in part because of the Bahamian accent of the teller, Wilbur Roberts. The transcription includes two ellipses to indicate passages that I was unable to puzzle out and three words that I was not sure I transcribed correctly (these words are enclosed in brackets). At the end of the tale, Wilbur Roberts refers to "squint eyes." I have listened to these words multiple times, and as I hear them, Mr. Roberts is saying "slit eyes." Yet the written notes provided by Stetson Kennedy and Robert Cook, who were present in person to record the performance, refer to "squint eyes." My personal experience with both recording and transcribing tales has led me to the conclusion that what one hears during a live performance tends to be more accurate than what one gleans from a recording of "poor" sound quality (as the American Folklife Center has labeled many of the online performances transcribed in this book). Hence, I have deferred to Kennedy and Cook and retained their wording, "squint eyes."

I encourage readers who have consulted the audio recordings and who would like to offer corrections of and suggestions regarding these transcriptions to contact the transcriber at lindahlc9@aol.com.

I have done the best I could to decipher the speech of the storytellers whose art is presented here, yet in some cases I am particularly disappointed that I have not done better. I have listened to certain passages in the performances of Joshua Alley, John Davis, Sam Harmon, and J.D. Suggs, to name the most difficult examples, 100 times or more, yet I still find crucial parts of their performances unintelligible. None of the tales of these men is yet available online, but I request that any researcher who visits the American Folklife Center to listen to any of their tales (or any of the tales published here) contact me with corrections.

Although I have striven for consistency in these transcriptions, I am aware that other listeners, attempting to follow precisely the rules that I outline here, could easily (and inevitably) render the same sounds substantially differently than I have. Still others could rightly object to my list of exceptions to the basic rules set forth above: if, for example, I am generally against dialect spellings, why include any? Or, having included the few mentioned above, why not include others that could just as logically be defended? I confess that there is a certain arbitrary, and certainly subjective, quality to my choices.

Nevertheless, I believe that the transcriptions in this book reflect the words and sense of the storytellers about as accurately as they can, without sacrificing readability. I have sought to balance, without compromise, the two often-conflicting goals of faithfulness to the storyteller and accessibility to the reader. I was certain that if I came reasonably close to both goals, a third—the reader's enjoyment and appreciation of these remarkable stories—would be guaranteed. I owed it to the storytellers (most of whom have now gone unheard for decades and past the limits of their lives) to try to make their words live again. If they do, they are certain to satisfy.

AMERICAN FOLKTALES: THEIR STUFF AND STYLES

There is no form of human expression more general, or more personal, than oral storytelling. Many of us associate such tales as "Cinderella" and "Jack the Giant-Killer" with timeless and universal themes; at the same time, we often experience our parents' family anecdotes as the unique records of our own personal identity. In storytelling, the universal and the unique typically appear in combination. An individual may find important private meanings in a tale that has been told before, in numberless different ways, to literally millions of listeners. Similarly, in telling a family story to a stranger, we often rely upon the conviction that such an intensely personal account nevertheless possesses a broad appeal that will allow it to speak meaningfully to virtually anyone.

The demonstrated power of stories to speak *for* one gifted narrator, but also *to* innumerable listeners who have never met the teller, dictates the form of this book. On the one hand, it is my hope that each tale will speak for itself; on the other hand, it is my conviction that each tale speaks even more effectively when we begin to know the teller.

THE STUFF OF FOLKTALES

Most Americans associate the term "folktale" either with pure fantasy or unenlightened falsehood. For many, a folktale is the equivalent of "fairy tale": an escapist narrative from oral tradition reworked into bedtime reading for children or transformed into feature-length Disney cartoons. To just as many others, "folktale" signifies a piece of spurious popular wisdom, an "old wives' tale" that, though popularly believed to be true, is actually false.

Neither of these characterizations comes very close to what today's folklorists mean by folktale. This book takes a view both narrower and broader than the one common street definitions embrace. Although many readers make no distinction between a spoken version of "Cinderella" and a storybook treatment of the same plot, the tales featured here were created as oral performances by speakers accustomed to entertaining live audiences. True to its name, a folktale is shared by a "folk," a narrative community. In a folktale, the narrator speaks not only for her- or himself but also for the friends, neighbors, and relatives who first passed it on to the storyteller and who have often since gathered around the teller to hear it again. This book, then, focuses upon the individual storyteller as a community artist who communicates shared values and esthetics in a uniquely artful way.

These shared values and esthetics are part of the narrator's *tradition*: it is not just the plot that makes a folktale. Even a story with "new" content—for example, the personal narratives of Will Gilchrist (stories 71–75)—may be a folktale if it unfolds in a traditional context (in Gilchrist's day, the barbershop, known by many groups as a place to congregate and tell tales) and conveys traditional subject matter and themes (even if they had not heard Gilchrist's stories before, his African American listeners were familiar with the racist attitudes and actions he described) in a form and style valued by the group. By relying both upon the time-tested expectations of his audience and upon his own powerfully understated art of description, Will Gilchrist told tales that were simultaneously old and fresh.

Although the folktales appear here in written form, the tellers did not write them down, nor did they intend to. These stories are not literary creations and are not meant to be, though there are certainly important continuities between American folklore and American literature. Major American writers have often drawn upon oral traditions for their materials: Mark Twain, for example, established his reputation through his skillful translations of oral tall tale subjects and styles into "The Celebrated Jumping Frog of Calavaras County," "Baker's Blue Jay Yarn," and other short stories; similarly, Nathaniel Hawthorne drew upon oral New England legends to create such eerie and allegorical tales as "The Minister's Black Veil" and "Young Goodman Brown"; and Washington Irving converted Colonial Dutch legends like "Rip Van Winkle" and "The Legend of Sleepy Hollow" into brilliant legend parodies. The notes at the end of this book point out literary and film treatments of certain oral tales presented here. The tales themselves, however, are the spoken creations of everyday artists far less famous than Twain, Hawthorne, and Irving, but far more artful than their anonymity might lead readers to suspect.

Most of the storytellers anthologized here were acknowledged as major performers within their own communities. Typically, they had entertained their families, friends, and neighbors with their tales for decades before folklorists recorded them. Maud Long's daughter Jane Douglas recalls that Maud's neighbors would come calling regularly, day and night, asking Maud to tell them Jack Tales. Will Gilchrist's friends described how his barbershop was continually crowded, not only with paying customers but also with listeners, people who visited just to hear Will perform his inimitable tales. For the small groups that gathered to listen to these storytellers, these tales assumed an importance equal to that enjoyed by books, films, and television in the United States today. If the canon of major American writers has been selected by generations of critics, accomplished oral storytellers have had to pass through their own selection process: Most of the performers featured in this book were chosen by their own communities as master narrators. In this sense, each performance here represents both the artistry of a single narrator and the esthetics of the community that cherished that individual's tales.

If this book narrows one popular definition of folktale by focusing exclusively on oral creations, it significantly expands upon another common definition. Although many people regard a "folktale" as a fictional form, I use the term here to apply to any traditional tale, whether its tellers consider it true, or false, or both. Thus, the scope of this book extends far beyond fiction to encompass belief tales, personal experience stories, and accounts of major historical events.

Some of the finest American narrators specialize in nonfiction. All the surviving tales of the great African American raconteur Will Gilchrist, for example, are firsthand accounts of personal experiences involving brushes with the law. Other tellers devote themselves more or less exclusively to one fictional genre: all but one of Maud Long's recorded stories are Jack Tales, fantasy adventures of an every-boy named Jack.

Yet it is far more common for great storytellers to lend their skills to many different types of stories, ranging from personal experience and family history to magical fantasy. J.D. Suggs (stories 47–61), for example, tells a magic tale about a man who marries the Devil's daughter, a belief tale concerning a witch who can slip out of her skin, animal tales featuring Brer Rabbit and Brother Fox, jokes centering on clever slaves who outwit their masters, a tall tale about a giant watermelon, and another whopper about a superhumanly powerful African American Texas gunslinger.

To concentrate simply on the "fictional" stories while ignoring the "factual" ones would amount to creating a skewed impression of the storytellers and their arts. Perhaps the best justification for viewing folktales as both fact and fantasy is provided by the Maine storyteller Joshua Alley, who combines truth and fiction in all his verbal creations. Good stories, Alley reminds us, "ain't all one kind of stuff." It is the storyteller's job to mingle just enough fact and just enough art to make the tale "stick together." Meticulously remembered history and artful invention blend together in Alley's accounts. To better appreciate the arts of those who don't just always tell the same stuff all the time, this book devotes about half its length to the personal and family repertoires of nine great storytellers—Sam Harmon, Maud Long, Ray Hicks, Sara Cleveland, J.D. Suggs, Joshua Alley, Will Gilchrist, Jane Muncy Fugate, and Aunt Molly Jackson—all of whom possess narrative voices that set them distinctively apart from others, and most of whom exercise their spoken arts over a wide range of topics and genres. Rather than breaking the stories into generic or topical categories, I have grouped them together and framed them by discussions of the narrator's life and art, allowing readers to experience the diversity and power of these special storytellers and their stories.

THE STYLES OF FOLKTALES

Anticipating that many readers will come to this book in search of one particular narrative genre or theme, I now address the thematic and generic range of the tales presented here. Folklorists have long recognized that any given traditional narrative performance will possess at least three kinds of style: personal, cultural, and generic. An accomplished narrator telling "Cinderella," for example, will imbue the performance with his or her *personal* art. Furthermore, the tale will reflect the *cultural* environment in which it is told: in Sam and Alberta Harmon's version of "Cinderella" ("Catskins," story 11), the king lives in a house, not a castle, and he attends prayer meetings regularly, just as Sam and Alberta's Appalachian neighbors did. Yet, wherever "Cinderella" is told, it nearly always takes on the *generic* form of a magic tale, or märchen, the oral equivalent of the literary fairy tale. We have evidence that oral versions of "Cinderella" were circulating at least as early as the ninth century in China, and more than four hundred years ago in Europe. These early tales varied extraordinarily from the Perrault and Disney versions told today, and yet those familiar with Disney's version would instantly recognize any of these enormously diverse oral tales as relatives of "Cinderella."

Personal Styles

This book is designed to highlight the personal styles of great American narrators. In the 1800s, during the early years of folktale scholarship, researchers devoted almost all their attention to the tale itself and not to the teller. It was often assumed that each tale represented ancient dimensions of human imagination, and that a folklorist's most important project was to discover the original form, point of origin, and meaning of the tale. In the heat of their search for the story's roots, researchers neglected the folk artists who had actually told them the tales. Throughout the twentieth century, however, folklorists expressed increasing doubt that they could discover the ancient origins of folktales. Fieldworkers turned their attentions progressively toward the storytellers and discovered much about how the stories spoke not only of a distant past but also for the storyteller and her or his living communities, who were often full partners in the storytelling process.

Like every literary artist, every folktale teller possesses a personal style. No matter how reverently a community guards a certain story, no matter how doggedly a given storyteller tries to emulate the style of her father or his grandmother, every teller will inevitably set a unique stamp on her or his performance. From teller to teller, and even from one teller's performance to the next, the tale will change to fit the social situation, to accommodate the teller's mood, the interests and expectations of the audience, and the climate of the times. One of the best measures of this fact is the repertoire of the Hicks-Harmon family, to whom a large section of this book is devoted. One of the family's favorite tales was "Jack and the Heifer Hide" (story 23), sometimes also called "Jack, Tom, and Will" (story 5). As a child, Daron Douglas often heard the tale from her grandmother, Maud Long. Daron heard the tale so often and listened so attentively to her grandmother that she could have repeated it in much the same form as she first heard it. But when, as an adult, Daron began to share "Jack and the Heifer Hide" with young listeners, she shortened the tale considerably. She felt that the early sections of her grandmother's story, which recount the wanton slaughter of animals, were too raw for her audience of children, so she dropped the opening scenes, developed the final episode of her grandmother's tale into an independent story, and changed the story's title to "Jack and the River" (story 24), effectively creating a new tale suitable for her personal style and informed by her views concerning the tastes and values of her audience.

Accomplished narrators often alter their tales from telling to telling to suit their developing notions of the tale's meaning as well as the expectations of their listeners. The two performances of "Tailipoe" presented by Jane Muncy in this book (stories 84 and 85) reveal how dramatically a teller may alter her tale from one telling to the next. In Jane's family tradition, "Tailipoe" and its close cousin "Grown Toe" were two similarly plotted tales that were commonly told by her grandmother and her aunts. Both tales concern a hungry mountaineer who eats part of the body of an extraordinary being (the severed toe of a corpse or the tail of a strange creature). The being then returns to reclaim its missing member and kills the mountaineer. Jane's Aunt, Glen Muncy Anderson, was most familiar with the severed-toe version (see story 180), but Jane preferred the tale of the creature with the sliced-off tail. In her performance of 1955, Jane ended the story with an eerie suggestion that the murderous creature was still stalking the Kentucky hills and that on dark nights listeners could still hear the sounds of the beast crying out for its "tailipoe." In a performance of the "same tale" recorded forty-six years later, Jane provides a radically different ending: As the creature reappears to claim its tail from the mountaineer, Jane lets out a screechy scream calculated to unsettle her audience. She then concludes, "He [the mountaineer] didn't live happily ever after," a comic twist on the traditional fairy tale ending. Jane's 2001 telling of "Tailipoe" is thus more startling and more humorous than her 1955 performance. In this collection, headnotes to the individual folktales frequently point out notable aspects of the tellers' personal styles and contrast the styles of one teller and another, as well as point out the differences that emerge from one tale to the next in a narrator's repertoire.

Generic and Cultural Styles

The following brief survey introduces the folktale genres most richly represented in this book: märchen (magic tales), animal tales, jokes, tall tales, legends, and personal experience narratives. All these folktale forms are found not only in the United States but throughout the world. Thus I will discuss the basic traits of each genre as they are found in international circulation, but I will focus more closely on those aspects of cultural style most characteristic of the tales when told in specific American settings.

The *märchen* or *magic tale* (popularly known by the name of its literary offshoot, "fairy tale") is to some synonymous with "folktale." Most Americans know the genre through the storybook adaptations of the Brothers Grimm,

Helen Hartness Flanders (collector of stories 194 and 201) sharing stories with Mrs. Olive May of Stowe, Vermont, 1950s. (Photo by Bob Bourdon, courtesy of Nancy-Jean Siegel)

Hans Christian Andersen, Charles Perrault, Italo Calvino, and numerous other authors who have transformed traditional oral tales into works of literary art. Indeed, many Americans assume that such tales never thrived in the United States, a view supported to some extent by the meager historical evidence of the märchen's existence in the New World.

Magic tales seem to have been popular among the British and Irish immigrant populations that colonized the Appalachian region before the Revolutionary War, but as early as 1820, at least one expert expressed his belief that the tales had already died out. Folklorists did not question this claim until the 1920s, when Isabel Gordon Carter (1925) collected a number of tales in Madison County, North Carolina. Since that time, folklorists have found märchen tellers almost everywhere they have sought them in the Appalachians. The tradition was indeed significantly richer than the experts had believed. The profusion in which these tales are now found among families who were not asked to tell them in past generations constitutes significant evidence that the märchen was always more popular than folklorists once believed it to be.

Although the oral American märchen is not particularly well known among Americans outside the Appalachians, nearly all Americans are familiar with storybook märchen. Through these literary versions, we can readily identify some of the leading traits of the oral magic tale.

The märchen is an invitation to imagine the impossible. It begins with a conventional phrase ("Once upon a time") or a long nonsense introduction ("Once upon a time, and a long time ago it was—if I was alive then, I wouldn't be alive now, and if I'm alive now, I surely wasn't living then, there was a king and a queen in Ireland") that signals to its audience that a flight of fantasy will follow. In American oral tradition, these opening formulas tend to be spare. A few narrators use "Once upon a time," but others abbreviate the opening formula to "One time" or simply start the story off without any such marker.

The märchen then moves on to focus on one major character, most often an adolescent boy or girl (Jack or Catskins, for example) who faces an enormous challenge (poverty or the attacks of an otherworldly creature) and must eventually leave home to attempt to better his or her lot. The journey carries the protagonist into a world-turned-upside-down populated with talking animals, enormous beasts, glass mountains, or any of a number of other magical beings and props, some of which challenge and others of which aid the hero.

Some readers and listeners consider the märchen sheer fantasy because of the memorable instances of magic that befall the heroes on their journeys. But folklorists have long noted that even these presumably pure flights of fancy carry a great deal of specific cultural information reflecting the knowledge and surroundings of each community in which the tale is shared. The märchen is in effect a magic sandwich, a tale that begins and ends at home, no matter how many magical experiences its heroes encounter on the journeys that fill the middle of the tale. In storybook tradition, home is typically an extravagant castle in a distant land, but in the oral tales of American tradition home takes on the nature of the storyteller's immediate surroundings. Appalachian tales most often begin in a mountain cabin, and the circumstance that most often causes the leading figure to leave home is poverty, a condition all too familiar to the storyteller. When Ray Hicks begins "Grinding the at the Mill" (story 31) by saying that "Jack and his mother were having it hard," he is telling the story of his family and many of his neighbors, who were no strangers to hard times.

After the hero hits the road, even the most escapist magic of the American märchen is inflected with the everyday knowledge and values of the storytelling community. For example, the cannibal giants in Lee Wallin's "Little Nippy" (story 191) practice a lifestyle identical to that of Wallin's more prosperous neighbors: They own a farm, not a castle, and the giant wife uses a "half-moon" pitcher to fetch washing and drinking water from a nearby spring, just as Wallin's neighbors did. Wallin's giant couple even attend evening prayer meetings conducted by a circuit-riding preacher. The point is that people do not have fantasies about things that do not concern them. We learn at least as much about a culture from its favorite fictions as we do from its houses and its shopping lists.

As the venturesome märchen hero enters the magic world, he or she encounters otherworldly helpers and enemies. In American märchen, help tends to come early in the hero's adventure, often before he or she realizes, and it does not exactly come free. Most often in the märchen presented here, help takes the form of a hungry old man. The hero generously shares food with this man, who in return becomes a "donor" bestowing the hero with magical powers or a magic object. The unnamed female protagonist of Jane Muncy's "Rawhead and Bloody-bones" (story 81) receives enhanced beauty from the old man she feeds; in Maud Long's "Jack and the Northwest Wind" (story 19), the old man grants Jack a tablecloth that furnishes endless food, a hen that lays golden eggs, and a stick that answers the hero's command by flying through the air to drub the villain.

In American tradition, the hero generally receives far less magic help than does the European hero. The boy protagonists of Jane Muncy Fugate's "Old Greasybeard" (story 79), Lee Wallin's "Little Nippy" (story 191), and Sam Harmon's "Stiff Dick" (story 7) overcome their powerful adversaries through the power of their own wits or through sheer good luck. Dwarfed by two enormous giants, Jack may hide in a log and throw rocks at the head of one giant, who then blames the other giant for attacking him; the two giants fight among themselves until both die, and Jack escapes unscathed.

This collection reflects the general body of American märchen in that the most common magic foes of the märchen heroes are giants, followed by witches, and the devil. Myriad other beings, real or imagined—including lions, wicked kings, a unicorn, a cruel old bearded man—make occasional appearances. But the dragon, a fixture of storybook tradition, is not to be found among the tales assembled here and is extremely rare in American tradition in general.

Once the hero has overcome these daunting foes, she or he is rewarded with riches or marriage. In European märchen, the hero nearly always finds a spouse at the story's end; in American tradition, however, marriage occurs far less frequently. Among the twenty-two märchen told by Sara Cleveland, Maud Long, Sam Harmon, Daron Douglas, and Jane Muncy Fugate in this book, only nine end with a marriage, a very low count by worldwide standards, and one that may say something significant about the place of marriage in American, as compared to European, folk tradition. The Appalachian märchen, particularly, tend to end without marriage, especially when the protagonist is a male. The young Appalachian hero ends his adventures not only unmarried but also without great wealth: No palaces, gold, or noble titles await him. Typically, modest gains spell success. Jack is alive, and he now has enough money to keep starvation from the door. Sometimes, he has also accumulated sufficient wealth to keep from having to work. These tales, generally passed on by families that had to work hard and endlessly simply to survive, reflect a world in which the slightest rise in prosperity is viewed as an almost magical gift.

The märchen typically ends with a closing formula: "They lived happily ever after" is the standard storybook ending. Such markers could be seen as the tellers' attempt to draw a hard and fast line between the story's magic world and the everyday world of the listeners, a signal that shuts the door of the magic kingdom and drops the listeners back to earth. But in American storytelling tradition, as in many others worldwide, the narrator often ends the tale playfully, blurring the boundaries between the two worlds by pretending to have actually participated in the action of the tale and to have witnessed the hero's return from the magic world and the celebration marking the family reunion that concludes the action. Thus, Maud Long often ended her Jack Tales, "and when I left there, Jack and his mother were doing just fine."

Americans tend to associate märchen with Old World peasants and to think of these tales in terms of medieval European characters and fixtures including kings, princesses, castles, knights, and dragons. Many assume that such tales never thrived in the United States—but this book offers rich evidence to the contrary.

In much of the world, particularly in nonliterate regions, magic tales constituted a major form of entertainment for the entire community, young and old alike. In the United States, however, märchen are told primarily by parents and grandparents to young children. Among the märchen tellers represented in this book, Sam Harmon, Maud Long, Ray Hicks, Sara Cleveland, and Jane Muncy Fugate learned their tales as young children from their elderly relatives and, as adults, told them in turn to young children as well. The storyteller's adult friends and relatives are often left entirely out of the storytelling process. For example, Jane Muncy Fugate learned "Merrywise," her favorite märchen, at age 4 from her grandmother; in subsequent years, she shared the tale frequently with her own children and grandchildren, but her husband of forty-four years had never heard it until Jane performed it for me in 2000, some fifty-eight years after she had first heard it.

A second form of traditional fantasy represented in this collection is the *animal tale.* Like the märchen, the animal tale makes no pretense at presenting an ordinary, believable world; rather—true to its name—it features remarkable fauna: Brer Rabbit, Brother Bear, Mr. Buzzard, and many more. These characters, if decidedly nonhuman in form, are uncannily human in other ways: they speak, sing, plant crops, build houses, hold weddings, and form complex societies.

The world inhabited by these inhuman beings is ironically in many ways more realistic than that of the magic tale. Märchen heroes may appear entirely human, but they are often superhumanly virtuous, displaying measures of innocence, generosity, courage, or trust seldom found within ourselves or among our neighbors. In contrast, the protagonists of animal tales may not look like us, but they tend to embody all-too-common human shortcomings: suspicion, greed, cowardice, and treachery, for example. These creatures of nature represent human nature more effectively than they represent themselves. In "Mr. Snake and the Farmer" (story 48), a rattlesnake, half dead from the cold, begs a farmer to open his shirt and warm it with his own body heat. The farmer repeatedly states, "But you're a snake. You'll bite me." The snake, however, swears again and again that it won't bite the man and ultimately persuades him to open his shirt and hold the creature to his heart. Once warm, the snake bites its human helper. The stunned victim asks the reptile for an explanation. "You see, I'm a snake. I'm *supposed* to bite you." This creature is, of course, not simply a snake, but a human voice wrapped in snakeskin. At the end of the tale, master narrator J.D. Suggs makes it clear that "Mr. Snake and the Farmer" conveys a "real lesson" about human behavior: "When you know that a fellow is a crook or a thief, a robber, . . . don't never put him in your bosom, for when he gets warm, first chance, he going to trip you." When presented by an acute moralist like J.D. Suggs, the animal tale often takes on the coloring of a fable, a serious moral lesson cloaked in fiction.

Animal tales point out and sometimes even celebrate the negative potential of human beings. Many of the animal figures, like the snake in J.D. Suggs's tale, are villainous, but others are more heroic. The animal protagonist's status depends largely on the nature of his opponent. When tricking a decent, generous victim (like the farmer bitten to death by Mr. Snake), the self-serving animal emerges as the villain. But, when standing up to powerful and abusive foes, animal tricksters are transformed into heroes. Such is the case with Brer Rabbit, who employs his trickery against the clever exploiter Brother Fox and the stupid brute Brother Bear. In many Brer Rabbit tales, African American narrators cast Brother Fox and Brother Bear into the roles of slave-owner and overseer. In such contexts, the wily Rabbit employs his treachery to rectify an unjust situation, and his triumph over his more powerful opponents triggers the congratulatory laughter of the African American audience.

The choice of the rabbit as protagonist is not uniquely African American. Some Native American animal tales feature trickster rabbits, and many other cultures worldwide cast the physically weak but mentally adept rabbit in the role of underdog hero (in Cambodia, for example, the clever rabbit is known as "Judge Hare"). The popular cartoon trickster figure Bugs Bunny represents a pop culture spin-off of the long-standing identification of rabbits as clever tricksters. Yet Brer Rabbit is unique in the sense that he is by far America's best-known animal tale hero.

In the collections of the American Folklife Center, as in American tradition in general, animal tales are far more popular among African Americans than among European Americans. J.D. Suggs, Mose Platt, and Cora Jackson are some of the narrators who feature animal tales prominently in their repertoires. Other American groups that nurture animal tales include Hispanics (see, for example, "Miss Martina Cockroach and Mr. Perez Mouse" [story 186] as told by Cuban American Evelia Andux) and many Native American cultures, which often use them (as J.D. Suggs uses "Mr. Snake") as allegories and lessons on appropriate conduct.

American animal tales possess a much more richly documented history than do American märchen. Forty-five years before folklorists published the first Appalachian märchen, Georgia newspaper correspondent Joel Chandler Harris published *Nights of Uncle Remus: His Songs and His Sayings* (1880), one of the best-selling literary adaptations of oral folktales ever printed in the United States. Harris, a European American, drew upon his childhood memories of African American narrators to craft the character of Uncle Remus, an artful slave who uses the Brer Rabbit tales to amuse and instruct a young white child. Thanks largely to the Uncle Remus collection, animal tales, nearly universally known among southern blacks and widely popular among southern whites (who, like Harris, generally heard them from blacks), now found an even wider audience among northern whites, most of whom had not previously been exposed to these tales. Within a few years of the publication of this enormously successful book, several other collections, including Alcée Fortier's edition of French-language animal tales from Louisiana Creoles, appeared.

Throughout the late nineteenth and early twentieth centuries, European Americans made the great majority of the collections of these African American tales. The more closely one examines the cultural history of the Brer Rabbit tales, the less surprising this fact becomes. African American slaves and nannies regularly passed on these tales to white children. Black nannies and white nannies exchanged the tales with each other. In the years before 1900, many African Americans learned Brer Rabbit tales from whites. In an interview with John A. Lomax in 1937, Aunt Florida Hampton, an African American, explained, "Every time I stayed with a new set of white people, I learned some." Aunt Florida learned the tales from white children who had learned them from their black house servants (see AFC recording AFS 1324). Long before the South was legally integrated, it became narratively integrated. The Brer Rabbit tales of the nineteenth century, like the blues and jazz of the twentieth, were black artistic creations that crossed color barriers and drew blacks and whites closer together. Interestingly, Brer Rabbit, himself often shaped into a figure of black resistance to white oppression, became one of the most beloved characters in white storytelling tradition. The figure of the clever underdog—whose witty acts and words made fools of his powerful opponents—attracted white readers, and white authors kept up with the demand by printing written versions of the tales. Yet even in these European American retellings, the tales do not completely lose the flavor of their African American creators, "a people seeking to express their humanity" in conditions of oppression and paradoxically using an animal as the vehicle for conveying the most sacred human values (Hemenway 1982: 31).

A substantial breakthrough occurred in 1935 with the appearance of *Mules and Men*, a compendium of African American lore, including many animal tales, collected by African American folklorist Zora Neale Hurston. Hurston would later come to be known as one of the great authors of the twentieth century. Her love of fiction had begun with her childhood exposure to oral storytelling in the northern Florida town of Eatonville. Local "men folks" would gather in public places for "lying" sessions, "straining against each other in telling folks tales" that conjured up a time before time when "Lion, Tiger, Buzzard, and all the wood folks walked and talked like natural men" (Hurston 1942: 47).

JOKES, a third form of folk fiction anthologized here, are far more common than märchen or animal tales in contemporary American oral culture. That fact notwithstanding, many of the oral jokes that appear in this book will seem foreign to most modern American readers. Like all other active folklore genres, jokes are a measure of the times in which they are told and the attitudes and values of their tellers. Most of the jokes in this book were learned by the tellers at the end of the nineteenth century and recorded by folklorists in the early and middle decades of the twentieth; thus, they reflect the vanished worlds of subsistence farming, slavery, and local religious rivalries. Many of these comic tales had already enjoyed two centuries of popularity in America by the time they were recorded, but today most are verbal time capsules that tell us more about our past than about our present.

It is impossible to know the exact nature of the oral joke tradition during the Colonial period, but a close approximation may be found in the chapbooks, almanacs, and other printed ephemera that circulated broadly in the eighteenth and nineteenth centuries. Among these publications we find no evidence that British Americans, who made up the bulk of the U.S. population at the end of the Revolutionary War, read märchen such as "Jack and the Bean Stalk" (even though pamphlet versions of this and other Jack Tales were enormously popular in Britain during this period). To the contrary, the Colonial public enormously preferred reading narrative jokes.

The major printed vehicle for jokes in the eighteenth and nineteenth centuries was the almanac. Benjamin Franklin's *Poor Richard's Almanac* is by far the best known of these, but there were literally hundreds of others published annually during Colonial times. Almanacs predicted the weather for the year and passed on folk wisdom in the form of proverbs, but they typically devoted most of their verbiage to storytelling. Humorous narratives constituted the most popular type of story. In their subjects, themes, and plots, the jokes found in 200-year-old almanacs closely resemble those found in the Library of Congress field recordings of the 1930s and 1940s, as attested in J. Michael Stitt and Robert K. Dodge's painstaking research (1991).

These jokes present a vanished rural America and portray, in stereotyped fashion, some of the most common characters of the farm and the frontier: greedy farmers, circuit-riding preachers, rival religious denominations, resourceful Indians, wily prospectors, and shepherds who care a little too much for their sheep. Most often, the jokes amplify to the point of ridiculousness the daily tensions and rivalries within rural communities, pitting husbands against wives, preachers against their congregations, Baptists against Methodists, masters against slaves. Typically, though not always, in these tales the relatively powerless figure, the "little man," ends up on top, deflating the pretensions of the more powerful figure: the game warden, preacher, landowner, or slaveholder. Such jokes are contests in deceit: A sneaky, treacherous authority figure seeks to exploit a weak individual, but the underdog proves even more sneaky than the villain and eventually turns the tables on the man of power. Folklorists identify this underdog as a "trickster figure," and American folklore is rife with them. We have already encountered a nonhuman form of this figure in the animal tale, which features such four-legged tricksters as Brer Rabbit.

The circuit-riding preacher attracts a great many jokes in both African American and European American traditions. In rural communities too small or poor to support a minister on a permanent basis, circuit riders made periodic visits, conducting worship services perhaps every third or fourth Sunday; while in the community they would stay at the home of one of the church deacons or elders. This outsider, who enjoyed his hosts' hospitality without contributing to their material well-being, was often viewed with a certain measure of suspicion. The jokes about preachers, then, are not as a rule antireligious, but they are often stridently anticlerical: the stories cast continual doubt on the motives and morals of the traveling preachers. In "The Preacher Who Could Always Be Trapped by Women" (story 95), the circuit rider attempts to sleep with his parishioner's wife; in "Cold as Hell" (story 151), he basks in the heat of the fire while the host's son shivers in the corner of the room. In both of these tales, the preacher eventually gets his comeuppance at the hands of the "little people" he has tried to exploit.

In some tales, the sneaky preacher joins forces with another stock villain, the adulterous wife. In "Little Dicky Whigburn" (story 10), a farmer's wife strikes up a liaison with a hypocritical preacher in the farmer's absence. Eventually, and often with the help of a beggar or another lowly soul, the cuckolded farmer exposes the adultery and the little man comes out on top. (In other tales—for example, stories 8 and 23, both versions of the Heifer Hide tale—the two-timing wife performs her infidelities without the preacher's help.)

The preacher may be rural America's all-purpose joke villain, the figure most generally shared by the diverse groups that contributed to the nation's old-time humor traditions, but certain groups—notably migrant farmworkers, sharecroppers, and subsistence farmers—reserved their most pointed ridicule for landlords, overseers, and others who amassed wealth from the farmers' labor while the farmers themselves had to struggle for the barest necessities. Various American rural communities have nurtured stock trickster figures to challenge the landlords. In Mexican American tradition, as well as throughout Central and South American, a character named Pedro de Urdemalas thrives. In jokes told along the Mexican border, Pedro sometimes plays the fool, but he generally converts his powerful opponents into his dupes through the sheer force of his wits: as when Pedro takes the ears and tails of butchered pigs and sticks them in the ground, tells the government agent that these protruding animal parts belong to whole pigs buried in mud up to their ears, and then sells these "pigs" to the farm agents for a tidy sum (story 157).

Another enormously popular rural trickster is an old slave named John (or, less commonly, Jack or Efan) who matches wits with "Old Master" (sometimes identified in dialect as "Old Marster"), the slaveholder. Hundreds of John and Old Master tales have been collected from African American communities throughout the country, and this book is proportionately rich with them: John Davis of Georgia, Son House of Louisiana, Ulisses Jefferson of Mississippi, and J.D. Suggs of Michigan are all masters of this form. To modern readers, many of these tales may seem too realistic to be funny; it is particularly realistic, for example, that the slave underdog is often caught and punished. John can be enormously clever, but sometimes he falls into the trap of his own cleverness, as in the tale of "John and the Coon": John eavesdrops on his Old Master to learn the master's plans. Suggesting he has learned the master's secrets through supernatural means, John awes his white owner. Eventually, Old Master comes to believe that John does indeed possess extrasensory powers; in a wager with another white planter, he stakes his entire plantation that John can guess the identity of an animal hidden in a box. The box is produced and now John is on the hot seat. Admitting defeat, John sighs, "You got the old coon at last." But a raccoon is indeed the animal hidden in the box; John has lucked into the right answer, and all goes well, at least for a time, between master and slave. John Davis's performance (story 171) drew roars of laughter from Zora Neale Hurston and the other African American members of Davis's audience. For all of its obvious comic value, "John and the Coon," like many other John and Old Master tales, provides canny observations on the daily struggles of slaves. The story asks listeners to consider strategies for survival in a world of subservience, the limitations of such strategies, and certain boundaries between master and slave that a slave can seldom cross successfully. Sometimes, it may be a good idea for a slave to create a mystique that leads his master to wonder how much the slave knows and how he has come to know it. But how far can the slave carry this idea without being punished for it? The finest jokes in this collection—including the best John and Old Master jokes—offer the reader not just an opportunity to laugh but also an education in how to strategize and how to succeed in difficult social situations.

If any one narrative form can claim the title of America's definitive folktale, it is the *tall tale* (also known among storytellers as the windy, the yarn, the whopper, the lie, the dying truth, and dozens of other names). In a meticulous survey of British and North American folktales, Ernest Baughman (1966) found that tall tales were 100 times more common in the United States than in Britain. From the earliest printed records of American humor, the almanacs of Colonial times, to the weekly national papers of the mid-nineteenth century, tall tales

Herbert Halpert (collector of stories 1–12) recording a folktale from James L. Conklin, New York, 1946. (Photo by Violetta Maloney Halpert)

entertained the entire population. During the 1830s, frontiersman and congressman Davy Crockett became the subject of numerous Crockett Almanacs that celebrated his career with tall tales in which he appeared as the hero. Later in the nineteenth century, Mark Twain became America's most popular writer largely on the strength of his genius for converting tall tales into written form. In the early twentieth century, a lumber company began publishing tall tales featuring a giant woodsman named Paul Bunyan. By the end of the twentieth century, Paul Bunyan had become the best-known figure in American folk tradition, his popularity enhanced by cartoon and other media treatments.

These famous printed and animated tall tales, however, are just the tip of the iceberg, a rough surface measure of the prevalence of a folktale form far more widespread in oral culture than even in its numerous print and film spin-offs. The popularity of the tall tale is so great that it begs us to ask why it has become America's favored folktale form. A brief consideration of the tall tale's style and content offers some clues to its pervasiveness.

The tall tale is a joke masquerading as a true story. In American tradition it is almost always a man who mounts this masquerade, and males make up most of his audience. The teller typically begins his tale in sincere tones and with a straight face, claiming that he is narrating an actual happening, usually an event he has experienced himself. As a rule the story starts out realistically enough. The tale usually opens in an environment thoroughly familiar to the storyteller's audience. In Sam Harmon's "Great Pumpkin" tale (story 3), for example, the action unfolds in Sam's backyard, a patch of newground that he has cleared to serve as the family vegetable farm. Once the teller has set his thoroughly ordinary scene, exaggerations invade the tale. These exaggerations most often take the form of the forces and creatures of nature: days so hot that the sun pops the popcorn growing in the fields, or mosquitoes so large that they fly off with dogs and small children. Sometimes the teller introduces his exaggerations slowly and incrementally, beginning with slightly improbable assertions and then adding increasingly outrageous claims until no sane person would believe the tale true. L.A. Ledford (story 136) uses this strategy of slow-building to great effect. Beginning with the account that he talked the U.S. Cavalry into letting him bring his horse with him into the army, he goes on to narrate how only his horse and he survived a dead-on hit from an enemy shell. Although improbable, these events fall within most listeners' notion of the possible. When Ledford mentions that the bomb blast blew "the little horse out of the harness and it didn't even hurt him," he is pushing us to the outer limits of our credulity. Then, as Ledford narrates how his one little horse had to pull a boxcar uphill and pulled so hard that he "bogged . . . up to his knees in solid rock," he has taken us completely into the realm of fantasy.

In a second tall tale strategy, the teller starts out with an absolutely unbelievable detail, but continues to pile one impossibility on top of another until he has exhausted his listeners. A third scenario involves two or more narrators engaged in a liar's contest, with each trying to top the other. In one such contest (story 137), one liar claims he grew a pumpkin big enough to house a whole community: "I hired me three carpenters to put partitions in it, and we made forty-two three-room apartments." A second liar claims, "That ain't nothing. . . . I made a big old steel pot: twenty-five miles around it, five miles deep." When the first liar asks, "What are you gonna do with a big pot like that?" the second responds, "Cook the pumpkin you raised in it."

No matter which strategy the teller uses, he continues to narrate even the most outrageous details in the most down-to-earth and matter-of-fact voice, as if there were nothing unusual about his preposterous claims. This deceptively calm storytelling style has much to do with the tall tale's enormous popularity. And the disproportion between the wild details of the story and the teller's low-key presentation is a major factor in creating the tall tale's comic effect.

The tall tale has been particularly popular in all-male occupational groups—lumberjacks, cowboys, and soldiers, for example—as well as in male recreational communities, most notably hunters and fishermen. These groups regularly encountered dangers, many of which were life-threatening. An attitude commonly fostered in such working conditions was to recognize life's daily dangers but not to get too worked up over them. For all its comic qualities, the tall tale presents a model for cool detached thinking in the face of danger.

In all-male communities, tall tales also often served as a form of initiation. Lumber camp veterans, for example, would often tell rookies about some of the less unbelievable adventures of an imaginary lumberjack named Paul Bunyan. In such situations, the tall tale served as a test of the newcomer's gullibility as well as his grace under pressure: How well could he take a joke, once he found out that the veteran was putting one over on him?

We Always Lie to Strangers, proclaims the title of Vance Randolph's famous study of tall tale telling in the Ozarks (Randolph 1951). Randolph reports that groups of men clustered in rural general stores and other public places would often begin creating tall tales communally as soon a stranger came within earshot. Without speaking directly to the newcomer, and even pretending that they do not wish to be overheard, the men treat the stranger to a group lie performed so smoothly that the stranger immediately assumes that the men are speaking sincerely. Another way, then, in which men on the frontier have used the tall tale is to mark territory, thereby separating the insiders from the outsiders.

Even more than the strategies of tall tale telling, the content and themes of these narratives suggest reasons why they have become so popular throughout the United States. Nature is the principal topic of the tall tale: the bounty of nature and the hazards of nature are the genre's two most pervasive themes. To the various immigrant populations, who left behind overcrowded conditions in the Old World and who, often as not, had never before owned the land they worked, the American landscape seemed a tall tale in itself. Here was unimaginable bounty, but also risks and threats almost unimaginable in the old country.

One of the most popular American tall tales, "The Lucky Shot" (story 20 in this book has a related plot), encapsulates both the threat and the gifts of nature with remarkable economy. A hungry man down to the last two bullets of his double-barreled, muzzle-loading rifle is combing the woods for the game that will save him from starvation. All at once, he sees more game than he can handle—a bear, a boar, and a mountain lion—all rushing at him at the same time from three directions. He loads his bullets, but he doesn't have time to remove the ramrod. He fires just as the bear reaches him. The ramrod hits the bear in the eye and kills him just as the bear's paw splits apart the gun's two barrels in opposite directions. The bullets fly out of the twisted barrels and kill the other two attacking animals. In one day, the hero has had two close calls with death—death from starvation and death from animal attack—but by nightfall he is prosperous and happy, blessed by more food than he can possibly eat. Such tall tales are comic presentations of the real dangers of the frontier, but they are also, and even more so, expressions of an optimistic attitude—one is tempted to say, a faith—that nature will ultimately provide.

Characteristically, all but one of the tall tale tellers featured in this book are male. Characteristically, the narrators hail from all regions of the country and from several different ethnic groups. Perhaps most characteristically, the tall tale was particularly popular among the migrant workers of the Dust Bowl era whose stories appear in this anthology. These Dust Bowl refugees had been forced by some of nature's most destructive acts to leave their homes and farms and to travel on to a place where they finally found nature's bounty. Exiled from their homes, living in tents, working for cutthroat wages when employed at all, the men of the camps had no shortage of reasons for despair. Yet they entertained each other with tall tales, many of which held out the hope that even a man down to his last bullet can find sudden prosperity in the bounty of nature.

Belief legends—sometimes called "ghost stories" or "scary stories" by their tellers in America—focus on the hazy boundary that divides everyday reality from the realm of the supernatural. Such tales explore the limits of the possible. Depending on the cultural context and belief system, the central figures of these tales may be ghosts, witches, angels, saints—in short, figures whose existence is debatable. A culture's rational laws and science can neither prove nor disprove that these beings exist. Their reality is a question of belief.

Content alone cannot distinguish a legend from a märchen. Both genres feature situations in which ordinary people pursuing everyday activities encounter otherworldly beings and baffling situations. More than the content of the tale, it is the attitude of the teller and the audience—the degree of their willingness to consider the tale as either fact or fiction, an entertaining fantasy or a disturbing truth—that determines the generic status of the tale. Ray Hicks, for example, tells "Grinding at the Mill" (story 31) as a märchen, but many American narrators tell very similar tales featuring old women who take the form of cats and are discovered after the hero has chopped off the cat's paw and the woman is found the next day with her hand chopped off. At the end of "Grinding at the Mill," Ray jokingly mentions that many of his neighbors believed in witches. These neighbors might easily retell Ray's story as a true account.

By converting a legend into a märchen, Ray Hicks's "Grinding at the Mill" represents a relatively rare development. In American tradition it is far more common to convert a märchen into a legend than vice versa. One typical example is the tale type known by folklorists as "The Youth Who Set Out to Learn What Fear Is," which appears to be the most popular märchen plot in the United States. "Shiver and Shake" (story 44), Sara Cleveland's version of the tale, learned from her Irish family members, is told in märchen style. The hero, who knows no fear, sets out to learn how to shiver and shake. He spends the night in a haunted house and encounters talking skeletons and other terrifying beings, but these creatures fail to scare him. Later, he marries a girl; the morning after their wedding, she awakens him by emptying a bucket of cold water on him. The hero finally learns how to shiver and shake.

Most American versions of this plot leave off the humorous coda and convert the tale into a belief legend. As in Laurie Hance's performance of "A Haunted House" (story 117), the teller typically asserts that the story is true, identifies the hero by name, and cites the exact location of the house, usually an abandoned building known to the teller's neighbors.

Legends raise questions and take stands on the fundamental mysteries of life: Is there life after death, can humans acquire supernatural powers, are there supernatural explanations for human suffering, is there such a thing as divine intervention? If märchen are blatant fantasies, no matter how many cultural truths they embed, teller and audience alike agree on their make-believe nature. Legends, by contrast, come attached to the notion of belief. These stories possess a strong "what if?" component. Whether or not the teller believes it, the story is presented as a "truth claim"; that is, *someone* asserts that it is true. In beginning a legend performance, the narrator often expresses a measure of doubt, but almost always leaves the door open for belief, as when saying, "I wouldn't believe this story at all, but my cousin, who doesn't kid around, swears that it happened to her."

Legends that explore the negative potential of the supernatural tend to focus on boundaries. If a mortal crosses the acceptable boundaries of space, time, or morality, the veil between the everyday and the otherworldly is lifted, the "rules" of life change, and more often than not a supernatural being appears. A man may move beyond the limits of the community to an abandoned cabin in the woods, and a ghost appears (stories 119–123). Or he may take a lonely walk during the "witching hour" and see an evil woman step out of her skin (story 58). Or he may violate a moral law and eat a human body part, only to invite the vengeance of the corpse whose toe he has consumed (story 180).

In the legend traditions of the Old World countries that fed the American migrations, there are myriad types of supernatural beings—elves, gnomes, fairies, mermaids, trolls, and so on—that seldom became focal figures in New World legendry. In this book, the fairies and banshees of Irish tradition are among the few Old World beings that make a substantial showing. It is significant that the three Irish American storytellers who contributed fairy legends to this volume— Sara Cleveland (story 41), Margaret Sullivan (story 131), and Father Sarsfield O'Sullivan (story 132)—were either born in Ireland or learned their fairy legends from elders who were born there. Aside from the Irish materials, there are few indications that the specific beliefs of the Old World took root in American. The German American tradition of *The Seventh Book of Moses*—a magic manual employed by sorcerers to invoke the devil's help to effect their evil plans, is one of the few such instances (story 125, headnote).

Typical of American tradition, the three supernatural beings that appear most often in this book are ghosts, witches, and the devil (or one of Satan's demons).

In most of the tales printed here, the ghost is a sympathetic figure. Its presence often frightens the mortals who happen across it in the wilds or, more often, in an abandoned house, but those brave enough to stand their ground usually discover that the ghost is searching not for innocent victims, but for justice, and is seeking the aid of the human hero to attain that justice. Many of the ghosts that appear here are reluctant haunters who harbor secrets. Most often, the ghost's secret concerns hidden treasure or the identity of his own murderer, the criminal who has created the ghost. These ghosts are condemned to inhabit the human world until unburdened of their secrets. The soul brave enough to hear out the ghost and follow its instructions then digs up the treasure (usually retaining much or all of it as a reward) or identifies the murderer of the ghost, and the haunting stops. In one dramatic tale, the hero recovers the ghost's buried treasure and then brings the ghost's murderer to trial; to make sure that the criminal is punished, the ghosts itself shows up in the courtroom for the trial and helps win a speedy conviction (story 117).

The witches of American legend differ considerably from the beings pictured in bedtime storybooks or seen parading in costume on Halloween. In the oral legends of the Appalachians, witches do not wear black pointed hats or fly through the air on broomsticks. Rather, the legend witch is most often a neighbor, even a relative of the intended victim. In appearance, she (for the great majority of American legend witches are female) is largely indistinguishable from her neighbors, although she may be more cruel or envious or engage in unusual behavior.

The American legend witch typically dwells in rural areas, feeds on envy, and thrives on the misfortune of her foes. She may cause a farmer's sheep to die or a cow to stop giving milk (stories 108, 127). She may transform herself into a spider to ride on the back of a man (story 128). She may slip out of her skin and through a keyhole to steal a piece of jewelry (story 58). To all but the poorest members of today's overwhelmingly urban society, the goals and powers of this villain may seem unbelievably modest. Why would a woman sell her soul to the devil in return for astonishing powers, only to use them to gain such small material rewards? The answer lies in the rural areas where such legends once thrived and where they are still told today. The rural African Americans and Anglo Americans who shared these tales lived subsistence lifestyles: The health of one cow could mean the difference between relatively prosperity and near starvation. In such environments, witch legends are used to explore and explain the causes of misfortune and poverty.

The third most common American legend villain is some manifestation of the devil or the evil spirits he commands. In this anthology, the devil never appears in his stereotypical form: red in color, with horns on his head, and a pointed tail. Sometimes, the devil simply announces his presence with eerie sounds (story 70); at other times, he assumes the form of a dapper stranger who tricks a mortal into surrendering his soul (story 122).

The popularity of ghost, witch, and devil legends should not obscure the fact that many legends feature benevolent supernatural beings. Even ghosts, as earlier mentioned, often appear as helpers in these tales. Other positive legends focus on miracle-working agents of the divine. In Mormon tradition, the Three Ne-phites appear magically to offer aid to mortals who are lost or endangered (story 133). The far more terrifying figure of death personified may appear in a vision sent by God to effect the salvation of wayward souls (story 126).

Legends typically raise more questions than they answer. In Lula Davis's tale of "The Child and the Snake" (story 116), a boy shares bread and milk with a rattlesnake. Discovering the two together, the terrified mother kills the snake, but then the child grows weak and soon follows the snake in death. Related tales have been reported with great frequency in both African American and British American communities. Lula Davis's father, from whom she learned the legend, attempted to find an explanation for the child's death based on his understanding of the principles of the natural world: According to his way of thinking, the child had consumed regular doses of poisonous venom when eating from the same spoon as the snake, but when the snake died, the boy's diet was upset; the child actually died from a lack of poison. Other people, telling the same tale, have offered a supernatural explanation: a mystical bond, a common soul shared by the child and the snake, which caused one to die when the other did.

Belief legends dwell on the boundary between this world and the next; *historical legends*, by contrast, unfold fully in this world, but focus on the most remarkable and memorable figures and features of the past: the most heroic acts, most heinous crimes, extremes of cruelty and courage. Many of these legends, like tall tales, concern the constant challenge of life on the frontier. Among the most popular are family accounts of ancestors who endured assaults of nature as well as human rivals to establish claim to the land that the family ultimately came to consider their home. W.D. Casey (story 87) narrates a desert trek of almost 100 miles undertaken by his father, without water, and describes the outlaw who nearly ended his father's life once he reached the end of the trail. Both Joshua Alley of Maine (story 65) and Roby Monroe Hicks of North Carolina (story 25) tell tales in which European American settlers struggled with Native Americans for control of the land. The family traditions of both tellers bear memories of a man who survived an Indian raid that wiped out his family. In both tales, the survivor devotes the rest of his life to exacting vengeance upon the Indians. Other settlement stories include accounts of positive relations between Indians and settlers: Flora Robertson (story 211) recalls the generosity extended to her family by the Cheyenne of western Oklahoma.

Many of the most dramatic historical accounts relate the personal experiences of the tellers themselves: Sloan Matthews (story 88) recalls how his brother died during a cattle drive accident, Woody Guthrie relates his experiences of the Dust Bowl (stories 209–210), and Janet Freeman (story 212) and Lillie Hawes (stories 213–215) recount how they experienced the terrorist attacks of September 11, 2001.

In historical legends, the great social and ecological movements that molded the nation are given an anecdotal dimension and a human face. The ecological nightmare that was the Dust Bowl created millions of refugees. In this book, two of them—one famous and one nearly unknown—use their personal experiences and narrative skills to bring the reader closer to the everyday dimensions of this disaster: what it was like to try to keep a house clean with winds sweeping dust through the walls, what it was like to have to leave one's ancestral land and travel hundreds of miles with no money, only to find a migrant camp—and no paying work—at the end of the line.

Beyond the natural tragedies of famine, drought, and fire, historical legend also features such human disasters as murder, war, and terrorist attack. In most such tales, the details or the scale of the bloodshed play only a minor part. Rather, and again, it is the personal dimensions of the story that predominate in the collections of the Library of Congress. Civil War stories are told from the point of view of unbloodied victims such as the women (for example, Lee Winniford's Aunt Becky and Aunt Sara, stories 198–199) left behind when their fathers, husbands, sons, and suitors left home to fight. One of the two women who relate their September 11 experiences in this book actually saw the Trade Towers in flames, but it is her personal relationship with the firefighters, including one who did not return, that is focal to her telling (stories 213–215). The second woman experienced September 11 in the safety of her home, with only the TV for company (story 212). All of these accounts are saturated with the tiny details of everyday life: cooking, cleaning, tending bar. Each tale seems at least to imply lessons in survival—one of the points frequently made by the tellers of these disaster accounts is the necessity of sticking it out, attending to the everyday actions of life as a way of asserting a threatened normalcy and overcoming the horrors of violence.

Sometimes these personal accounts of lived experience seem every bit as magical and plotted as folk fiction. Early in her account of September 11, 2001, Lillie Haws tells of standing on a pier in Brooklyn, watching plane tickets—debris from the fallen towers—floating down from the sky (story 213). Later (story 215), Lillie recalls how, in a moment of mourning for a lost firefighter friend, she calls out for a sign that her friend has made it safely to a better world—and how then, seemingly from nowhere and in seeming answer to her prayer, a feather falls into her hand. Miracle or coincidence, it is a moment Lillie Haws will never forget—nor will anyone who listens to her story.

AMERICAN FOLKTALES

THE NATION'S MOST CELEBRATED STORYTELLING FAMILY

THE HICKSES AND THE HARMONS

For over sixty years, the Library of Congress has been accumulating tales and songs from the far-flung and enormously talented Hicks-Harmon family of the southern Appalachians. In 1939, when Herbert Halpert first recorded stories from balladeer and banjo-player Samuel Harmon, few folklorists imagined that his family possessed—in addition to its stunning musical repertoire—a vast stock of rare tales. By 2001, when the American Folklife Center acquired the collections of the International Storytelling Center, one family member, Ray Hicks, had become the most famous traditional storyteller in America. During the 1970s, 1980s, and 1990s, Ray was the focal presence at the National Storytelling Festival in Jonesborough, Tennessee, where story-lovers from around the world gathered every October to enjoy his remarkable narrative art.

As the AFC collections richly attest, Ray Hicks did not learn his arts in a vacuum. Storytelling was a staple in the various Hicks and Harmon homes. When the family ancestors emigrated from Europe, they brought with them a body of *märchen*, or magic tales, that they nurtured from generation to generation with at least as much care as they devoted to their most important material possessions. The Hickses came from England, the Harmons from Germany; both families had settled in Watauga County, North Carolina by the end of the 1700s. Their tales (or at least the most common tales in the families' twentieth-century repertoire) were probably, at first, more English than German, for even in the twentieth century England is the only foreign nation reflected with any frequency in the tellings, which feature references to English people (the giants of Maud Long's tales love to kill "Englishmen"), coins ("guineas"), and locales (London appears in Samuel Harmon's "Little Dicky Whigburn" [story 10]). As the Har-

Ray Hicks (teller of stories 28–32) dancing as Buna Hicks (teller of story 27) plays the fiddle. Beech Mountain, North Carolina, 1959. (Photo by Frank Warner, from the Anne and Frank Warner Collection)

mons and the Hickses combined their families and their considerable verbal skills, they continued to nurture a shared store of tales, which became thoroughly localized through the generations. When Maud Long or Ray Hicks or Daron Douglas tells one of these tales, the characters wander through landscapes filled with mountains, forests, hollows, deserted cabins, itinerant workers, and poor farmers—a world much like that which the Hickses and Harmons have inhabited since the late eighteenth century. As Ray Hicks says of his family tale treasure, "Just listen. They's a lot that's not true, but a lot that is." Ray sees himself and his surroundings in the stories he tells, as when the hero "Jack and his mother was seeing it hard" and Jack took a dare to work in a haunted gristmill. The gristmill in the tale is modeled on the building that Ray visited as a boy to grind grain.

These stories have long outlived their earliest tellers, as well as most of the family lands, deeds, and houses. As the Hicks-Harmon clan branched out from Beech Mountain, North Carolina, to find homes along the towering ridge that marks the North Carolina–Tennessee border, they carefully maintained the plots of their tales. Samuel Harmon's version of "Stiff Dick" (story 7, told in Maryville, Tennessee, in 1939) is easily recognizable as a close cousin of Maud Long's "Jack and the Varmints" (story 16, learned in Hot Springs, North Carolina, and recorded in 1947), and of Ray Hicks's "The Unicorn and the Wild Boar" (story 29, learned in Watauga County, North Carolina, and recorded in 1951). The three tales share special aspects of vocabulary, phrasing, and characterization, even though the tellers had never met each other, and even though they endowed their separate performances with distinctive, personalized twists of style.

The Hicks-Harmon family is best known for its "Jack Tales." Few, if any, types of American folktales have been considered as rare or as precious as these long, magic-saturated stories, in which a boy-hero named Jack relies on nothing more than native wit or innate goodness to fend off larger and more powerful opponents: giants, witches, evil kings, and even sometimes his two older brothers.

Known in England at least since the Middle Ages, Jack Tales had become enormously popular in England, Scotland, and Ireland by the time the American colonies were first settled. In the early eighteenth century, when the major waves of immigration into the Appalachian Mountains began, published versions of "Jack the Giantkiller" (*The History of Jack and the Giants*, 1711) and "Jack and the Beanstalk" (*The Story of Jack Spriggins and the Enchanted Bean*, 1734) were widespread in England. Great literary artists, including Henry Fielding and Samuel Johnson, read and wrote about Jack. But the English, Scottish, and Irish settlers of the Appalachians did not read these stories; rather, they spoke them from memory to avid listeners. And by the 1760s, in the region now known as West Virginia, apparently everyone was telling them.

Reverend Joseph Doddridge, who grew up in the Appalachians in the eighteenth century, remembered how popular these tales had been when he was a boy:

> Dramatic narrations, chiefly concerning Jack and the Giant, furnished our young people with another source of amusement during their leisure hours. Many of those tales were lengthy, and embraced a considerable range of incident. Jack, always the hero of the story, after encountering many diffi-

culties, and performing many great achievements, came off conqueror of the Giant. . . . These dramatic narrations . . . were so arranged as to the different incidents of the narration, that they were easily committed to memory. They certainly have been handed down from generation to generation from time immemorial.

Yet, by 1824, when Doddridge published his recollections, he thought that the Jack Tales had already disappeared. When "civilization" entered the frontier, he explained, the settlers began reading novels and romances and stopped telling "those ancient tales."

Doddridge was wrong. Although many Appalachian families and communities abandoned the Jack Tales, many others have continued telling them up to the present day. But because the storytellers generally did not share these tales outside of their family and neighborhood circles, and because folklorists were not looking for them, the stories did not surface. In 1922, nearly a century after Doddridge had declared the Jack Tales dead, sociologist Isabel Gordon Carter found eleven of them alive and well on the lips of a celebrated ballad singer in Hot Springs, North Carolina.

The storyteller was Jane Hicks Gentry, daughter of Ransom Hicks and Emoline Harmon. On both sides of her family tree, she was a member of the now-celebrated Hicks-Harmon family, which had yet to become the most famous family in American storytelling history. Apparently, Jane had learned her Jack Tales from her grandfather Council Harmon (ca. 1807–1896) of Beech Mountain, North Carolina, a man whose tales were never recorded by or dictated to folklorists, but still a legendary figure in the minds of those who remembered his storytelling almost fifty years after his death. "Counce" loved to sing and dance, with such enthusiasm that he sometimes became the focus of disparaging sermons by Beech Mountain preachers. But Counce's storytelling enraptured the children of the family. Grandson Miles A. Ward told collector Richard Chase, "Ever-when I'd see Old Counce a-coming, I'd run to meet him so I could walk with him back to the house. Then he'd sit and take me up on his lap, and I'd ask him right off for a Jack Tale. He'd tell me one, too; never did fail me. He loved to tell about Jack."

Some twenty years after Jane Hicks Gentry dictated her stories, other grandchildren of Council Harmon were telling their versions of the same tales to a young man from Alabama named Richard Chase. Chase wrote notes on the tales he heard on Beech Mountain, combined them with notes from other folktale performances from other families, and assembled them in a book titled *The Jack*

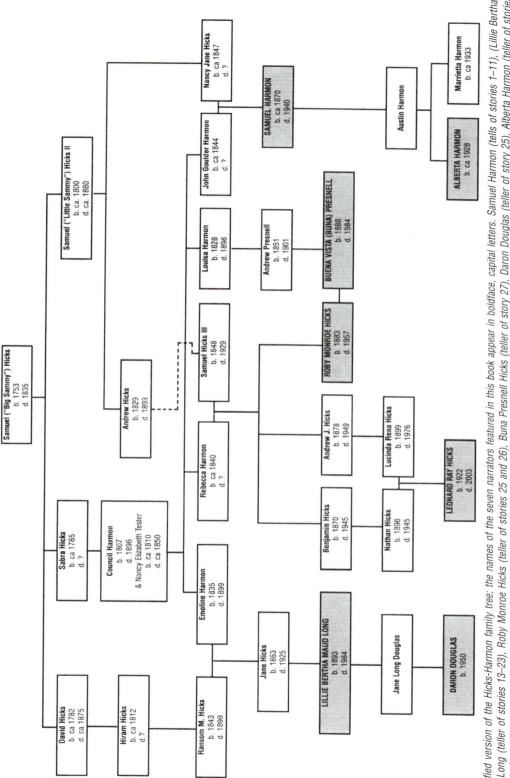

Simplified version of the Hicks-Harmon family tree; the names of the seven narrators featured in this book appear in boldface, capital letters. Samuel Harmon (tells of stories 1–11), (Lillie Bertha) Maud Long (teller of stories 13–23), Roby Monroe Hicks (teller of stories 25 and 26), Buna Presnell Hicks (teller of story 27), Daron Douglas (teller of story 27), Alberta Harmon (teller of stories 11 and 12), and (Leonard) Ray Hicks (teller of stories 28–32) are all direct descendants of both Council Harmon and Samuel ("Big Sammy") Hicks. Maud Long's mother, Jane Hicks (Gentry), was the first memeber of the family from whom folklorists collected Jack tales; Jane stated that she had heard her stories from Council Harmon, direct progenitor of all seven storytellers featured here. In contrast, Samuel Harmon learned his tales from Samuel ("Little Sammy") Hicks II, a direct progenitor of five of the narrators, but not of Maud Long or Daron Douglas.

Tales (1943), which has become the most famous collection of American folktales ever published, still in print today, sixty years after it was first issued.

The enormous popularity of Chase's book inspired folklorists to return, again and again, to members of the Hicks-Harmon family, to listen to their Jack Tales. The storytellers shared not only the tales but also detailed descriptions of the circumstances in which the stories were told. In the following pages, Samuel Harmon, Maud Long, Daron Douglas, Roby Monroe Hicks, and Ray Hicks speak about where and when they heard and told Jack Tales. Two themes sound repeatedly throughout these recollections. One is the important function served by the stories in motivating children to work. Most of the Hickses and Harmons have been subsistence farmers who had to labor incessantly at agriculture, cloth making, lumbering, and various odd jobs to feed their families and to buy the few necessities they could not grow or make themselves. Even in early childhood, the Hickses and Harmons were doing grown-up work (for example, in story 1, Sam Harmon tells of how he was put to work babysitting at age 5). Parents and grandparents got more work from the children when telling them stories. In the 1920s, Ray Hicks's grandmother Julie Hicks put Ray to work shelling beans and rewarded the boy with tales as he labored; in the 1950s, Maud Long used the same ritual to entertain granddaughter Daron Douglas in her kitchen.

The second theme has less to do with material sustenance than with emotional bonding. Among the recorded reminiscences, the most detailed and affectionate accounts involve grandparents. For Samuel Harmon, Roby Hicks, Daron Douglas, and others, the stories they tell here are expressions of a special bond with their grandparents and a way of keeping those they have lost alive in their hearts. In accounts of grandfather-grandchild storytelling, work is seldom mentioned; rather, the speakers tend to invoke leisurely and quiet times, a picture of grandparent and grandchild alone together. As family member Austin Harmon put it, "Seemed to me that I couldn't be contented nowhere else but with grandfather, because he was always telling tales, and singing songs, roaming the woods, and it seems like he took up with me. . . . We was always together, and no one else but us alone, out in the woods somewhere."

The Library of Congress preserves some special performances by Ray Hicks, as well as equally artful tellings by his near and more distant relations. The AFC holdings of Hicks-Harmon tales are extensive enough to fill a book devoted entirely to the family repertoire, and they cannot all be printed here. Remarkably, only four of the tales presented in this section have been previously transcribed and published, and only four have been previously released as sound recordings. Ironically, the first family member to record his voice for the Library of

Congress was among the last to be heard. Although Samuel Harmon's tales have been housed in the American Folklife Center for more than six decades, only one of his tales has been previously published. It is fitting to begin with the oldest and longest-neglected family voice that we still have the power to hear.

Samuel Harmon (1870–1940)

Sam Patterson Harmon was a quick and copious learner. "I used to have as good a recollection as anybody ever lived, I reckon," he told folklorist Herpert Halpert in April 1939. Sam's words could be mistaken for idle boasts had he not backed them up by performing for Halpert's recording machine virtually nonstop, filling sixty-four disks with songs and tales in a seven-day period.

As a young boy, Sam listened to his grandfather, Samuel ("Little Sammy") Hicks II, tell tales and sing songs. Sam Harmon was named after his grandfather, and there was a special bond between them. Sam obviously shared the old man's talents for stories and songs. The grandfather would perform a piece twice, "and then I could sing it just as good as he could." Sam Harmon credited "Old Granddaddy Hicks" with teaching him nearly all the old songs and stories he knew. This attribution is a tribute to the verbal and memorial arts of both men. Sam Harmon's feats of memory grow all the more remarkable when we discover that Granddaddy Hicks died about 1880, when Sam was 10 years old. By the time of Sam's marathon recording session, his special teacher had been dead nearly sixty years.

Samuel Harmon was 68 years old when he shared his stories and songs with the Library of Congress. By that time he was gaunt and hollow-faced; by the end of the following year, he would be dead. He no longer trusted his prodigious memory. He confided to Halpert that his powers of recollection had faded, but his memories of the old days still held: "I can remember things back then a heap better than I can remember things that passed yesterday anymore." And listening to the scratchy six-decade-old recordings of Sam telling tales, one gets the sense that he has forgotten very little about these tales or the special circumstances in which he learned them. Occasionally, he drops the thread of the plot or leaves out a given detail, but he always ties up his tale tidily by the time he has finished it.

In one of the few instances in which Sam seems to suffer a genuine memory lapse, he is describing his grandfather's youth. According to Sam, Old Grand-daddy Hicks "come from England. His father brought him across the waters

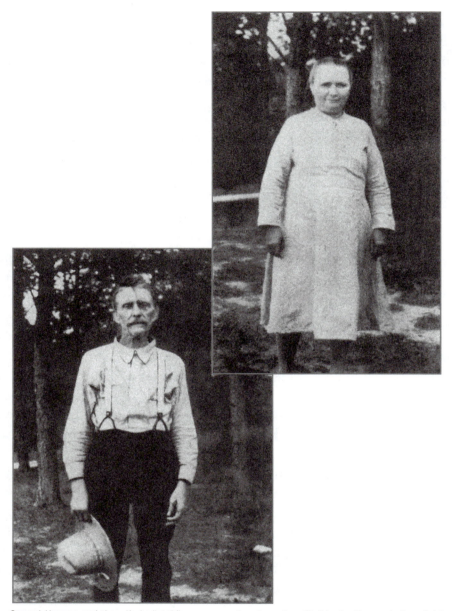

Samuel Harmon and the wife he "stole" as a young boy (see story 1). (Used with permission of J.J. Augustin, Inc.)

when he was four years old, and he learned all of them old songs, I reckon, from my old great granddaddy. Learned em all. . . . And then *his* father lived a good while after he come here. He was a young man, grown, my old Granddaddy Hicks was, when his father died and he left him these songs . . . that he knew."

Genealogical research indicates, to the contrary, that Granddaddy Hicks was born around 1800 in Watauga County, North Carolina, long after his family first arrived in the New World. One possible reason for Sam's misremembering is the intensity of the bond formed between grandfather and grandson, coupled with their shared love of stories: his grandfather had told him that the Jack Tales came from England; therefore, Granddaddy Hicks did too, for the man and his tales seem to have been inseparable in Sam's mind.

After "Little Sammy" Hicks died (about 1880), Sam quickly followed in his grandfather's footsteps to become a popular local entertainer, widely known for his singing and banjo-playing skills. Shortly after Sam was married at age 17, his home became a magnet for Saturday-night dancers. "I used to do lots of singing. I never went nowhere to sing. They always come to *me* to listen at em. . . . Every Saturday night and sometimes through the week, they'd come . . . over to my house. And I had a banjo then and kept a banjo in good practice, and they'd want me to pick the banjo and sing songs, and I'd set em up many a night, and sleep the day for singing songs for them—for the young folks, you know, girls, young girls and boys." Sam kept up this weekly entertainment for about twenty years.

Sam was born in the ancestral Hicks-Harmon homeplace, Watauga County, North Carolina. But when Sam was still a boy, his father, Samuel Goulder Harmon, moved the family across the Blue Ridge to the neighborhood of Cades Cove, Tennessee. In the 1930s, when the federal government evicted the residents of Cades Cove in order to create the Great Smoky Mountains National Park, the Harmons were forced to leave their home. After a period of traveling, Samuel moved to Maryville, Tennessee, to live with his son Austin. It was at Austin's home that folklorist Herbert Halpert found Samuel and recorded his tales in 1939.

1. How I Bought and Stole My Wife	SAMUEL HARMON Maryville, Tennessee Recorded by Herbert Halpert, April 25, 1939

This autobiographical description of Sam's marriage to his stepsister Polly has all the twists and turns of an elaborate joke, but it also illustrates harsh conditions of daily life in the Appalachians in the 1880s. At age 12, and soon to be married, Polly Haggerman had already left home and was working as a live-in servant for twenty-five cents a week. The story also bears

A mountain cabin at the foot of the Great Smoky Mountains in Tennessee, in the region where Samuel Harmon grew up and told his tales. (Library of Congress, Wittemann Collection)

witness that Sam and his neighbors played as hard as they worked. Sam chuckles to himself repeatedly as he relates the pranks played on the newlyweds during their wedding night, the prank he played by stealing his friend's whiskey, and the pranks he and his young friends played on themselves by downing half a gallon of whiskey and suffering the consequences.

Perhaps more than anything else, the tale illustrates Sam's character: he is fearless in standing up to the squire, the wedding-night pranksters, and his outraged stepmother, and he shows an artful knack for using a few well-chosen words to defuse a volatile situation. Sam was a master of quick, one-liner comebacks. Among them is his answer to those who thought he'd married too young: "They asked me one time what made me marry so soon, and I told em . . . 'To get the good out of married life, I reckon.' That's all that I knew to tell em."

Apparently, this tale was a family favorite. Folksong collector Mellinger G. Henry heard it told during his visits with Sam and Polly in the 1920s and 1930s. In 1938, Henry published a somewhat different version, as told from Polly's perspective: Polly's mother and Sam's mother were having a needlework contest; 5-year-old Sam and baby Polly were in the room with the women. Polly cried so much that her frustrated mother turned to Sam and told him that she would sell Polly to him for three sticks of wood. "Samuel soberly brought in the three sticks, laid them at her feet, took the baby out on the steps and quieted her." Later Polly's father and Samuel's mother died, and Polly's mother married Samuel's father. Sam and Polly were now stepbrother and stepsister. After Sam and Polly fell in love and eloped, Sam "stopped all objections from her mother (Sam's own stepmother) by reminding her that he had bought Polly when she was a baby for three sticks of wood."

By the time that Sam Harmon told his own version to Herbert Halpert, Polly was dead.

My half brother is my wife's half brother. How are you going to unpuzzle that? Well, my wife's mother married and had one kid, Haggerman. And then my mother died, and my father married my wife's mother, and I married the girl.

[Herbert Halpert: How did you get her to marry you?]

Why, I stoled her. . . . Why, she's a-staying away from home and was hired out from home. And her mother never knowed that we loved one another at all. [When her mother was around,] we never had nothing to say to one another or nothing before her.

Well, I told her mother that I was going back to North Carolina to see my people, and she hunted up lots of scraps of her dresses and one thing or another, you know, for me to take back to show *her* mother.

Well, I got outside of the house, I throwed them old rags all down, you know, and I went on to Maryville and got my license and come back by where [Polly] was a-staying and got her and took her down to Happy Valley . . . and was married. . . . I was seventeen. . . . She was twelve the seventh day of May, and we was married the twentieth of next September. [She was] just that much over twelve years old. I'd known her for about ten years.

[Herbert Halpert: Isn't there a story about how you bought her? . . .]

Her mother . . . brought her to my mother's house on a carding and spinning contest back years ago when I was a boy, when they wove cloth. And she hadn't quit nursing yet, and I was five years old. I was five years older than my wife.

Well, her mother told me, if I'd rock her and see to her that day, she'd *give her* to me and buy me a pound of candy. I was a little feller, I sucked my thumb then all the time, and picked this titty nipple, had it pulled out a-way long. So I went up to the cradle and looked at her, and I said, "Well, she's a awful ugly little old thing, but maybe she'd be some use to me sometime. I'll just do that."

Well, I'll tell you the whole rigmarole of it, being as I started it.

Well, when we went to marry, why, there was nobody there but just a squire and his old folks. . . . And then he commenced talking to us, and he said he didn't want to marry us. Says, "You're just children, you're just kids. And . . . when you come to be men and women, you'll see people that . . . you'll love better. . . ."

"Well," I said, "if you don't marry me," I said, "there's other squires that will."

"Well," he says, "I'll marry you," he said, "but I'll just give you six months to live together."

[Polly's] mother would never let her go to a-playing or nothing. Just kept her cowed down, let her hired out around and about [to] people for twenty-five cents a week, . . . working herself to death. And I didn't like that at all. I loved the girl.

[On their wedding night, Sam and Polly's friends subject them to a playful ritual called a chivaree, in which they try to "plague out" the newlyweds with pranks and teasing.]

Well, we went to Alvin Smith the first night after we was married. Well, we were just kids, you know, and the other ones took to plague us out. But they couldn't make nothing off of me. Of course, they got her fine, but they couldn't make a thing off of me, if I was a kid. Well, they kept us in after supper. Said, "Well, we must turn in now and get these children to bed."

And I says, "All right, I'm a-getting wearied. I'd like to get to bed as quick as possible."

Well, finally at last, they seed that I didn't care for that. Well, they didn't strip us and put us to bed like they said they would, and Alvin Smith said he was going to tie cowbells to the bed-cord that night. I said, "It don't make any difference." I said, "You don't need to do that." I says, "It'll make racket enough without any bells to it." [Sam laughs.]

And the old bed, every time you moved, it just *ricka-racka-ricka-racka-ricka-racka-ricka-racka*, you know. I just kept a-rolling, a-twisting, you know, and at last about midnight, Alvin says [laughing], "I just want you to lay still and go to sleep," he says. "We can't get to sleep a wink tonight." And so, he told us then to come back next Saturday night, and he'd have us a wedding supper. Well, I told him, "All right."

And he went to Knoxville and got a half a gallon of whiskey, and he's a-going to keep that whiskey till all left but his just, best friends, and he was going to bring it out and treat em all. . . .

Well, I got a little hint of [where he hid] the whiskey, and I knowed he come right to that little old barn. . . . And there's a window you had to crawl up there and go in.

And way long about midnight, the crowd begin to break up, and me and my wife and Allen J. Crumbley and his sisters was going up the same road together—had about two mile to go—and we went to that little barn, and I says to them, I says, "I bet you a dollar right in here is where's he hid that whiskey. I'm going to get up and hunt it and see if I can find it." Well, I crawled into the little window and I hunted everywhere. And I was started to get out, and happened to put my hand right on the jug setting right beside the window. The seal had never been broke on it.

Well, back then, my wife and . . . the Crumbley sisters didn't know anything about whiskey. . . . And I brought it down, there's half a gallon of it. Us four, now, was going to have to drink every drop in this jug. Well, my wife says, "I heard em say, whiskey'd make you drunk, wouldn't it?"

I said, "No. *This* won't." I said, "This won't." I said, "You could drink a half a gallon. It wouldn't make you drunk."

Well, we set into drinking, you know, and kept on drinking, till we drunk the last drop of it. And there was a branch running out beside the barn, and I went out there and filled the jug up again, and fixed the seal back on, and put it right back where it was.

We had about two miles to go. . . . They got to staggering and reeling around, the women did. Said [high-pitched, female voice], "What's the matter with me? I can't stand up!" [Laughing]

We got to laughing at em and finally they's just up and [falling] down, up and down, up and down. And finally Irene Crumbley got so drunk she couldn't go. Me and her brother got her up by the arm and just drug her along about two hundred yards through the mud and everything, you know. And [her] old man and the old woman's old, and they's in the house asleep, and they had the plank [path] to the log house right at the road. And that's where she always slept. We drug her in there and tucked her in there and put her into bed. She was just dead drunk. Just no life in her, hardly. And the old man and the old woman never knowed it. Well, Allen stopped there too.

And we started on then up, me and my wife. . . . There was a little trail around the bank [of a creek]. She'd fall off some time. The creek was as high as this loft, nearly.

I looked in there. I says, "What are you doing down there, partner?" [Laughing]

And Old Man Buttshanks lived about a hundred yards below where we did and had an old black one-eyed dog that'd just eat you up, if you didn't knock him down. It was way midnight. And they had the fence right along the trail, and right where you passed the fence, there was one end of an old rail come out in the trail and you had to lean around to get around that rail. I got me some good rocks and come on, and he had the plank in to his log house right next to the trail. Well, I got up there, and that old dog come out and here he come, just yelling, you know, and I [threw one] at him and didn't hit him, throwed through the fence crack and hit the end of that house. And you never heard such a racket in the world. Old Man Buttshanks jumped up, lit the lantern and come out on the porch, and I broke to run. I forgot that darned rail was a sticking out there and it just hit me right in the stomach, just knocked the breath out of me. I'd just get a breath about every fifteen minutes.

And finally at last my wife come up and says, "What? Are you laying there, Pardner?" I couldn't speak to her, you know. I laid there awhile.

[Then we sneaked into] a little room of the house my father lived in. And they all thought I was in North Carolina, you know. . . . And my half-sister slept in that room, and so we went in. The old folks was asleep and I slipped and got into bed, and my wife, she slipped and got into bed. . . .

[My half-sister] waked up, . . . and she looked up and she commenced hollering, "Hey, mother, mother! Polly's getting to bed with Sam!" She kept a-hollering at em and got em to wake up.

[My stepmother] said, "Lay down there and shut your lying mouth," and said, "You just a-dreaming." Said, "Sam's in North Carolina, and Polly's over across the mountain at Penny Yardwood's."

[But my half-sister] just kept on and kept on and kept on, and [my stepmother] says to my father, says, "That child's a-dreaming, or in a trance or something. I'll go in and wake her up." She lit the light and come in there, you know, and sure enough, right there we was, you know. She jumped at my wife, and she got her by the hair of the head, you know, and she's just attacking her everywhere. "I'll give you 'married,' durn you! Now I'll give you 'married'! I'm going to let you know now what 'married' is. I'm a-going to take a warrant for you for stealing that young'un."

I said, "Look-a here, Mama." I says, "I can prove by your own self, and by other witnesses, that I bought her when she was a baby and paid for her." I said, "Just go ahead and take the warrant if you want to."

And she cut a big shine [to me], and it wasn't a year after that that she thought more of me . . . honestly, than she did of her own young'uns. And she said she wished . . . she'd got all of her son-in-laws just like me. . . .

[Herbert Halpert: How had you bought your wife? . . .]

By rocking her and seeing to her while [her mother] was a-carding that day, you know. Paid-worked her out.

2. Telling Tales to My Grandkids

SAMUEL HARMON
Maryville, Tennessee
Recorded by Herbert Halpert,
April 27, 1939

Herbert Halpert not only registered the earliest surviving audio recordings of Appalachian Jack Tales but also elicited some of the earliest accounts of how, when, why, and to whom these tales were told. The following passage was recorded after Samuel Harmon had already told Halpert ten tales. Halpert then asked Harmon to talk about the situations in which he normally heard and retold his family's tales. In the course of describing his storytelling practices, he slips in a brief Jack Tale to demonstrate how he alludes to the actions in his tales in his attempts to divert his audience into letting him sleep. In a rhythmic whisper, he imitates the sound of the impact of a thrown rock and runs it together with a sentence describing Jack picking up the rock ("He tuck [took] it") or his victory over the giants ("He tuck em") to create a hypnotic nonsense phrase that he repeats until he and—with luck—his grandchildren fall asleep as they lie in their dugout shelter.

Herbert Halpert: Was it to the children that you told this story?]

My . . . grandchildren—my son's children.

[Herbert Halpert: How did you come . . . to have to make up your own stories?]

Why, I told all I knowed, and then I had to go to make em up myself and telling em. We—

[Herbert Halpert: Did they used to pester you, bother you to tell stories?]

Yeah. I stayed with my son and he had a house dug in the ground. And through the summertime, why, me and the kids would lay in that house down in the ground there—it's called a storm house. And they'd just wear the life out of me to tell em tales. And I told em tales and tales and tales. I told all that I

Herbert Halpert with his "sound wagon," an ambulance converted into a portable recording studio. During three months in the spring of 1939, he drove through ten southern states, often sleeping in the ambulance next to the recording machine. By his journey's end, Halpert had recorded 416 disks, including the first twelve folktale performances presented in this book. (Courtesy of Violetta Maloney Halpert)

did know, and then I just had to go to making em up some and telling em, to get shut of em, to get rid of em. . . .

Why, they'd say, "Grandpa, do tell us another tale. Grandpa, do please tell us one more tale and we'll let you alone."

Well, I'd get so sleepy that it appeared to me like I just couldn't keep my eyes open. And I told em one about two old giants that went out to carry a big log of wood in, . . . a big log, and it's hollow.

And there's a young man by the name of Jack. The king would give him . . . a thousand dollar each for—if he could destroy these giants. Well, Jack he slipped out and heared em a-talking about the log of wood, and he goes gets some rocks and crawled in the hollow of this big log. Well, they picked it up on their shoulders and started. And Jack, he went and throwed the rocks out the end of the log and hit one on the head. And [the lead giant] thought it was the other giant behind him. He said, "What did you hit me that way for?"

The other says, "I ain't hitting you."

He says, "I know better. You *did* hit me."

And Jack, he'd sit in there, and he hit the other'n.

And so he said, "Now you hit *me!* What'd you hit me for?"

The other say, "Why, I ain't hitting you."

They kept on that way until they got mad and throwed the log down and got to fighting. And they fit, and they couldn't nary one get up. And Jack took his tomahawk and killed em. And he'd go to the end of the log. And I'd always say, "*Ka-thump-he-tuck-im.*" And he'd go back there at the end of the log: "*Ka-thump-he-tuck-im.*"

Well, I told tales to them till I got so sleepy, you know, I'd go to sleep and they'd keep on at me. And I'd kind of wake me up, I'd say, "*Ka-thump-he-tuck-im.*" Then I'd go to snoring again, get back to sleep. And they'd keep on, trying to wake me up again. I'd say, "*Kathump-he-tuck-it,*" I'd [do that again and again] before I ever did get sound sleep.

[Herbert Halpert: What was that you were saying to them?]

"*Kathump-he-tuck-it.*"

[Herbert Halpert: What does that mean?]

I'd be throwing rocks. I told them in the tale, you know, that Jack would slip up and then hit one: "*Ka-thump,* he'd take him." Then he'd get the other one: "*Ka-thump,* he'd take him." And after I was asleep, they'd keep on at me, and I'd kind of wake up, you know, and again I'd say, "*Ka-thump-he-tuck-em.*" Then I was off asleep again. Snore awhile, and then they'd get me awake again. I'd say, "*Ka-thump-he-tuck-em.*"

3. The Great Pumpkin

SAMUEL HARMON
Maryville, Tennessee
Recorded by Herbert Halpert,
April 27, 1939

This tall tale is one of the stories that Sam made up to tell his children. When the interviewer asked him where he learned the story, Harmon answered, "I learned it from experience." In the classic manner of American tall tale narrators, Harmon speaks his story in flat and earnest tones, his voice giving no hint that he is telling an outrageous lie.

What called me to start this—why *everybody* that God sent to this earth, he sent him with a different gift. And I was studying to try and to find out my gift, that I was gifted. Every person has got a different gift, and if they . . . start on the gift that God give em, they prosper. And I got to study—and the way my mind led—that my gift was raising pumpkins. And I started out that-a-way. And I lived . . . on the Mississippi River, where the land is terrible rich. I bought a acre lot there. Put up a little cabin on it before I was married, and so I decided to try my luck on raising pumpkins right there. Well, I cleaned up me a little patch, fixed it, got it in good shape. I planted me seventeen pumpkins here. And they come up, and they come a cold spell and killed em all but one. . . . And I went out and I seed my pumpkins all covered [with ice] and I was expecting another cold spell. And I went and protected that [last pumpkin] from the cold.

Well, it didn't agree with me there very well. My health, somehow or another, I didn't have my health good. And so I just locked my doors and thought I'd take a trip out and stay a month or two, and maybe till fall, and see if it couldn't improve my health some way or another. Well, I did that, and went to Florida, and stayed six months, I believe it was. . . . The climate suit me better there, and I got to feeling better and long about time that I knew that pumpkin was matured, if it made anything, I went back. I went back there and where I'd planted that seed, and I seed a big mossy log, looked like it was stretched out over the fields. . . .

And I think to myself, that pumpkin's never done no good. It's died or something has destroyed it. Well, I think I'll get on this log and walk out a piece and see what I can discover out there. I was active then and young and I got out and started and kept going and going and going, I seen it just kept going on. Well, I come back, and, uh, got me a lot of provisions and I think I'll take me another trip and see if I can find the end of that. Well I got all the stuff that I could carry. I traveled on and traveled on till I seen that I just had enough to get back to where I could get something more to turn around and come back again. I hadn't yet found no end. . . .

The second trip I come back, I took my tomahawk with me. And I discovered after so long a time that this log . . . was hollow. I taked the tomahawk and cut a hole in it, and I seen that this was hollow. The log seemed to be likely to be about six foot through, with a big hollow in there, and I studied out a plan now, how would I manage to get rations along so that I could follow to the end of it.

Well, I think to myself, now I know what I'll do. I'll just take my tomahawk and I'll carry a load as far as I can go, and get back in one day, and I'll cut a hole in this log and drop my provisions down in there and well, then, I'll go back and get another load, and then I'll go as far as I can and go and cut a hole and drop it in there. And as I come back, I can stop *here* and eat something and stop *here* and eat something. And so, I was *three weeks* a-cutting holes and putting provisions along in this log so I could eat along my travels. And so, the fourth week—it was on a Saturday evening, as well as I recollect—I got where I could see the other side. And I seed a big yellow mountain in front of me. A big yellow mountain. I think to myself, that surely is a world of gold. I'm lucky now, sure enough.

Well, when I got over there and got to it, it was a pumpkin. It took me four days and nights to walk around that pumpkin.

And so, I had an old sow that'd been gone a year. Good old sow. The best . . . I'd ever had in my life. Well, I discovered after all of this that this log that was hollow [ended] here. So I went up to that, found out it was a pumpkin. I walked four days and nights walking around it. And I got around on the far side, and there's a hole in this pumpkin. I looked in there, and that damned old sow had got in that vine and went clean across and had eat a hole in that pumpkin and she was in there yet. And she went and had a hundred and ten shoats right there in the pumpkin, where she'd raised them right there in that pumpkin. And yet you couldn't tell any of them'd been there.

And so, I learned that my gift was raising pumpkins.

4. Giant Mosquitoes

SAMUEL HARMON
Maryville, Tennessee
Recorded by Herbert Halpert,
April 27, 1939

Samuel Harmon did not claim to have invented this story, but as tall tale tellers often do, he did claim it to be a true account from his own past.

[Herbert Halpert: Where'd you get this story?]
I got it through experience.
[Herbert Halpert: All right.]
I used to be a great mineral hunter. I put in the biggest part of my life a-hunting minerals, and I always had a tomahawk that I used, with a hammer on one end and a blade on the other end, to test the stones and things with. And I was coming up the Mississippi River one time and—along in . . . July or August, one or the other. I disremember what time it was. And the mosquitoes there was so thick, you couldn't rest nowhere you could get.

And I didn't work for two weeks. I hadn't got a night's sleep for the mosquitoes. And I'd run out of money and I wasn't able to go to a hotel, or even to a private house. And, in that country, why, you had to pay for what you got there. I was just tired and wore out, and I was going up the river one evening right late, and happened to discover a big wash kettle beside the river where this lady'd been washing.

I seed that and . . . I think to myself, "Right there I'll get one night's rest." I go over on up there, and I turn the kettle over, got in under it, and turned it back down on me, and I was a-feeling good. Hadn't been there but a little bit, a heard one *tap*, *tap*, on the kettle that a-way. And by golly that blamed thing socked its bill clean through that kettle. I don't know how. . . . And I'll be durned if the thing didn't fly off with the kettle and left me laying there naked again. Well, I laid there awhile, and I didn't think what in the world that I would do. [But I got off out of there.]

Well, I goes on up the river a piece further and I come to a little cow stable, built pretty close to the river. And I think to myself, maybe I'll get a little rest there, maybe if I can get under the boards. I get under the boards. It was covered with boards, some kind of boards. I don't know what the timber growth was there, I just forget. But anyhow, I got in there and crawled up in the little loft they had, it was pretty close to the boards there. And I hadn't laid there but a little bit, and they's four [mosquitoes; claps loudly, then] *tap*, *tap*. I think to myself, by gosh, if you hit them seasoned boards, it may break your bill. . . . Them four stuck their blamed bills through that board and I reckon I'll be damned if they didn't fly off with the roof.

So I just give up trying to rest or sleep or anything, and I just thinks to myself, I'll have to die right on this big river. But finally I got through into a good settlement where the people turned to me and give me something to eat. I finally got to a railroad station and got back on the train and got back into my own country.

I just give up my job of mineral hunting. I never hunted any more after that.

[Herbert Halpert: A true story, isn't it, Mr. Harmon?]
Yeah. Yeah.

5. Jack, Tom, and Will

SAMUEL HARMON
Maryville, Tennessee
Recorded by Herbert Halpert,
April 26, 1939

This, the first Jack Tale told by Samuel Harmon to Herbert Halpert, appears to be the overall favorite of the Hicks-Harmon family. Halpert asks, "Mr. Harmon, will you tell us a story?" Samuel Harmon answers, with transparent eagerness, "Yes, sir."

One time they's a family and they was three sons, and they's named Jack, Tom, and Will. And the father died—they was poor folks—and he willed . . . Tom and Will a horse apiece—fine horses—and give Jack a little old heifer.

Jack was lazy, he wouldn't do nothing, he just laid around. He wasn't no account. And Tom and Will was good workers. And they went to working and was out a-clearing one day, and cut a tree on Jack's little heifer and killed it.

He went out and drug it down in the house and just laid there. He got plumb naked. There wasn't a rag on him. And he'd skin a piece out, and he'd cut it out and boil it and eat it—eat that heifer up. Well, he went out then and took the hide and filled it up full of straw and leaves and went to dragging it about over the settlement. Drug it around till it got to stinking. And then a crow flew and lit on it one day, and he catched the crow and put it under his arm and left his cow skin.

He goes on to a fellow's house—where a man lived, that the old preacher was coming to stay with his wife that night. And he was gone, her husband was. And Jack, he come up to the door late and hollered to stay all night.

She told him that she never kept nobody when her husband was gone, especially strangers. He said, *bedad*, he's going to stay anyhow.

"Well," she said, "if you're going to stay anyhow," said, "you go upstairs and go to bed."

And so she had all kinds of good cooking fixed, you know, and was fixing up for a good supper for her and the preacher. And she's dressed neat and fine, you know. And Jack, he went upstairs. There was a knothole in the ceiling—and he laid awake and peeked down and watched her and what all she done with these goodies she had cooked.

Way late in the night her husband come in unexpected and knocked at the door, and he come in and says, "I want a bite to eat."

"Well," she says, "there's a little piece bread back in the kitchen there—you're just going to be without meat. I didn't cook anything this evening."

And so he went in—and fixing to eat a bite, and Jack, he begin to fuss around upstairs.

[The husband] says, [raising his voice] "Who is that upstairs?"

"Why," she says, "an old naked crazy man come here to stay all night last night, and I told him I couldn't keep him, and he says he's good to stay anyhow, and I told him to go upstairs."

And her husband says, "*Hello, stranger!* Come down and have some supper with me."

Said, "Bedad," he believed he would. He was hungry. He come down with his old crow under his arm, you know, and he set down at the table and he sort of mashed his arm down on the crow, and the old crow says, [high pitched] *Squawk!*

[Jack said,] "Shut your mouth. You gab around here and you'll have the woman of the house mad directly."

Her husband said, "What did he say, Jack?"

(He'd watched her put all these goodies away, you know. And hid em.) "Ah, he said there's a little baked pig and a little stuffed turkey and one thing or another in the cupboard."

"Is there, old woman?"

"Yeah, a little I saved for my kinfolk. I was *sure* they'd be over today."

"Bring it out and let me and Jack eat it. Blamed kinfolks."

He made her get it out, and him and Jack been going at it awhile. And Jack squeezed, and that old crow went, *Squawk.* And he said, "Didn't I tell you to shut your mouth. You'll have the woman of the house mad directly."

"What'd he say, Jack?"

"Ah," he said, "there's some fried eggs," he said, "and egg custard, and one thing and another in the cupboard."

Says, "Is there, old woman?"

"Yes," says, but says she's saving for her kinfolks. She was *sure* they'd be over that day. "Blame my kinfolk." She set it down and let him and Jack eat it. He made her get it out. And [Jack] squeezed his old crow again and: *Squawk.*

He said, "I told you to shut your blamed mouth. You're going to have the woman of the house mad directly."

Said, "What did he say, Jack?"

"Ah, he said there's a little speck of butter and a little sweetened rum and one thing or another in the cupboard."

"Is there, old woman?"

Said, "Yeah, a little I saved for the kinfolk. I was sure they'd be over today. Ah," she said, "blame my kinfolk."

Husband said, "Let me and Jack eat it."

Well they eat and eat till Jack's whole stomach just looked [swollen], you know, he just eat so much. Stayed all night. Next morning, he got up, and the husband wanted to know what he'd take for that talking bird.

Oh, he said, he wouldn't sell that at all.

Well, he said, money *enough* would buy it, wouldn't it?

Oh, yes, he said, money *enough* would buy it.

"Well," he said, "what'll you take for it?"

(He seed this old preacher get in this big chest there [the night before] and she'd locked him up.) And so, well, he said, "I'll take a thousand dollars and that big chest a sitting there."

His wife said, "You're not a-going to *get* that chest. My father's father give it to my father and my father give it to me, and *nobody'll* get that chest." Her husband said, yes, he could have that blamed chest if he wants it. He paid him a thousand dollars and all, and [Jack] got this old preacher up on his back in the chest and he went out and he bought him a nice suit of clothes and fixed up, you know, and dragged this old chest a piece till he come to an old open well.

And, "Ah," he said, "this blamed old heavy chest." Says, "I'm going to throw it in this well," he says. "I ain't got no use for it."

The old preacher says, "*Please! Please don't*, Jack. Don't, Jack. I'll poke you out five hundred dollars more at the keyhole."

Jack said, "Poke it out in a hurry, then."

He poked him out five hundred dollars more at the keyhole. And then [Jack] rested awhile and he picked [the preacher] up on his back . . . and he's going around and he carried it around this big, high river bank. "Ah," he says, "I'm going to throw this blamed old chest in the river." Says, "I ain't going to carry it no further."

The old preacher says, "*Do please*, Jack." He says, "Please don't throw me in the river." Says, "I'll poke you out five hundred dollars more at the keyhole and you unlock the chest." Jack told him he would. He poked him out the money and he set it down and unlocked the chest. That made him two thousand dollars.

He goes in, you know, and Tom and Will seed him a-coming all dressed up. They didn't know him for a while. And after he come up, they said, "Jack, where in the world did you get all that money?"

"Ah," he said, bedad, he got it from his cow's skin.

Well, they said, "Now, Jack." they says. They went up to the stable and killed their horses, you know, and got the hide and stuffed it full of stuff and straw and started dragging it around over the settlement. It got to stinking and nobody'd let em come up to the house and let em come in. They told Jack now that he'd told them a lie and . . . they was going to drown him.

Jack says, "Well," he says, "bedads," he says, "you can drown me if you want to, but I told you how I got my money."

Well, they got a sack, and Tom and Will took him down to the riverbank, put him in the sack and tied him up. And they forgot something or other they had to do before they drowned him. And while they's setting back, there's an old, gray-headed man come up the river with a big herd of sheep. He's driving his sheep and: "*Ho, sheep there. Ho, sheep there.*" Come up there, and Jack is wiggling around there. And they got to talking and he wanted to know if somebody in there, and [Jack] told him yes and he wanted to know what was he a-doing there.

Ah, said he's just fixing to go to heaven.

The old man let into arguing and said, "Jack, you're young," said, "and I'm old." He says, "please let me go in your place."

Jack said no. "Bedad," he said, he might get none other chance. He said he'd better go while he had a chance to go.

The old man kept arguing with him till at last, "Well," [Jack] says, "if nothing else will do you," he says, "come and untie the sack and let me get out." And he jumped up out of the sack and said, "Let me tie you up."

He untied the sack and Jack got out and the old man got in there and [Jack] tied him up and he said, "Now, before you start," he said, "you'll hear two angels come talking."

Well, Jack he drove his sheep on back down the river out of here. . . . And Tom and Will come, and just knowed it was Jack, and picked the old man up and threw him in the river and drownded him.

Well, after they went back, Jack went down and got around his sheep, you know, and come a-driving four or five hundred head of sheep up toward the house. And so Tom and Will are standing in the door and they say, "That *is* Jack," and "it can't be Jack! No, we drowned him."

They kept arguing that-a-way back and forth till he got up, and they knowed that it was Jack. Says, "Jack. We drowned you. Where in the world did you get all of that fine herd of sheep?"

Ah, said, bedad, he got em by the river where they throwed em. That's where he a-got em.

"Well," they said, "Now, Jack," said, "you caused us to kill our horses and everything," they said . . . "you pick us up and throw us in there to get us a herd of sheep."

Oh, he said he wasn't going to do it.

"Well," they said, "if you don't, we'll shoot you. We know we can kill you that way."

Kept on arguing. Jack says, "Well, if nothing else'll do you, get you a sack apiece and come on."

Well, they got em a sack apiece, you know, and they went on down there and Jack put em in and tied em up, you know, and they picked up Tom and throwed him in the river, and he was a kicking around a-drowning.

And Will says, "What's he doing now, Jack?"

Oh, he said, "He's got a hell of a wether by the tail. I forget to throw him a little further, he'd a got ten thousand."

Will said, "Pitch me in, just as far as ever you can, Jack."

Jack picked, just picked him up and threwed him in the river as far as he could and drowned them both, and went back down and had a fortune.

6. The Marriage of the King's Daughter

SAMUEL HARMON
Maryville, Tennessee
Recorded by Herbert Halpert,
April 27, 1939

This was the third tale told by Sam Harmon to Halpert. It seems to represent one of the most deeply submerged strands of the Hicks-Harmon family narrative tradition. The fact that the tale contains both risqué situations and scatological scenes has probably kept it from surfacing more often in command performances presented by mountain people for folktale collections from outside the region. This is only the second version of this tale to emerge in British American tradition. The other version was told by Hicks-Harmon family member Marshall Ward in 1981, shortly before his death.

Halpert was anxious to hear this tale, but Sam hesitated to tell it. He whispered to Harmon that there was "something wrong" about it. Puzzled, Halpert asked, "What's wrong with it?" After Sam offers that the tale is "a little smutty" and has "some ugly words about it," Halpert presses Sam to continue and simultaneously tries to reassure him: "Oh, don't worry about that. . . . You just go on ahead. They won't pay any attention to that. . . . When it gets to [the ugly] part, we'll just turn off the machine. Go on, tell me." After a reluctant start, however, Sam shows obvious enjoyment in telling the tale, and before the tale is over he is laughing to himself as he speaks.

The "tumblebug" that appears in the tale is a dung beetle, an insect that rolls up balls of dung to encase its eggs; this is what Sam is referring to when he says that the tumblebug "nasties up" the princess's bed.

Ohne time there's a king, had a fair daughter, and so—there's Jack, Tom, and Will, and Tom first went to see her and they was three questions that if he'd answer, why, the one that could answer either one of them questions—why, he offered to give his girl to.

Tom went. He couldn't answer the questions.

Will went and *he* couldn't answer the questions.

And finally *Jack* went, and he answered the question. And the king give him up his daughter, and he married her.

And there's another young man that saw every sight of the world of her. He *loved* her. And he wanted her too, and when they was married, he told Jack that if he wouldn't turn over to her or speak to her for three nights, he'd give him ten thousand dollars. And Jack told him he would.

Well, when they was married, and went to bed, why, Jack wouldn't turn over to her or speak to her the whole night.

Next morning, her father came down to her, the king, and says, "Well, daughter, how'd your man do last night?"

"Oh," she said. "He didn't do no way. He wouldn't turn over or speak to me, or nothing."

King says, "Well, in two more nights, and if he don't do no better, we'll throw him in the lion's den."

Well, next night, just the same. The old king come down next morning and said, . . . "How'd your husband do last night, daughter?"

"Ah," she said, just like [before], she said he wouldn't turn over or speak to her or nothing.

"Well," he says, "one more night, and if he don't do better we'll throw him in the lion's den."

When Jack's father's died, he gave him a tumblebug and a mouse—was all he give him.

Well, the third night he come down, and just the same thing. They took him and throwed him in the lion's den and Jack, he just took this piece of lace, put it over the lion's mouth, and the lion couldn't eat him.

So this other fellow married her and so that night, why, after they're married, why—Jack sent his tumblebug over to smear the bed, all over.

And so [laughs], the old king come down next morning. Says, "How'd the new man do last night, daughter?"

"Oh," she said, "he just nastied the bed all over." She said, "He's worse than Jack."

"Well," he said, "two more nights. If he don't do no better, we'll throw him in the lion's den."

He goes next day and had a patch stuck over [his rear], you know where. So he know'd he couldn't do nothing, then, in the bed.

So Jack sent his little mouse . . . to cut a hole through the patch, and the tumblebug nastied the bed again. Well, he got up next morning. The bed was just the same way.

The old king come down, "Well," says, "how'd your man do last night, daughter?"

"Oh," she says, "just the same thing." [S]he says, "He just nastied the bed all over."

"Well," he said, "one more night," says, "if he don't do no better, throw him in the lion's den."

He went back then, had a plug put over in him, so he knowed he *couldn't* do nothing then.

So Jack sent the little mouse to whip his tail in his nose to make him sneeze, you know.

And so the old king is going to stay up at the foot of the bed that night to see how he's done these things.

Well, Jack's little mouse went and whipped his tale on his nose, he makes a big sneeze, and the cork flew out and hit the old man right between the eyes and knocked him over. And he got up and went home and [laughing] come back the next morning, said, "Daughter, how'd your man do last night?"

She said, "He done worse than ever."

He says, "Take him and throw him in the lion's den and let Jack stay with you. For God's sake, bring Jack back."

They took him and put him in the lion's den and the lion devoured him right down. (You see, Jack took his lace off his mouth, you know.) And Jack wasn't hurt a bit.

And they took Jack back then, to her.

And so he come down next morning and said, "So, daughter, how'd Jack do last night?"

"Oh, Daddy," she said, "he just done fine." She said, "Just go off and let us alone." She said, "We're all right."

[Audience laughs.]

So Jack got his ten thousand dollars and the king's daughter back too, you see.

7. Stiff Dick

SAMUEL HARMON
Maryville, Tennessee
Recorded by Herbert Halpert,
April 27, 1939

If "The Marriage of the King's Daughter" (story 6) is a risqué tale with an innocent title, "Stiff Dick" is just the opposite. The title and the rhyme on which it is based suggest an x-rated performance, but the story itself is a straightforward adventure tale. The earthy incident that gives Sam's tale its title—the scene in which Jack swats seven flies buzzing around a pile of cat manure—has been cleaned up by all the other Hicks-Harmon narrators whose stories have been printed, except one: Ray Hicks tells a version in which Jack kills seven flies clustered on a cow pie. In Ray's tale, Jack celebrates his feat with a rhyme ("Big man Jack / Killed seven at a whack") more delicate than Sam's "Stiff Dick: / Killed seven at a lick."

In his telling, Sam's voice reveals his pure delight with the plot, and with a hero so resourceful with his words that he uses them to conceal his cowardice and fool the king and all the king's men. The way in which Jack "wins with words," using one-liners to convert losing situations into triumphs, bears a strong resemblance to Sam's own talents for using a few well-chosen words to overcome his challengers (see, for example, "How I Bought and Stole My Wife," story 1).

One time this orphan boy raised up, he just made what he made out of hisself. His mother wasn't much, and he had no father and he just roved here and yonder everywhere till . . . he got to be a young man.

And he's a going along one day, traveling, he didn't know where he was at. He was way out in a strange country, he didn't know whereabouts he's at or nothing.

And [it's] summertime; he had him a paddle. Walking along where the cat had been and this, this—seven of these big old green flies a-setting. And he upped his paddle and killed seven at the lick. He traveled on and—then he went and had a buckle put on his belt and had it printed on his buckle,

Stiff Dick:
Killed Seven at a Lick.

First thing he knowed, he rambled around, got to the king's house, and he went in and stayed till dinner and so pulled his belt off and laid it on the bed when he went into dinner. And the king, he got done eating and went out, and he happened to notice this on his belt. When he got done eating, he come out, he said, "You must be a terrible warrior." Says, "Here it is on your belt,

'Stiff Dick:
Killed Seven at a Lick.' "

Said, bedad, he was.
Says, "You're the very man I've been looking, looking for for years." Says, "I've . . . got a job for you."
He want to know what it was.
"Well," he says, "there's a unicorn and a lion and a wild boar in these woods that destroyed—no telling the people and stock that they destroyed. I never could run across no man brave enough to destroy em—till you."
"Ah," he said, "bedad," he said, he would.
He says, "I'll give you a thousand dollars for the boar, a thousand dollars for the unicorn, and a thousand dollars for the lion." Said, "I'll pay you five hundred down and the [rest] when you bring em in."
He told em, Jack told him, that it was all right.
He paid him five hundred dollars, just pleased the poor boy to death, you know—he never did have no money, and he thinks now he'll slip around and get out of there and not run across em. He's easing through the woods and got away out in the forest and the unicorn out in the side of the mountain, here they come—just as hard as they could run and took after Jack, and Jack just run as hard as he could run and he come to a big oak tree. And he got to running around that tree and the unicorn after him (and the unicorn just had one straight horn in its forehead, right out this way) and he's jabbing at him and at last he made a big lunge and jabbed his horn into that tree and couldn't pull it out.
Jack, he got him a little hickory and he reached around the tree and [looked],

you know, to see if he could get loose, and seed he's fast. Goes on back to the king's house and—

"Well," the king said, "did you get him, Jack?"

"Get him?" He said he'd never seed nothing to get. He said, hisself, he's a-going out there through the woods, said a little old bull come yelling, come busting out there. And he picked up the end of the tail, stove his horn in that tree out there. "If you want to kill it, go kill it."

Well, the king sent a fellow out there and shot it and paid Jack the other five hundred. That made him a thousand.

And there's a wild boar, the next one he's a-going to get. So he made sure he'd get out that time. He had all the money he thought he'd ever need. And so there's an old big log house out in the forest and where the campers used to stay, and the roof had about rottened off, all of it and he's a-going along, and the old wild boar heard him. And here they come a-bellowing, and Jack broke into a run and as hard as he could fly and he just did get in the old house— before the hog got him, he clumb up on the joists.

The hog—he run in the house. He's hot and tired and he laid down, and he went to sleep, the old hog did, and Stiff Dick—Jack—he slipped around and eased down and shut the door and shut him up out there and eased out while the hog's asleep. And goes back to the king's house. . . .

The king says, "Well, did you get him, Jack?"

"Ah," says, "Get him?" He said he didn't see nothing to get. He says he's going out there through the woods, said a little old boar shoat come bristling at him, said he picked up the tail in the air, he said, and pitched it in that old house out there. Said, "If you want to kill it, go out there and kill it." The king, he sent a fellow out there and shot it. And they paid him his other five hundred. That made him two thousand.

The lion was yet to get. He just knowed in his own mind that he'd get around that lion and not find it out. He started and traveled on and begin to think he's out of reach of the lion, [but] about between sundown and dark the lion found him out.

Here they come. Jack, he run up a tree. And the lion, he went to gnawing the tree. He gnawed the tree and gnawed, kept gnawing—had the tree until it was weaving backwards and forwards. Just about daylight, the old lion got so tired and sleepy and he just laid down beneath the tree and went to sleep.

And Jack thought: *now, while's he's asleep.* He'd ease down and get away while the lion is asleep. He kept clumbing on down, clumbing on down—he got down. There's a dead limb on the tree about ten foot above the lion and he got down and went to get down that dead limb to peep over, to see if the lion's eyes—he was well, good asleep.

He stepped on that limb. And the limb broke and fell right astraddle the lion, and he wound [caught] his hands in this wood and went to hollering and screaming as hard as he could scream and got the lion excited and [chuckling] the lion went . . . just as hard as he could fly through the woods.

And he happened to run right through the king's yard. And the king demanded to run out and shoot him quick. And they run out and shot the lion. And Jack said, "Now," he said, "you have to pay me another thousand dollars." Says, "I'm just a-breaking this lion," said, "for the king's riding horse." [Chuckles]

That's all of it.

8. The Mad King

SAMUEL HARMON
Maryville, Tennessee
Recorded by Herbert Halpert,
April 27, 1939

This tale of a very cruel king who receives an equally cruel comeuppance is perhaps the most violent story in the Hicks-Harmon family repertoire. It is also perhaps the most difficult of Samuel Harmon's tales for today's readers to follow because it contains many details relating to old-time farming practices. Sam refers to a "jenny," or female donkey. When Jack matches the jenny to a full-grown horse and hitches them both to his plow, the jenny cannot keep up with the much more powerful horse and eventually dies of exhaustion. Jack ties the dead jenny to the neck of the plow horse, and the horse drags its dead body through the fields. Jack later explains to the king that the jenny is his harrow, a farm implement used to even the ground after the plow has broken it into ridges.

As Sam Harmon has demonstrated in his telling of "The Marriage of the King's Daughter" (story 6), he does not shy from describing scatological matters in his tales. Yet Sam is very delicate in discussing sexual situations. In the final episode of this tale, the king is tricked into ordering the queen to sleep with Jack. Sam is so reluctant to explain the sexual dimensions of the tale that the reader can easily become confused about what, exactly, finally inspires the anger of the king.

One time there was a king and he'd hire a man to work for him, and he wouldn't give him nothing to eat.

And he hired Jack. Jack told a fellow that he'd hire to [the king]. The fellow told [Jack] he couldn't work for him. He'd starve to death. He'd get nothing to eat.

[Jack] said, bedad, he wouldn't. Well, he went and hired to the king. The agreement [the king] always made . . . with em—the first one got mad, the other laid him down and cut a leather strop out of his back, skin a piece of skin off of [the] back [of the] first one that got mad. And so the king would always get em mad and get a leather strop out of their back. And then nobody couldn't work for him.

Well, he asked Jack if he's a good hand to herd sheep.

Jack told him, yes, he was the best hand in the world to herd sheep. [The king] put him out with his sheep, and so he come in to dinner that day and want something to eat.

The king said, "I didn't hire you to eat. I hired you to herd sheep."

Jack told him that it was all right. He went back and he killed one of the finest wethers they had and cut a piece out of his ham and boiled it and eat it. And stayed out there about a week and never come in.

King . . . went out one day to see how he was a getting along. He went out and he . . . he finds his sheep laying here and yonder, pieces cut out of them, and them all spoilt and everything.

Said, "Jack, what in the world do you mean?" Said, "You've destroyed the best sheep I've got."

"Why," he said, "Bedad, why didn't you give me something to eat then?" Jack said, "You mad, King?"

No, he said he wasn't a bit mad.

"Well," he says, "Jack, are you a good hand to plow?"

[Jack] said, yes, the best hand that ever took hold of a plow handle, he reckoned, to plow.

Well, he said, he seed he wasn't fit to herd sheep—he put him to plowing. Well, he had a big, fine team of horses and put him out to plow. And [Jack] was plowing along—and one day there was an old man coming, riding along on a little old poor jenny.

Jack stops, says, "Hello, stranger. I want to swap horses."

The old man says, "Ah," he says, "Jack, you needn't be making fun of me, because I'm poor and ain't got nothing except a little old jenny."

Oh, he said, he wasn't making fun of him. He says, "I'll swap with you."

"Oh," he says, "I know better than that." Says, "I ain't got no money to pay no boot."

"Oh," he says, "I don't want no boot." Says, "I'll swap even with you."

"Well," the old man says, "All right. If you mean it," he said, "I'll swap."

So [Jack] took the fine horse out and put this old, this little old poor jenny on the side of the other'n and drug her around a round or two, and the little old jenny died. And he took then the other horse and hitched [the jenny] up to the other'n by the neck and dragged and dragged her about over the ground where he'd plowed.

The king come out and said, "*What in the world, Jack, have you done?*"

"Why," Jack says, "I'm a-harrowing." He says, "I always just plowed a bit and I'm harrowing . . . awhile," he says. "Keep it harrowed as I plow it."

[King] says, "What did you do with the other horse?"

Well, he said, he swapped it off for that harrow to harrow the ground with. Jack says, "You mad, King?"

No, he says, he wasn't a bit mad.

"Well," the king says, "are you a good hand to . . . cut wood?"

That was his job, he said, cutting wood. [The king] got him another team and his wagon and sent him out to cut wood, and Jack, he drove the horses [and wagon] out under a main, big tree. . . . And he set into chopping and finally chopped [the tree] down all across the wagon and horses.

The old king went out to see how he was a getting along. He says, "Well, Jack," he says, "there you are." He said, "*What in the world,*" he said, "did you cut that tree on them horses and wagon for?"

Oh, he said, bedad, how could he load that tree, he said, without cutting it [so it would fall] *on* the wagon?

King says, "Well," he says, "I see you ain't no account for that." And he says, "Are you a good hand to gather apples?"

"Yes, sir," he said, "the best hand in the world. Well," Jack said, "You mad, King?"

He says, "No," he said, "I'm not a bit mad." He sent [Jack] out gathering apples. And he went out and had about half of this fine orchard cut done. Cut [the trees] down and picked the apples off em.

King went out and he said, "Jack, what in the world do you mean?" He says, "Here you are, now. Spoilt my whole orchard nearly. Cut my finest trees down."

"Ah," Jack said. "Bedad"—had to cut em down just for he could get the apples. Said he couldn't reach up to the top of the tree to get em. That's the way he always get at apples.

The king said, "Let me show you, Jack, how to gather apples." Says, "You go get a ladder. Let me show you."

Jack went and got a ladder, and the king, he clumb up in the apple tree. . . . Jack jerked the ladder down. Wouldn't let him down. And [the king] stayed up there till he was about to fall down anyhow. Well, . . . he tried to make Jack get the ladder and let him down.

"Well," Jack says, ". . . whenever you give me something to eat, I'll let you down."

[So the king] stayed up there—went up early in the morning and stayed till getting late in the evening.

Last he seed that he couldn't stay any longer. Said, "Well, go up to the house and tell my wife to give you something to eat."

He went down there and didn't tell her to give him something to eat. Told her the king said something else. And she got awful mad. And Jack went to the door, says, *She won't do it, . . . King.*"

Says, "You tell her damn well she better do it, cause if I live to get down here she'll do it."

And she done what Jack wanted to do, you know. [Laughs]

He took the ladder. [Chuckling] King got down and he went down to her. And she says, "What in the world did you send that old nasty old ragged tramp here," says, "on me" (for what he said).

The king says, "Well, I never said that—I told him to give you something to eat."

Jack says, "You mad, King?"

Says, yes, by god, he's mad, and good and mad.

And Jack throwed him down and [laughing] cut a little strap out of his back [laughing] and went about his business. [Laughs heartily]

God, [the king] put up with everything else, but [come] to *that*. . . . He's mad and *damn* good and mad.

9. The Bean Tree

SAMUEL HARMON
Maryville, Tennessee
Recorded by Herbert Halpert,
April 27, 1939

Readers will recognize this tale as a close relative of "Jack and the Beanstalk." Sam recognized this tale as "a giant tale," but not as a Jack Tale. It may seem curious that Sam Harmon, a member of a family famous for Jack Tales, does not remember the name of the hero of "The Bean Tree." Evidently, the world's best-known Jack Tale was not considered a Jack Tale by Sam.

As close in plot as "The Bean Tree" comes to "Jack and the Beanstalk," Harmon's tale ends differently. On the recording, we hear collector Herbert Halpert express astonishment at the way Harmon ends the story; most of today's readers are likely to be similarly surprised.

One time there's a family had a little boy. I don't recollect their names. And his mother was a-sweeping house one morning, and she come across a bean. And she told the little boy to go out, plant it, and make a bean tree.

He got up the next morning, went out and planted it, and then the next morning he got up, went and looked, and said, "Lord a mercy, Mama," says, "my bean tree's higher than my head."

"Oh," she said, "that's not so," and she whipped him.

He says, "You come out and look."

She went out and looked and then she gave him a piece of bread and butter to hush his crying.

Next morning he got up and goes out and says, "Lord, mama, my bean tree's clean out of sight."

So she says, "You little lying rascal, you," says, "I'm going to beat you good." She give him a good beating.

He says, "Mama, come out and see."

She went out and seed, and sure enough it's out of sight. She give him a piece of bread and butter to get him to hush up crying.

Well, the next day he told his mother, said he'd, he's a going to climb his bean tree and see just how high it went, if he could find any top to it.

Well, he started up his bean tree and he kept climbing and climbing and climbing, and when he got up to the top, the giant had built a house in the top of his bean tree. And so he went in.

And an old woman giant says, "My husband's an old giant and he come and eat every little boy that come up there." Well, she hid him under a sifter. And the old giant come and said:

"Fee Faw Fum,
I smell English meat here."

"Ah," she said, "It's nothing but that sheep you killed the other day." He kept on thinking he smelled meat.

Well, after the old giant left, the little boy, he slipped out and he was going back to go down his bean tree. When he got down a piece, that old giant come and find out he's a-going, leaving—he took down the bean tree after him. And the little boy hit the ground, says, "Get an ax, Mammy, get an ax, Mammy, cut it down quick."

She got the ax and cut the bean tree down—and the bean tree fell and killed em both.

[Herbert Halpert: Killed both of them? Is that what happened? Both of them got killed?]

Yeah. Yeah.

[Herbert Halpert: Nothing else happened in the story?]

No.

10. Little Dicky Whigburn

SAMUEL HARMON
Maryville, Tennessee
Recorded by Herbert Halpert,
April 2, 1939

This is a *cante-fable*, a story intended to be both spoken and sung. The tale ends with a scene very familiar to the storyteller and his mountain community, with the characters entertaining each other, exchanging songs as they sit around the fire. At the outset of the tale, Sam tells us that the story is set in a town named Whigburn, but he doesn't tell us where Whigburn is. Dicky sets out from Whigburn and travels through a "wilderness" in search of a spring. In the song, however, we hear Dicky's wife sing that Dickie has gone to London. It appears that in Sam's performance, the originally English setting of the story has been transformed into a mountain landscape, with only the word "London" to remind us that this is one of the many stories that his forebears brought over from England.

In a trick to get her husband out of the house, Dicky's wife sends him to fetch some special water with healing properties. The term Sam uses in the tale appears to be "aphtha" or "naphthum." Here I spell the word "naphtha," because many people in Harmon's time believed naphtha water to have the power to cure illnesses.

Sam sings the closing scene zestfully, laughing as he sings the last verse.

Well, one time there's a little town by the name of Whigburn. There's a little man lived in that town by the name of Dicky Whigburn. And there was a naphtha spring away far off in the wilderness, and when one got sick why they'd go there and get this water to cure em.

And Little Dicky Whigburn's wife got bad one time, and she wanted him to go to the naphtha spring and get her some water. And so he got the bottle and started, and he goes on, he gets out in the wilderness a piece, and meets up with a peddler that he was well acquainted with once, and [the peddler] asked him where he's a-going. [Dicky] told him he's a-going . . . to the naphtha springs, to get some water for his wife. She was bad off. Well, the peddler got to talking to him, and told him there wasn't anything wrong with his wife, that she just wanted to get shut of him, and the old parson was going to be there that night, and she didn't want [Dicky] to be there.

Well, [Dicky] couldn't believe it for a long time, unless [the peddler] kept on arguing with him and finally got him to agree to go back with him. He told [Dicky] to go back with him so he could see the whole thing with his own eyes. Well, he agreed to go at last. And [the peddler] told him he'd put him in one of his goods sacks, and he put him in a sack and tied him up and he went on.

And he got there at Little Dicky Whigburn's about sundown, and called to stay all night. [Dicky's] wife said she hardly ever kept anybody when her husband was gone. He wasn't there, but then she was well acquainted. He had stayed there so much, why, to drive on to the barn and put up his team and come on in. Well, he done so, and he come on in, why, there wasn't a thing the matter with the woman. She's all rigged up, you know, so fine a fly couldn't stick to her hardly, and the old preacher he's there, you know, fixing to have a good time.

Well, this peddler says to Mrs. Whigburn, says, "Mrs. Whigburn," says, "I've got a sack of goods wet in crossing the river today. If there are no objections, I'd like to set em in by the fire and let em dry out tonight."

She told him to bring em in and he took Little Dicky and set him up in the corner, you know, by the fire. And they eat supper. And after supper . . . Mrs. Whigburn says, "Suppose we all sing a song apiece tonight and to enjoy ourselves." They all agreed, and [the peddler] says, "Well, you're the woman of the house, Mrs. Whigburn. You sing the first one":

[Mrs. Whigburn sings:]

> Oh, Little Dicky Whigburn, to London he's gone
> To bring me a bottle of clear aphthum;
> The Lord send him a long journey to never return.
> And it's through the woods and the willows.

"Pretty good, Mrs. Whigburn. Sing that again":

> Oh, Little Dicky Whigburn to London he's gone
> To bring me a bottle of clear aphthum;
> The Lord send him a long journey to never return.
> And it's through the woods and the willows.

"Well—Mr. Preacher, it come to your turn."

> Oh, Little Dicky know a little dirty fink
> Who eats of his eats and drinks of his drinks;
> The Lord spare me my life,
> This night I'll lie with his wife.
> And it's through the woods and the willows.

"Pretty good, Mr. Preacher. Sing that again."

> Oh, Little Dicky know a little dirty fink
> Who eats of his eats and drinks all the drink
> The Lord spare me my life,
> This night I'll lie with his wife.
> And it's through the woods and the willows.

"Well, Mr. Peddler, it's come to your turn."

> Oh, Little Dicky Whigburn, he is not far
> And out of my hopsack I'll have him to repair [return]
> And if a friend he does lack,

I will stand at his back.
And it's through the woods and the willows.

The old preacher looks up and he says, "It's—late, I'd better be a-going."
"Oh, no. Oh, no," the peddler says, "I heard your verse twice. Now you can hear mine twice." . . .

Oh, Little Dicky Whigburn he is not far,
And out of my hopsack I'll have him to repair.
And if a friend he does lack,
I will stand at his back.
And it's through the woods and the willows.

Now, this is Little Dicky Whigburn. Then he walked out [of the sack]. That's his'n. Next one is his verse:

Good morning, fine gentlemen, all in a row,
The chief of your secret I very well know.
And the price of a guinea I very well know.
And it's through the woods and the willow.

[The dirty old parson] stayed away,
And stayed with his wife on the very next day.
And Dicky and the peddler together did stay.
And it's through the woods and the willows.

[Laughter]

11. Catskins

**ALBERTA HARMON AND
SAMUEL HARMON**
Maryville, Tennessee
**Recorded by Herbert Halpert,
April 27, 1939**

The Hicks-Harmon Jack Tales have enjoyed such popularity that listeners often forget that the family also told a number of tales featuring female characters. Given the family's enormous store of narrative tradition, it is not surprising to find an earthy version of the Cinderella story among its treasures. Just as Sam Harmon's Jack Tales were passed on primarily from grandfather to grandson, "Catskins" was passed on from grandmother to granddaughter. Nevertheless, stories with male heroes were not told solely among males, nor were stories with female heroes told exclusively among females. Sam Harmon obviously knew "Catskins" well, as the following performance affirms.

During the recording of "Catskins," collector Herbert Halpert played the part of emcee, directing Sam and his granddaughter Alberta Harmon to take turns telling parts of the tale. In the end, Sam tells the lion's share of the story, possibly because Alberta felt shy in front of the visiting outsider, his recording machine, or both. There is a measure of reserve in her voice that is not heard in the grandfather's. Nevertheless, Alberta performs her part of the tale well. At the end, she adds an episode that changes the focus of the tale from Catskins's happiness to her getting even with her sisters. Like Sam Harmon's version of Jack and the Beanstalk (story 9), Alberta's version of Cinderella undercuts the magic of the tale by ending on a surprising and realistically cynical note.

Sam Harmon:] One time there was three sisters. They had no father and no mother. They just was out by theyselves. And they's two of the sisters was smart and good girls, and one of em was lazy and tired and slothful and wasn't no count—she wouldn't work. Well, this Catskins, why, she wouldn't work and wouldn't do nothing, and she just lolled about and just got practically naked and her clothes all off of her. And she had some cats and she got to killing cats and killing cats and throwing the hides together to make her a dress out of catskin to put on. Well, she stayed around there, till she about *had* to do something, she's about to starve. And she decided she'd go up to the king's house and be a servant and the king'd let her—

[Herbert Halpert: Alberta, you go on and tell us what happened then, go on. . . .]

[Alberta Harmon:] She said she'd go out into the woods and starve to death, lay down somewhere to starve to death. And she went out into the woods and there's a man come by and he give her a box and three dresses.

[Herbert Halpert: Why'd he give her the box?]

[Alberta Harmon:] Told her she could take that box and get in it and tell it to lock and it'd fly off with her and she said that it'd go anywhere she wanted it to, and so when she got to where she wanted it to stop, just tell it to, light and then to unlock and she could get out. And she said she'd go to the king's house and—

[Sam Harmon resumes:] She thought she'd go to the king's house to see if she couldn't get in to be the king's wife's servant. Well, she goes and tells her condition and with her catskin dress on and the queen didn't want her at all at the start and she said that they wouldn't eat her cooking if they knowed she cooked it nohow, and she didn't see that she could keep her. And she kept on. At last the king's wife told her that if she'd be sure to stay in the kitchen so nobody could see her, she'd try her a little while.

Well, she went in the kitchen and stayed there right smart a little while, maybe a month or two. They's having a meeting one time and—

[Herbert Halpert: Is there anything wrong, Alberta?]

[Alberta Harmon:] No, sir.

[Herbert Halpert: Go on, Mr. Harmon. What kind of meeting were they having?]

[Samuel Harmon:] A gospel meeting.

[Herbert Halpert: Uh, huh. Go ahead.]

[Samuel Harmon:] And Catskins wanted the queen to let her go.

"Oh," she says, "You can't go." Says, "You wouldn't want to be kicked out in the crowd—you old nasty, dirty thing," she said, "with that old catskin dress on."

She kept on pleading with the queen to let her go. And at last the queen said, "Well, I can let you wear one of my old dresses; you can go tonight."

Well, she put on this here dress of the queen's and she slipped out to her box, and it was the color of every bird that ever flew in the air. She put it on, got in her box and told it to go to the meeting, fly to the meeting house. Took her there and lit and unlocked. And she gets out, and she goed in. . . . And the king's son was there, and he seen her . . . the beautifullest thing he ever seen in his life. And he fell in love with her. And he talked to her that night, too. And so whenever she got ready to leave, she slips out her box and gets in her box and strips and go back to the queen, with just the old dress on, that she wore off.

And so a month or two after that, there was another meeting. And the king's son went every time there was a meeting and never could find this girl, no more. He never could find her anymore. It was worrying him to death.

And Catskins wanted the queen to let her go again and she told her, well, to put on one of her oldest dresses, reckon she'd let her go again. Well, she went to her box and put on this dress that had the color of every fish that ever floated in the water. And went in, and the king's son seed her again, and he just fell in love with her, deeper all the time. Every time he seed her, the better he'd love her.

And he put a gold ring on her finger. And she slipped off and she got ready to go.

[Herbert Halpert: Who put the gold ring—]

[Samuel Harmon:] This king's son.

[Herbert Halpert: Put the gold ring on her finger?]

[Samuel Harmon:] Yes, sir. . . . A notable ring that he'd know. And, so, he'd go to meeting. Every meeting he'd come a-looking for this girl. And never could find her. At last he got lovesick. He was a-going to die. It was wearing the life out of him. And he'd tell his mother and father if he could only see that girl again that had that dress on, and the ring that he'd put on her finger, he'd be a happy soul, and if he didn't he never would be anymore. But they never could find her. And at last he just give up and went to bed—going to die, and he wouldn't eat nothing hardly. They couldn't do a thing with him.

And so, Catskins told his mother, one time, she says, "You let me bake him a cake."

"Oh," said, "you nasty thing." Says, "You reckon he'd eat anything that he knowed you cooked?"

"Why," she said, "then not let him know that I cooked it. . . ."

Well, she agreed. She thought he was going to die anyhow. She said he'd be gone if there couldn't be something done and so she baked him a cake and put this ring right in the middle of the dough and told her mother to tell him now, to break this cake right in the middle the first time they broke it.

She took it to him and he broke the cake and he discovered this ring. He knowed it. That revived him up, and he said if he could only find the girl that wore that ring and that dress he seed at meeting, he was a happy soul. He's all right.

Well, Catskin she slipped out to her box and put on that dress, you know, and walked in, and when he seed that, he jumped out of bed and grabbed her and he hugged her and he kissed her and took on and over. And, so, next day or two, they was married. And that's all of it, I think, that I know.

[Herbert Halpert: Alberta. . . . Go on ahead.]

[Alberta Harmon:] And she writ her sisters a letter and told em that she'd married the king's son and was—well off, and better off than they'd ever been.

[Herbert Halpert: What she'd do that for?]

[Alberta Harmon, laughing:] I don't know.

12. Old Black Dog

ALBERTA HARMON
Maryville, Tennessee
Recorded by Herbert Halpert,
April 27, 1939

This story belongs to a large body of tales told primarily to children by their elders for the purpose of reinforcing a strong work ethic and good behavior in general. Like Alberta's version of "Catskins" (story 11), "Old Black Dog" was passed down from female to female, from Polly Harmon to her granddaughter Alberta.

As with her performance of "Catskins," Alberta gives this tale a surprise ending.

Herbert Halpert: What do you call this story?]
"Old Black Dog" is the only name I ever knowed for it.
[Herbert Halpert: And from whom did you hear it?]
My Grandma Harmon.
[Herbert Halpert: All right, go ahead.]
One time there's a old dog and a little girl, and this little girl and the old dog made em a flower bed. And the little girl, she was lazy, laid around the house all the time, wouldn't work her flowers. Old dog, he'd get out and he would bite and pull the weeds out of his flowerbed.

One day when his flowers got just great big and hers was little old bitsy things, she went out and says, "I'm going to collect flowers."

And the old dog says, "Yes, now I'll collect flowers too."

The little girl says, "Now I'll collect *yours*."

And the old dog says, "Now I'll collect *you*."

And so he got her up on his back and took her out to an old hollow log. He got her up in that old hollow log and she laid there till morning. And he said, "What will you call me if I take you back to your mommy and daddy one more time?"

Said, " 'Honey,' as long as you live."

And he got her up on his back and took her up back to the house and set her up on the porch, and he says, "What do you call me now?"

Said, "Old Black Dog."

And he grabbed her up on his back and set off with her and took her to an old haunted house, and she just laid there all night, and the next morning he said, "What will you . . . call me if I take you back to your mommy and daddy one more time?"

She told him she'd call him "Honey" as long as she lived.

He took her back and put her on the porch and he asked her what did she call him.

"Honey," as long as she lived.

One day she went on the porch and picked him up and pitched him off and break his neck. And every time she start to go back to the flowerbed to get her flowers, she could see the dogs coming.

Maud Long (1893–1984)

Lillie Bertha Maud Long and Samuel Harmon were both children of the western North Carolina mountains, but they came of age in two vastly different worlds. Maud Long's mother, Jane Hicks Gentry, was born in 1863 and her first cousin Sam Harmon in 1870, both in Watauga County. Sam left the ancestral home when still a young child and spent almost all of the rest of his life near Cades Cove, Maryville, and other locales in eastern Tennessee. Sam had already gone by 1875, when Cousin Jane left, her family traveling south and west on a path parallel to Sam's, toward the Great Smoky Mountains. But whereas Sam's family crossed into Tennessee, Jane Gentry stayed on the eastern slopes in Madison County, on the North Carolina side. It was in rural Madison County, not far from Hot Springs, that Jane's daughter, Maud Gentry Long, was born in 1893. As the crow flies, Hot Springs was less than sixty miles from Sam Harmon's home, and Maud passed the first few years of her life in an environment similar to Sam's; but when her mother moved into town, Maud's life changed radically.

In 1898, when five-year-old Maud moved to town, Hot Springs was the site of the grand Mountain Park hotel where wealthy city people came to "take the waters," and a far more cosmopolitan place than Cades Cove. More important, Hot Springs was also the home of the Dorland Institute, a school founded expressly to educate "girls from remote mountain districts." Jane wanted her children to attend the school eight months a year; all nine of them attended and eight graduated. Maud Long became a dedicated student and a devoted alumna who raised funds for the school, which set her on a new course in life, as she was continually and progressively exposed to educational and social activities that would remain foreign to Sam Harmon his entire life. This is one major reason

Maud Long, teller of stories 13–23. (Courtesy of Daron Douglas)

why Maud Long's tales resemble literary fairy tales far more closely than do Sam Harmon's.

At the same time that Jane brought Maud and her other children to "civilization," however, she also brought with her an enormous store of folk traditions. Jane was often called upon to tell her tales and sing her songs at school activities, and she became known as the "mountain friend of Dorland." As her children were given a formal education, she gave a rich folkloric education to their teachers. The staff developed a deep respect for Jane's folk arts, another reason why Maud Long grew up revering what she had learned both from the school and from the family.

Thus, Maud Long came of age in an environment where both modern educational techniques and the folk traditions of her family were taught and respected. In many respects, mother and daughter were "cultural translators," artists who made it their mission to demonstrate and explain the values of their community heritage to outsiders who had never experienced it firsthand. This is another reason why Maud Long's performances of the Jack Tales sound so familiar in comparison with Sam Harmon's. By 1947, when she recorded the following tales, she had spent more than four decades, all her adult life, entertaining outsiders.

Yet another reason for the differences between Maud's and Sam's tales is that Maud was very strongly affected by Richard Chase's famous book, *The Jack Tales*, which had appeared in 1943. In that book, Chase used a popular storybook idiom to retell tales he had heard from Maud and other family members. Chase and Maud became friends before the book was published, and his influence on her performances was so great that every one of the Jack Tales she told for the Library of Congress in 1947 is more similar in diction and general flavor to Chase's published stories than to the stories her mother dictated to Isabel Gordon Carter in 1923.

As deeply as Maud Long revered her family narrative tradition, she did not put it on a pedestal; for her, the Jack Tales remained an integral part of ordinary day-to-day life. Maud spent most of her adult years in Hot Springs, running an inn that hosted tourists and railroad and lumber company employees. Maud's daughter, Jane Douglas, recalls that the Jack Tales were a constant part of the informal entertainment that took place at the inn. Guests often asked Maud for stories, and neighbors who had known Maud since her childhood would drop by and ask to hear them too. Maud did not stage these tellings; rather, they flowed naturally from the give and take of conversation around the inn. As Jane Douglas remembers, Maud "didn't perform the tales, you

Sunnybank Inn, Hot Springs, North Carolina, where Maud Long often told her tales to neighbors and tourists. (Courtesy of Daron Douglas)

know. This was a very cozy, easy, relaxed environment, whether she stood on a stage and told it to a group of schoolchildren, or sat in our living room and told them to friends, or whoever. It was just the natural thing to do. No pretense. No pretense, whatsoever." Seemingly without even trying, Maud "could just entrance a group."

Maud Long tells her tales with animation and relish. She is more emphatic in her delivery than Sam Harmon is. In dialogue passages, she changes her tone and pitch to impersonate, and sometimes to differentiate, the various fictional characters. In Maud's tellings, Jack becomes a willful, forthright, indomitable figure. Maud's relatives Sam Harmon and Ray Hicks portray the pervasive poverty of Jack's background and the hero's occasional flashes of vulnerability and fear; Maud, however, projects a Jack who is almost invariably light-hearted and snappy in his actions and speech. Maud's hero is an unflappable optimist who is almost never worried about his prospects, no matter how grim they may seem to the tale's other characters or to its listeners. This aspect of Jack's personality could well have been passed on to Maud by her mother, Jane Gentry, who was once described by author Irving Bacheller as "the happiest person I ever knew."

13. When My Mother Told Jack Tales

MAUD LONG
Hot Springs, North Carolina
Recorded by Duncan Emrich,
Washington, D.C., 1947

I cannot remember when I heard the Jack, Will, and Tom tales for the first time. For we grew up on them like we did the mountain air and the lovely old ballads that my mother used to sing to us. But the occasion for the tales is a very vivid memory.

It would be on a long winter evening when, after supper, all of us were gathered before the big open fire, my mother taking care of the baby—or else the baby was in the cradle very near to Mother. And she would be sewing or carding. My father would be mending someone's shoes, or maybe a bit of harness. The older girls were helping with the carding or the sewing, and all of us little ones would either have a lap full or a basket full of wool, out of which we must pick all the burrs and the Spanish needles, and the bits of briars and dirt against the next day's carding, for my mother wove all of this wool that had been shorn from the backs of our own sheep (raised there on the farm that was in the heart of the Great Smoky Mountains of North Carolina) into linsey-woolsey, for hers and our dresses, or into blue jeans for my father's and brother's suits, or into blankets to keep us warm, or into the beautiful patterned coverlets, to say nothing of all the socks and stockings and mitts and hoods that it took for a large family of nine children. And so she needed every bit of the wool that she could get ready. And to keep our eyes open and our fingers busy and our hearts merry, my mother would tell these marvelous tales, the Jack, Will and Tom Tales.

14. Jack and the Giants' Newground

MAUD LONG
Hot Springs, North Carolina
Recorded by Duncan Emrich,
Washington, D.C., 1947

This is Maud Long's longest tale. She lavishes extraordinary detail on almost every aspect of the telling, particularly in her portrayal of Jack, who emerges as more introspective, fearful, and vulnerable in this tale than in any of the others in Maud's recorded repertoire.

During the performance, the recording technicians discovered that they had accidentally erased a portion of the story by taping over it. They

Duncan Emrich (chief of the Library of Congress Folklore Section, 1945–55), recorded the tales of Maud Long (stories 13–23) in 1947. Here he appears, standing on right, in Coolidge Auditorium, Library of Congress, 1948. Also pictured are, standing, Harold Spivacke, chief of Library of Congress Music Division, and folklorist Helen Hartness Flanders (collector of stories 194 and 201); seated New England singers Charles Fennimore (Maine), Elmer George and Asa Davis (both from Vermont). (American Folklife Center, Nancy-Jean Seigel Collection)

stopped Maud as she was nearing the end of her tale and asked if she would retell the part that had been erased. "That's all right," Maud said, "I don't mind [retelling part of the tale]. No. I won't tell it the same anyway, so it doesn't matter." She laughed and added, "I never do," but went on to say, "I'd rather have one [complete tale] told well." Her responses reveal two marks of an accomplished folk performer: flexibility and perfectionism. Apparently, the technicians opted for flexibility because the surviving tape does not contain one complete performance; the following transcription combines the two partial performances that took place on the same day.

This is the story of Jack and the Giants' Newground.

Long time ago, Jack and his folks lived way back in the mountains, and they were just as poor as people could be. Will and Tom, the two older brothers, were just fine workers. They helped in everything, but Jack was just so lazy, half the time, they couldn't get a lick of work out of him. Now, of course, this made for a lot of quarreling and fussing with the two older brothers and his father and mother. So one day, Jack said, "You know what I'm going to do? I'm going to clear out of this place. I'm going out into the world and see if I can't find me a fortune. I'm tired of this little old rocky farm."

So his mother fixed him up a poke of vittles, and he threw em over his back and away he went. He walked and he walked, and the sun just a-beating down on him so hard. He got hungry and ate up his poke of vittles, and went walking on, and the sun getting hotter and hotter every step he took. And yet it wasn't twelve o'clock. And he thought, "I wonder where I'm going to get a bite of dinner, for I sure am getting hungry."

And just then, he noticed a nice-looking road that turned off from the main highway, and he thinks to himself, "I'll just follow this a little ways and see where it leads to." And pretty soon, he came to a great big rock wall with a gate of pure gold. "Hmm," says Jack to himself. "They's well-doing folks a-living here. I just wonder if they'd give me a bite of dinner. I believe I'll holler and find out. [Bellows] *Uh-oh!*"

Pretty soon, a man came out onto the porch, said, "Hello, stranger. What are you doing? What are you looking for?"

"Well, I'm a-looking for a job of work," says Jack.

"Well, I don't know as I'm hiring anybody right now, but come on in anyway, stranger, and sit a while."

Jack pushed that gate open, marched right in. Oh, [the] man reached around, brought out two chairs, said, "Come on, sit down. I reckon you can rest a little while, can't you? You're not in much of a hurry."

"No," Jack says, "I guess I can rest a little while, anyway." So he took out his old corncob pipe and leaned back and went to smoking. Looked around after a while, and he says, "And what did you say your name was, Mister?"

"Why, I'm the king. What's your name?"

"Jack's my name. Now, Mr. King, I'm just *mighty* glad to know you. I'm mighty glad. And I know with all of this land that you have around here, you got a sight of work. Don't you want to hire somebody?"

"Well," the old king says, "now Jack, I'd like to know, are you a good worker?"

"Oh, yes, sir!" Jack says, "I'm the finest worker there is back home."

"Well, can you plow?"

"Sure I can."

"Well, can you clear a newground?"

"Why, you know, King, that's just all I do back home. I just clear newgrounds."

"Well, can you kill a giant?"

"Huh?" says Jack. Dropped his old pipe. He reached down and picked it up. Said, "Well, I ain't never killed one yet, but I guess I could try."

"Well, now," the king says, "if you can clear a newground, and if you're a giantkiller, you're just the man I've been looking for. For I tell you, Jack, I have a newground at the top of that mountain yonder that I've been trying to get cleared for years. I've sent more than a dozen men up there, and they've every one been killed by the giants. Because you see, down in that other hollow, there lives a family of giants that claims that newground is theirs, and they won't let anybody clear it. Well, if you can go up there and kill em and then clear that newground, Jack, I tell you what, you're the man I'm looking for. Besides paying you good wages for clearing that newground, I'll pay you a thousand dollars for every giant head you bring here to the house, and I'll give you ten cents a hour for every bit of work you do besides, and that's a good price."

"Yes, sir," Jack says, "that's a good price, and that just suits me fine. I'll be ready to go up there and see what I can do."

"Yes," the king says, "after you eat a bite of dinner. Now come on in. I think the old woman has us some dinner ready. And let's see if we can't eat a little and then you can go up there and see what you can do."

Jack went in to the table and, my, it was just loaded with good things to eat. Chicken and ham and pie and cake and biscuit and butter and honey. Oh, Jack just ate such a dinner. But he looked across, and the old king was still eating, and the queen just piled his plate up full of food again. Law, Jack didn't want those folks to think that he couldn't eat as much as the king. So he reached down under the table and drew up that little old leather apron that he always wore, fastened it good in his pants belt, and drew his belt right good and tight to hold it down good and strong, and he begun eating all over again. He'd take a bite, and then he'd slip a whole lot down into that old leather apron. Poured four or five glasses of milk down in there and bread and chicken and cake, just everything. After a while, the king pushed back his chair and said he was through, and Jack pushed back his chair.

Went out on the porch and he said, "Now I guess, bedads, I'd better be about that giantkilling." "Yes," the king said, "go on down yonder to the wood pile, and you'll see they're some axes. Pick you up the sharpest-edged looking one you can find and go on. Up on the top of the mountain there, you'll find a tree with a chip or two taken out of it where the other fellows had tried to begin chipping. But just about the time you begin a-whacking, Jack, right then, the giants will be a-coming."

Well, Jack went on down to the woodpile. Looked back and waved to him, said, "I'll be back in time for supper."

Picked him up a little old bit of a tommy hatchet there, and the king said, "Jack, Jack, you'll need one of them big axes. Don't take that little old thing."

"No," Jack says, "bedads, this axe is just what I want." Stuck it in his belt and went a-climbing on to the top of the mountain.

Now when Jack got up there, he was sure worried. He didn't know what he was going to do. Gracious sakes, he didn't want to begin a-hacking on that tree, for those giants would come a-running up on him. And he knew if he didn't hack some, . . . the king would know that he hadn't been a-doing any kind of work, and he wouldn't give him any supper. Well, he thought and he thought, what could he do? He just didn't know. Looked around and he saw a tall, slim poplar tree, the highest thing on the mountain. Climbed right into the very tip-top of that, took off that little old tommy hatchet from out of his belt and begun hacking at the little bitty limbs, right in the tip-top. *Ka-whack. Ka-whack.*

He hadn't made more than six whacks till he heard something coming through the underbrush. And he looked down there, and gracious sakes alive, there was that two-headed giant that the king had told him about. Yes, sir, this one just had two heads, but the twins had three heads apiece, the old mother had three heads, and the old daddy had four.

"Oh, boy," Jack says, "there comes two thousand dollars. But do you reckon I'll ever get em?"

He just kept right on a-whacking, though, just like he didn't know a thing was down underneath. The old giant came right to the very tree where he was a-whacking, looked up there, and he said, "Howdy, stranger. What in the world are you doing up there?"

"Oh," Jack says, "bedads, I'm clearing a newground."

"Clearing a newground?"

"Yeah, I'm clearing a newground for the king."

He said, "Now, look-y here, stranger, what's your name?"

"Jack's my name, bedads."

"Well, Jack, you must be plum crazy, clearing a newground, and a-beginning at the top of a tree. I never heard tell of no such."

"Why," Jack says, "that's the way we clear the newgrounds back home all the time."

"Well," the man says, "listen, Jack. We're not having that newground cleared. No, sir-ree, we're not. This newground belongs to us, and the king nor nobody else is going to clear it. Now, you just come down on out of that tree and go on home with me for supper."

Well, that old giant thought Jack wouldn't understand what he meant, but Jack did. Well, he came sliding down the tree, but he stayed well up in the limbs above that old giant's reach. He looked down at him, and he said, "I tell you I've always heard that giants is powerful strong. How about it, sir?"

"Well," the old giant says, "some of us is and some of us ain't. Now's for me, I can kill any thousand Englishmen that ever dare face me, just bare handed."

"Well," Jack says, "I'll tell you what. I bet you I can do something that you can't do."

"Huh?" the old giant says. "What is that?"

"Why," Jack says, "I can squeeze milk out of a flint rock."

"Eh, you can't do it, and I know it."

"Well," Jack says, "just—hunt me up a flint rock down there and chunk it up here. I'll show you."

So while the old giant was hunting around to find a flint rock, Jack took a little old knife, sharp point of it, and jabbed a little hole in that old leather apron. Giant threw him up the flint rock, and Jack caught in his hand, squeezed it right up tight next to that little old hole in the leather apron, and *drip, drip, drip* went the milk right down at the old giant's feet.

"Well," he says, "land's sakes, Jack! Do that again."

So Jack pushed it up good and tight against the little old apron and *squirt*, the milk came out just like he's a-milking a cow!

"Well," that giant says, "throw that rock down here to me. If you can do that, I can do it."

He threw the rock down to the giant, and he squeezed down on it, and he didn't get a drop of milk. And he squeezed again, and—didn't any milk come. And the old giant got so mad, he just squeezed down with all his might, and just ground that flint rock into powder in his hand.

"Well," Jack says, "I can do something else you can't do, too, giant."

"Now," the giant says, "what can you do this time?"

"Why, Law's a-mercy, I can just take my knife and rip my stomach right open, sew it up again, and I'm just as good as new."

"Ha! Now," the old giant says, "Now I know you're lying, Jack."

"All right," Jack says, "bedads, just watch me." Took his knife and he ripped open that little old leather apron and out came pouring milk and chicken and everything, and Jack just took him a little old rawhide string that he had and punched him some holes and sewed that old leather apron right back up again.

The old giant says, "Jack, for land's sakes, throw me down that knife. I *know* if you can do that, I can do it."

Jack threw him down the knife. The old giant picked it up and ripped open his stomach, and blood and everything begun flying out and first thing you know, the old giant just reeled around there and keeled over dead. Jack slipped down that tree, took his little old tommy hatchet, hacked off those two heads, went a-dragging them down to the king's house.

Well, when the king saw him coming, he says, "Land a-sakes, Jack, if you're not the finest giantkiller I ever saw! You're sure the man I've been a-looking for, and here's your two thousand dollars for those two heads. Now, come on in, Jack, and eat you some supper and rest up a bit."

Well, Jack went in, and he had him a good a supper, and he had a good bed to sleep in, and, oh, he had two thousand dollars. "Huh," Jack thinks to himself, "Boy, as soon as I can get away from here, I'm a-lighting back out home." After breakfast, he said to the king, "Now, I tell you. I'd better be going home. Uh, the folks are missing me powerful back there, and I bet you my pappy's a-wanting me to help him set out tobacco. I'd better be just a-going on back."

"Oh no," the king says, "Jack, you can't go back now. Why gracious sakes, you're the finest giantkiller that there is. No, sir, you go back up in that new-ground and kill me some more of those giants. That's what you do. Why, I believe you can destroy the whole bunch of them."

"Well," Jack says, "bedads, I guess I can go back and try."

So he started back up the mountain. Oh my, how he wished he could get out of there some way without passing back by that king's house. He didn't want to mix up with those giants anymore, but he didn't have much time to think, because just about the time he reached there, off a-coming up the hollow, he heard *tramp, break, scrape, brush,* down through the thicket there. He looked and there came the twins with the three heads, just a-stepping over those big old rocks and laurel thickets, a-coming, just a-brushing up that mountain.

"Law," Jack thought, "what will I do, what will I do?" He was just shaking all over. Saw a great old big hollow log over there, ran into that just as hard as he could go, scooping his shirttail up full of rocks as he went in. Got in there, and he laid down. It was so big, why, he could stand right up in it. He just crawled down in slow, among some of the big old leaves and things that had blown in there and lay as still as a mouse.

When those two giants came up and saw their brother lying there with his head cut off, oh, my lands, such a taking on you've never heard! They screamed, and they cried, and they said, "Oh, what will Pappy and Mammy say when they know about this? And don't we wish we knew who did it. Look, the ground's not tore up a bit. It don't look like there's been a sign of a fight, and yet his head's whacked clear off and gone. Oh, if we could just find the fellow that did that, wouldn't we go for him? You know he could've killed a thousand Englishmen, if everyone of them had come at him at one time. Now, who do you reckon could've done that?"

"Well," they said, "we'd better pick him up . . . and take him on down home." And he said, "You know what? Mammy sent us up here for some firewood. We'd better not go back without it, either. But let's just pick the handiest thing that there is. Let's take this old big hollow log over here. That'll just be fine."

"All right." One of the twins got at one end of it, and the other at the other. Of course, Jack got jostled around a good bit laying in there, but finally they kind of got it up on their shoulders and settled down a little bit. The giant in front had it just laying right up on his shoulders, just right with his head showing right square to Jack.

Jack waited until they got down the hill a little ways. He picked him out one of those pretty good-sized rocks and with all of his strength, *ka-bam!* He took the old giant right in the back of the head. The old giant stumbled a little, and he said, "Look-y here! Don't you be a-rocking me!" Said, "Goodness knows, we've got enough carrying this old log with brother laying on top of it. Don't go a-rocking me now, sir!"

"Oh," the other giant said, "why I didn't touch you with no rock. What's the matter with you? I don't got a rock anyway. So go on down that mountain."

Well, they started on down the mountain a little. Traveled a little bit further, and Jack picked him out a little bit bigger rock. And *ka-whack!* He took him right in the back of the head. Oh boy, that hurt, I know! And the old giant stumbled around, and he said, "Now listen here, that's the second time you've done it! You hit me with another rock, and if you don't take a licking, it'll be because I can't give it to you. Now you mind what you're doing."

His brother said, "Well, what in the world are you a-talking about? I've not hit you with no rock."

Now, they just bust and quarreled and gave each other the line, everything you could think about. And they finally started on down the hill though—carrying the big old log with the brother laying on top of it. Well, Jack reached around in among his rocks, and he got a real sharp-edged one, the biggest one of the whole bunch. And just let go with it, *ker-wham!* Right in the same spot. He just cut that old giant's head till the blood begun to ooze down there. Oh, it just almost knocked him down.

And he threw down that log, and he took back at that brother—other giant, and he said, "I'll tell you, I told you I'd whipped you if it was in me, if you hit me with another rock, and you cut the blood out of my head!"

And such a fight you've never seen! Why they clawed and kicked and bit and pulled hair and finally, they got clenched so tight, they rolled over and over on the ground. They kicked up great trees and rocks and they just fought until they were so weak, they couldn't even let go of each other.

When Jack saw them in that kind of a fix, he just crawled out of that—end of that old log and *ker-whack, ker-whack, ker-whack, ker-whack, ker-whack, ker-whack*, and the six heads of those giants were off. Jack took the six heads, and he went a-walking back down to the king's house. Well, there was six thousand dollars more. Oh boy, Jack was feeling good.

The king says, "Now, Jack, you've killed all the young ones. There's just the old man and the old woman, and I know good and well, you can go back up there and get them."

"Well," Jack says, "I tell you this is enough. I—I guess I'd better be going for home. Sure, I know my folks is worried about me by now. If they're expecting me back to house, I'd better go on."

"No, now Jack," the king says, "go on back up there and kill the rest of those giants. And then the only thing in the world you'll have to do is clear that newground."

"Well," Jack says, "bedads, I'll go on back up there and try." So back up the mountain he started. And this time, he didn't climb no tree. He wasn't a-shaking, he wasn't scared, he just took his little old tommy hatchet, and he begun a-hacking on that tree, *ker-whack, ker-whack!* And my lands, it sounded like thunder coming up that mountain.

This old big giant with four heads just right charging on in. When he saw his boys lying there dead, their heads cut off, he said, "Uh—uh, stranger, howdy. What's your name?"

Says, "Mr. Jack is my name, sir."

"Well," he says, "Mr. Jack, do you know anything about who's killed my boys here?"

"Yes, sir," Jack says, "you're looking right at the man now. I killed em. Come up here a-sassing me and a-cussing me around. I'm not taking that off of anybody. And you want to be mighty careful, sir, what you say to me, or I'll fix you the same way."

"Oh yes," the old giant pappy says, "come on, Mr. Jack, come on down to the house with me and meet the old lady. Why no, I'm not going to sass you nor say nothing bad at all. I'm going to be powerful careful what I say."

"Well," Jack says, "bedads, I don't care if I do then. Let's go."

And down the mountain they started to the old giant's house. And the old giant said, when they got pretty close, he says, "Now Jack, you'd better wait out here and let me go in, for when I tell the old woman about these boys being killed, and you being out here, she's a-going to take on powerful. Law, there's no telling what she might do. So Jack, you just stay out here and wait on me a little while, and I'll go in. And then, if it's all right, why, we'd be glad to have you come in for some supper."

"Well," Jack says, "bedads, I'll just wait out here on you."

And he just waited until the old giant got in the house. And then he's went a-slipping to the door as fast as he could and put his ear right to the keyhole. And he heard the old man say, "Old woman, they's a little old man out there named Mr. Jack that's killed all three of our boys. He's cut their heads off. You've never seen such a fight in your life as there's been up on that mountain. It's just cleared up pretty near." And he said, "This Mr. Jack says he done it. Now, I don't know whether he did or not. He don't look powerful strong to me, but out there's the boys. I brought em down. They're laying out there in the yard."

Well, the old woman *did* throw a fit. She screamed and she cried and she raved, and then she said she'd kill Mr. Jack. And, "Now, now, now," the old man said, "don't you go out there! He's killed those three boys. Now, don't you dare go. Oh, and you're kind of weak and feeble compared to them. Don't you get out that—way. You just wait. I'll test out Jack's strength. I'll see if he's as strong as he says he is."

So the old woman calmed down a little, and he says, "And besides that, I think we might have him for a little supper. And so," he said, "I'm going out to find out about him. You just kind of straighten up the house in here and get the oven good and hot."

So, Jack went a-flying back out into the yard, and was a-standing out at the edge just like he'd—was a-walking up to where the old giant in the house was. The old giant came out, and he reached there in the yard, and he picked up four great big old buckets. You've never seen such things. Slung them on his arm, and said, "Come on, Jack, let's go down here to the creek and bring the old woman a little bit of water so she can get her some supper."

So they went down to the creek. The old man giant reached in with one hand, and he dipped up one big piggin full, and he reached in the other hand, and he dipped up the other. He said, "Now, Jack, over there is your two buckets."

Jack didn't pay him a bit of attention. He just rolled up his britches leg, and he rolled up his shirtsleeves way up to his elbows, and he went wading right out into the middle of that creek. Feeling around in under a big old rock that was out there.

And the old giant says, "Jack, what in the world are you doing out there?"

"Why," he says, "bedads, just as soon as I can find a place to take hold of, I'm going to tote this creek up there to the old woman, so she won't have to—we won't have to little old dabs water up there. She can just come out here and get it when she wants it."

"Oh Law, no!" the old giant says. "Don't be getting this creek up there, Jack. No, no, don't do that." Said, "Land's sakes, don't you know it would ruin my cornfield. And besides, the old woman's getting kind of old and tottery. She might fall in it and drown. Now Jack, just leave that creek out there and come on, come on back to the house."

"Well," Jack says, "bedads, if I can't take the creek up there, I'm not taking no little old piggin of water."

"Well," the old giant says, "just leave the creek alone, Jack, and you don't need to mind about them little old buckets of water. Come on. These two's enough for her anyway." And on back up to the house they went.

The old man went into the house again, and he said, "Land's sakes, old woman! I had the hardest time in the world getting Jack not to bring that creek up here! Law, he's the mightiest man I ever did hear tell of. I just had to beg him to leave it down there." Says, "Now listen, you see if you can't do something with him. I'll get him to come in the house here, and you see if you can't get him in that oven over there, and I'll go out, and I'll be out here some-where."

"Well," the old man says, "Wait a minute! Let me—let me try him at throw-ing that crowbar. Just wait a minute. I'll see what he can do with that."

So he comes on back out. And Jack had heard every word that he said, but he's standing way off down in the yard just like he hadn't heard a thing. The old man says, "Come on, Jack, this is what me and the boys used to do while the old woman was a-getting supper. We'd pick up this crowbar here and see who could throw it the furthest. Now come on, I'll give it a send way out yonder in the field, and you go out there and get it and bring it on back over here. Throw it on back over here to me."

So, the old man picked up this great old big crowbar. Why, it must've weighed a half a ton. And give it a sling through the air, went about a hundred and fifty feet out there. Well, Jack went a-running on out to where the old crowbar laid up in the ground. Standing there, he didn't even pay a bit of attention to the old giant. He cupped his hands up to his mouth, and he said, [calls out] "*Uncle! Uncle!*"

"Ah," the old giant says, "what you call me 'Uncle' for?"

"Ah," he says, "I'm not a-talking to you. I'm not a-talking to you at all. *Uncle!* I'm a-hollering to my uncle way over yonder in Ohio. Why, I got an uncle over there that's a blacksmith, and he needs this here crowbar about making some horseshoes. The very thing. I'm just getting ready to throw it over there to him, and I want him to be ready to catch it. *Uncle!*"

"Listen, Jack, Jack, don't throw that crowbar away. Why that's all the one I've got. Don't—don't do that. No, take your hand off of that crowbar and come on back here. Come on to the house. Let's go on in. I think the old woman has got some supper ready. If she ain't, she pretty soon will have."

So the old giant took Jack into the house and said, "Now, old woman, here's Mr. Jack. And he's going to come and have a little supper with us. I'll go out and split you up a little bit of wood while you go on and finish the supper."

Well, the old woman, she made like she was real glad to see Jack and she picked up a comb and a wash rag and said, "Come on here now, Jacky. Let me comb your hair and wash your face and get you nice and cleaned up ready for supper."

"Oh no, bedads," Jack says, "I can wash my own face, and I can comb my own hair, too."

"Oh no, no, now," the old woman says, "come on and just let me do it. This is they way I always fixed up my own boys. Now, come on, let me do it, Jacky. You—just get right up there on that shelf, and uh, I can reach right over and get you without having to stoop over a bit."

And Jack looked, and he saw that that shelf was right where he could be tipped right off into the old oven. Well, Jack, he—he kind-y acted like he'd like to get up on the shelf, and he couldn't, and he wiggled off, and he'd get off always on the wrong side, and the old woman said, "Well, Jack, didn't you ever sit on a shelf before in your life?"

"No, sir," but Jack—but Jack says, "bedads, I never did. I don't know a bit more . . . how to sit on this shelf than anything. You get up here and show me."

"Well," the old woman says, "I'm powerful heavy to get up on that little shelf, but you just put your shoulder right under the edge of it there and hold it up so it won't break, and I'll get up there and show you how to sit on a shelf."

So the old woman, the old giant, got up onto that shelf, and Jack just gave his shoulder a little hunch and a good push, and right into that old oven he threw the old giant mother. And he worked around there with a great big old iron hook, and he finally pulled the lid on it. Went over and hid in behind the door.

After awhile, the old man pushed open the door, came walking in, says, "Old woman, old woman, Jack's a-burning! I smell him. I smell him."

Jack didn't say a thing. The old man run over and pulled the top of the big old—uh, furnace there, and "Law have mercy," he said, "that's not Jack, that's my old woman! And she's burned to a coal! There's her three heads, there's her three heads. That's her!"

"Yes," and Jack stepped from behind the door, and he said, "Mind what you say to me. I just sure put you in there, too."

"Oh yes, Jack, I'm a-minding what I say to you. I'm not going to say a thing in this world out of the way. No sir, Jack, I'm not! But," he says, "listen, Jack, help me to get out of this country some way." He says, "Here you've killed my boys, and now you've killed the old woman. Just help me out of the country."

"Well," Jack says, "I'd be glad to, sir, but you know, I'm afraid it's a little too late."

"Too late? What do you mean?"

"Why," Jack said, "the king's a-sending a thousand soldiers down here right now. Maybe two or three thousand of em, and they're going to kill you just as soon as they get down here."

"Oh, Jack, Jack, can't you hide me somewhere? Can't you do something for me, Jack?"

"Yeah," Jack says, "get into that big old chest over there, and I'll see what I can do."

So they got the old giant down in the chest, and Jack ran out on the back side of the house, and he took up big sticks of wood and he thumped and he beat on the old house and he hollered and he whooped and he—you would've thought there's two or three thousand men out there, the noise Jack was a-making. And he was a-fussing with them. "Now go on back, go on back, I tell you I've done done away with all of them. You go on back home. Tell the king just, he didn't need to send you over here. Go on back, every one of you."

He made just like they pushed right in on the house, and Jack come on in the house, throwing over the chairs and breaking up the tables and *ker-whacking* and *ka-banging* and—and finally Jack acted like he was just driving them every-one back out, and he took up a big stick, and he said, "Now, if you don't get on out of here, I'm going to do you just like I did the giants. Get out, I tell you! I've already killed the old giant. Go on out of here!" Finally, he went like they all went all off, and the noise kind of died down. And Jack went over to the chest and raised up the . . . lid a little bit, and he said, "Now crawl out there." Says, "The last one of them is gone. You get out of there, easy-like, and get away from here."

The old giant came out. He was just trembling and a-shaking. "Oh, Jack," he said, "what'll I do for you, what'll I do? Here you've saved my life from all them three thousand Englishmen." Said, "I know they'd have killed me. They would've tore me limb from limb. Now Jack, what do you want me to do?"

Jack says, "Mister, just start right over that mountain, and don't let me see you stop anywhere. Just keep a-walking. And that'll be all I ever ask of you. Just don't you ever come back here."

The old giant said, "Jack, I'll be so glad to get away from here that I'll never want to come back." And great steps he went, taking right over that mountain, and the last Jack saw of him, he just tipped the ridge and right, right down on the other side.

Well, Jack looked around. There was the three old heads of the old woman giant. He could take them in. But boy, what was he going to do about the old man? He sent him away. Took those three heads back down to the king, and the king says, "Now, Jack, I just owe you three thousand dollars more, for sure I can't pay you a thing for them giant's heads that went walking right over the mountain. You just lost four thousand dollars right that-a-way."

"Well," Jack says, "bedads, this is plenty to do me and my folks the rest of our lives anyway." And he says, "Now listen, king, I'm kind of tired and wore out fighting. I'm going on back home, and tomorrow, I'll send Will and Tom to clear that newground for you."

15. Jack and the Drill

MAUD LONG
Hot Springs, North Carolina
Recorded by Duncan Emrich,
Washington, D.C., 1947

This is the story of Jack and the Drill.

Once upon a time, there was a king who had an enchanted daughter. He just didn't know what was wrong with her. But anyway, he put out an oration that the boy who could come and break the enchantment could have all the gold in his kingdom and whichever one of his girls he wanted for his wife. Well, Will and Tom, the two oldest boys in Jack's family, wanted to go and see if they could break that enchantment. The mother and the father tried their best to get them not to do it, but nothing would do Will and Tom but they must go.

Yes, but then the mother said, "Don't you know if you fail, why then the king has your head cut off." Said, "Just right straight. That's in the bargain."

"Oh," Tom says, "I know it, but bedads, I won't have my head cut off. And I want to win all that gold and that pretty girl for my wife."

Well, the old man and the old woman couldn't do a thing with him, so the old mother baked Tom up a nice little cake and gave him a bottle of wine, and he started off, up to the king's house to break this enchantment. As he walked along, he got kind of hungry, and he sat down to eat him a little bite.

Little old man came along, and he said, "Uh, good morning, son."

"Morning," said Tom.

"Don't reckon you could give me a little bite of that to eat?"

"No, no, just got enough for myself."

"Well, good day then, sir." And on the little old man went.

So Tom got over to the king's house, and the king said, "Now, Tom, you understand that you brought your rabbit with you."

"Oh yes, yes, yeah," Tom says, "I brought the rabbit."

"All right now," he says, "I'm going out into the yard, and I'm going to draw a *big* circle ten feet in diameter. And you're going to put your rabbit down in that. And if you don't keep your eye right on that rabbit for a half an hour and you stay right in that circle, why then, you're just a goner."

"Oh yes," Tom says, "I understand all about it, but *I* can keep up with this rabbit."

"All right," the old man says, "here's your big circle. Now, you see it. Now turn your rabbit loose."

. . . Tom turned his rabbit loose and, bless me, why that rabbit just lit out and was gone before you could say "Jack Robinson." Tom just looked around everywhere. The rabbit was gone. The soldiers came out, and off went Tom's head. Well, that was the last of him.

When he didn't come back home, why, Will said, "Now, I knew that crazy Tom would never do anything. Let me go over there. Let me show that king how to watch a rabbit. The very idea! Why, I run a rabbit all day. And I know good and well I could watch one for thirty minutes."

"Well," the father said, "now Will, Tom's gone. Stay on here at the house. Don't—don't go like that."

"No sir, now," Will says, "bedads, you let Tom go, and I'm a-going."

So the mother baked him a nice little cake, gave him a bottle of wine, and *he* started out. Well, after he walked until he was tired, he sat down to eat.

Along came a little old bit of a man. Said, "Good morning, son."

[In an irritated tone:] "Morning."

"I don't reckon you got a little bite there that you could spare me to eat, have you?"

"No, no," Will says, "I just bare got enough for myself."

"Well, then, good day, sir." And on down the road the little old man went.

Will went on to the king's house, and the *very same thing* happened to him. Off went Will's head, because his rabbit ran right out of that ring. Why, he couldn't keep up with it.

Well, they waited and waited, and when Will didn't come back, "Now," Jack says, "there they are, both gone. And I *knew* that's what had happened. Now, bedads, I'm going over there and get that gold and bring you back a mighty good looking girl for my wife, too."

"No," the mother says, "you're not a-going, Jack. Now, to begin with, you don't have right and good sense. And Will and Tom, as smart as they were, they couldn't do that. You're not going over there and get yourself killed."

"Well, bedads," Jack says, "I'm a-going to go. And I know good and well I can *do* whatever it is that I've got to do, and that's just watch a rabbit for thirty minutes. I know good and well I can keep up with a rabbit for thirty minutes."

"Well," the mother says, "now you can go, Jack, if you want to, but I'm *sure* not giving you anything at all to take with you to eat."

Jack says, "Don't differ a bit in the world. Bedads, I can bake myself an ashcake, and I'll just take me a bottle of water." Took it, and out he started.

Well, he came to the same place, about, that his brothers had sat down to eat, and he got hungry. Sat down there to eat a little. He's sitting there, eating away on his ashcake and he's drinking his bottle of water.

The little old man came walking by. He said, "Good morning, son."

[Enthusiastic and respectful tone:] "Oh, good morning, father. Good morning, father. How are you today? Now, I've not got much here to eat, but don't you want to sit down and eat a little bit of it with me?"

"Well," the little old man said, "that's mighty nice. I guess I could. What's your name, son?"

"Jack. That's my name."

And the little old man says, "And where are you going?"

"Why," he says, "I'm going over to the king's house to break the enchantment."

"Yes, but," he says, "Jack, do you know what you got to do?"

"Why sure," Jack says, "got my rabbit right here in the poke. I'm just taking this rabbit along, going to turn it loose, and keep in sight of it for thirty minutes. And then I get half of the . . . gold of the kingdom. And besides that, I get whichever one of the girls that I want for my wife."

"Well," the little old man says, "Jack, you talk mighty brave, but there's many a nice fellow lost his head over it."

"Yes, but," Jack says, "bedads, I guess they didn't know just how to go about it."

"Well," the little old man said, "now, Jack, you've been mighty nice to me. I might help you a little bit." He said, "Right here is a little old drill. Now when that king comes out and makes his *great* old big circle, you just reach over and about the center of that circle, you just stick down this drill. Then turn your rabbit loose, and you'll stay right in sight of him from sunup to sundown."

"Oh, well," Jack says, "bedads, now that is sure a-going to help, and I'm much obliged to you, father, for this little kindness."

"Well," the old man says, "good luck to you, son, and I'll be getting on my way." And on down the road he went.

Jack stuck his little old drill down in his pocket and pretty soon came to the king's house. "Well," the king says, "now, Jack, it's too late to begin now. But in the morning, bright and early, get yourself up and get out here. You've got your rabbit, have you?"

"Oh yes," Jack says, "my rabbit's right here in this poke, and I'm not turning him loose until morning."

So when morning came, the old king came out, made a great big ring, and he said, "Now, Jack, turn your rabbit loose and remember, you've got to keep in sight of him for thirty minutes."

"Oh yes," Jack says, "bedads, I know all about it." And as he said that, he just reached over and stuck his drill down in . . . the earth and stepped back a little ways, opened his poke, and turned his rabbit loose. And the rabbit went making a circle, right round and round and round that drill, just as hard as he could go, and Jack a-standing there.

And the old king stood there, and his eyes just came out on stems, almost, a-looking. "Law," he said, "what about that, what about that. What—what's going to happen now? Jack's going to get it, just as sure as anything." And he stood there until he just was so anxious and worried, he didn't know what to do. Went running into the house, and he says, "Listen here. Come over—come right quick to me, old woman. And girls, come here. Jack's got a drill out there that he's stuck down in the ground. That rabbit's just running himself to death right around and around and around it. For goodness sakes, go out there and see if you can't do something about it."

"Well," the oldest girl said, "I'll tell you, I'll go out and see if I can *buy* that drill from him." So she went down, and she said, "Uh, uh, Jack [clearing her throat to get Jack's attention], reckon you won't sell that drill?"

"Yes," Jack says, "I've got a drill for sale in just about thirty minutes."

"No, no, no," she says, "I want it right now, Jack, I want it right now."

"Oh no, no," Jack says, "not a thing a-doing. Not a thing. No, I can't sell this drill yet."

Well, she couldn't get it, so she turned on around, went back into the house. "No," she says, "Jack won't even *talk* about it." Says, "Sister, you're prettier than I am. You go out and see if you can do it."

Well, the youngest girl went down, and she *was* really beautiful. And she walked up pretty close to Jack, and she said [clearing her throat], "Uh, Jack, I don't reckon that you have a drill that you want to sell, do you?"

"Oh, yes," Jack says, "I've got a drill that I want to sell *you*, but I can't sell it for a few minutes yet, but you just stand around and pretty soon, I'll have it ready for sale."

"No, no," the girl says, "if I can't have it now, Jack, I don't want it at all."

"Well," Jack says, "bedads, I like your looks mighty well, but I can't give you that drill."

Well, she went back in the house. And the king says, "Old woman, old woman, go out there and see if you can get the drill."

And the old woman went marching down. She was a good-looking queen, too. And she said, "Young man, I've come out here to see if I can buy that drill."

"Oh no," he said, "Madam, I'm mighty sorry. I'll give you that drill in a few minutes, but right now, it's not for sale."

Well, she went back in the house. "Well," the old king says, "I might just as well go on down there. He's sure going to cut my head off this time."

And as he went, he picked him up a bowl. And he went down, he said, "Jack, you're going to get it. Pretty soon, you're going to just take this sword here and whack off my head. But," he said, "Jack, listen, I want you to sing to this bowl full of lies, if you can, before you, before you do that."

"Well," Jack says, "bedads, I'll try. Hold the bowl."

So the old king held the bowl, and Jack, he reared back, he said: [singing]

"Your oldest daughter, she came down
For to buy my drill.
I hugged her and I kissed her well,
Fill, bowl, fill."

"Is it full yet?"
"No, Jack, it's just got a drop in it."
"Well, bedads, just hold the bowl."
And Jack reared back, and he sang:

"Your youngest daughter, she came down,
For to buy my drill.
I hugged her and I kissed her well,
Fill, bowl, fill."

"Full yet?"
"Nope, Jack, just got two drops."
"Well, just keep on holding the bowl." Jack reared back, and he said: [sings]

"Your old queen, she came down
For to buy my drill.
I hugged—"

"Uh, uh, uh! Jack, Jack, Jack! Hush, hush, hush! It's running over, it's running over! Just take this sword and cut off my head."

16. Jack and the Varmints

MAUD LONG
Hot Springs, North Carolina
Recorded by Duncan Emrich,
Washington, D.C., 1947

Maud uses a more precise local geography in this tale than in the others. She seems to situate the king's palace in her own hometown of Hot Springs, North Carolina, for when the king and Jack set out after the boar, they move north toward "the Tennessee side" of the mountains, just as one would do if traveling from Hot Springs toward the wilderness region now named the Cherokee National Forest.

Jack was one of those boys that just simply didn't like to work. He could do most anything in the world to get out of it. And one day as he was walking along the road, he had a little old stick. Whittling along on it. Nice little old soft piece of pine. Didn't know what he was making. He was just a-whittling. But the first thing he knew he had a good-looking little paddle made out of it.

He came alongside of a good cold spring and he knelt down to get him a drink. And there was a whole lot of little blue butterflies, flew up as he laid down to drink. And he thought, "I'm going to watch and let them settle again. And I'm going to see how many of them I can get at one whack."

Took his little paddle, and the butterflies settled down, and *slam!* He came down. Raised up his paddle, and there were seven of the little butterflies he'd killed.

"Hmm," he said. "I know what I'll do. I'll go down here to this blacksmith and get him to make me a nice big broad belt. And on it he'll say,

Little Man Jack
Killed Seven at a Whack

Won't that look good on that belt? My, that will make me look like something and somebody."

He went down to the blacksmith's shop, and, sure enough, the blacksmith said, "Sure, I can make that kind of a belt." And in just no time Jack put on his new belt and went strutting on down the road, feeling mighty fine and big.

After a while he said, "Well, believe I'll just walk up to the king's house and see what I can do for him."

When the king saw him, he said, "Jack, I like the looks of that belt:

Little Man Jack
Killed Seven at a Whack

Do you really mean that you can do that?"

"Well," Jack says, "bedads, I've done done it. Sure I can kill seven at a whack. What is it you'd like to have killed, King?"

"Well," the king said, "I'll tell you something I'd like to have killed. Way back over here in the north part of the kingdom, there's a big wild hog that is just ruining everything. Why, people are getting scared to go out, Jack. They're afraid of that wild hog. I guess he just wandered over from Tennessee, but they sure are scared of him, and he's causing a lot of trouble. Now, Jack, listen. If you'll get on my horse, I'll take you over there, pretty close to the place where he's been a-working. And then I'll let you off. And you go on and kill that hog for me, come back to the palace, and I'll pay you a thousand dollars."

"Well," Jack says, "bedads, let's get going. Where's your horse?" So Jack climbed up behind the king on his horse, and he rode away into the north country.

The king was beginning to get pretty nervous. Jack could tell that. He came to a certain place, and he said, "Now listen, Jack. I can't take my horse and go any further. You slide off. And now be careful, Jack, for that hog is a monster and, I'm telling you, he's a mean one."

"Oh," Jack says, "don't you worry about me and that hog. We'll get along all right." King turned around and whippity-cut back down the road he went just as hard as he could, cause he didn't want that hog to get wind of him and that horse.

Jack went a-walking on a little ways and he said, "Now, bedads, how can I get out of this country? I'm not a-going to mix up with no big hog. I can tell the world that. But I don't know where to go. I'll just ease along and maybe he'll never even hear me."

So Jack was walking along just as soft as he knew how when all of a sudden up through the brush he heard a mighty crashing and a-tramping and a-scraping. "Oh, Law," he said, "he's smelled me, he's smelled me sure as anything. Now what can I do? I don't know a thing in the world but just to take to my heels." He turned around and back down the mountain he went, just as hard as he could go, and right behind him come this monster of a hog. He looked over his shoulder one time and, oh my, he didn't take time to look any more. That was the biggest hog he'd ever seen in his life. Great long tusks and just coming right straight at him, just a-snorting.

Oh, Jack just stirred up the ground. He just *flew*. And as he was going by, he saw an old kind of a waste-house, and he thought, "Well, I'll run into this little old house, and maybe I can get away from that hog." He ran into this little old house, but right behind him he heard that hog a-coming.

But the top had all been blown off of the old house, and it was just great high walls, without any roof. Jack was going so fast, he just gave one mighty leap and right up the wall he went, sitting on the top. And the old hog run right in at the door after him, right behind him.

Oh, Jack just fell off of that wall, and around and slammed that door as quick as could be! There he had the big old hog all just fastened up in that little old house. Turned around and begun kind of whistling and walking on back towards the palace. He walked and he walked, and finally the king saw him coming and came running out. He said, "Jack, Jack, did you see that hog?"

"Oh, well," Jack said, "there was a little old shoat up there come running around after me, messing around, wanting like it wanted to play. Is that what you're talking about, you reckon, King?"

"Why," king said, "I guess that's what it is. That's the only hog up there that I know anything of. What did you do with him, Jack? What did you do with him?"

"Why, I picked him up by the tail and flung him into the little old shed up there. If you want him, send your soldiers up there and let them kill it."

The king called twelve soldiers and gave them guns and sent them up to the little old house to see, sure enough, if Jack had put that big wild hog in there. When the men came and looked in, they just couldn't believe their eyes. There he was, just charging and snorting and, oh my, he looked like he could tear all twelve of them up.

Finally, they got him killed.

When they got that hog out of there and scalded him and dressed him, cut him up, he made a wagonload of the finest hog meat you've ever seen in your life. They went hauling it on back down to the palace. Well, the king paid Jack his thousand dollars, and Jack thanked him and was ever so much obliged to him. Says now he'd better be getting on his way.

"Oh, no. No," the king says. "You just wait a minute, Jack. I tell you, we've got another varmint. It is just worrying the people down in the south part of the kingdom to death. They can't stay there, their horses can't get out, their cattle can't get out, they're afraid to go work their farms. It's just awful, Jack. You'll have to go down there and try to kill that unicorn."

"Oh," Jack says, "a little old unicorn? Who's scared of that?"

"Well," the king said, "*you'll* be when you see him. But now listen, get up on my horse here, and I'll take you just as far as I dare go. And then, Jack, you'll just have to do the rest of it on foot."

"Oh, yes," Jack said, "bedads, that's all right. Come on, let's get going." So Jack climbed up on the horse.

The king went riding off and rode just as far as he dared into the country where that unicorn was loose. He said, "Now, Jack, slide off, and the rest of it's up to you, son. And I just wish you the best of luck in the world. But you be careful of that unicorn. I'm telling you, that horn's killed more men than you can think of. Now you just be careful."

"Oh, yes," Jack says, "bedads, I'll be careful. I know how to do that."

And the king left him, turned on his horse and *clickety-cut* back down the road he went just as hard as he could tear, leaving Jack standing there.

And after the dust had kind of died down, Jack looked around and he thought, "Unicorn, you can stay right here for all I care. I've got a thousand dollars and that's all I want. I'm leaving here, too. But I'll wait till the king's out of sight."

Well, he didn't have time to wait till the king was out of sight. Just as he turned around, he heard a great noise and a pawing, and there came the unicorn charging down the mountain on him just like a streak of red lightning. Oh, *my*, but Jack took to his heels again. And down he went just as hard as he could go through this big field, around this tree and over that one, and the unicorn right behind him. He was getting so close, he could almost feel his breath on his back.

Out in front of Jack there, he saw a little young tree. Too little to climb, but he thought, "I believe I'll dodge behind it. Maybe it might save me." And as he dodged right behind the little tree, *ker-slam!* The old unicorn just rammed his horn right through it.

Now, you know a unicorn's old horn has rings all on it. And it just fastened in there just exactly like a screw had fastened it. And the unicorn couldn't get loose. He just pawed and he snorted. Jack stood off and looked at him a little while, picked him up a little brush, and gave him one good little lick to see if he'd hold. And that unicorn was fast. Right there. By his horn.

Jack went to the palace.

The king said, "Jack, did you find that unicorn?"

"Uh, well, yes. I guess I did. I found a little old pony up there with a horn out in the middle of his head. I tied him up and fastened him up there a little sapling. If you want him, let your men go up there and get him."

"Well," the king says, "come on. Take fifty of the soldiers out there and go and see if you can find him."

Well, when they came near, that unicorn was just pawing and snorting and cutting up so, the men were just scared. They were scared almost to get close enough to kill him.

Jack picked him up a little switch and walking up and he gave him a switch or two on the rump, and said, "See, he can't hurt you. Come on up here and shoot him." Well, the men came up, killed the little old unicorn.

"Well," the king says, "Jack, I'm telling you, you're the finest fella to go out after varmints that ever I seen. Now, listen, we've got one more thing. Over on the east side of the kingdom, there is a lion loose, a lion that has eaten up men that I've sent over there to kill him. Now I want to know if you think you can go over and kill that lion."

"Oh, why Law, yes," Jack says, "a little old lion. Ha, anybody can kill a lion if they just know how."

"Well, all right," the king says, "here's your thousand dollars for the unicorn. Now just go on over there and make away with that lion for me. And that's the last varmint that I know of that you'll have to kill."

So Jack got started. The king didn't even take him on the horse that time. He said, "Jack, you'll just have to go ahead on foot. That lion has killed too many men. I'm not going over there."

"Oh," Jack says, "bedads, I don't mind a bit in the world. I'll just go over on foot." And so he went walking away. He waited until he got good and out of the sight of the king. And he said, "Hmm, lion. No. I'm not looking for you. And I hope you're not looking for me, cause if I can get past you, I'm leaving this country."

He was walking along just as soft and easy as he knew how to walk. But he couldn't walk soft enough to get past the lion.

With an awful roar, Jack heard him coming.

"Oh," he says, "I'm gone-for now! What'll I do? What'll I do? I'll climb up this tree." And up the tree he went, just as hard and fast as he could go.

The old lion had seen him. He reached up just as high as those long sharp claws of his could reach and scraped down the bark of that tree. And growled and roared. My gracious, he roared until he just shook the earth.

Jack just sat up in that tree and trembled. "Whew," he said, "I just don't know what I'm a-going to do, but just as long as that lion stays here, *I'm* staying here." So he sat down on a limb.

Well, then, he waited, and the old lion run around that tree, and he'd reach up and he'd roar and he'd pull off more bark. And finally he was just given out. Layed down right at the foot of the tree and went sound asleep.

"Boy," Jack says, "here's my chance. If I can just light down out of this tree and get away from that lion while he's asleep and worn out, I'll be all right." So he was slipping down the tree with his eye right on that old lion all the time. He wasn't looking where his feet was a-going. And the first thing you know, one foot went right down on a little old dead limb, and *ker-whack*—it broke off, and Jack dropped right down on the back of that lion.

Oh, with an awful roar that lion was up and just flying. Jack holding on to his mane just as hard as he could, just laying there. Didn't know what in the world was going to happen. But anyway, he was hanging on to that lion. And the lion just ripping right down through the road, just as hard as he could go, right into the town and right round and round the palace, and the people all scared to death. They just fell into the houses, and the men hollering, "Get your gun! Get your gun!"

Here the men were all running out, peeping around to see where in the world Jack was riding that lion. Round the palace they went, Jack just holding on to his mane for dear life.

Well, the men were just so excited. Finally, one of em got a good aim, and *ker-bang!* Killed that lion dead, with just one shot.

When the lion fell out from under Jack, Jack stood up there, and by that time all the noise and confusion had brought the king. The king came walking over and he says, "Jack, what in the world were you doing?"

"Well," Jack says, "what I was doing is nothing to what I'm a-going to do now. For I'm mad, and I'm plenty mad."

"Well, what are you mad about, Jack?"

"Good land, what in the world did they go and kill that lion for? My lands, don't you know I was a-breaking that lion for you a ridey-horse? Great day, what did they go and kill him for? I just had him pretty near tame, and he'd have made you the finest ridey-horse. I'm mad. I tell you, they'll pay me, and they'll pay me plenty. They can just fork over three thousand dollars for killing that lion on me."

So the king went over to the men and he says, "I tell you, Jack is mad, and he's plenty mad." And he said, "We've got to give him three thousand extra dollars for you shooting that lion. He was breaking that lion for me a ridey-horse. Now, I tell you, there's just nothing to do. Let's pay him and get rid of him."

And the men all began chipping in their money.

First thing you know, they had three thousand dollars made up for Jack. The king paid him the thousand dollars he owed him, and gave him that other three thousand.

Well, Jack told them all goodbye and went a-walking off down the road. And ever after that, Jack was known as

Little Man Jack
Killed Seven at a Whack.

17. Jack and the Bull

MAUD LONG
Hot Springs, North Carolina
Recorded by Duncan Emrich,
Washington, D.C., 1947

Maud Long's second-longest tale (after "Jack and the Giants' Newground," story 14) apparently did not come from her mother's story stock. It is possible that she learned the tale from collector Richard Chase, who had found a very similar story in Wise County, Virginia, and inserted it into his book, *The Jack Tales*.

Though rare in Hicks-Harmon family tradition, "Jack and the Bull" is popular in eastern Kentucky and extreme western Virginia, and it has also been found in parts of North Carolina and Tennessee.

This is the story of Jack and the Bull.

One time Jack hired out to an old farmer to do a piece of work for him. And the farmer liked Jack just fine, and Jack was a good worker, but the old woman just couldn't hardly stand the boy. She just fairly hated him. And they had three girls, and the girls didn't like him either. So the old woman said, "Now, I tell you what. I know what I'm going to do. I'm going to get rid of this Jack. I'm going to starve him to death. Every morning, while he's out a-milking and a-feeding the critters, I'm going to have breakfast. And the dishes'll all be done up and there won't be a sign of anything to eat when Jack comes in. And then when he goes to milk and feeds the critters at night, I'll have supper. And I just won't call him to any dinner at all."

Well, she did that way. And poor old Jack, he was just about to starve to death. He got as thin as a rail and could hardly walk. The old man couldn't do a thing with his old woman. She just wouldn't listen to a thing that he said. And so it looked like, sure enough, Jack was going to die.

And one evening he started out up on to the top of the mountain there to bring in the cattle. He was just so weak he could hardly put one foot in front of the other. And he sat down on a big old rock and begun to cry. And he noticed coming out of the woods, a great big old, fine-looking black bull. Jumped right over that fence and come and stood right alongside Jack and said, "Jack, what's the matter?"

Well, Jack told him he was just starved to death. That he hadn't had a bite to eat in so long, he didn't hardly know what food looked like.

"Hmmph," the old bull says, "if that's all that's a-bothering you, you're fixed." Says, "Listen. Just unscrew my right horn there, and you'll find all the bread you want. And you just unscrew my left horn and pour you out milk and eat every bite you can hold."

Well, Jack unscrewed the right horn of the big old bull. There fell out the nicest loaf of bread you ever saw. And Jack's eyes just like to have popped out of his head. He unscrewed the left horn, took it out, turned it up a little bit, and the milk just poured out, just like it was coming out of a big old cup. Well, Jack just ate bread and milk till he was full as a tick. He couldn't move.

He sat there on the rock a little while and he said, "I tell you. You're the best friend that I ever had."

Well, the big old black bull says, "I'm going to stay right with you, Jack. I'm just here in this pasture along with the rest of the cattle, and nobody never need know it, and you never will go hungry another day as long as *I* live."

Well, the old woman kept wondering how could Jack get fat when she wasn't feeding him a bite in the world. She thought that sure enough he was about ready to die, when all at once he begun to mend. And she noticed that Jack and that old big black strange bull seemed *mighty, mighty* pals. They were always standing around together, or Jack would pick him a little fresh bunch of clover and go over and give it to that old black bull or something. And the old woman says to one of her little girls—you know those girls were a little bit peculiar. One of em had one eye, right in the middle of her forehead. And one of em had two eyes, just like me and you. And the other one had three eyes: two eyes just like we have and then one right in the middle of her forehead. So she said to One-Eye, "Now, listen. You go out and slip along behind Jack. Now, don't let him see you. But hide in the woods or in the grass or somewhere when it comes meal time, and see where Jack gets something to eat."

Well, the little girl went along. But, Law, Jack saw her before she'd been following him more than a hundred yards. And when it came dinnertime, he reached around there and picked up his little old fiddle that he kept always under a little old dry rock where he sat down to eat, took that fiddle out, and picked it up, and begun playing the softest, sweetest little tune you've ever heard in your life. And the first thing you know, that little girl with the one eye was sound asleep. When Jack saw she was sound asleep, he just took off the old bull's horns and ate his bread and milk, and fastened it back on. After a while, the little girl waked up, went back home, and she said to her mother, "I tell you, I didn't see a thing."

"Oh, well," she said, "you're no good anyway. Just that one little old eye." She said, "Now, Two-Eyes, you watch him tomorrow. You go every step Jack goes. And don't you go to sleep. I bet you that's what One-Eye did. You stay awake, now, and watch, and see where Jack gets him something to eat."

So Two-Eyes started out. She slipped along through the weeds and the bushes and followed, but, hmm, Jack saw her before she'd gone as far as One-Eye had. She made a lot of noise. And so he played around, watching the cattle and doing his work. And after a while, he sat down on this old rock and reached around and took out his fiddle out of the little old case and he begun to play. He played a piece twice as long as he played the day before, sweet and soft, and first thing you knew, little old Two-Eyes was sound asleep.

Jack went over to his bull, unscrewed the horns, and got his bread and milk and ate his dinner, all in the world that he wanted. And everything was just as usual when little Two-Eyes waked up. She ran back to the house and she says, "Mother, I tell you, I don't know where he gets anything to eat. I didn't see him eat a bite."

"No," mother said, "I'll bet you pretty *you* went to sleep. Now, Three-Eyes, tomorrow you follow him, and if you go to sleep I'm going to whip you when you come home."

Well, Three-Eyes slipped along. She did better following Jack. Jack thought no one was following him for a long time, and then he saw Three-Eyes slip behind a tree. So he didn't pay a bit of mind to her. He just went on and looked after the sheep and the cattle and what he was supposed to do, and the old black bull eating around in the field just as usual. But he always got around to where that big old rock was about noontime. And Jack reached around, picked out his little old fiddle, begun playing away, oh, the sweetest tune in the world. And he played it three times as long as he did the first day. But, you know, two of those eyes of Three-Eyes went to sleep just like you or I would go to sleep, and then that third eye kept popping open every once in awhile, because she didn't want to be whipped. She kept a-popping that eye open. And course, Jack, when he looked and saw her *two eyes* was shut, and that third eye looked like it was closed, he thought he was safe, so he went over to the black bull and unfastened his horns and got him some bread and milk and ate. *Oh, boy*, old Three-Eyes just a-went a-clippity back to that house just as hard as she could go.

"Oh, mother. I can tell you exactly where Jack's been getting his eats."

"Um, hum," the old mother said. "I *thought* he and that old black bull was too friendly. All right, I guess I can fix that." And so that night when her old man came into supper, she says, "I'm kind of sick. I'm just not a-feeling a bit well. I want the melt of a bull to eat, and I don't want any but that big old black one."

"Aw," the old man says, "now listen, that's Jack's bull. Nobody knows anything about where it came from or anything. It just seems to have taken up with Jack. Why, you . . . can't go and kill that little old boy's bull. That's all he has."

"Why," the little old woman says, "I *will* have it. I've *got* to have it. I'm sick and I've got to have that."

Well, . . . the old man couldn't talk her out of it. So, finally, he went and told Jack. He says, "I tell you, the old woman says she's just got to have the melt out of this big black bull to eat. That she's about to die and nothing else will save her."

Well, Jack sat down on this rock, and he sure enough cried then. After a while, when the old man had gone away, the old big black bull came walking up to him and said, "Now, Jack, what's the matter?"

Well, Jack told him. The old bull tramped around there a little while and then came back up to Jack and he says, "Now listen, Jack. We'll fix that. That's all right. You just go on and act like you don't care about me being killed or anything. And when you drive me down to the barnyard—but that's all right, I'll go, but I won't let *anybody* at all come close to me, excepting the old woman. I won't let anybody else come and then she'll come up to me." And says, "Now, you have your big old broad-ax ready and go like you're going to hit me right in the head. And you just make a miss-lick, and kill her. And, boy, you can light on my back, and we'll leave here."

Well, Jack says, "It's all right. But don't you think I'm going to kill you."

"Nah," the bull says. "I know you'll do all right. Now go on."

So, after a while the old man came back to see if Jack was willing to drive his bull down to the barnyard to be killed. And, "Well," Jack says, "bedads, I hate to mighty bad, but I guess if I've got to, I've got to."

"Well," the old man says, "drive him on down. Let's get it over with just as quick as we can."

So Jack drove the old black bull down, and when he got in the barnyard, the old man came out to catch hold of his horns, to hold him while Jack killed him. Oh, you've never seen such snorting and pawing and prancing around and bellowing and lowering his horns at that old man. Why, it had the old farmer just about scared to death.

And the old woman heard all of that rumpus going on out there, and she thought, "Well, my lands. What in the world is the matter?" She went out and she saw what was a-happening and she says, "Aw, Saw buck. Saw. Saw. Stand still now. Saw, buck, saw."

She went back to the house and got the gourd with some salt in it, and she came back with some of that salt, poured it out in her hand. "Saw buck. Saw. Stand still now. Stand still." And she kept easing up a little closer to him and a little closer to him with that handful of salt and finally she reached up the other hand and grabbed a hold of his horn. "All right," she says, "Jack, come on, right quick now. Hurry up. Kill him! Kill him while I've got hold of him."

And Jack came running just as hard as he could with that big old ax drawn back, just like he was going to hit the bull in the head, and *Ker-splick*, he just let it come right down in the very center of that old woman's face and chopped off her head. That was the end of her.

Jack jumped on to the black bull's back and away they went, just lickity split down the road. Well, they had everything in the world they wanted. There was plenty of grass along by the road, and there was plenty of water in the branches that they passed, and Jack had all the milk and the bread that he wanted, and they were just getting along fine, happy as they could be. But one day when that big old black bull bent his head down to a big creek to drink, he saw queer grayish-bluish bubbles come bubbling up out of the water. And he raised up his head from drinking and he gave a, kind of a long sigh, and he says, "Bad sign, Jack. Bad sign. Get on my back." He said, "Just as sure as anything in this world, I've got a bull to fight right up the road. And he'll be grayish-blue. Now you look and see."

Well, they went on up the road a little ways and, sure enough, about around two curves, and they heard a bull bellowing. You've never heard anything like it. Well, the old bull said, "Now listen, Jack. Don't you get scared. I can fight that bull, but you climb off of my back. Don't you be around on the ground anywhere. We might kill you. You just shinny right up a tree somewhere, stay there till I get this bull out of the way, and then we'll go on."

So, when they got around the next curve, there he stood, just a-pawing the earth. Just not letting a thing pass without a fight. So Jack shinnied up a tree just as hard as he could go and the old black bull lowered his head, and he made at that old bluish-gray bull, and you've never seen such a fight. Oh, my lands. Just this way and that way and the other, but *finally* the old big black bull just downed the old blue-gray one and gored him to death. Now Jack climbed down out of the tree (Oh [boy], he certainly had been a-shaking up in there), got onto his back, and away they went riding again, just as happy as they could be.

But the very next day, as the big old black bull was drinking out of another creek, there came up queer old reddish-looking bubbles. *Um, um.* The old bull says, "Jack, that's another bad sign. I'm telling you, I've got a big old red bull right up the road here to fight, but I think I can whip him. I think I can." Said, "Now you do just like you did yesterday. Shinny up that tree there, get out of the way, and just give me plenty of room, and I bet you I'll fix him."

And so, when they met the big old red bull, he was the biggest thing that Jack had ever seen. He wasn't quite as broad as Jack's big old black bull, but he was a mean-looking thing, pawing the earth and snorting and bellowing. You've never heard anything like it. And the two old bulls just locked horns and up and down that road they went, back and forth and under and over. Once or twice, Jack's big old black bull got brought right down to his knees, but he come up again and down and finally he got the old red bull and broke his neck.

Well, Jack got down and he patted his big old black bull, and he loved him, and he hugged his neck, and he says, "I tell you, you're the finest bull in the world. But you're getting kind of tired, aren't you?"

"Yes," big old black bull says, "I tell you, I can't do much more of this."

Well, they went on for several days and had a good time, but somehow or other, the big old black bull couldn't get back quite as strong as he was, and that—about the fourth day, when he bent his head down to drink out of this creek, big old white blubbers came bubbling up. The big old black bull just raised up his head and he didn't say a word. Jack climbed onto his back and they went walking on up the road. A little ways on up there, the old black bull stopped. He says, "Jack, there's a big old white bull right around this curve here."

Says, "Don't you hear him a-bellowing? And I've got him to fight. And, Jack, I may not make it this time, for I tell you I'm kind of tired and weak. But now you listen to me close. If he does kill me, when he's gone on off, you climb down out of the tree, and you just take a strop from the tip of my tail clear up to the end of my nose, and be sure and get my horns on it. And roll that up and take it on with you. And then, Jack, the rest of your life, if anybody ever does bother you, all in this world you've got to do or say is, 'Tie, hide, tie. Beat, horns, beat.' And that hide will tie anything in this world that's a-bothering you and the horns will beat it to death."

"Well," Jack says, "Now I do *hope* that you're going to whip that old white bull and that we can go on forever, being happy just like we are. But," he says, "I'll sure remember and you've been mighty, mighty good to me." And just then, that big old white bull came in sight. Three times as big as the big black bull. And the fiercest, angriest-looking bull Jack had ever known in his life.

So up the tree he went, and together you could hear their big old horns and heads hit for a mile along that road. You've never seen such a fight. Oh, Jack's bull put up the finest fight you've ever seen, but he just wasn't strong enough for that big old white bull. And [the white bull] finally downed him, and gored him to death. And went on off down the road, just a-bellowing as loud as could be, as far as Jack could hear him.

Jack waited till he was clear out of hearing. Then he climbed down off, out of the tree. He'd been sitting up there crying ever since his bull had been killed, but he remembered what [the bull had] told him, so he said, "Well, I guess I better do it." So he took his hunting knife and he just—from the tip of that bull's tail right straight up to the tip of his nose, and taking in the horns—he cut him out a big strop of leather.

Jack rolled up his strop of leather and horns, stuck it in his pocket, and went a-walking on up the road. But, you know, after a while he begun to get hungry. And he said, "Well, my best friend's gone, but he said that this thing'll take care of me. And I guess he knows what he's talking about. So, I guess I'll just stop here and see, though, if I can get a little job of work to do, at least enough to get me something to eat."

So he went in and knocked at this nice-looking farmhouse, and an old, haggy witch-of-a-looking woman came to the door. Jack says, "Madam, have you got any work to do, that a boy like me could have, get him something to eat?"

"Yes," the old woman says, "can you tend sheep?"

"Oh, sure," Jack says, "I can tend sheep."

"Well, get right on up on that mountain there. Then you'll find a whole flock. Round em up up there, and I'll be up to see you after a while. Bring you something to eat." So Jack went on up on the mountain. Sure enough, the sheep were just scattered all over, everywhere. He begun kind of humming and whistling and calling to them, and the first thing you know, he had the sheep all rounded up, and just as happy eating away as could be.

And a farmer came along through the field and stopped and talked to Jack a little while, and Jack told him about hiring out to the old woman.

"Ah," the man says, "Jack, you'll never, never in this world do a bit of good of her. She's a witch."

"Well, bedads," Jack says, "I guess I can manage her. I guess I can."

"Well," the man says, "if you do, you'll be the first one that's ever managed her." Said, "I tell you, she's been the death of more men around here than I know of, let alone little boys."

"Well," Jack says, "bedads, I'll, I'll try it out for a little while."

So the farmer went on down through the fields, and it wasn't very long till he saw the old woman a-coming. Well, he thought she'd bring him something to eat. She got up kind of close to him, and she had something, looked like, in a basket, and she's holding that in one hand, and walked up kind of close to Jack and she said, "Which are you going to take, hard tacks or sharp shins?"

"Well," Jack says, "I'll take hard tacks."

And boy, she grabbed him at the throat and was just about to choke him to death. Jack just bare had breath enough to holler, "Tie, hide, tie. Beat, horns, beat." Boys, that old strop of leather just wrapped itself up around that old woman just like a big black snake, and those horns begun beating her this way and that way, and in the face and in the back, knocking her over, and she began hollering, "Oh, Jack, Jack! Take this off, take this off of me. What is it you want? What is it you want?"

"Oh," Jack says, "bedads, I guess I want me a fine-looking suit of clothes."

"Oh," she says, "you can have it, you can have it. Take this thing off of me."

Well, Jack took it off and stuck it back in his pocket, rolled it up good and tight and the old woman went beating it down the hill—oh, she was just cursing and swearing (you've never heard anything like it) just as long as Jack could hear her. But when he got in that evening, there on the table sat a good supper for him, and when he got up in the loft to where his pile of straw was that he was to sleep [in], hanging right up over it was as nice a looking suit of clothes as anybody'd ever want to wear.

Well, next morning, Jack put em on. He went back . . . with his sheep up on to the mountain. Just at noontime, here came the old woman back again. She didn't get quite so close to Jack this time, but she was pretty close. And she says, "All right, what it's going to be, hard tacks or sharp shins?"

"Bedads, I'll just take hard tacks again."

And with that, the old witch started out to grab Jack, but, hmm, before she got her hands on him, he hollered, "Tie, hide, tie! Beat, horns, beat!" And out came that old strop of leather and those horns and, I'm telling you, they just fairly beat the life out of that old woman, after the strop got her tied down good. She begun yelling for Jack to let her loose, let her loose, let loose. She said, "Oh, Jack, what will [you] take, what will you take? Get this thing off of me. I'll just give you anything."

"Oh, well," he says, "bedads," he says, "I guess I could do pretty well with a bag of gold."

"All right, sir," she says, "it'll be right waiting for you when you come in tonight." So Jack took the old horns and the strop off of her, and she went down the hill. My, she was mad.

Well, when Jack went in, there was another good supper for him. When he went up to his pallet of straw up there, right there set a bag of gold, in the middle of his straw bed. There was some silver in it, but it was most all gold.

Well, Jack thought he was doing pretty well. So he took his gold with him the next morning, and he started back up on the hill with the sheep again. Just at noontime, here comes the old woman. I'm telling you, she was mad. You could tell she was mad long before she got to Jack. And she was just a-gritting her teeth and a-shaking her fists, and when she came in hearing of him, she says, "All right, what are you taking this time, hard tack or sharp shins."

"Why," Jack says, "bedads, I'll just take hard tacks again." And with that, she made at him, and Jack made like he was going to go at her. And instead, he hollered, "Tie, hide, tie! Beat, horns, beat!" And out they came, and he says, "Give it to her this time. Give it to her." And they beat her all the way back down that hill, clear down to the [barns]. And Jack followed along, the sheep scared to death—they stayed way on top of the mountain. And every breath that she's getting, she's a-hollering to Jack to get that thing off of her. "Get it off, get it off," she said. "Jack, what do you want? What do you want this time? Get this thing off of me."

"Well," Jack says, "bedads, I'll tell you. I want that fine horse you've got, that brand new saddle, and that shiny bridle." "All right," the old woman says, "they're yours." And with her last breath, she says, "They've done killed me anyway." And sure enough, there lay the old witch dead as a doornail.

Well, Jack got on his pony. Oh, but he was a handsome thing. That bright, shiny new saddle and the bright shiny bridle, his bag of gold, and he was all dressed up just as fine as anything you've ever seen in your life. And down the road he went. Oh, didn't Jack have him a good time? He stopped at the best hotels, he ate at the finest café, and he spent his money, and he had a good time, and, Law, he just—he was having the best time that anybody could ever have. But you know one thing? Why, after a while, his clothes begun to look shabby. And his horse, he fed him pretty good, all along, but he's kindly beginning to look poor. And he looked in his money bag, and it was about all gone. In another day or two, he didn't have a thing.

"Well, now," Jack says, "bedads, I've played the fool. Why didn't I save a little of that money? I've just now got to get back to work again. So I guess I'll just stop up here at this farmer's house and see if he's got a little job of work I can do."

So he stopped at the house and the old farmer looked him over. "Well," he says, "you're kind of a poor-looking specimen, but can you mind pigs?"

"Law, yes," Jack says, "I can mind pigs just about the best thing of anything I can do. Sure, I can mind pigs."

"Well now," the old man says, "listen. I want you to climb up in these apple trees around here and shake on down plenty of apples during the day—you can eat some of the apples too, and then when night comes, I want you to keep your eyes open. For something's been going with some of my pigs here. Every night, I lose two or three. First thing you know, I'm not going to have a hog left. Well," he said, "I tell you, Jack. If you can just find out who's getting my pigs, you sure are going to be well set up in life."

"All right," Jack says, "bedads, Father, I'll sure find em for you." So all day long, he climbed from one apple tree to another and shook down the big old juicy ripe apples for the hogs to eat, down in underneath. And every once in a while, he'd eat him one too. And then he had a good supper up at the house, and came back down to the orchard and climbed up in a big, low-spreading tree in a nice easy crotch there, where he was just hidden from anybody that was down underneath. But he could see everything that was going on. Now, it was getting kindly late, beginning to be dark, but there was a big, bright moon and Jack was just sitting up in there, watching for all he was worth. And he didn't have long to wait, for in just a little while, here came the queerest-looking old witch of a woman, up over the fence, and down into the orchard, feeling around the pigs' shoulders and their bellies to see if they was nice and fat, so she could get her a nice, good, a nice, good one. Finally found two that just suited her, grabbed em up in under her arms and was a-starting on off, back over the fence. And Jack hollered, "Hey there, old woman. Just wait a minute. What you think you're doing with our pigs like that?" Said, "Put them pigs down, and just wait till I get down there."

The old woman dropped the pigs just like they were hot, grabbed her up two old big rocks, and she just begun grinding those rocks together. I'm telling you, the sand just flew from them, and the sparks. She said, "Yes, you little devil, you can come down here if you want to. I'll grind you up between these two rocks." And Jack just reached in his back pocket there, and he said, "Tie, hide, tie! Beat, horns, beat!" and before you could say "scat" they had that old woman tied hand and foot, and the horns begun beating her and banging her and knocking her down. The pigs run up and bite her, and stomp on her and squeal, and the dogs begun to bark. You've never heard such a noise in your life. It waked up the old farmer. He came running down to the pig lot there in the orchard, just as hard as he could go, with his great old big broad-ax. When he saw that old witch tied there, he whacked off her head, and that was the end of her.

He gave Jack a big, fine mare, another sack full of gold, and a brand new suit of clothes. Jack says, "Now, I'm a-going home to my little farm, where I can live the rest of my days without having to work too hard. I'm not going to waste my money like I did before." And so he took his horse and his money, and he rode on off down the road, and as far as I know, he's living right there at home yet.

18. Jack and the Doctor's Girl

MAUD LONG
Hot Springs, North Carolina
Recorded by Duncan Emrich,
Washington, D.C., 1947

This is the story of Jack and the Doctor's Girl.

In the same settlement where Jack and his folks lived, there lived a rich doctor, and he had the nicest looking girl. Jack was just beginning to kind of get grown, and he just naturally was falling in love with the girl. But the old doctor said to Jack's father, "Now look-y here. There's no sense in Jack coming down to see *my girl*. He's too poor, entirely. I wouldn't think of letting anybody come to see her that wasn't worth at least a thousand dollars."

"Well," Jack's father says, "I'll tell him."

So when Jack's father told him that there was just no need in the world of his thinking about the doctor's girl—"why," he said, "you have to have a thousand dollars, Jack, before you can go back up there."

"Well, bedads," Jack says, "I'll have to think about it a little then." He sat around kind of blue-like and glum and not saying much, but he's doing a lot of thinking. He decided he'd never be able to make a thousand dollars there in that neighborhood. He might just as well get out in the world and hunt him up a job.

So he started out. His mother fixed him up a great sack of rations. He slung em across his back and he started walking. He walked and he walked and he walked and he walked and he was just getting into a regular wilderness—a great, dark forest. All day he'd traveled and he hadn't as much as seen a house. And he thought, "Well, night's coming on. I don't know what I'm going to do, but I'll just keep a-walking, I guess."

And as he walked on through these woods, the rain began to pour like it was just coming down out of a bucket. And not even a little wink of a light anywhere. Till way up in a holler, he saw one little gleam of light, and he made right straight for it. Soon as he got to the house, he was banging on the door, and a little old, bent-over woman came to the door, and she said, "Why, stranger, what in the world are you doing here?"

"Bedads," Jack says [laughing], "that's just what I'd like to know myself. I'm lost. But I saw your light way down the road yonder and I made for it. I want to come in, get out of this rain."

"Oh, no, no," she said [whispering], "you can't come in here. Why this is . . . a highway robbers' house. They'd kill you, Jack, just as sure as anything, if you come in here."

"Oh, well, bedads, I'd just as soon they'd kill me as to stand out here and get drowned in this rain. Let me in, I tell you. I'm just *bound* to come in."

"Well," she says, "but I'm telling you the truth now. They'll kill you."

"Well," he says, "just let em kill me." Walked on over to the back end of the little room and laid down on a pile of straw there, and went sound asleep.

Wasn't long after that till the robbers sure enough came home. Had great big old sacks of things they'd stolen from here and there and everywhere, and they'd begun opening the sacks and dividing out the loot, and long in the time of it, Jack begun to *snore*, you've never heard such a noise. And one of the men jumped up right quick, said, "What in the world is that?"

"Oh, Law," the old woman says, "I forgot to tell you. Little old boy come here about in the middle of the storm, and he just *would* come in. Nothing else would do him. And he went right back there in the back of the room and laid down and he's been asleep ever since."

One of the robbers says, "Well, that's the end of that. We'll just kill him. Can't let any man live that's ever been in here."

"Oh, well," the woman says, "listen. Don't kill him, and him asleep. I never did like to see anybody killed and them asleep. Wake him up."

So they waked up Jack, said, "Jack, get up from there. Get up. We've got to kill you. We can't have anybody that's ever been in here, live."

Well [in a tired voice], Jack sat up and rubbed his eyes, and he said, "Now, listen here. You can kill me if you want to. I ain't got a thing in the world but just these clothes I got on. And if you want them, why, just kill me. But what in the world do you want with just these old clothes? Better let me live, hadn't you? I might be a little help to you."

"Well," they said, "nah. I don't know. Are you any good at stealing?"

"Well," Jack says, "don't know. I guess I could try."

"Well," they said, "now listen. There's an old farmer lives up the road here. He's going to go to market tomorrow, with one of those big, fat oxen that he has. If you can steal that ox away from that farmer, we'll pay you good money for him."

"All right," Jack says, "Just wait till morning comes and I'll do my very best."

Morning came. Jack had a good breakfast, started off the porch, saw a good old big strong rope a hanging there and he picked it up and threw it along on his shoulder and went walking on up the road.

He hadn't gone so very far from this very house till he heard the old farmer coming a-whistling and a-singing down the road, driving his ox.

Well, he thought, what in the world will I do? How am I going to steal that ox from a man like that? And just right out ahead of him, at a kind of a turn in the road, there was a little old tree that bent *way* out right over the road, and Jack had a thought. Up that tree he went, just as quick as he could, made him a noose and fastened it in under his arm, like, and pulled his coat up round over it well, and twisted it around his neck and threw it up over the truck of the tree, and hung his head over on one side, just like he'd been hung—hanging there in the air.

Well, the old farmer, driving along, singing away, whistling, looked up and he said, "Law, I wish you'd look what's there. Right now those highway robbers have hung a man. And I bet you there don't a soul in the world know a thing about it. I'll just tie Old Buck right over here to this tree and I'll hit her back to the village just as fast as I can go and let the word be known."

So he tied his oxen up to the tree, hit her back up the road just as far as he could go—and Jack waited until he was well out of sight, pulled that rope loose from that tree, swung down to the ground, untied Old Buck, and down the road he started, just as hard as he could go, to the highway robbers' house.

Well, when they saw him a-coming, they said, "Jack, let me tell you. You sure are a slick one. That's fine stealing as far as we know."

"Now," Jack says, "listen. That same farmer will come with another oxen in the morning. Just as sure as anything. But I wonder what he's a-doing now."

Well, one of the highwaymen said, "I bet you I know what he's a-doing, for I heard it back in the village, that he told that there's a man hung down here in the road and the whole town came running out to find him and he run them up and down that road all morning trying to find the man that was hung and his ox."

Well, they all had them a big laugh about it and says, "Now, Jack, see what you can do in the morning."

So, they paid Jack three hundred dollars for stealing that ox. He put that money away, and the next morning he was up ready and bright early to go. He wanted to steal another ox if he could and get another three hundred dollars. And as he started out through the yard, there laid a pretty shoe, brand new woman's shoe, that the men had dropped out of their bag that they'd been bringing in where they'd stolen from one of the merchants. And Jack picked the thing up, says, "Well, bedads, let's take this along. Might use it."

Walked on up the road a little ways and he heard the farmer coming, whistling and a-singing, driving another one of his big fat oxen down to the market to sell it. So, Jack got in a pretty good little spot and he ran out into the middle of the road, put this shoe down, and he hit back into the bushes there, and hid, waited till the old farmer came by. And he was driving along—*almost* didn't see the shoe—and just as he got by it, he said, "Whoa, here Buck, whoa, whoa. Let me see. What is this? Well, I declare to you—a brand new woman's shoe." Said, "You know, if I just had the mate of that, that'd make my old woman a good pair of shoes, last her a whole year. But Law," he says, "where's the mate? One old shoe's no good. I just don't know. Well, no need to carry one old shoe. Just throw it down."

Jack waited until he got around the bend in the road, and out he hopped into the middle of the road and grabbed this shoe, and struck across a little old path that he knew right through the woods, that went *way* on down the road further, and he got there long before the old farmer could, driving that slow ox—he slipped out in the middle of the road and dropped down the shoe. Hid in the bushes to see what the old farmer would do.

When the old farmer come alongside of it, he said, "Look. If there's not the mate of that shoe that I saw *way* back up the road. [Calling his ox:] *Saw, Buck, saw.* Here. I'll just tie you over here to this little old sapling, and I'll hit her back there, but I'm going to tie you *good and tight* now. I don't want you getting away while I'm gone. And I'm going to run back up there and get that other shoe. Why, I could take those shoes to town and sell em for maybe three dollars. Yeah, I'll go back and get it."

By that time he had Old Buck tied up, and back up the road he went.

Well, Jack waited until he was out of sight, and he slipped down, untied Buck, and head off into the woods with him just as hard as he could go, toward the old robbers' house.

That man ran up and down the road *all* that whole day, hunting for that other shoe.

Well, the robbers said, "Well, Jack, I'm telling you. You sure are showing what kind of a stealer you are. I'm telling you, you're all right. Now, here's your other three hundred dollars. Now, there's just one more ox that that farmer has. He's going to go to town tomorrow with it, to sell. If you'll get that one, we'll make it a even thousand dollars. And we'll give you the name of the best thief that we've ever known."

"Well," Jack says, "bedads, I don't know, but I'll do my best. I'll try, come morning."

So when morning came, Jack started out. He didn't see a thing he felt like he wanted to take with him. Well, he just didn't know what he's a-going to do. But he'd get up the road and see if he could see anything that'd help him out any. He saw the farmer coming, but he wasn't a-whistling and a-singing this morning. He was a-wondering and a-worrying about those two big fine fat oxen that he'd lost. He's kind of sad-like, walking down the road.

Jack saw him. He took off into the woods and way out up through the brush he went, just a-making the most noise, and

MOO-OOO

MOO-OOO

MOO-OOO

"Why," the old farmer says, "Listen. Listen. That's one of those oxen just as sure as anything. That's Old Buck."

And about that time, Jack was over on the other side of the mountain, breaking brush and a-knocking the trees around and a-shaking the bushes and a bellowing and—"Well," the old farmer says, "If there's not Bill on that other side! There's Buck and Bill, both, right out there in the woods. They're just running up and down trying to get home. Now, I'll just tie you right over here to this sapling and I'll go bring those other two down, and I'll have all three of you to take to the market." And Jack was up one holler and down the other and up one side of the hill and down another, and in through the laurel thicket just a-thrashing and a-making the most noise that you possibly could. Never could quite tell where Buck nor Bill was, by the way Jack was a-bawling and a-bellowing. And the old farmer was just running his legs off and Jack got him twisted around there so in a big old clump of laurel thicket that he didn't hardly see how to get out. And Jack gave him a side-slip and slipped away from him, back to the road, untied his third oxen, and drove him down to the robbers' house.

"All right," the robber says, "here's your thousand dollars, Jack. And if we ever want a thief, we'll know right where to come to find one."

Jack took his thousand dollars and thanked him, and he started for home. My, he was proud. When he got in, he told his father all about how he'd gotten the thousand dollars.

"Now," he says, "I want you to take this and go up to the doctor's house, and see if it's all right for me to come up and see the girl. Well, the old farmer— Jack took the—Jack's father took the thousand dollars and went up to the old doctor's house. And the doctor said, "Well, heard anything from Jack since he been gone?"

"Oh, yes," his father said, "he come in last night."

"Well, gone a might little short time. Don't reckon he got any thousand dollars while he's gone, did he?"

"Well, yes," Jack's father said, "bedads, he did. He brought the thousand dollars in. Got it right here in my pocket."

"Now, how in the world did Jack make a thousand dollars in just those few days he was gone?"

"Well," the old father said, "I'll just tell you exactly how he did it." And so he told him how Jack had stolen the oxen and how the old robbers had paid him a thousand dollars.

"Hum," doctor says. "Jack's a pretty good thief, isn't he? I guess I'd just like to see him do a little stealing around *me*, before he comes up here to see this girl of mine." Said, "You tell Jack, if he wants to come see this girl, why he can just come up here to my barn and steal the horses out from under twelve men that'll be riding em. I've got twelve horses, and I'm going to have twelve men ride em tonight, down in the lot. And if he can steal those horses from under those men, then you tell him I'll talk to him."

Well, Jack's father went back down home and he said, "Now, son, I told you from the first. You're just a-wasting your time. *Now* the doctor says you've got to come up there and steal twelve horses from under twelve men tonight, or you can't come see that girl."

"Well, bedads," Jack says, "I guess I can go *try*." So Jack fooled around till about dark, went up to the doctor's barn. Had him a little old keg under his arm, and as he started to go in at the gate. "No," one of the men says, "Just don't come in here, Jack. You're not to come in."

"Well," Jack says, "bedads, I'll just climb up on the fence then and sit here a little while."

Well, he climbed up on the fence. And it was getting pretty cold. Jack opened the old keg, turned it up to his lips like he's getting him a good drink, and [Maud makes a smacking noise] smacked his lips and put it down back on his knees again and sit there. And those men watched him all the time. Every now and then Jack'd turn that keg up to his lips like he was drinking. Finally, the men begun to get so cold, they—one of em rode up to him and says, "Jack, listen here. Hand me over that keg and let me have just a—one dram."

"Why, sure," Jack says. "Just help yourself. Drink as much as you want to."

"No, bedads, I'm not going to take but one dram, because I know what you're thinking about." So the man turned the keg up and drunk him one dram and went riding on off.

Well, when the other men saw that this one had had a dram, why, they decided that they would all take-em *one drink* out of Jack's keg. So they all took-em one drink. And by the time that first man had ridden back around to where Jack was, he was sound asleep on his horse's neck, because Jack had been down to the—bought him a little chloroform and put in that whiskey, and it just put the men all to sleep. There were all twelve of em—as fast as they rode around by Jack, he just lifted em off and put em over there in the trough and held on to the horses' bridles. And in just a little while, here he had the twelve horses. Took em on down to the house and went to bed.

Next morning, his father got up, and Jack told him what had happened. He took the twelve horses and went riding up to the old doctor's house. "Well," he says, "now I reckon, Jack can come up and see her, can't he?"

"Well, I'll bedads. No, he can't. He can't come yet and see her. I tell you he's got to do something that he'll never get done. Tonight he's got to come up here to our house, steal a rabbit right out of the pot that's a-cooking, and me and my old woman and the girl a-sitting there a-watching it."

Well, the father went back down home and he says, "Now, Jack, you see, he's just going to keep on. You'll never be able to get the best of him. Now he wants you to come up there and steal a rabbit out of the pot where it's a-cooking. And him and his old woman and the girl all a-sitting there a-looking at it."

"Well," Jack says, "I guess I can *try*." Night came along. There sat the old doctor and his wife and the girl all right in front of a big open fireplace where there was a big black kettle on the coals a-cooking. And every once in a while the old lady'd lift off the lid and look in, and there was the rabbit. Well, as the girl looked out at the window, she said, "Law, Pappy, there went a big rabbit jumping right through the yard."

"Now," the old doctor says, "don't you worry about that rabbit. You keep your eyes right on that one in the pot. That's the only rabbit I'm interested in."

Well, they all sat there for a little while. Jack let another, great, big rabbit go hopping past the window.

"Law," the woman says, "there went the biggest rabbit I ever did see in my life, doctor. That's the biggest rabbit, I know, that ever was. Twice as big as this one is in the pot."

"Well," the doctor says, "keep your mind off of that rabbit and keep it on the one in the pot. That's what I'm a-telling you."

And they sat there for a little bit longer. And Jack had *eased* right up to the door and eased the screen open and put in the biggest rabbit that he had. When he hopped right up in front of the doctor, the old doctor said, "Law-a-mercy, that *is* the biggest rabbit I ever did see in my life. Help me catch it here, old woman, you and the girl."

And there they went, over the chairs and the table, and in under the bed and just everywhere you could think of after that rabbit. He's always keeping right out of their reach. And around and around over the house he went. Finally, he bumped it up against the screen door and pushed it open and out he was gone.

"*Pshew*," the doctor says, "I'm awful sorry we missed that rabbit. I've never seen such a rabbit in my life." He said, "I tell you what, old woman, you better look over at this one that's in the pot and see if it's needing any more water."

The old woman went over and lifted up the lid of her pot and she said, "There's nothing in here but just the gravy! The rabbit's gone."

"Yes," and the doctor says, "and *I* know where the rabbit is. That's a 'Jack' rabbit by now. Well," he says, "nothing can be done about it."

Morning came and the father came right up to the old doctor's with that cooked rabbit . . . in a bucket.

"All right," he said, "now here's your rabbit. Jack got him right out from under all of you a-looking at it."

"Yes, but," the old doctor says, "he tricked us. That's what he done. He tricked us. Now, I tell you. If he can come up here tonight and steal the sheet off of the bed where me and the old woman's a-sleeping, then I'll think about Jack coming to see our girl."

Well, the father went back and told Jack. "Now," he says, "Jack, listen. He said he's a-going to have every window nailed down and every door locked. And if you come fooling around up there tonight, he's going to kill you."

"Well," Jack says, "I guess, bedads, I can just go and *try*. I don't think he'll kill me, and I bet you I can get the sheet."

So along, way up in the night, the old doctor and his wife are lying there in bed and they weren't asleep, because they was kind of wondering if Jack was going to be coming around. They was about to give him up when they heard a *thump, thump, thump* right outside one of their windows. And they looked, and there was Jack's head with a big old hat on, peeping in at the window. And the old doctor raised up in bed, and he said, "Now, listen, Jack, I give you fair warning. If you break out one of those lights, I'll shoot you just as sure as I'm in this bed—I've got my gun with me. Now, you better just get on away from here."

Well, the head bobbed back down. Everything was quiet for a little while and back up the head come again and *ka-thump* against the window.

And the doctor set right up in bed and he says, "Now, Jack, that's you, and I know it. And I'm telling you, you break a window light out of there, and just that sure, I'm going to shoot you."

Head bobbed back down again. A few minutes it came—*bang*—back up again and hit against that window frame and just simply broke out every windowpane in it.

And just as soon as he did that, *bang, bang, bang*, went the old doctor with his gun, three times. And then they heard an awful noise.

"Well," the old woman says, "doctor, just as sure as you're living, you've killed Jack. I heard him hit the ground."

"Well," the old doctor says, "I didn't mean to kill him. I was just a-trying to scare him away."

"Yeah," but the old woman says, "I bet you pretty he's dead." And says, "You know, come morning, why they'll find him lying down there, and the sheriff'll be down here and get you, and you'll hang for that, just as sure as anything. That's *murder*."

"Oh, Law," the old doctor says, "you know, I hadn't thought about *that*." He said, "I guess I had better get out of here and go down there and drag him off somewhere away from the house and kind of hide him, especially till morning." So the old doctor was so excited and so nervous as he went running down the steps, he left every door standing wide open.

And after a while, the old woman heard something—heard somebody downstairs. "Old woman, old woman, listen. Throw me down something here to wrap him up in."

"Oh, Lawdy, what'll I throw you down? I don't see a thing."

"Oh," he said, "just the handiest thing that you've got, but be quick about it. You know, if I get this blood all over me, that'll look bad. I've got to get him wrapped up so that none of the blood'll get on my clothes. Hurry up. Oh," he says, "just reach me the old sheet there, and throw it down to me."

And down went the sheet just as hard as the old woman could throw it, down the steps. And after a while, the old doctor came back up the steps just killing himself a-laughing.

"Now," his old woman says, "Now what in the world's tickled you now? I don't reckon killing Jack'd do the likes of that to you."

"Oh, law," he said. "I didn't kill Jack." He said, "Don't you know, that's an old dummy head he had stuck up there! And he had it weighted down with a big old rock, and that was what we heard hit the ground," he says. "There's not a thing in the world down there, but just that dummy head and that rock."

"Well," the old woman says, "what in the world did you need a-coming in here and hollering for me to throw you down the sheet for?"

"Oh, I didn't holler to you to throw me down anything at all. I haven't hollered to you at all."

Said, "You did too. You run in there and told me it'd keep the blood off of you, to throw you something to wrap him up in. And I couldn't find anything else, and you said—hollered up and said, 'Oh, just throw me down the sheet.'"

92

"Well," the old doctor says, "that fixes it. We know who got the sheet. I bet you I know right now where it is."

Next morning, Jack's father came up to the house, and he said, "Well, here's your sheet. And Jack wants to know now if he can come up and see the girl." He said, "You know, he has evidence that you tried to kill him, because they's three shot right from your pistol through his hat, and he's going down to town to see the law about it. But he said to tell you that he wasn't going to be in any great hurry about going, and you could let him know what to do."

Oh, the doctor wiped his brow with his handkerchief and he says, "Listen here. You go home and tell Jack I said, come right up here and get this girl. She's his'n, from now on. And tell him I said just not to say anything about that shooting."

And so, Jack and the doctor's daughter—girl—was married, and as far as I know, they lived happy ever after.

19. Jack and the Northwest Wind

MAUD LONG
Hot Springs, North Carolina
Recorded by Duncan Emrich,
Washington, D.C., 1947

A long time ago, Jack and his folks lived on a high windy hill. And at the time I'm going to tell you about now, just Jack and his mammy were there. The father'd gone off on a long trip and was working on helping build the road, and Will and Tom, the older brothers, had gone off into a neighboring settlement to try to find a job of work.

And so Jack was doing the best that he could to look after his mammy and the feeding and cutting the wood and all the things that had to be done around the little old farm. But wintertime was coming on, and it was getting colder and colder and colder. At last the north wind just begun to whistle through that old house, and Jack's mammy said, "I'll tell you, Jack, what you'll have to do. Get you some boards and nails and a hammer and get out there and see if you can't fasten up some of these awful cracks around here. We're going to freeze to death, boy."

Well, Jack sat down, and he studied a little while, and he allowed as how Will had broke the head off of the hammer the last time he was cracking walnuts, and Tom had used up the last nail they had, fixing that old fence. And they didn't have any planks was worth a thing in the world. Was all just old rotten pieces. So he pulled his old hat down on his head, and he says, "Mammy, I tell you what I'm going to do. I'm going to cut you up a passel of firewood and I'm going to *leave* here and stop that Northwest Wind."

She says, "Now, Jack, listen here son. You know you can't do that."

"Bedads I can. Just let me find the hole it's coming out at, and I'm gonna stuff my old hat in it. And we'll have no more Northwest Wind."

So Jack got just as busy as could be, all the rest of that day and the next, fixing up a big pile of firewood for his mother. The morning after that, he pulled his old raggedy hat down . . . on his head and away he started to stop the Northwest Wind. He traveled and he traveled and he traveled and he traveled. And it was beginning to get along up in the evening. Jack was kind of beginning to wonder what he was going to do for the night, for he sure hadn't found the hole that the Northwest Wind came out of. And as he was a-standing there trying to kind of think, the wind just whistling around him like everything, saw a little old gray man standing there by the side of the road, and when he come alongside of him, the man seemed to know him right from the very first.

"Why," he says, "howdy, Jack. Where in the world are you going on this blustery, windy day?"

"Well," Jack says, "bedads, Uncle, I tell you what I'm going to do. I'm going to stop this Northwest Wind a-blowing."

"Ah," the little old man said, "Jack, you know, you can't do that." Says, "It's a long piece where that north wind's coming from."

"Well, bedads, I know, but I'm going on to find it anyway."

"Now, listen, son. You just come up to the house and sit down a little while with me and get yourself good and warm, and let's talk this thing over. You may not have to go on to find the Northwest Wind." Well, Jack was pretty tired, and he was pretty hungry, so he just let the old man have his way and went on home with him.

The old man stirred around, and after a while had a good hot supper on the table. And Jack didn't have to be coaxed to sit down. Now, after they had eaten a *fine* meal, Jack had washed up the dishes, they were sitting there before the fire, and Jack was just good and rested. The old man says, "Now, son, let me tell you what to do. You take this little present that I've got here for your mammy, and you go on back home. Here's a nice tablecloth. And all in the world that you have to do, when you spread it out on the table, is to say, 'Spread, tablecloth, spread.' And you'll have as fine a feast as you'd want ever to find in your life."

"Well," Jack says, "bedads, that really is something. We don't have much to eat at our house these days. I'll just take it, sir, and go on back home."

The old man says, "Now, listen, Jack. Don't stop at the next house down the road. They's devilish boys there, and they'll torment you to death. Now don't stop there, Jack."

"All right, Uncle. I'll just remember that, and I'll not stop." So he thanked him for his nice tablecloth, put it under his arm and started down the road.

Well, it *was* real late, and by the time he came to that next house, the boys was out in the yard a-playing around, and they begun hollering at Jack to stop and play with em a while. And he stopped and played with em a while. And one of em says, "Jack, what's that you got under your arm? What is that tablecloth?"

"Oh," Jack says, "it's just a little present the old man that lives up at the next house give me."

"Well, Jack. What is it? What is it? Tell us about it."

"Well," Jack says, "now stop pestering me and I'll tell you. You spread it out and you say, 'Spread, tablecloth, spread,' and you've got just as nice a meal as you'd ever want."

"Aw," they said. "Naw. We'll believe that when we see it. Suppose you spread out your tablecloth."

"Well," Jack says, "bedads, I'll just show you." So he went in the house, spread the tablecloth on the table and said, "Spread, tablecloth, spread," and you've never seen such a nice meal in your life. They all sat down and *ate* every bite they wanted. They were just as full as could be.

"Well," one of the boys said, "look-y here. You just have to wait now and show this to Pappy when he comes. Why, he'd be tickled to death to see table-cloths like this."

"Well," Jack said, "maybe I'll wait a little while."

They said, "Listen, Jack. Just lay up with us for the night. No need to where you're going home tonight." It was pitch-black dark by that time.

"Well," Jack says, "bedads, I guess I could, and I can go home early in the morning." And so Jack went to bed. Went sound asleep, of course, just like a boy would. And away in the middle of the night, the old man gets up and puts a tablecloth exactly like Jack's right there on the table by him, and takes Jack's tablecloth.

Well, come morning, Jack was awake bright and early, and he thought about his old mammy back at home and the Northwest Wind a-blowing so. He grabbed that tablecloth and he started for home just as hard as he could tear. Got it just at real, good day.

His mammy said, "Well, I see, you're back and that wind's just a-blowing as cold as it ever did."

"Yes, bedads," Jack says, "I didn't get to the place where it's coming out. Met a little old man, and he give me a nice present for you, Mammy, and I just brought it home."

"Well," she says, "what is it?"

"It's a tablecloth. And all I got to do is put it here on the table and say, 'Spread, tablecloth, spread,' and we'll have just as fine a breakfast as you ever saw."

"Well," his mammy says, "I'll know more about that when I see it, son. Do your work."

Jack spread the tablecloth on the table, said, "Spread, tablecloth, spread."

Hmmp. Not a thing in the world happened.

"Well," Mammy says, "just about like I expected, son. I'll just take that old tablecloth and make you a shirt."

So Jack stayed around home another, about another week. And the Northwest Wind kind of let up for about a week. And then it begin to blow *harder than ever.* Oh, just like a gale, blowing through the cracks in that old house.

Mammy says, "Jack, you're just bound to do something, son. Now, I can't stand it any longer."

"All right, bedads, Mammy, I got you plenty of firewood ready, and *this* time I'm going to find where the Northwest Wind's a-coming out, and I'll stop it." So he started. Now, he knew right where the old man was living this time, so when he got pretty close to the house, he just decided he'd split right out through that field and go clear around the old man's house, and he would never see him, and he could get on to where the Northwest Wind was coming out. He just had gotten all away around through that field and come back to the road, and there was a water mill right along by the side of the road there, and who was going out the door but the little old gray man with his turn of meal on his shoulder.

"Well," he says, "Jack, what in this world are you doing out on such a day as today? Now where are you going?"

"Well," Jack says, "bedads, now this time I'm going to find that Northwest Wind. I'm going to stop up the hole so me and Mammy won't freeze to death, and you are not going to stop me."

"Oh," the man says, "don't you know, it's too cold and too far a piece. You don't know how long a ways it is to that place. And besides that, you're about to freeze to death. This is a cold day, so now turn around, and come back home with me. I got a lot of good stuff to eat, and I might have another present for you."

[Dismissive tone] "Ah," Jack says, "another present. I don't want your presents." Says, "That old tablecloth wouldn't do a thing when I got it home."

The little old man says, "Now listen, Jack. Did you stop down at that house that I told you not to?"

"Yes," Jack says, "I stopped and stayed all night with em."

"Well, son," he says, "*they've* got your tablecloth." Says, "Come on home with me now. I've got something else that's mighty good for you, if you'll just come home and leave off this Northwest Wind business."

So Jack turned around and went on home with the little old man. They had another fine supper. And Jack sat down by the good warm fire and got all so rested and easy-feeling. And the old man says, "Now, listen. This time, I got a rooster to give you. As fine a rooster as you ever saw in your life, and all you have to do is take your hat, hold it right under that rooster, and say, 'Come, gold, come.' And your hat'll be plum full of gold eggs."

"Well," Jack says, "bedads. Now that *will* be something for Mammy, won't it. And I'm much obliged to you, mister. And I'll just go on home now." Took the rooster under his arm, and he started down the road.

And the old man ran out the door and said, "Hey, Jack! Listen to what I'm saying to you. Don't stop down there at that thievish house again. Go on. Get past them boys."

"Oh, yes," Jack hollered back. "You may be sure I'll never stop there again." And on down the road he went.

Well, sure enough, he got by the house, and was way on down the road, when he met all four of the boys a-coming from the store. "Well, Jack," they said. "Glad to see you again. What's that you got under your arm?"

"Now," Jack said, "that's none of your business."

"Oh, well," says, "you don't need to be so huffy about it. So I guess that's something the little old man gave you, is it?"

"Yes," Jack says, "it is, if you got to know."

"Well," he says, "what's that old rooster fit for?"

"Well," Jack says, "he's fit for plenty. I just put my hand under him and say, 'Come, gold, come,' and he'll lay a hatful of gold eggs."

"Law, Jack," he says, "come on back to the house. Show that to Pappy. He'd just love to see a rooster that laid gold eggs." But he says, "You know what? Rooster can't lay eggs at all, let alone a gold un."

"All right," Jack says, "let's go to the house and I'll just show you."

Set the rooster on the table, put his hand under him, and said, "Come, gold, come." There was a hatful of gold eggs. Well, the old man just took on. "Why," he says, "Jack, you got the finest rooster that ever was in the world. Now son, it's too dark and late. Thieves might waylay you along the road somewhere. You just better spend the night here."

"Yes," Jack says, "I guess I had better. But I sure want to take good care of this rooster."

"Well," the old man says, "that's all right son. I'll get you a box, and you can put the rooster right into it." Got him a box, put the rooster right into it, right alongside of Jack's bed, and Jack laid his hand right on top of the box. And he meant to stay awake all night and watch his rooster. But, Law, you know how a boy is. Why, he was sound asleep in ten minutes. And the first thing you know, the old man tripped out to his barnyard, brought in a rooster that looked *exactly* like the one that Jack had, and he put his into the box and took Jack's and out he went.

Well, the next morning, Jack got up. Didn't know a thing in the world about what had taken place in the night. Took his rooster, thanked the old man for being so nice to him, and give him the box and went on home. As he went into the house, the wind just a-whistling, Mammy said, "Jack, here you are back, and that wind still a-blowing."

"Yes, bedads, Mammy, I didn't get past the little old gray man again. I went clear around his house and I met him at the mill. And he brought me back and he bring me another present to . . . home." And he says, "Now, we've got something this time."

[Impatiently:] "All right," Mammy says, "what is it?"

"This rooster will lay my hat full of gold eggs for me. Just all I got to do is set him on the table, put my hand under him, and: 'Come, gold, come.' "

[Whispering:] Wasn't a thing in the world.

The old rooster flapped his wings and flew up on the back of a rocking chair, and gave a great big crow. And his mammy says, "Well, son, you've just played the fool again. Now you got nothing but an old rooster. We'll eat him for dinner."

Well, Jack stayed around the house a-working and a-thinking, and a-thinking and a-working and a-wondering whatever would become of him and his mammy. And the wind got to blowing. Oh, this time it bout blew the old house over. And it . . . in the meantime, and the snow just blew through that house, and it looked like a regular hurricane was coming.

"Well," Jack says, "Mammy, this is the end of it. I've got to go this time, and I'm going to go till I find that Northwest Wind. We'll freeze to death sure, before the winter's over."

And his mammy says, "And be sure that you don't let the little old gray man stop you this time."

So Jack started. Now he wasn't going to go around to even near where the mill was, for fraid the little old man would meet him there again. So he took off on the other side of the little old gray man's house, out through the woods— and about half-way through the woods, run right square on the little old man, a-rabbit hunting.

And the man laughed, and he says, "Jack, what in this world are you doing out in all this snow? The cold west, Northwest Wind is blowing harder today than it's ever blowed."

Jack says, "Bedads, that's what I know. That's why I'm here. I'm on my way to stop the blamed stuff. We're about to freeze to death back at our house."

The little old man says, "Jack, don't you know that you'll freeze to death before you'll get there? Here you are, wet to the knees a-wading through this snow. You're as tired as you can be. Come on home with me, son. And I might have another present for you."

Now, Jack says, "Bedads, your presents, there's nothing to em. That rooster couldn't do a thing when I got him home. We ate him for our dinner."

"Yes," the little old man says. "Did you stop down at the house where those thieves are?" Says, "Jack, I told you they were devilish boys."

"Yes," Jack says, "Bedads, I know it. But I thought I'd keep my hands on the old rooster all night. And it was pitch-black dark, and they was awful nice to me and he asked me to stay."

"Well," the little old man says, "they've got your rooster as well as your tablecloth."

But he says, "Come on, now. Let's eat our supper. And let's talk this thing over good." And, he says, "I tell you. I've got one more present for you, and I believe you're going to like it, Jack."

Well, after they'd eaten their supper and sat there in front of the fire and got good and warm, the little old man reached on top of the mantle and took a little old knotty club.

Said, "Now, Jack, this club will just sure be the thing you're wanting. Come out into the yard. I want to show you how it works before I give it to you, and maybe you'll hang on to it."

So he took the little old club out in the back yard, and he said, "Play away, club, play away."

And that club just knocked down as big a tree as you've ever seen in your life, whacked it right up into stovewood, and even split some of it into kindling. All right there in the yard before their eyes.

"Law," Jack slapped his hands and he whooped and he hollered. "Boys," he said, "that's the thing I been a-wanting. That sure is the thing for me. Give it to me, mister, and I sure do thank you. Now, I'm going to take my club and I'm going home."

"Yes," and the little old man says, "and be sure that you don't stop at that house."

"Oh, no," Jack says, "Bedads, I'm going home with my club." He took his little old club and started down the road.

Well, just as he got to the house, out came the old man and the boys. And they said, "Now, Jack. You been up to the little old man's house again. And what do you reckon he's given you this time?"

"Well," Jack says, "Bedads, he didn't give me anything much this time."

"Well," they said, "What is it? Show it to us."

"Ah," Jack says, "just a little old club. Nothing else in the world."

"Sure enough? Well, what's it good for, Jack? What's it worth, just a little old club? Anybody could give you that."

"Eh, Law, but," Jack says, "Boys, this is one more club. I could just tell it to get to work here, and the first thing you know, you would have as fine a pile of stove wood as ever you'd want in your life."

"Law," the boys say, "we ain't got a stick. Here, Jack. Show us what it will do. Show us what it'll do."

"Well," Jack says, "come round to the backyard." And they went around the backyard and he says, "Play away, stick. Play away. Cut em up some firewood."

And that old club just knocked down a big old dead chestnut and banged it up into stovewood before you could hardly say "scat," right there before their eyes. Well, they all took on. They whooped and they hollered and they laughed and they slapped Jack on the back.

"Jack, you're the finest fellow I've ever seen in my life. Now, listen. It's just pitch-black dark. It's too dark for you to go on. Just stay here."

The old man says, "Yes. I've got to go on to the mill. I'll be back in just a little bit. Jack, stay till I get back. Stay, son. I want to see you a little bit longer."

"Well," Jack says, "I, I maybe can stay till you get back. Go on. I'll stay if I can." He sat down in his chair with his club in his hand and a-waiting on the old man, he went sound asleep. Well, just as the boys was tipping around just as quiet as could be around to keep Jack asleep, the old man came back in. He said, "I want to see that club work again. Boys, let's see if we can do it. Slip it out of his hand there, and let's see if it'll bust up this log here."

They slipped it out of Jack's hand right easy-like and says, "Play away, club. Play away."

It began to thumping on that old log there, just knocking it into splinters, but it was making so much noise it just waked Jack up. Jack saw exactly what was a-happening. He made a running go for that door, and when he got into the yard, he hollered back, "Play away, stick. Play away. Knock down their old house! Tear it to pieces! Kill every last one of em, unless they give me back my tablecloth and my rooster, right quick!"

And that club begun knocking the logs out of that house, had em all out of one side and began playing on the roof. And the boys come a-running out just as fast as they could. One of em took the tablecloth and the old man with the rooster here, "Jack! Here, Jack! Take your things, take your things right quick, and stop that stick. Stop it before it tears our house plumb down. And the first thing you know, it'll be killing us."

"All right." Jack took his things, called his stick, and away they went, just to the house as hard as they could go. Well, when they got into the house, his poor old mother was a-shivering over in one corner just about to froze too death. She said, "Jack, that Northwest Wind is freezing me to death, and you've not done a thing about it."

"No, but," Jack says, "Mammy, I've got everything we'll need for the rest of our lives. Come out of that place over there, come out of that corner. I'm going to show you what we've got."

So his Mammy came out. Jack spread the tablecloth on the table and said, "Spread, tablecloth, spread."

My, you've never seen such a breakfast in your life. They sat down and ate until they were just so full they was about to burst. Then Jack says, "Now, Mammy, look here." He set his rooster up on another table and he took his hat and he said, "Come, gold, come." And there was a hat full of gold. Jack says, "You see, Mammy. That's why I'm not going to worry about the Northwest Wind anymore. Right here is all the gold in the world we'll ever need, and besides, we've got the rooster to lay us some more. Why, we can go to town to buy nails, planks, and hammers, and so we can fix up this old house. I tell you, we're just fixed."

"Well," but the Mammy says, "what's that little old knotty stick you got there in your pocket?"

"Come out into the yard, Mammy. Come out into the yard. I've just got one more thing to show you."

They went out into the yard, and he said, "Play away, club! Play away!" And boy, that stick was on the mountainside before you could say "scat," had a old big tree rolling down right to the chipyard. Cut it up just as fine as could be, and the old mammy just laughing and a-hollering. She says, "Jack, I've never seen such a sight in my life, boy, and I'm telling you, you've done well." And so Jack and his mammy had all that they wanted the rest of the days of their life. They was doing real well when I left there, and besides that, they had that house fixed just as nice and as tight against that old Northwest Wind as ever you'd a-wanted it.

20. Jack and One of His Hunting Trips

MAUD LONG
Hot Springs, North Carolina
Recorded by Duncan Emrich,
Washington, D.C., 1947

One day Jack decided he'd just make him a little hunt. He took the big old hog rifle down off the pegs, threw him a powder horn around his neck, and took his hunting knife and started. He traveled and traveled out through the woods and through fields and hadn't seen much of anything, not even hardly enough to shoot at. And then when he came out in the edge of a clearing, standing way on the other side was the finest big buck deer you ever seen in your life. Oh, he was a handsome critter. And just right up above him and a little behind him, on a big old oak limb, there was twelve of the prettiest turkeys you've ever laid your eyes on.

So—Law [laughing]—Jack didn't know what to do. He sure did want to get that deer, but, Law, how he'd love to have those turkeys too. So he grabbed out his old ramrod and cut it in two, and poked him in a bullet and some powder, and then the ramrod. Poked him in another bullet and some powder. And he said, "Now, I, I think this'll do it all right. I just believe it will." And so he took a good sight, just a extra good sight, and he saw that—after he shot that first bullet out, he could just bare, tip the gun the least little bit, and it would go right down that row of turkeys, and he thought surely he'd get him five or six out of that dozen that was up there. And so he took a good fine bead and— *ka-bang*—and just as he, the bullet left the barrel, up he jerked the gun just the least little bit. Well, he got the deer all right, just dropped dead in his tracks.

And Jack was so excited he didn't hardly wait to see how many of the turkeys he got.

But you know what happened? That second bullet just ripped open that big old oak limb that those turkeys was a-sitting on, and . . . of course, the bullet running through just sprung it open—and when it clapped back together, if it didn't catch the middle toe of every one of those twelve turkeys. There they were, all caught squawking right on top of the limb. Well, when Jack saw . . . they's all sure enough caught, he went around to look at his deer. Oh, he was a magnificent animal—great big antlers, and the finest coat you've ever seen.

"Boy," Jack says, "that'll make a pretty rug. That'll make a pretty rug." And then he saw something right there at his feet a-ticking, and he looked and, bless me, if that bullet hadn't gone right through the deer and had killed a rabbit right there in the weeds. Well, Jack threw the little old rabbit out of his way and decided he'd climb up that tree and cut that limb off, and get those turkeys. He could tie em all together some way, he figured, and get em home. And when he put his hand out on to the tree, he felt something sticky, and looked at it, and stuck it up to his tongue. That was a bee tree, and honey was a-oozing out where the bullet had bounced up and gone right in through the tree, bark of the tree.

Well, Jack says, "Bedads. This is my lucky day. Here I've got me a deer, a rabbit, a bee tree, and now if I can just get em home, I've got me some turkeys. So he climbed up there with his big old hunting knife. He was a-whacking away, cutting that big old oak limb off. And he just was hanging on to it for dear life, cause he didn't hardly know how he was going to manage those turkeys. And just as he got it whacked off, all twelve of those turkeys spread their wings at once. The limb, Jack, and all just went sailing right off through the air. "Pshew," Jack says, "Where do you reckon they'll take me? But, boys, I've got to hang on, I've got to hang on. [Laughing] I can't turn loose."

But . . . it just didn't look they was going to light at all. Jack says, "Well, I guess, first good place I see, I better try to drop off." And way out ahead of him, he saw what looked like a big, old chestnut stump. "Oh," he says, "that's the very place. When I get right over that, I'm going to turn loose and drop right on to that stump."

So when the old turkeys sure enough flew right over that big old stump, when he got right above it, Jack just turned loose and dropped right down. But, boy, that old stump was holler, and he went *ker-plunk* right down to the very bottom of it. Black as Egypt down in there. And he could feel something a kind of roughing around his legs and muzzling up to him, and ooh, Law, he thought, what is it, what is it, what is it? Finally, his eyes got used to that big, black hole down in there, and it was three of the cutest little old cub bears you ever seen. But, Law, Jack says, "You know what? That old mammy bear'll be coming in here the first thing I know, and what in the world have I got to fight with? Not one thing: I left my gun by the deer. I dropped my knife when I cut off that limb." And he felt in his pocket to see if he had a single thing. Yes, sir, there was an old kitchen fork with just one prong on it. "Well," Jack says, "bedads, I got to use what I got. So I'll just wait till that old bear starts down."

And when the old bear started down, he heard her. Clawing, clawing, clawing, coming up, and then he knew right then she was beginning to come down, and he knew she'd have to come down that holler log backwards. And so he just reached up as far as he could and got hold of her tail just as soon as it got near enough to him, and then he begun jabbing that old bear with that one prong of that old kitchen fork. And, of course, the old bear just went tearing right back up out the, the hollow tree just as hard as she could go, and Jack a-hanging right on to her tail, jabbing her every, every breath he was drawing. And the old bear was so befuddled and bemuddled when she got on the outside there, instead of turning around and a-giving Jack a slap, why Jack gave her a push, and down she fell and broke her neck.

"Well," Jack says, "bedads, I got me a bear too. Now that's something. I just wonder where all them turkeys went. Well," he said, "I'll never see them again. I guess they'll fly clear out of the country. But," he said, "I'd better go on home now. I guess I've hunted enough. And get the boys to come and bring the wagon and help me get up this meat."

So he started on home, going down by the river. There, in a little smooth place of kind of an eddy like, he saw the prettiest flock of ducks that you ever seen just so pretty sailing around over that smooth still water. "Law," Jack says, "I can't go on home. I've got to have those ducks. But it'll never do in the world to scare em up. I've got nothing in the world to shoot with. So I just wade right into this river way down here, and I'll wade up to where it's beginning to get deep, and I'll just swim up in there under those ducks. I know how to get em."

So he tied the legs of his overalls good and tight, so he could swim better. And waded in down there as quiet as could be, way down below the ducks, and then down in under the water he went, swimming right around in under those ducks, and with a big old rawhide thong that he had there in his pocket, he tied those ducks' legs, every one together—with this old big string and went over and tied the string to the edge of a big old sycamore root over there. And then he stood up, right in the middle of em. And the ducks squawked and started to fly up, but of course the old rawhide leather thong would just jerk em right back down into the water.

Well, Jack saw he had his ducks good and fast, so he wasn't worried about them, but he thought, "What's that a-flopping around in my old overall legs?" and begun a-feeling, a-looking around. He waded out up into the road, and bless me, he'd been down in under that water so long, his old overalls was chock full of fine fish. And he begun taking em out, stringing em on a string there, and when he got em all caught and on to that string he had about thirty pounds of fish. He took his ducks and his fish and went on home. Told the boys about his deer and his rabbit and the bee tree—and told em to come on—and his bear—help him get that meat in.

So they hitched up the old wagon, and went to where the deer and the rabbit and the bee tree was. Took em two big old barrels to get the honey in. Hot dog. Those two barrels just held half of that honey. But they filled it up just as full as they could get it, and skinned the deer—oh, such a handsome hide as they had. Had a whole wagonload of that deer meat and he threw the rabbit up on it. Thought now we'll just go on around and see if we can pick up the bear, and we'll be getting for home. He'd already taken his ducks and had them staked in a pen down there.

And as he went along, they skinned the bear, oh, and that was the finest bear hide you've ever seen. Jack says, "When I get that tanned, we'll have the finest rug there is in the country anywhere." And the bear was even bigger than the deer. They had more meat in it—you've never seen such a wagonload of meat in your life as they were a-taking home. And before they got out of that woods, on that old trail, if they didn't hear the awfullest squawking and a calling you ever heard in your life. And over there was that whole rail full of turkeys, all down in the big old bramble briars where they'd tried to light. Well, Jack didn't do a thing in the world, but take him a little old knot of a pole, go over there and just thump each one of them a little bit in the head till he had em all kind of addled, picked those turkeys up and tied em all together and throw em up onto the wagon, and away they went riding home.

And, I tell you, Jack and his folks had deer meat and bear meat and turkey meat and duck meat and fish for a long, long time. And they took two more barrels and went back to that bee tree and got the rest of that honey. And I just can't even begin to tell you how long they were eating on that honey.

21. Old Fire Dragaman

MAUD LONG
Hot Springs, North Carolina
Recorded by Duncan Emrich,
Washington, D.C., 1947

The name of this Jack story is "Old Fire Dragaman."

One time Jack and Will and Tom was just laying around the house, not doing a bit of good, not a lick of work could their father get out of em. And so he said, "Now, I'm tired of this. Do you boys know that big new boundary of timber that I bought way yonder in the wilderness on the top of that mountain? All right, sir, you can have every single bit of that. I'll give it to you, but you've got to get up there and clear it off, and build you a house and make you some crops. But now it's yours, if you'll just on up there and look after it.

Oh, well, that suited the boys fine. That was a long ways off from where anybody lived, so they fixed em up a wagon, loaded it up with rations, and took em some tools, the best that they had, and, and started on up there.

And pretty soon they found the place and—oh, *my*—it was a fine, fine piece of timberland. Of course there was no house on the place at all, but they soon had holes cut out and notched em, and fixed em up a very nice whole house. And they were just going to let that do, because they had to begin clearing and getting ready to put in a crop if they was going to have any food for the winter.

So they started out to their work and then they said, "Now, look-y here. This'll never do. One of us will have to stay at the house till twelve o'clock, and get something cooked up. And then that one can come on to the field and we'll all work together. Then come back home and they'll be plenty left from dinner for supper."

So they decided that Tom ought to stay first. He was the oldest. So Tom worked around as hard as he could fixing up as fine a dinner, and he wanted to have plenty so he'd have all they wanted for their supper too. And after—he got it all on the table, setting it up as nice as could be, he walked out into the yard and took the old dinner horn down and gave a big toot on it. That called the men from the fields so that they'd have plenty of time to get in and get washed up by the time Jack brought in the milk from the springhouse—they'd bought em up a cow along with em. Oh, they were really fixed to *live.* So . . . Tom was going down to the springhouse to bring up the milk, and he looked—coming out of the wilderness, down there, was the biggest, old stepping giant—half giant and half man. He'd never seen anything like it. Just a monster of a thing. With a big old long four-foot pipe in his mouth. And a big long blue beard that reached from his chin and was dragging the ground. And his hands stuffed behind him. Oh, Law.

Tom says, "I'll never get to the springhouse, but let me hide in that house if I can somewhere any from that thing. Why, he's coming right toward us. He's just coming right at this house."

He run in through the door just as hard as he could, got right in behind it and pulled the door up against him just as flat as he could, and just a-shaking in there.

Old Fire Dragaman came right on into the house and looked all around, walked over to that table, and he gave one big swipe, and he just lifted up everybody's food that was on it, and into his big old mouth it went. Walked over to the coal fireplace there where he had a big hot bed of coals that he was going to cover up to keep for back-cooking their supper. Reached in and got him the biggest old chunk in the whole thing, laid it up in the bowl of that old pipe, and stuck his hands behind him, and went a marching out the door, the smoke a-rolling back there like it was a-coming out of an engine.

Well, poor old Tom, he just stood him behind there and shook. After a while, here Jack and Will came walking in. Looked in there, and there was the dishes cleaned out as slick as a whistle. And by that time Tom had come from behind the door. He was still pale through as ashes.

And Will said, "Well, what in the world have you done with our dinner? Where is it?"

Tom says, "Dinner, the nation! If you'd a seed what I've seen, you wouldn't be a-thinking about dinner. Old Fire Dragaman come right out of that wilderness into this house here and he's with one lick sopped up every bit I had cooked. Grabbed him a big old chunk of fire out of the fireplace over here and stuck it down in that old pipe, and went a-marching off down the road."

"Well," Will says, "Come on. Let's just dish up what little we had left for supper here. Now let's eat and get on back to the newground."

They ate. Will kind of snickered every once in awhile.

"All right," Tom says. "You needn't a-snicker about it. It'll be your time tomorrow. I just wonder what you'll do."

Well, Will stayed at the house the next day. He got up another good dinner. Oh, my, it was a fine one. He stepped out and took the old dinner horn down and gave it a blow, and Tom and Jack was kind of anxious to know what had happened so down they came from the mountain, just a-tearing. And just as that horn stopped blowing, Will looked down toward the wilderness and here came

Old Fire Dragaman just stepping *the longest, biggest* steps you've ever seen in your life.

Will didn't even wait to get behind the door. He slid in under the bed. And just lay there trembling like he was *scared to death.*

Old Fire Dragaman come right on into the kitchen, just scooped up everything there was to eat, and picked up the plates and licked them. Went over to the pots and licked them out. Reached in the big old fireplace there and picked him up a big old chunk of fire, put it down in his pipe and he went on back down to the wilderness, smoking—smoke a-rolling out of there like fire out of a chimney.

Well, when the boys got in, they looked and saw the table, and knew what had happened. And then old Will come crawling out from under the bed.

"All right," Tom said, "Happened to you, has it?" And Jack kind of laughed.

And they said, "All right. You, you laugh, Jack, if you want to. It's your turn tomorrow, and you little old snipe you, I bet you he'll eat you up."

Well, Jack said, "Bedads. We'll just *see* about that."

So the next day they were kind of anxious to get off to work. Will and Tom talked *all morning,* laughing, just laughed to each other about how poor little old Jack'd get along with Old Fire Dragaman. They could just see that boy scared to death.

Well, Jack got his dinner cooked. Oh, he cooked up a good one. But he hadn't dished it up. He went out, took out the dinner horn, gave it a toot, and went on back into the, back into the kitchen, but waited long enough on the porch to see if he could see Old Fire Dragaman a-coming. And, boys, there he was, walking *right out of the wilderness, just a stepping along big, high long steps,* looked like he could just eat up everything, that big old blue beard flowing right down to the ground, and his hands stuck behind him. Walked right up to the door just as hard as he could go, but Jack didn't hide. He just ran on back to the kitchen and began dishing up the beans and the turnip greens and the hog jowl, and everything—cornbread—and getting it all on the table.

Old Fire Dragaman walked right in. And Jack, without turning around even, says, "Why howdy, Pappy, howdy. Howdy. *Mighty* glad to see you. Come on in and sit down now. We're just about to be getting ready for dinner."

"No, no," Fire Dragaman says, "I've not got any time to stay and eat. I just wanted me a chunk of fire for my old pipe." Reached over in the grate and got him up a big old chuck of fire and stuck it down in his pipe and went a-walking on back off down the road. Jack had the dinner all served up. Tried his *best* to get him to stay. No, no. Old Fire Dragaman wasn't about to stay. Down the road he started.

And Jack just kind of *eased* along behind. He could follow him *easy, easy* with all of that smoke a-boiling out of that old big pipe. You could just see it a long ways after you lost sight of him. And then all at once, Jack saw him go right down in a hole in the ground. Well, Jack waited a few minutes, and he ran up to that hole, and he looked—and sure enough, it was just a great big hole. You could still see smoke coming, bubbling out of it.

Well, Will and Tom got to the house after laughing themselves sick two or three times coming down the mountain, just at what poor little old Jack was doing. And they walked in. There was the dinner, but there was no Jack.

"Um, hum," Will says, "It's just what I thought. Old Fire Dragaman has eat Jack up. That's the last we'll ever see of him. Well," he said, "we might just as well set on down here and eat. There's nothing we can do about it. Let's eat and get on back to work."

So they's sitting there eating their dinner, and Jack came in. "Law, Jack," they says, "Where've you been?"

"Why," he says, "I've been following Old Fire Dragaman. Where'd you think I've been?" And he said, "You know, I saw *right* where he went down a big hole right into the ground." He said, "Come on, boys. Get that old big split basket over there and that big hickory rope that—we tied it last night, out of that hickory bark. Come on, let's go down to that hole and see what's down there."

Well, the boys said they'd believe they would. So down they all went. "Now," they said, "Tom, you're the oldest. We're going to put you in this basket and we're going to let you down in this hole. But, now, the rope's fastened good on both sides of it. And it—whenever you get a little scared or you feel like you want to come back, you just shake this—the handles of this basket, and we'll bring you right back up."

"All right," Tom says, "Now, that's fair enough, and I think I'm the one to go down first." So they put him into the basket, and down in this big old deep hole they stuck him. Down, down—they's playing out the rope. Down he went. Down he went. After a while—*shake, shake, shake*—and up they jerked the basket and Tom.

Jack says, "What'd you see, Tom?"

[In an awestruck whisper] "Oh," he says, "I saw a great big house."

"Well now," Will says, "Let me in the basket. Let me go down there and see what I can see."

So they let Will in the basket. Told him, now, when he was ready, just to shake either side of the, of the big old hickory rope, and they'd bring him right back up. So they played the rope out, and down Will and the basket went, and down, down, down. And after awhile—*shake, shake, shake, shake*—and up they jerked the basket and Will.

Jack says, "What'd you see, Will?"

[Awestruck whisper] "*Oh,*" he says, "I saw the biggest, finest house, and a *great big barn.*"

"Oh," Jack says, "bedads. Let me in this basket." So they let Jack in the basket. And now Jack says, "Hold on to the rope and when I shake, you fellows pull up."

"Yeah," they said, "We will, Jack. Go on, now, and see what you can see."

Jack let that basket come right down over the ridge of that house, right down over the eves, and right on down to the ground. Oh, it was a beautiful house. The prettiest house he'd ever seen. The other boys had told him it was like another world down there, but he didn't know it *could* be so fine-looking. He walked right up to that door, and knocked at the door. *And the most beautiful girl* came to the door. Jack just fell in love with her the very first minute. "Oh," he said, "you are the loveliest person I've ever seen in my life. Oh, you're so pretty. Won't you marry me?"

"Oh," she said, "I have a sister in that next room that's far prettier than I am."

And Jack just left off courting her right straight and went and knocked on the other door. They girl came to the door, and, oh, she was lovely to look at. Jack forgot all about the first girl that he'd seen and he begun making love with this girl, and asked her right straight off would she marry him, and she said, "Oh, I have a sister in the next room that's far lovelier than I am."

"Why," Jack said, "I didn't know they could make anybody prettier than you are."

"Well," she says, "Go and see."

So Jack went on and knocked at that door, and, honestly, it was a dream girl. Oh, she was just the loveliest thing to look at you've ever seen in your life. And Jack just fell down on his knees before her, and he says, "Oh, you'll just have to marry me. Now, you *will* marry me, won't—"

She says, "Look-y here. You get up from there. Why," she says, "don't you know Old Fire Dragaman will come in here and the first thing you know, he'll begin spitting balls of fire all over this place. And Jack, listen here. There's not but one thing that'll keep him from burning you to death. I'm going to give you a little tube of ointment here and every time one of those balls of fire hits you, rub a little of this on and it won't even blister. And look here, Jack, here's the only sword in the world that could kill Old Fire Dragaman. And kill him if you can, Jack, so we can get free."

Well, she had hardly gotten the words out of her mouth when Old Fire Dragaman came a-spluttering in and, I'm telling you, balls of fire he was a-spitting. Why, some of em was as big as pumpkins, and he's trying his best to make em all hit Jack. And when one would, he'd rub that ointment on right quick, and didn't blister a bit, and Jack kept a-working in just as much nearer to Old Fire Dragaman as he could for the balls of fire, till he finally got a good whack at him and *ker-lick*— off went Old Fire Dragaman's head. The balls of fire stopped rolling, and Jack looked at the girl.

"Yes," she says, "Jack, I'll marry you. I'll marry you. Now, listen. Plait this red ribbon in my hair, so that we can be sure—and I can be sure to remember that I'm going to marry you."

"All right," Jack says, "I'll plait the ribbon into your hair for you. Come on, now. Let's, let's get the other girls and get out of here."

Why, the girls told Jack they couldn't hardly remember when the Old Fire Dragaman caught them and brought them down into this place in under the earth. They'd lived here *all their lives*. They'd forgotten even how it looked up on earth almost. But, oh, they were so glad to think they were going to get out of there. And so they went over to the big old basket. There it sat, just as—like Jack left it. And they put the oldest girl into it. And Jack shook the, the rope, and up they took—and when Will and Tom saw that beautiful woman, they begun fighting each other right straight as to which one of em was going to get to marry her. And she said, "Oh, I have a sister that's down there that's prettier than I am."

"Why," Will says, "I didn't know that could be."

"Well," Tom says, "let's put that basket down."

So they let the basket down, brought up the other girl. And then they both begun fighting to see which one of em would get to have *her*.

And she says, "There's a little sister that's down there, younger than either of us."

And Will says, "Is she prettier than you?"

The girl says, "I ain't a-saying."

Well, . . . Will says, "Let's let this basket back down there, and Jack'll put her in."

So they put the youngest girl in. Oh, when they saw *her*, they really did begin to fighting and quarreling with each other as to which one of em was going to get the youngest girl. She said, "Now, I'm not going to marry either one of you. I'm going to marry *Jack.* I've already promised him."

"Hmmp," they says, "Jack—the nation. Jack can stay down in that hole." And with that they threw the rope all right down into the hole.

"Well," she said, "My lands. There's not much to eat down there. Jack'll starve to death."

"Why, that's just what we want. Let him starve to death."

"Well," she said, "I don't think that's a bit nice. I just don't think it's a bit nice."

And then, wasn't she glad that she had given Jack a little wishing ring after he had put that ribbon in her hair. She thought, *Now maybe Jack'll get out.* But Jack didn't think a thing in the world about that. He just didn't think that was a bit nice, the way Will and Tom had done. Got the three beautiful girls out and then threw the rope back down in the hole so he couldn't even climb out. Well, he looked around in the pantry and everywhere and found all the things that he could to eat, and after awhile, though, it all gave out. And he got so thin and poor, he sat down on a little old seat that was there, and was holding his hands, looking at them, seeing how poor and thin they were getting. And, why, his ring that the girl had given him was about to fall off his finger, it was so loose. And he took that ring, he rubbed it a little bit. "Oh, me," he said, "I wish I was back at my mammy's home in the chimney corner a-smoking my old chunky pipe."

Oh, no sooner did he say it then right there he was a-sitting, right at home in the chimney corner, at his mother's a-smoking his old chunky pipe.

She says, "Jack, what in the world are you doing here? I thought you was at the newground." And, "Bedads, Mammy," he says, "that's just where I'm a-going." And up to the newground he went just as hard as he could go—and you know Will and Tom was *still* a-fighting, trying to see which one of them was going to get to marry that pretty girl. And when she saw Jack, she spread out her arms and she says, "Oh, Jack, I'm so glad you got out of there."

"Yes, bedads, honey," he says, "and *I'm* glad I got out too."

Well, when Will and Tom saw that Jack was there and that he got the prettiest girl, then they said, "Well, we just better act sensible about it."

Will, before Tom could say a thing, Will says, "Now, I'm going to marry this girl"—that was the second prettiest one. And so that left the oldest one for Tom. But that was just like it ought to have been. And so they built them three fine log houses, and when I left there, they were just as happy as they could be, and every one was doing well.

22. Love: A Riddle Tale

MAUD LONG
Hot Springs, North Carolina
Recorded by Duncan Emrich,
Washington, D.C., 1947

Some of the tales that Maud Long learned from her mother centered on riddles. "Love" is an example of what folklorists call a "neck riddle": A man is condemned to death, and the only way he can save his neck is to pose a riddle that his captors cannot solve.

My mother knew a great many riddles and she could say them so fast that it would just make your head swim. I'm going to give you a few of those, but I'm not going to go as fast as she would go in saying them.

Maybe the first one that I always liked was—

> Through a rock, through a reel,
> Through an old spinning wheel,
> Through a sheepshank bone.
> Such a riddle never known.

And the answer to that was lightning.
Another one was—

> Hackemore
> Hanging over the kitchen door.
> Nothing so long and nothing so strong
> As Hickemore, Hackemore
> Hanging over the kitchen door.

And that was the sun.
Then another that I liked was—

> Love I sit, and Love I stand.
> Love I hold in my right hand.
> I love Love, and Love loves me.
> Guess this riddle and you may hang me.

And the reason for that riddle was a young man was going to be hung if he could not make a riddle that the king's courtiers couldn't guess. And so he had a beautiful collie dog that he loved very much, and the dog's name was Love. He took some of the hair from his ruff and sewed it into his glove, put some in his shoes, sewed some in the seat of his pants, and then he made his riddle, was—

> Love I sit, Love I stand
> Love I hold in my right hand.
> I love Love, and Love loves me.
> Guess this riddle and you may hang me.

Well, they didn't guess it, and so the young man got to live.

23. Jack and the Heifer Hide

MAUD LONG
Hot Springs, North Carolina
Recorded by Duncan Emrich,
Washington, D.C., 1947

Once upon a time there was a man who had three sons: Jack, Will, and Tom. Will and Tom, the two older boys, were great big fine strapping fellows, and the father knew they'd be able to take care of their farm when he was gone, with all the horses and cattle and sheep that he could leave them. But poor little old Jack, he just wondered what in the world would become of that boy, for he never had seemed quite right. So he just left to him one little old heifer calf.

Jack said, "That's all right, bedads," if that's just what his father wanted him to have, that's what he wanted. The two older boys were to take care of Jack and look after him. But soon after the father's death, they begun to mistreat him. And they imposed upon him. They made him do all the housework, all the cooking, and just everything. And they were out in the fields, in the woods and, as Jack thought, having a real good time.

One day when they'd come home to the noon meal, Will said, "Jack, when you've finished up these dishes, I guess you'd better go down yonder by the wood lot, skin your little old calf. Done cut a tree down on her and killed her."

"Well, bedads, I will then." And so after he'd finished his dishes, down to the wood lot he went, and sure enough, there laid his little old heifer calf, dead. He skinned her hide, brought it back up to the barn, tacked it up to the barn to dry. In about two weeks, he went down, and that hide was just as dry as a bone. He took it down, got him a little piece of rawhide and a peg and awl and sewed that calf hide up, stuffed it with chips and straw, took it by its tail, and went dragging it up to the house. *Thumpity-bump, bumpity-thump.*

Will and Tom said, "Jack, what in the world are you going to do with that little old calf hide?"

"Oh, bedads, this is my fortune. I'm going out into the world in the morning, and when *I* come back, I'll come back with pockets of gold."

"Hmph, you'd better stay here. You'll be coming back about nighttime starved to death, and not a bite of food cooked in the house."

"No, bedads," Jack says, "I'll not be coming back that-a-way."

So morning came. Took his little old calf hide and started off down the road. *Thumpity-bump, bumpity-thump.* Walked *all* day, dragging that thing behind him. And about night, he begun to get hungry and tired. He wished he could find a place to spend the night. And along then he saw a nice-looking little house by the side of the road, and one light shining out of the window. Walked up to the door and knocked. When a nice looking lady came, he said, "Kind lady, would you let a little old boy named Jack spend the night here with you?"

"Oh no, son! I can't be bothered with you. Why, my husband isn't home, and no, I can't be bothered with you. Just run on down the road."

"Oh," he says, "kind lady, I'm just so tired. I won't be a mite of trouble. Please take me in. Just give me a place to sleep. That's all I want."

"Oh, well, Jack, come on in then. Go on upstairs to that room right at the head of the steps; you'll find a bed there—and go on to sleep."

Jack thanked her and went on up the steps. And when he got into that room, he saw—coming right up through the middle of the floor, through a knothole—a beam of light. Went over and put his eye down to that light and saw, down below, that he was looking right into a dining room. And there was a nice-looking table spread with all the good things you can think of to eat, a nice-looking young man sitting on one side of the table, and a nice-looking lady on the other. And they were just having the best time. Oh, there was chicken and ham and pie and cake and preserves and honey. Just everything you could think of that a person wanted to eat. And they were having such a good time.

Jack just looked, and his mouth watered.

About that time, out in the yard, they heard a great commotion. "*Whoa, whoa, whoa here!*"

"Ooh, ooh, quick, quick, quick," she says. "That's my husband! He's come home! Hurry, hurry! Get into something right quick! Here! Here, jump into this great old big case." He jumped over there into a great old big chest. She let the lid down all but just a little bit and begun pushing those things over the table as fast as she could into a little cupboard over there. And about that time, somebody was knocking on the door.

"*Old woman, old woman, let me in here.* Here I am, come home early."

She just whisked her things all off the table and folded up the nice linen tablecloth and finally got to the door, and he said, "Well, what makes you so long a-coming to the door?"

"Oh," she said, "my rheumatism hurts me tonight."

"Well," he said, "rheumatism or no rheumatism, get me something to eat. I'm starved to death."

"Well," she said, "there's not a thing in the world in this house but just bread and milk."

"Oh well, cornbread and milk is just good enough for anybody. Bring it out here."

And she brought out a great big bowl and a big pitcher of cold milk and a great big platter of cornbread. And Jack all the time had his eye glued right to that knothole, just watching it, every bit. He waited until the man had eaten one big bowl of milk and bread, and he just couldn't stand it any longer. Reached around, and took a hold of the tail of that calf hide and gave him a great shake over the floor.

The old man looked up and said, "Old woman, what is that?"

"Oh, poor little old simple boy that I let go upstairs to sleep, dragging a little old calf hide or something behind him."

"Yeah," and he said, "and I bet you didn't even offer him any supper." Stepped out into the hall and he said, "Jack, Jack, don't you want to come down here, son, and have some bread and milk?"

"Well, bedads, I don't care if I do!" And so Jack took his calf hide by the tail and came dragging him down the stairs. *Bumpity-thump, thumpity-bump,* right up to the side of his chair and sat down. The lady had brought out another big bowl of porridge, bread, and milk and brought him another pitcher of milk and, oh, didn't Jack have a good time with that first bowl. He'd eaten that and started on the second one. Reached down and took that calf hide by the tail and gave him a good thumping rattle right on the floor. "No," he said, "you hush up! Don't you say another word to me, sir. Now shut your mouth, and don't let me hear you open it again. Now you just be quiet."

The old man said, "Jack? Well, what did he say?"

"Oh no, sir!" Jack said. "I'm sorry, I can't tell you. Oh no, no. This bread and milk sure is good!" Finished up the second bowl. Reached down and he gave that calf hide another good rattle. "Now," he said, "didn't I tell you to keep your mouth shut? You just shut that up right now and don't let me hear you speak again. Now, you understand me, don't you?"

The old man says, "Now listen, Jack. Why, I want to know what *is* that he's saying to you!"

"Oh no," Jack said, "if it might hurt the nice lady's feelings, and she's been awful good to me. No sir, I'm sorry, I just can't tell you."

The old man says, "Now, listen, Jack, you *can* tell me, too, sir!" He said, "You come on and tell me. It won't hurt your feelings, will it, old lady?"

"Oh, no, I guess not," she said.

"Oh, well then," Jack said, "if it won't hurt her feelings, I'll just tell you what he said. Over in that corner cupboard, there's all kinds of good things to eat. There's chicken, there's pie, there's ham, there's cake, there's jelly and preserves and honey."

The old man said, "Old woman, is that so?"

"Oh well, they's just a few little things over there that I had for me and my poor kinfolks."

"Well, bedads, me and Jack is your poor kinfolks. Get that out here!"

And she spread the tablecloth and brought out *all* of those good things to eat. And Jack and the old man just began all over again. Oh my, but Jack had one good meal. The old man said, "Now I'll tell you, Jack, I want to buy that hide from you."

"Oh, no, sir!" Jack said. "I'm sorry, that's my fortune. No, sir, I can't part with that."

"Aw," he says, "now come, Jack. You can." Said, "Listen. I'll give you anything in the world you want. Just name your price. Look around you. Just anything you see. Why, I—I'll just give you anything for that, Jack. I'm bound to have it." Says, "It'll talk to me just like it talked to you, won't it?"

"Sure," Jack says. "It'll talk just the same to you as it talked to me."

Well, the old man said then, "Bedads, I'm just *bound* to have it. Now what will you take for it?"

"Well," Jack said, "you've been awfully good to me. I tell you what I'll do. I'll take that old big chest over there. I'll swap even with you for it."

"Oh, Law, yes," the man said, "just take the old chest, Jack, and give me that hide."

He gave the old man over the hide, picked up that big chest, *slung* it on his shoulder, and walked out the door. Walked on down the road and then begun talking to himself, and he said, "Now, I played it. Here I've sold my fortune for this old empty chest. I'm going to throw the thing into the well just soon as I come on down the road a little piece."

And inside the chest there was a great knocking. "No, no, Jack, Jack, Jack. Don't throw this into the well! Don't you know I'm in here?"

"Oh, Law," Jack says, "bedads, that's right, I was about to forget, you are in there! Well, what'll you take for me not throwing you in the well?"

"Oh," the passenger says, "well, I'll just give you all the gold you want, Jack."

"Bedads, that's just what I'm a-looking for. I'll ease you right down here off my shoulder, and you just begin handing me out the gold."

And the passenger handed out gold till Jack had his pockets full, tied the pants legs and filled the pants legs just as full of gold as he could walk with, and started back home. Now, he got home just as Will and Tom were finishing up breakfast one morning. Walked in, and they said, "Why, what are you doing back here?"

"Well," Jack says, "bedads, I've made my fortune, that's what am I doing back here." And he begun pulling out hands full of gold and putting them on that table, and . . . Will's and Tom's eyes just liked to pop out of their head.

They said, "Where did you get all that gold, Jack?"

"Hmmph, told you. I sold my calf hide for it. That's where I got it."

They looked at each other right quick. Said, "Come on, let's go to the barn and kill the finest horse that we have. You know good and well if Jack could get all of that gold for a little old measly heifer hide, what will we get for one of our big old fine horses? Come on, right quick!"

And before you could say "Jack Robinson," down they went and had killed the finest horse that each of them had. Now, they couldn't wait for it to dry, oh no. They sewed it up right then. Stuffed em full of straw and chips and started off to the nearest village. And they got there and went up and down the streets, calling [singing], "Horse hides for sale! Horse hides for sale!" Just up and down the streets, and the people looked at them like they thought they must be crazy men. And they just kept doing that, day after day. Now, you know it was summertime, and oh my, those old horse hides were *green*. And the first thing you know it begun to leave a terrible smell, and the people had just stood it as long as they were going to. And they came out with sticks and stones, and they told those two men to get out of their town and get in a hurry with those old smelly horse hides.

And they started back home, *mad*. Every step they took, they got madder. When they'd come to the house, they said, "Now, look here, Jack, you just plain lied to us. Why those people even drove us out of—out of the town. And here you said you sold your little old calf hide for it."

"Well," Jack says, "I'm just telling you just exactly what I'd done."

"Well now," they said, "listen, you didn't either, and we're going to throw you in the river. That's what's going to become of you. So just come right on, we've got the sheet here to tie you up in." They took Jack by the hand and the sheet and started to the river bridge. Oh, but they forgot to take a rope to tie it with. And when they got there, they begun to fuss which one was to go back and get the rope.

Will said, "Now, Tom, you ought to go because you're the oldest."

"No," Tom says, "Will, you ought to go because you're *not* the oldest. Now, you just go on back and get the rope."

Well, they fussed and they quarreled, and Jack just stood there.

Said, "Get down in here, Jack, lay down in this sheet. We're going to roll you up, and we going to leave you laying right on this bridge. And now believe me, you'd better be there when we come back, and we'll go together back and get that rope." They rolled Jack up in the big old sheet, left him laying there on the side of the bridge, and went back to the house.

Well, Jack kind of wormed his way along out to the edge of—of the big old sheet and was laying there with his head sticking out just about like a terrapin. And he saw, coming on the other end of the bridge, oh, the *prettiest* flock of sheep you've ever seen. And a little old bit of a man with a long, gray beard kind of shooing them on [low voice], "*Sheep, sheep, sheep!*" Getting them up onto the bridge, because they saw something kind of strange lying out there in the middle of the bridge, but Jack just stayed as still as could be, and the sheep came right on by him, and when the little man got alongside of him, he said, "Son, what in the world are you doing in that sheet?"

"Well," Jack says, "Father, I'm going to heaven. That's just what I'm a-doing."

"Oh," the old man said, "Jack, I've wanted to go to heaven for so long. Listen, son, well you're just a boy. Get out of there, won't you please, and let me get in your place, and let me go to heaven?"

"Well," Jack says, "my father always *did* tell me to be nice to old people. Yes, I'll get out, and you lay down here on this sheet, and I'll roll you up, and you stay just as still as you can be. After a while, they'll come back, two fellows, and they'll tie you up and send you off to heaven."

He says, "Now, Jack, all those sheep are yours. Just take them, son."

Jack took those sheep and he got them back off of that bridge just as hard as he could and around a great big old rock cliff. And he stayed just as still as could be. He kept peeping around the rock every once in a while, and after a while, he saw Will and Tom turn around and go back home. Well, he waited until they'd had a little time to about get there. He started his sheep across the bridge again. [Low voice] *"Sheep, sheep."* And the sheep just obeyed him just like he'd always driven them. Right across that bridge they went without a bit of trouble, Jack just having the best time. Drove those sheep right on up to his gate.

He said, "Will, Tom, come on out here, can't you, and help me get these sheep in."

Well, when they bounced on to . . . the porch, and saw Jack with all of those sheep, they just came flying down and opened the bars, and they said, "Jack, where in this world did you get those sheep?"

"In the river. Where do you think I got them?" Says, "Come on, though, and open those bars a little better and help me get em in."

"Listen Jack, listen," Will said, "Will you throw me in the river if I—if-if-if-if, if I get my sheet?"

"Well sure," Jack said. "I'll throw you in the river if you'll get your sheet."

"But, uh," well Tom says, "then if you're going to throw him, you'll just simply have to throw me, too."

"Sure, sure, I'll throw you in, too. That's all right. You just go on and get your sheet, Will. But now listen, both of you get you a rope, you understand? I'm not going to carry nobody's rope for him."

"Oh sure, we'll get us a sheet and a rope, too."

And away they went just as hard as they could go to get them a sheet and a rope. And down to the river bridge they went. And all the way down there, they were fussing which one was going to be thrown in first. Tom said that he ought to be, because he is the oldest, and Will said, "No, sir, I ought to be because I'm the youngest. Now, you just let him throw me in first."

"Oh," Jack says, "let's just hush! I'm going to throw you both in, and there's plenty of sheep for both of you."

And so they finally worked it out. Tom was to go first. Got down and got into his sheet, and Jack tied a great big old hard knot, picked that sheet up and gave it a swing back and forth, back and forth, and—*ka-bang*—out into the river he went. Of course, he begun kind of kicking around. Will says, "What's he doing, Jack, what's he doing?"

"Why," Jack says, "I just know he's gathering in sheep."

"Oh," he said, "hurry, hurry, quick, tie me in a hurry! Throw me in there before he gets them all."

Jack gave him a good old swing and a hard tie and *out* into the river he went. Turned on around and went back home. And, you know, when I left there, Jack was just one of the richest men there was in that country.

24. Jack and the River

DARON DOUGLAS
Blaine, Tennessee
Recorded by Carl Lindahl,
May 6, 1997

Daron Douglas learned this tale from her maternal grandmother, Maud Long. Born in 1950, Daron spent much of her childhood at Maud's inn in Hot Springs, North Carolina. Maud often told Daron Jack Tales as they shelled beans together in the inn's kitchen and as they went about other household tasks. Daron went on to become an expert musician, and today she often performs on stage or at schools, playing traditional Appalachian fiddle as well as other musical styles. For many years, she did not retell the tales that her grandmother had shared with her, but her memory and love of them did not fade.

Eventually, Daron began telling tales to complement her musical performances. According to Jane Douglas, mother of Daron and daughter of Maud Long, it was natural that Daron would eventually choose to continue Maud's storytelling tradition. Jane sees a close affinity between the personalities and the narrative styles of the two women: Daron possesses "the same sort of confident, but unpretentious way" that marked Maud Long's storytelling art.

The tale that follows is a shortened version of Maud's "Jack and the Heifer Hide" (story 23), a family favorite. This is the first of her grandmother's stories that Daron introduced into her performances at public schools. Daron explained that although she likes the whole tale, she shortened it to avoid the early scenes in which Jack's brothers kill Jack's heifer and two of their own horses: "I didn't want to kill off three good animals right in the first story I ever told." She then added, while laughing, that her version does manage to kill off Jack's two brothers, a situation that is nevertheless more tolerable than the slaughter of the three animals because Will and Tom have tried to kill Jack.

Daron Douglas with her fiddle. (Courtesy of Daron Douglas)

Daron tends to tell her Jack Tales to young children. When I visited her, she expressed surprise that an adult folklorist would ask her to perform one. Yet her grandmother had brought her up to expect to deliver an occasional command performance for visitors, a fact to which she alludes as she prepares to tell her tale.

When there'd be company at my grandmother's house, she would say, "Well, now, why don't you play your violin for company," and what happened was, you got up and you played your violin. No matter what. And there was no, no question of "no, not this time" or "I don't feel like it" or "I'm busy." None of that! It was not questioned. You get up. You play. And so—however many times, I just, okay, I can do it. So if somebody asks you to tell a tale, you tell a tale. If somebody asks you to sing, you sing. So yeah, I'll tell you. It'll just be what I call "Jack and the River," the end of the "Heifer Hide" story.

One time, years ago, there lived a boy named Jack. Now Jack had two brothers, Will and Tom. And they lived way back in the mountains. And Will and Tom were hard workers. They'd get up of a morning and they'd go out, they'd clear newground, they'd build, they'd feed. They'd do their work.

And Jack was more the kind that—he liked to sing, he liked to stay around the house, and he liked to eat, and he just did what he wanted.

Well, this made Will and Tom so mad, they figured, "Jack's at home, he's eating up all our food, he's in our way, he doesn't do a lick of work." And they came back to the house and said, "Jack, we're just mad at you and we're going to kill you."

Jack says, "That's okay."

So Will and Tom got a big sack, put Jack in the sack, and took him on down to the river. And got ready to throw him in. And Will says, "Wait a minute. We need a little piece of rope to tie the bag shut."

Tom says, "Go back to the house and get a rope."

Will says, "No, you go back to the house and get a rope."

Tom says, "No, you go back to the house and get a rope."

Will and Tom decided they'd better go back to the house together and get a piece of rope.

They put Jack down, rolled a log across the open end of the sack, and just left him right there. Went back to the house.

About that time came an old man leading some sheep down the road. He saw that sack sitting by the side of the road and he thought he heard some whistling. He leaned down to the sack. He said, "Hello?"

And Jack says, "Howdy."

Old man says, "Why, what are you doing sitting there in a sack?"

Jack says, "Well, I'm fixing to die. Angels'll be back any minute."

Old man says, "A-fixing to die? Why you sound like a mighty young man to die."

Jack says, "Roll this log off the opening and we'll talk about it."

Old man rolled the log off the opening of the sack. Jack popped his head out and says, "See? I am a young man."

Old man says, "Well, let me go in your place, son. I'm an old man. I'm ready to die. I been *wanting* to die. I'm *trying* to die."

Jack says, "Oh, no. Oh, no. I couldn't possibly do that."

Old man says, "Look. I tell you. I'll make you a deal. You can let me in that sack and you go free, and you can have all my sheep too."

Jack says, "Well. Well. Okay." He got out. Old man climbed in. Jack put the log across the opening of the sack, and said, "Now, don't say a word. The angels'll be back any minute." Jack took his sheep and went on down the road around a curve so Tom and Will wouldn't see him.

Before long, Will and Tom came back, tied that sack shut, threw it far out in the river, went on back to the house.

A little bit later, Tom says, "You know, Will, I can almost hear Jack a-whistling, coming down the road."

Tom looks out the window and: "My Law, look-a here, here comes Jack! And he's got about a hundred sheep with him."

He got to the house and they said, "Jack, where in the world did you get those sheep?"

Jack says, "Well, now, boys, where did you leave me?"

Will and Tom says, "Why, we threw you way out in the river."

Jack says, "That's right. I'm mad too. If you'd thrown me about ten feet further, I could have gotten a hundred *more* sheep."

Will and Tom looked at each other and said, "Why, Jack, Jack. We want to die too. We want some sheep."

Jack says, "Well, get yourselves a sack apiece and get your own piece of rope and come on. I'll take you down there."

So they all went down to the river. Will got in his sack, tied it shut. Jack threw him as far out as he could.

Tom looks in there and says, "What's that—what's he kicking around for? What's all that kicking?"

And Jack says, "Well, he's gathering sheep."

Tom says, "Oh, Oh. Throw me in quick, before he gets em all!"

He climbed in his sack. Jack tied it shut, threw him far out as he could, and went on back to the house. Now, last I heard, Jack was at the house. He had as many sheep as he could handle, he could sing whenever he wanted. Nobody to bother him. He had plenty to eat. And he was doing real well.

Ta, dum. There you are. A Jack Tale!

25. Hooray for Old Sloosha!

ROBY MONROE HICKS
Beech Mountain, North Carolina
Recorded by Frank A. and Anne
Warner,
1951

Roby Monroe Hicks (1882–1957) was the son of Rebecca Harmon, who was in turn a first cousin to both Sam Harmon and Jane Hicks Gentry (Maud Long's mother). He was also the brother of Benjamin Hicks, Ray Hicks's grandfather. It was from Rebecca that Roby learned the following tale.

Roby was one of the many Hicks-Harmon family members who contributed to Richard Chase's famous book, *The Jack Tales* (1943). But by the time that this and the following tale were recorded for folksinger Frank A. Warner in 1951, Roby claimed that his memory of the Jack Tales had faded. Roby would eventually record one Jack Tale for Warner, but the stories that lingered most vividly in his memory were "bear tales," "Indian tales," and other historical legends describing the dangers of early North Carolina mountain life in the eighteenth and early nineteenth centuries.

Frank Warner and his wife, Anne, had been friends of the Hickses for twelve years when the following tales were collected from Roby. The stories are set in the neighborhood of Cherokee, North Carolina, in the Great Smoky Mountains, about 100 miles southwest of Beech Mountain, where Roby's grandparents were born. It is noteworthy that the name of the hero's gun survives in the family's tale tradition, though the name of the hero has long been forgotten.

[Frank A. Warner: These tales that you used to tell the children, you called em the Jack Tales. . . ?]

Well, the Jack Tales, and then there's the other tales, you know, bear tales and Indian tales, and all like that. . . . My mother was the first one that *I* heared em from. . . . She was raised in this country, but her parents come from back in Cherokee, I believe. She told me a many one. . . . We sat around the old fireplace. . . . A big fireplace, I guess six foot broad. And you could sit one on that side, and one on the other side—one on each side—and keep the fire between you and keep warm. [Laughs] . . . We'd sit by that fireplace of a night, and she would tell tales till midnight, to us young'uns.

[Frank A. Warner: Did she tell you where she learned the tales?]

Her daddy. Her parents told em to her. And they come from off yonder, but she was born in this country. . . . She would have been, if she'd lived on to now, about a hundred and twenty-five years old. . . .

[Frank A. Warner: Can you hear her telling you a story?]

Why, when I go to telling em myself, it seems like . . . she's a-telling em *now* to me, when I get to talking.

[Frank A. Warner: Why don't you do it now?]

Well, I just . . . quit telling em. When my young'uns all left and all, I just quit telling the tales and forgot the most of em. Now, . . . she told a sight of all kinds of tales, and she could tell em all night and never tell through em. I forgot em all, and can't hardly think of none now, but if I could study em up to start on em, to get em started, to tell em right, like they was. And there's some of em was true stories, and some wasn't. Now all those Jack Tales were just told. The bear tales and the Indian tales and such as that was nearly all true stories. . . .

There was . . . a Indian tale that a man traded . . . with the Indians . . . and he had up a little store of stuff he'd sell to the Indians. And the Indians would come and trade with him. Well, they got to buying: the whites sold em some guns. They used a bow and arrow to start, but the whites got to selling em some guns. And they come to him, and got to buying ammunition every time they come: they'd buy some powder, and caps, and stuff that way to shoot the guns with. (Well, they didn't buy no caps: they shot these old fire-up guns, used a flint.)

He kept noticing em . . . a-buying em, and he sold to em. Well, one night he dreamt that they come in and took his horses out from him, some of em did. Well, he told his wife, now, not to let em in. (They had log houses, and had em pens, locust pens, to keep the Indians out.)

And he went to the field to see about his horses, and when he got there, they was gone sure enough, the horses were. Well, he pulled back home, he was a-riding. And when he got there, the Indians was there [attacking] his house. And he run around the house three times. And [the Indians] were a-hollering and a-screaming. They hollered and screamed so [that his wife] couldn't hear him and let him in. See, he had guns and things; he could have killed em. Well, [my mother] said that they shot him off. He just run his horse off somewhere and got away. And that night he went back. They had tore his house down and burnt it, and killed em all but one little boy. They scalped [the boy] and struck him on top of the head with the things they call tomahawks. We call em hatchets now.

And he heared him a-crying, going, "Oh, Daddy, oh, Daddy." Said he found him. He was so weak he couldn't walk where they was going to, so he got him on his back and he crawled to . . . the neighbors' house. Well, he got him doctored up, and got doctored up hisself, and got him some guns, . . . and said he never ain't going to do nothing else in what time he lived, but kill Indians.

Well, he started out. There were two girls. The Indians had got two girls kidnapped. He started out to follow em, try to save em. He went out and he found em in the river, on a boat, where the Indians had em. He went, laid his gun down on the bank, and went in, swum in to cut em loose. He cut them loose and got em back to the bank, and by that time a Indian grabbed the gun, and he got it. And he said he jerked it out of the Indian's hand, knocked him on the head with it, and shot once.

And hollered, "Hooray for Sloosha!" Always called the gun "Sloosha" that he had on him. Well, all the rest broke and run. And he got them women and got em back in home. [My mother] said he killed the Indians that way as long as he lived . . . , that man did. That was all the tale, now, that she told on him.

[Frank A. Warner: What did he call his gun?]

Sloosha.

[Frank A. Warner: Sloosha?]

Named his gun Sloosha. And when the Indians found out the name of the gun, he said he could holler "Hooray for old Sloosha!" and said they'd break and run, didn't matter if there was a hundred of em.

[Frank A. Warner: He got a reputation.]

Yeah. And another time he was out, now, that [my mother] told me, he was out a-hunting for the Indians. He looked and he seed several Indians. Well, he said, they didn't see him, but he seed them. And he dodged behind a tree. He stuck his cap out on a stick. And walked up and down and made a noise, so they saw it.

Well, he said, they quieted down then. And he let it fall. Said they knowed his cap. Said, here they come. [Thinking the white man is dead, one of the Indians came closer.] Well, he said, he waited till he got [the Indian] just where he wanted him and said, "Now, say your prayers." And he shot and killed him. And he scared the rest of em away. If they'd have come on, they'd be too many of em for him. He hollered "Hooray for old Sloosha!" And he said they all broke and run. [Laughing]

[Frank A. Warner: That was enough to stop em?]

Yeah, he said they all stopped.

[Frank A. Warner: That's really a story.]

Yes it is. When he said that, they knowed what it meant and . . . they left right then.

[Frank A. Warner: Did you tell me who this man was?]

No. I don't know. She didn't know his name or nothing, you know. It was back, way back. They didn't know his name.

26. Feathers in Her Hair

ROBY MONROE HICKS
Beech Mountain, North Carolina
Recorded by Frank A. and Anne
Warner,
1951

The . . . white people would take . . . a whole crowd of men out and cut trees, just as long a fir trees as they could get and put em in holes. Take em in there and put up posts. Then they'd make their doors in there and they'd move in a dozen families in one of them forts, they called it. So the Indians couldn't get to em. When the men was out, the Indians come in, you know. . . .

Well, there was a whole crowd in one fort one day, and they go out to pick [greens for] salad, the women would, anything they could get, and watch and get back in there, when they see the Indians coming. . . . Called em a tribe. They went in tribes, they called em. They'd go about twelve together, she said, all the time, now my Granny said that. She was old Granny Presley, I heard her tell lots of tales. Susan Presley. And she come from Cherokee. And there was Indians out there, plenty of em. . . .

[A man warned Susan what to do if Indians started stalking her while she was picking salad greens:] "Now if you pick salad," says, "never let on like you see them at all." Said, "Pick up a little closer to em, make you a circle, and then pick up a little further from em. Pick up salad a little closer to em, and then when you goes the other way, pick off a little further from em, it's like if you didn't notice them," and says, "when you get to where you think you can run and get to the fort," he said, "drop your salad and go."

[Frank A. Warner: Yeah.]

Well, she said, she picked on. Finally she picked up right under [an Indian]. He was standing that close to her. As they were standing there, without saying anything or nothing . . . because she knowed he'd get her. Well, she said, that time, she said, she just kept picking and picking, said she was just a little afraid they'd start to run at her before she did start. When she got far enough, she said she dropped her salad and outrun em. . . . Got into the fort before they got at her. She said, when they got so close to the fort ([the settlers] had guns in there and all), they left and she got away. . . .

There's one that went out from the fort, a woman had, and she got off too far, and they got her. And they would scalp em, take the hair off down where the hair come to the skin on the head . . . , and then they struck em on top of the head with those things they called tomahawks to kill em. And they struck her and never killed her.

That's because when they left, there was an old house that people lived in— the Indians had killed out or something—just a small house. And she had crawled in there, got in there, and there was a tub of feathers. . . . And she crawled down in them feathers. And laid there about three days. Thinking she was a-going to die. Nothing to eat, you know. And she crawled out and said them feathers were stuck all over her head, where it bled, you know. There happened to be an old nag, a horse, there in the yard. And she got on that, and managed to get that [nag] to go to the fort, didn't happen to run across no Indians. ([You] didn't run across em every time you got out.) And the [people in the fort] hollered, "The Indians, the Indians!" And she just went on up. When they found out who it was, they got her all doctored up and saved. . . .

[Frank A. Warner: They thought she was an Indian because she had feathers on her head?]

Yeah. She had them feathers. The Indians *wore* feathers on their heads, most of em. . . . [My grandmother Presley] sat and told me tales that way. Now, if I was to tell em, for a week or two, I could think of half of em, maybe. Hundreds and hundreds of em.

27. The Yape

BUNA HICKS
Watauga County, North Carolina
Recorded by Frank A. and Anne Warner,
1951

Buena Vista (Buna) Presnell Hicks (1888–1984), wife of Roby Monroe Hicks, was a celebrated ballad singer. She taped a few brief stories for Frank and Anne Warner and other collectors who have contributed to the holdings of the American Folklife Center. This account of her mother's encounter with a hairy, humanoid creature resembles many tales about "Yahoos" that have circulated in the Appalachians for at least two centuries. In Buna's

Buna Hicks, teller of "The Yape" (story 27), with her homemade fretless banjo, Beech Mountain, North Carolina. (Courtesy of Archives of Appalachia, East Tennessee State University)

version, however, the monster is known as a "Yape," obviously a variant of the word "ape." The tale is set in the Civil War era.

Frank A. Warner: One more little thing, if you would tell me about that Yape?] That Yape, oh, yeah. . . . Well, back in them war times you know, way back years ago, my mother had to help get the work done and get out, and get in wood. And she went one evening to get her load . . . of wood, and she come to a place, she said, she's just picking up little old pieces of wood, here and yonder, and she come to an old brush fence that they had cut and made, and there stood a—what, she didn't really know what it was, a-standing up against the fence, called it—she called it a Yape. She really didn't know the name of it, but she thought—

[Frank A. Warner: Was it a big, hairy—]

Yeah, and it's hairy all over, just staring there, and its big eyes rolled around and looking around right at her. And [she] said she was scared so till it shocked her near to death, said she dropped her wood and she run for life. She tried to get in a home. In them war times, you know, they was all scared so.

[Frank A. Warner: What did she say it was?]

A Yape. And she got her in a home, and my grandma . . . , her mother, said, "Don't tell me what it is." She couldn't stand to hear it, says, "Wait till in the morning, because I can't stand for you to tell it tonight." And [my mother] said she hated it so bad that she couldn't tell her about what she had seed. She said it scared her so that when she got there she just fell in the door.

[Frank A. Warner: Um, um, um. Wasn't that something?]

It was awful.

Ray Hicks (1922–2003)

"Just listen," Ray Hicks once said of his stories, "there's a lot that's not true but a lot that is." For Ray, the Jack Tales embraced both a world of magical impossibilities and the story of his own life. Ray came to view and shape his life in such a way that magic and daily life were never far apart.

Poor as he was for most of his eighty years, he lived in a world of wonders. In his life, as in his tales, material poverty often presented seemingly insurmountable walls that inexplicably became doorways to inestimable spiritual treasures. Two of his favorite autobiographical tales portray such transformations. In both, Ray plays a role identical to his folktale hero Jack, offering his meager assets to an aged stranger and receiving a priceless gift in return. In the first tale, set in his boyhood, Ray gives his only nickel to an old woman on Beech Mountain, who then reads his fortune from a cup of coffee grounds. She tells him that he will marry a dark-haired beauty living in a box house covered with groundhog hides. Ray did not know of such a house or such a girl, but some years later he found them both. The house is gone, but until his death in the spring of 2003 Ray and his black-haired wife, Rosa, lived together in the house—built by his father, grandfather, and great-grandfather—where he was born and christened Leonard Ray Hicks in 1922.

In the second tale ("The Witch Woman on the Stone Mountain on the Tennessee Side," story 30), also set in Ray's boyhood, his father, Nathan, is strapped for cash to feed and clothe his family. Nathan leads Ray and a friend into the high country on an overnight trip to gather galax to sell. Carrying with them a poke filled with biscuits, potatoes, and "bought coffee," they camp on Stone Mountain, Tennessee. Ray encounters a distraught and famished "witch

Ray Hicks working his land, Beech Creek, North Carolina. (Photo by Herb E. Smith, Appalshop)

woman" who begs for his help. Ray offers her the campers' food and the warmth of their fire. The witch woman tells him, "Young man, you've got something in you, that's different from a lot of people. . . . I can feel the impression from your body and your soul. . . . I could ruin your life if I wanted to. But . . . you've offered to treat me good. . . . *I'll just go to put a little spell on you, so you can speak.*" In freeing Ray from the shyness that had dogged his boyhood, the woman opened the wellspring of Ray's storytelling art.

Of course, Ray already knew the Jack Tales, having heard them in many places. His grandfathers were brothers, Benjamin (1870–1945) and Andrew (1878–1949) Hicks. Ray credits both (along with another relative, Sam Ward) with teaching him Jack Tales. "I learned em from the old people, my Grandpa Ben and Grandpa Andy. . . . When I was little. Just hear some parts of em, you know. Just some would tell me parts of em and some another." But Ray learned most from Ben. Daily, as a child of six, and for many years after, Ray walked half a mile from his parents' house to visit Ben and his wife, Julia, to help with fetching water, chopping wood, and other odd jobs around their home as he absorbed their oral traditions. As Ray told writer Robert Isbell, "I've been telling these stories since my Grandpa Benjamin passed them on to me when I was a little boy shelling thrash beans on his porch. They ain't really to believe because a lot in them ain't true; but when you're listening, you got to believe."

Ray's life, like that of much of his family's, consisted largely of facing and overcoming great adversity through an even greater resourcefulness. The family's arts were not simply escapes from harsh reality but a means of creating a better reality. In 1928, when Ray was 5 years old, he rode a horse and his father, Nathan Talbert Hicks (1896–1945), walked beside him as they traveled miles to the closest city of any size (Boone, North Carolina) to raise money by singing on the street as Ray's father played a homemade dulcimer. On one such trip, a New York college professor admired Nathan's dulcimer and bought it from him.

A decade or so later, the man who bought the dulcimer would bring another New Yorker into Ray's life: Frank A. Warner, an officer in the YMCA and an avid folksinger, soon to be a loyal friend and supporter of the Hicks-Harmon family. In 1939, Warner met the professor who had purchased Nathan Hicks's dulcimer. Asking how to obtain a similar instrument for himself, Warner learned from the professor about the man and the small boy who sang for coins in the streets of a mountain town. The professor still had the craftsman's address. Warner wrote Nathan Hicks, asking to buy a dulcimer from him. Hicks wrote in reply that he did not have the money to acquire the necessary glue, stain, and postage to make and send him one. Warner immediately sent Nathan a check. After Nathan sent the finished instrument to Warner, several other Northerners ordered dulcimers from Nathan Hicks and his relatives, creating a short era of relative prosperity for the family, in which they received substantial incomes by practicing their treasured traditional arts.

Frank and his wife, Anne, became not only the Hickses' customers but also their friends. They visited the extended family within months of their first dulcimer purchase and returned to North Carolina to make several visits in subsequent years. The Warners were particularly interested in the family's store of folksongs and did much to focus the attention of folklorists and folk music aficionados on the traditional arts of the Hicks-Harmon family.

It was in 1951, during one of their visits, that the Warners recorded, for the first time, Ray Hicks telling Jack Tales. Two of Ray's first three recorded tales follow.

28. Jack and the Robbers

RAY HICKS
Watauga County, North Carolina
Recorded by Frank A. and Anne
Warner,
1951

Ray Hicks was 28 years old when he recorded "Jack and the Robbers" for Frank and Anne Warner. The Warners were in the midst of a protracted visit with various Hicks-Harmon family members, during which they recorded a handful of Jack Tales along with numerous folksongs, traditional instrumental pieces, plant lore, descriptions of occupational folklife, family legends, and autobiographical accounts. At these sessions, Ray contributed three Jack Tales and a fragmentary witch narrative, his earliest tape-recorded stories.

"Jack and the Robbers" is Ray's version of a tale known to Maud Long as "Jack and the Doctor's Girl" (see story 18). Even in this youthful performance, Ray shows himself a mature and accomplished verbal artist. Much of the tale is delivered in rhythmic, almost poetic style, marked by a tendency to stress the final word in a phrase or sentence, aspects of Harmon-Hicks family style familiar to the thousands of listeners who first heard Ray decades later at the National Storytelling Festival. In other regards, however, this intimate performance for a few friends and family members differs significantly from his later public tellings. In "Jack and the Robbers," Ray tends to speak quietly, without the enormous range of volume that characterized his later tales. Also, in this telling, Ray uses longer sentences and breath units than in his more recent recordings. Perhaps most noticeably, the young Ray often speaks very quickly, a performance trait missing from the later tellings, in which Ray draws out his words and lengthens the pauses between them. In the recordings of both tales that follow, Frank Warner is an avid and encouraging listener who often laughs and mumbles approvingly as Ray works his verbal magic.

Frank, I'm going to tell you another Jack Tale.
Jack and his mother, they got all out of anything to eat, and he started out on a job, and he got out in the woods and he got lost. And he crawled around. And fell down around, off the rocks. And stuck. And directly pried himself out of there. And he happened to see a little light down in the woods. And scrambled around and got down into that there light. And it was a little house. And he

went up hollering and says, "Howdy." This little woman come out, and says, "Law me, son. Little ragged boy." Says, "I hate it," says, "This is a robbers' house." Says, "They kill everybody that comes here."

Well, Jack stood there awhile and he studied, and just then it's pouring rain.

He says, "Well," he says, says, "Lady," he said, "bedad," he says, "I'd just as soon die with the robbers killing me than standing out in this rain and drown." He said, "Bedad, I'm a-coming in anyhow."

Says, "Well," she says, "if you come in here, go over there in that little pile of straw." Says, "That's what [we have] for the dog to lie in." Says, "You can lay down over there," and says, "they might not see you."

Well, the robbers come in about just a little before daylight, went to divide the money. And Jack was, wasn't really asleep, but he was making kind of a snoring fuss. And they happened to hear him and they up with their guns and says, says, "Woman, what's that a-making that racket?"

She says, "Ah," says, "just a little old boy," said, "come in here a while ago." Says, "I told him not to come in, you'uns would kill him."

Says, "Yeah." Says, "What's your name?"

Says, "My name's Jack."

Says, "Well, get up, Jack," says, "We'll kill everybody that comes." Says, "Dead men tell no tales."

Well, Jack got up and he said, with his little ragged clothes on, he says, "Well," he says, "You'uns can kill me if you want to." And says, "You see, I ain't got nothing but what's on me and it's just rags." He says, "You'uns robs for money, don't you?"

He said, "Yeah."

"You see, I ain't got nothing, all my little rags is all. I'm just a poor little humble boy."

And they got to looking at him. And got kind of, sort of sorry for Jack.

And says, "Well, Jack," said, "you a good hand to steal?"

"Well," he says, "Just to change it around the subject," he says, "bedad, I ought to be a good hand." Says, "A man ought to be a good hand to steal to save his life."

"Well," said, "I'll tell you what we'll do." Said, "A farmer's got three ox." Says, "He's going to the market with one of em in the morning." He says, "You steal that ox," and says, "I'll give you a hundred dollars for it." Said, "I'll pay you a hundred dollars."

Well, Jack he didn't know what to do. How to get that there stealing. He started down this little fence they'd built around the house, little old rail fence, and there's a piece of rope a-hanging on it. He just snapped that rope, and said, it seemed like his hand just reached out and got it, cut it and tied it around him and hid it. He didn't know what it'd be any use or not, and got on down the road.

And he heared the farmer coming. "*Saw Buck, hea Buck. Hea, hea. Saw Buck.*" And said he just looked up, and there was a stooping tree and he just run up that tree as quick as he could, tied hisself like a man that'd hung himself. Or at least a boy. Hanging there, like they'd hung a boy.

That farmer come along driving his steer. "*Saw Buck, how, how,* let's get to town." He looked up and seed Jack. "*Law, me,*" said. "Ain't that a pity." Says, "Them robbers want to kill everybody in my country." Says, "There hangs a poor little boy, dead." And says, says, "You've got to be buried." Says, "I've got to go back and tell my neighbors. We can take him down and bury him today."

Well, he just tied his steer there on the side of the road and run back for the neighbors, and Jack got his rope loose and got down and got the steer, and drove it on up to the robbers.

Said, "Law, me, Jack." He said, "Gosh." Said, "You are doing that good right on the start," he said, "coming in this quick with the first one."

Said, "Bedad," said, "I thought that was sorry." Says, "Thought I been gone a right smart time."

Said, "You ain't been gone a half hour."

Well, he said, he'd be a-going for the next one in the morning.

Said, "Sleep good tonight and take in the day. Have a good day." Said in the morning, he'd be going to the next one.

Well, Jack laid all that night studying how to get that next. He couldn't think next. Well, next morning he got up and the robbers'd been dividing up stuff there and they dropped a brand new woman's slipper. He just—his hand just reached out and snatched it in his pocket. He just put it in his pocket and went on down and he's sitting there, studying how to get that next steer.

And farmer come along: "*Saw Buck, hea Buck. Saw Buck, hea Buck. Hea, hea. Saw Buck.*" And just got right up agin him nearly. And Jack, he didn't think, didn't know what to do, he just reached back and got that slip and set it out in the road and dodged back in the woods and hid.

Farmer come out. "*Law, me.* Ain't that a sight? There's a pretty slipper." And says, "There is aught, no mate to it." Said, "If I had the mate for that," said, "it'd done my old woman all winter." But said, "What use is it? It ain't got no mate." And just throwed it back down in the road and got his steer and went on.

Jack run out and got the slipper he just left and took a near cut and throwed it at him again.

"*Law, me.* There's the mate to that slipper." He didn't keep it in his mind that, that it was the one for the left, it was for the left foot. And he didn't keep it in mind, you know that. He just said, "Law me, there's the"—[laughing] just like anybody'd be—says, "There's the mate for that slipper." And says, "I come a mile and left that." Says, "I'll just tie my steer here and run back and get that'un." Said, "That'll do my old woman all winter."

And he tied his steer and run back and get it, and while he's going back to get that other slipper, he got down there hunting for that slipper and walked an hour or two, running up and down thinking he was mistaken where he first found it. And he run an hour or two.

And Jack got the steer and went to the robbers while he's still hunting for that slipper. [Laughter]

And he come in and he says, "Boy, Jack! You's a hand to steal." He said, "With us a-talking about a-killing and a-stealing the likes of Jack." Said, "It just wasn't for us to kill you, was it?"

Said, "Bedad, don't look like it was."

Said, "Here's you another hundred," and Jack stuffed it down there in that little ragged pocket and had that two hundred dollars in it. [The robber tells Jack to steel the third animal.] "Get it and we'll let you off. Go home, anywhere you want to go," he says. "We'll spare your life. . . ."

And, well, Jack he couldn't think of nary a thing. . . . He didn't know *what to do*, and just went down through there, whistling the next morning, and felt so ill he didn't know, know—what to do. He set down side of the road, set down side of the road nearly ready to cry. Didn't know what, expecting to be killed yet, you know, when the robbers came up, for not getting that one, you know—the third one.

He's a-setting there and about that time farmer come around, and turn right on him. Just right agin him. "*Saw, Buck. Get up, Buck.* I done lost my other two ones, and now let's see if we can get to town with you." Talking mad.

Jack, he just happened to think right quick to strike up through the woods and go: "*Mooooo, Whaaa, Mooooo, Bwaaa. Blaaah.*"

"My two steers, they just got loose! That just got loose! I'll, I'll, I'll tie this'n and get them two and just take em all, all three together. That's what I thought. I thought they just got loose."

And Jack, farmer took up in the woods, there, and Jack is dodging like a rabbit, you know, and going, "*Meeehhh, Bwaa, Meehh, Bwaa.*"

"Yeah, that's them. That's them!"

He'd jump and take out after em. And Jack, Jack'd dodge like a rabbit, "*Myeh, Bwoo, Myeh, Bwoo,*" and led him further in. And directly he got him all tangled up across a log, and got his foot hung up in another one, and stumbled and turned his head down, the farmer did, and while he's all tangled around like that and Jack jumped out and got the other steer. [Laughter] And took that'n back to the robbers.

"Boy," he said, "that, that's the last one now." And said, "You ain't been no time."

Said, "No," said, "I hit him right in the road when I went." Said, "Just hit him right in the road."

Said, "Boy," said, "you wouldn't hire out to us, would you."

Says, "No," says, "I just stole this now to save my life, just like you'uns said. I ought to be a good hand at stealing."

"Well," he said, "Here's your other hundred." Said, "Well, that makes three hundred dollars."

Jack got the three hundred, put it in his pocket, and struck toward home, come in. Said, "Now, mother," he said, "we got three hundred dollars." And he said, "We could live good for a long time." Was said to live good from there out.

[Frank A. Warner: And that's the story?]

Yeah.

[Frank A. Warner: Well, dog, if it ain't about the best one I've ever heard.]

| 29. The Unicorn and the Wild Boar | RAY HICKS
Watauga County, North Carolina
Recorded by Frank A. and Anne Warner,
1951 |

"The Unicorn and the Wild Boar" was told immediately after "Jack and the Robbers." Frank Warner had just declared the robber story "about the best [Jack Tale] I've ever heard," and in response to this praise and encouragement Ray offered the "Unicorn" as an even better tale.

Perhaps in his haste to prove his point, Ray gets ahead of himself in the early stages of the performance, bringing Jack to the king's house before he has made his belt, and then backtracking to describe the incident leading to the hero's advertising himself as "Big Man Jack." After this relatively unsteady beginning, Ray quickly reaches the height of his form. Notable in this performance is the depiction of Jack as both extraordinarily resourceful and extraordinarily vulnerable. Ray creates a two-sided hero in this tale: a private Jack and a public Jack. When Jack tries to dodge the king's challenges and three charging animals, there are many moments of comedy and sensitivity that create a complex clash with the bravura of Jack's public boasts to the king.

I've got another'n, I believe it's better than that.
[Frank A. Warner: Well, all right. What's this one about?]

This one's about the unicorn and the wild boar.

[Frank A. Warner: All right, I'm a-listening.]

Well, Jack and his mother, they got hard up again. And he started out to hunt a job. And he come to a king's house, but he didn't know it was a king, and he asked, and—while he was going along to the king's house, he passed a, a muddy place in the road, and there's butterflies just all over that in the road.

[Frank A. Warner: Yes.]

And before he come to these butterflies, he was a-hewing on a little stick and first thing you know, he made a paddle. And just a paddle, and he come to them butterflies, and he decided to hit in em. And he hit in em, and he killed seven.

He just went on down to the blacksmith's shop, and had it printed on his belt:

> "Big Man Jack
> Killed Seven at a Whack

He come on to the king's house then, and asks, and he says, "Do you know where I could get a job?"

He says, "Well." He says, "You—turn around there, turn around there." Said, "I didn't get to see that good." He says, "Turn around there, and you might be the one that I been needing." He turned around and the king read that off, said,

> Big Man Jack
> Killed Seven at a Whack

He said, "You mean you big [as all that]—can you hold up to that what's on your belt?"

"Well," he said, "bedad, I reckon I can." He says, "I ain't very *big*, now, as far as the big—"

"Well," he said, "you can spend the night with me tonight," and says, says, "we'll talk over a job tonight." And Jack, he didn't know what it was going to be, you know. They went in to eat supper and he said, began to cringe just a little, thinking it was going to be something pretty bad. . . . After they eat supper, they come back in to the fireplace, and the king says, "Well, now," he says, "I've sent many men to the mountains. Took on my horse and sent em," and says, "they've hunt all for a wild boar out up there," and says, "it's a-killing everything. People, cattle, horses, don't leave nothing but what it runs on." And says, "I'm the king over the country," and says, "I have to get it killed." And says, "I've sent many of a man, many of men up there, and says, "it *killed* em," said, "I ain't seed no more of em. Took em up there on my horse."

And Jack got just a-trembling all over. Just a, just didn't think he'd live to see daylight come, and didn't know, didn't want to back out. Well, he went to bed, and he never slept a wink. Got up.

King said, "Do you feel like you can do that?"

"Well," he said, "bedad, I reckon I can try."

Says, "I'll give you three, three hundred bucks for killing that wild hog."

"Well," he said, "bedad, I reckon I can try. I just have to live till I die, any more than that." Said, "If I get killed, I'm killed."

And king says, "Well," he says, "it awful dangerous." And says, "I ain't a-telling you to go now." Said, "This is *you*."

He says, "I'm like to be killed."

"Why don't you get on my horse?" The king took Jack with him, [and then after riding a while told him] to light. . . . And Jack got off of the horse and . . . the king just whipped the horse to get back out of the woods, a-feared the hog'd get at him. And about that time, the hog smelled him. And said, here it comes after him, . . . just a-whickety-whack, and him a-whickety-whack, whickety-whack, and the hog run after around through the woods. So directly he come to a little old waste-house, it was a little old log house out in the field, and the hog got so close to him it bit off a end of his coattail, and just as he clumb up the outside of that log house, he clumb up, and the hog bit his coattail as he went up, and the hog shot in at the door, then. And Jack just jumped back off and shut the door up.

And come back down.

And [the king said], "Did you see anything, Jack?"

He said, "Bedad," he said, "*see* anything?" He said, "What is you'uns a-talking about?" Said, "Men a-being killed?" Said, "There's a little old shoat of a hog up there," said, "that kept prowling around me, playing with me, playing with me," says, "playing with me. Directly bit my coattail off and made me mad," and said, "I just picked it up by the tail and ears and stowed it in a little house up there and shut it up," and says, "you can go up there and see if that's what you wanted me to kill, or get." Says, "I didn't see nothing but a little old shoat."

The king knowed what it was. He sent and got his men, went up there, and all of the king's men didn't have nerve enough to shoot it, and Jack said, "Bedad, reach me the gun," says, "I can shoot it." Someone gave him one and he shot it and tore that whole building down on this pig. And they cleaned it out and made eight wagonloads of meat. And hauled it back down.

Well, Jack thought he was a-getting off to go home, thought that was all finished. He's setting there and in come some of the king's men and said, said, "Law, me," he said, "the hog is nothing." Said, "There's a unicorn out now, a wild unicorn," and says, "it's a, it *is* a sight."

King says, "Is that right?"

Says, "Yes." Says, says, "He's right."

Says, "Well," he says, "I've got the man here to do it." Said, "Here he is." Said, "He ain't big, but look on his belt," and says, "he's got the hog," and says, "he'll get that."

And Jack—next morning the king got him on the horse to go with . . . him to see the unicorn, and Jack, he didn't know what to do. Got up there, and he said, "Bedad," when the king let him off and run the horse as fast as he could to get back out before it could get after him.

Jacks says, "Bedads, I got three hundred dollars in my little old ragged pocket now," and says, "let me slip out of here." Says, "Before that unicorn gets after me," and says, "maybe I will get the good out of my three hundred," and says, "mess around here and get killed, it won't do me no good."

And he got trying to slip out, and the unicorn smelled him. Here it come, and making after him, with that horn, trying to gouge it in him. And Jack a-dodged from one tree to another'n, you know, . . . hid. And directly the unicorn made a big dive at him, and stuck that horn through a tree. Stuck it through it, and acted like it was [stuck] pretty good. And he just snatched some nails out of his pocket, and wedged it, on the other side with a rock, drove a wedge aside of the horn.

Run down and [the king] said, "Did you get it?"

He says, "I didn't see nothing much." Said, "A little old thing up there that looked like a colt, or filly, or something like that." Said, "It had a horn on the end of its head." And said, "It got to gouging that horn around at me like it was wanting to play, or a little something, got to gouging a little close, and made me mad," and said, "I picked her up by the tail and head and socked her through a tree up there."

"You mean you're sticking up to your belt, ain't you?" Said,

> " 'Big Man Jack,
> Killed Seven at a Whack.'

Did you mean you could do it?"

Said, "You can go up there and see if you want to." He just kept on pranking around. He says, "Don't guess what you want."

The king knowed it, and he just went and called his men and went and they went, and they wouldn't get as close to it than they did the wild hog, to shoot it.

Jack, he grabbed the gun out of their hand. "Let me show you how to shoot something," he said. When he shot that unicorn it grubbed that big white oak tree, took it right out of the ground.

And he went back in, and the king was turning him loose to go home. Jack had . . . another three hundred, and he had six hundred in his pocket.

Says, king says, "Well, you're through, Jack," and Jack had went through the [fence], got out a little piece, and one of the king's men just shot in just as Jack was going out again yet.

And says, "King!" Says, "It's a lion out." Says, "It's a lion out!"

King says, "Is it?"

"Yes, boy!" Says, "It's a-doing something, too." Says, "It's a-roaring so hard that it's a-busting rock off the mountain that's rolling and a-killing people," says it's so big.

Says, "Law, me!" Says, "Why wasn't you a little earlier." Said, "My man's gone." Said, "He's done killed the unicorn—got it, and killed it—and the wild hog." And says, "he's gone!" Says, "I bet he's gone."

And the king jumped on his horse and overtook Jack. He says, says, "Law, me, Jack, will you go back." Says, "Will you go back?"

"Well," Jack says, "I don't know." Jack figured he was out of that trouble, you know, and hadn't got hurt, and he'd better, he'd better not be so free to get back, and he says, "I don't know."

He says, "Do go back!" He says, "It's a lion out." Said, "I got word just as you was getting out again." Said, "There's a lion out."

"Well," Jack says, "I don't know," says, "but I reckon I'll go back."

Says, "I'll give you," says "I'll give you four hundred dollars if you go kill that lion. For killing it." (Jack boosted him on the trade, you know, by acting that he wasn't going back.)

Well, Jack went back, and king got him, and took him in the woods and said he'd see him.

Jack says, "Bedad," he said, "I've got six hundred in my pocket now, and I better get out of here. I better get out *this* time. And I mean, get out. Says, "If I mess around here and get killed now, and me with six hundred dollars in my pocket. . . ."

And he got trying to slip around there, and the lion smelled him, and said that beat any roaring you ever heared. Gree, just jarred his feet up off the ground, said here it come! And said he didn't see nary a way out of it, but a big ash, about six or seven feet through, and said he scaled that with his bare feet, went up in it, and that lion come, looked, smelled him up in there, and begin to gnaw that tree. Gnaw, gnaw, gnaw, gnaw on the tree, and the wood a-flying. And said, directly that lion give out, about the time it lacked two foot of having it cut down. Its jaws give out, and it just laid down and went to sleep.

And Jack said his heart was a-beating up in his neck. Just a-fluttering up in there, he was shaking so. And said he let his heart cool down just a little and decided he'd slip down *over* that lion, ease down over it while it was asleep and get out of there with his six hundred. He begin to ease down, his foot hit a brittle limb, and it broke, and it hit right on the lion's back. And when it hit on the lion's back, it woke. Now it scared the lion, and here it went! And him [on] the lion, clinching a hold of it. He come down, and he got in the town. In the town, all the people run in and hid. [The king] was having court, and it scared them all to death. And he stopped. And the king's men seed Jack, and they kept on trying to shoot it and keep from hitting Jack. It was a hard job. And directly, one made a good shot and hit the lion and killed it. It stove Jack in the ground. Mussed him up. King come.

Jack says, "King," he says, "I want to *tell* you something, what your men's done."

He says, "What have they done?"

"Well," says, "let me tell you." Says, "I had this lion," said, "now you'd a felt *big* around here being a king." Said, "I had this lion trained. I was . . . going to give you to make you a ridey-horse out of it, being you was a king." And says, "Here, your men *shot* it."

King says, "Boy, I'd," he said, "boy, I'd a looked big," he said, "around here a-riding on that. Men," he said, "now," he said, ". . . you'uns shot that," said, "you'll have to make Jack another hundred dollars extra money."

. . . Well, that made him eleven hundred dollars, he got out of it, for killing the lion and all. And he come back and the king thanked him. He come on home and him and his mother really lived good then. And that was the end of that.

30. The Witch Woman on the Stone Mountain on the Tennessee Side

RAY HICKS
Beech Mountain, North Carolina
Recorded at the National
Storytelling Festival,
Jonesborough, Tennessee,
October 3, 1998

The Ray Hicks of "Jack and the Robbers" and "The Unicorn and the Wild Boar" (stories 28 and 29, recorded in 1951) is already a great narrator, but not yet a celebrity. In the following three tales, we hear Ray forty-seven years later, at the height of his fame, entertaining an enthusiastic crowd gathered at the National Storytelling Festival in Jonesborough, Tennessee, the venue through which Ray became the best-known and most-admired traditional storyteller in America.

By the early 1970s, when Ray first took part in the National Storytelling Festival, he had already attracted the attention and respect of folklorists. In 1962, a Folk Legacy recording containing four of his tales appeared. In 1973, Elizabeth Barrett of Appalshop began filming Ray for a video later released under the title *Fixin' to Tell about Jack*. But the most important single factor in Ray's rise to fame was his role at the National Storytelling Festival, where he became the central presence, the only performer invited to entertain every year since the festival's inception. Between 1973 and 1999, Ray performed at twenty-five of these annual events, missing only twice.

Given the intensely intimate nature of traditional Jack Tale performances, typically shared in small groups of family and close friends, it is not surprising that Ray did not adjust immediately to a stage setting that required him to tell his tale to hundreds of assembled strangers. Friend and fellow storyteller Barbara Freeman, who witnessed Ray's first performance in Jonesborough, in 1973, recalls, "Ray was so nervous that he looked at the sky the whole time. And that microphone, and his voice, he was just shaking. . . . And I thought to myself . . . , boy, this seems cruel, you know, to bring somebody who is a front-porch storyteller out of their natural environment and subject them to a big microphone and big speakers and a great crowd of people."

As foreign and formidable as the Jonesborough setting may have been for Ray, it nevertheless possessed the essential human ingredient to avert disaster: a deeply sympathetic audience comprising amateur and professional storytellers, and story-lovers of many stripes, eager to listen to this man whose accent and appearance were so different from their own. The Festival's director, Jimmy Neil Smith, had been driven by the sheer love of story to mount this event, and from the beginning his mission attracted crowds that were avid, respectful, and open-minded. As one resident of Jonesborough has remarked, "The festival *seems* to be too big for the town. To count them, there are way too many people here; but because they are special people, they have what it takes to make the locals feel comfortable and each other feel at home." Ray soon overcame the strange surroundings and found a way to reach this welcoming audience.

After their debuts in 1973, Ray and the National Storytelling Festival grew to prominence together, and Jonesborough has become the medium through which more people are exposed to traditional storytelling than any other. At Jonesborough, Ray became the leading emissary of traditional mountain storytelling. Like his relative Maud Long, who in 1947 recorded the earliest commercially released Jack Tale performances (see stories 13–23), Ray was a cultural translator. But unlike Maud, whose extensive formal education led her to adopt a popular storybook style familiar to outsiders, Ray made outsiders come to him. He retained his distinctive accent and rhythmic phrasing, even though, as storytelling specialist Joseph Sobol has observed, "it can take an hour or more—roughly the length of one of his festival performances—for an outsider to begin to decipher his archaic mountain dialect."

Inevitably, however, the size of Ray's Jonesborough audiences caused him to adjust aspects of his delivery. In his later stage performances, Ray speaks more slowly and loudly than in his early recordings, and he pauses more frequently, using shorter sentences and phrases, and repeating himself more often—all devices that help his listeners keep pace with him. The content of his tales changes slightly as well, for Ray treats these festival performances not merely as entertainment but also as an education in an entire, nearly vanished way of life. For example, in the tale that follows, Ray pauses in his account to note the importance of galax as a source for money in his family, the uses of rubber rings from canning jars, and the value of owning a barlow knife when he was a boy.

"The Witch Woman" is one of Ray's favorite autobiographical tales, a story that explains, in part, how he became a storyteller. It carries with it lessons similar to those found in many of his Jack Tales: that one is never too poor to be generous, and that generosity is a gift to the giver as well as to the recipient.

After taking the stage at the National Storytelling Festival, Ray mentioned that he had been signing books and tapes, including a cassette that featured a story in which] I was with my dad, my father, on that cassette. And one lady that bought one was wanting me to sign it, and I signed it. . . . And she said, "Mr. Hicks, if you can think of it," said, "you try to tell that story." And so that's going to be my second [story] now, with the witch on Stone Mountain on the Tennessee side: "The Witch Woman on the Stone Mountain on the Tennessee Side."

And so we was without anything, nearly, to eat. Just had a little flour left, mother said, to bake a few biscuits, and a few Irish potatoes . . . and all the kids there, that was there. And Mama said, Mother said, "Nathan, you'd better take Ray in that old truck." It was a twenty-eight model, Chevrolet truck, three-quarter-ton with a four-cylinder motor and a back-end tank on it. . . . And I had learned to drive it, and so we went far as we could go with it, up them little old rough roads, and then we carried our eating, to pull galax. . . . And our quilts to sleep on.

And Daddy had been there, my father, had been there with *his* father, . . . my grandfather John Benjamin Hicks, and others, *back when they grew up*, a-pulling galax. . . . It was a evergreen. It sold old years ago, and it's selling now.

And so I had . . . up with me, my boyfriend, Carson Presnell. (He passed on. He was my age, close, but he went young.) And he said, "Tell Nathan that I want to go pull some galax and get *me* a little money."

"Well, Dad'd be glad for you to go," my father.

And so, Dad had bought a dog. . . . And the fellow that sold it to him said he didn't know it would run a coon, but he said he could see that dog would run anything. It was half bulldog. And we took the dog with us and went far as we could with a truck, and then we walked, seemed like it probably was farther than I thought it was, but seemed like, . . . I thought we walked five miles up that mountain. Four or five miles. And then down in to the Tennessee side.

And then [Dad] said, "You'uns stay here." Said, "I know down in it where it's a limestone spring, that ain't got much lime in it, where we used to camp in a covered wagon, pulling galax when *I* was young." And, and so he went down in it. It'd been *years*, some years. And he said, "I found it."

And we went down in there and built our camp. And the *lightning* and the electric storm, it had struck an old big twin wild chestnut tree, some time, and blowed off . . . a few slabs that broad, and *long*. And we carried some of them, and carried the broadest and made us a table, laid it on rock, and then we carried us two more and made us a seat on each side of it, and we had our fire on the end of it, on one end of it.

And so it was . . . in the evening when we got there. We're going camping to pull galax next day, or maybe two days. And so, with our supper, he put in some Irish potatoes to roast, and [Mom] had done sent the biscuits in a flour poke, done baked, and there's a cup and saucer apiece and a spoon and a fork to eat with, and a plate. . . . And so he added the taters in there, and he took a bucket just to boil him some plain-bought coffee, he took with him. (Now the coffee beans, where you ground em in that coffee mill you had to the side of the wall in that time. It wasn't no ground coffee we got, you just bought coffee beans, and ground em in the old coffee mill that was up on the side of the wall.)

And so he told me to take that dog up where there's an old field *way* up at the top of the woods, of the trees, a-growing up. And tie the dog and see to it. And so it got down a-getting dusky dark. Started to get dark in that mountain. And I heard that dog a-barking, like it was a-barking at some *body*. And I run. And here come a woman about fifty, looked like—to guess at it—or fifty-five years old, or maybe, if you'll ask her, forty. [Laughter] Forty, or forty-five, to guess at it. And with a black dress on, and her shoes, the soles had come loose, a-flapping [and she was using rubber rings from canning jars to hold her shoes together]. (And these old zinc can lids at that time had the rubber, you know, that went under them, and . . . you preserved with it. When you were canning your food. And then later on, and them's an antique now, if you had some good ones, them zinc ones there, these flipper ones come out, antique, worth a lot of money, if you had any.)

And so . . . there she come, and I hollered, "Whoever you are, don't go out to that dog, *please!* He'll eat you up." His mouth was that broad, about like this, about like that. He was about half bulldog, a fellow said.

And she just went out, and the dog put its nose up, kind of, and growled a little in its eye, and its bristles up, "*grrrrrr.*" And she just went around with her hand on top of its fur (and its nose up) round about two or three times. Dog just fell to the ground. With his tongue a-hanging out, like it was a-dying. "My God, you killed our dog!" [Laughter] "You killed our dog."

She said, "No! I ain't killed it." Said, "I just put it all to sleep for fifteen or twenty minutes." Said, "It won't bite nobody right now." And then she looked at me. In that dress, torn. You could see her thigh here, a little, and them there shoes with them there rubber around em to hold the soles from flapping. And she said, "You've got anything to eat?" She said, "I was a pulling galax in here, and I lost em." And said, "I've hunted," said, "I've hunted and pulled some more, nearly all this evening, and I can't find em." And said, "I happened to see your-uns' smoke." And said, "You got anything to eat?" She says, "I ain't had nothing to eat for the last three days here in this mountain, but three little raw onions. . . ."

"I heard you. Yes, ma'am. We've got some taters, Irish taters nearly done, and he's got some bought coffee a-boiling in his bucket, and got some biscuits that Mama, Mother sent with us in a flour poke."

And, and as we walked down, she said, "Young man, you've got something in you, that's different from a lot of people, young man." Said, "You're a *fine* young man to tell me to come on down to eat. And your feelings," said, "I can feel the impression from your body and your soul." Said, "Now, I could ruin your life if I wanted to. But," she said, "you've offered to treat me good, and your father and your boyfriend down there." And said, "*I'll just go to put a little spell on you,*" (I can feel that now) . . . said, "so you can *speak*."

I was shy from people. I could meet em in a little old road or path, and I'd *hide* till they went on. And from that day till now, I ain't been shy since, hardly.

[Audience laughter and applause]

And so, and so, Dad, my father, says to her, said, "Ma'am, you stay with the fire. And there's the rest of the potatoes and the coffee and . . . the biscuits." And said, "Stay, and make yourself at home. We've got to get out here in our quilt beds so we can lay and rest and pull galax tomorrow, next day."

And so she asked. My boyfriend had a barlow pocket knife. (. . . One big blade and one small one, and what they called a *barlow* pocket knife, and if you had one of them, good, now it's a antique. Worth a lot of money. And they just costed fifty cents or a dollar back then, but that was ten hours' work, a dollar a day.) And so she asked to use his knife to peel potatoes with, and to eat. I didn't have any knife. (A knife was hard to get a hold of. And then I'd lose mine a lot. I forgot it and it'd cut a hole in my overall pocket.)

And so we got out there in the bed. . . . I's a-dozing to go off to sleep, we were kindly worried, and Carson, my boyfriend, said, "Ray, how can you sleep, and a dang witch is setting down there." And said, "God, beside that, she's got my pocket knife." [Laughter] And said, "[If we] go to sleep, she might slip up here and cut our throats with it."

"*Gosh! Hush!* Be quiet! She don't have to cut our throats, the way she talked, and the little spell put on me. Why, she would witch you and ruin you."

And so, next morning, about four o'clock in the morning, it come a storm up on that mountain, and it was foggy, dark as a dungeon, and [Dad] told me to put the matches in the side of a old dead chestnut tree. You know, in that bark so they wouldn't get wet if it rained. And he told me to crawl out to the camp and hunt [up the matches], and get a fire started. And I crawled, and a-thinking that witch woman was setting there, but it seemed like I wasn't a-going to be a-feared of her, the way she'd talked to me. And so I found the tree and got the matches, and when I struck one on my overall button, the end just flew off of it, and . . . I struck two or three (they'd got damp). And I rubbed the end of one through my hair, with its tip right next to the [skin]. And struck it on my button, and she *went*—a kitchen match. And I grabbed then in there, and got a lot of that old sap bark that was in there, chestnut bark in there where it was dry, and got me a bundle of it, squeezed that in my hand, *lit it*, like a torch, and throwed some on a piece of bark then, and fixed me a fire on a piece of bark, and carried it and got then with a light, to where the fire [had been], where the rain had put it out, and I got there with the fire. And that woman was gone.

And they was a old barn, *way* down on the North Carolina side, kindly fell sideways, and I've studied it. I bet she was a-sleeping in that barn. And so, it rained us out. We just got to pull a few galax that day. It rained on, a-drizzling. And we had to come home with what we got, and never did go back to pull no more. And that's the end of "The Witch on the Stone Mountain."

31. Grinding at the Mill

RAY HICKS
Beech Mountain, North Carolina
Recorded at the National
Storytelling Festival,
Jonesborough, Tennessee,
October 3, 1998

Ray noted the resonance between this tale and his own boyhood. He told writer Robert Isbell that the grist mill featured in the tale was modeled on a similar mill in his own neighborhood. Ray also likened the poverty and hunger experienced by Jack and his mother to times in his boyhood when his family was "having it hard." As he explains at the end of his tale, belief in witchcraft was common in the mountains when he was a boy, but in his humorous explanation of how to become a witch, he implies that he doesn't set much stock in some of the beliefs current when he was a child.

And so here now is a Jack Tale story. Now back [then] they called it "Sop, Doll," they did, but I called it, of my way, "Grinding at the Mill." *Grist mill. Jack.*

And so Jack and his mother just lived together. Just her and Jack. And so they lived in a log cabin [with] a mudrock chimney, up on a cold ridge, of a mountain, was where they lived at. And it was *cold*. And so . . . they just had a little eating left. And what they called vittles, or food. And Jack's mother was a-crying, tears were running down out of her eyes. And Jack wasn't that old. He was pretty young. And he was humble-hearted, and looking at his mother a-crying, and he'd say, "Mother, let me go. I might hit [upon] somebody that might will *help* us."

"Well," she said, "if we don't get help, we won't see spring of the year," when the food grows again. "Well," she said, "You're too *young* to get out on your own." Finally, in a few days, she gave up, said, "Jack, take the pole-ax *today* and try to get you in *all* the wood you can get for me to use while you're gone."

And Jack worked, and carried wood all that day for the old mudrock fireplace. Next morning he started off, a-walking just at daylight.

And he come to a big forest, and what they called, when I grew up, was a lot of . . . what they called black mountain *panthers*. But, anymore, they call em mountain lion, or a *cougar*. And so Jack, one got on him, and he knowed how to shun it, and it didn't kill him. And he went on and got to the first log cabin. (They lived, some of em, pretty far apart, because they didn't know how to dig a well or nothing like that, just where the mountain springs was at. Well, it was limestone springs like in Tennessee and other states, like that, limestone springs. I've drunk out of some in Tennessee, a-working.)

And so, he run up on this first one, and he's out a-working, chopping wood or clearing a newground, and he went up and said, *"Hello. Hello, stranger!"*

And he looked around and seed that young lad. He said, "Son, why be *you* here? And you young as you is?"

He said, "Me and my mother is going to starve to death if somebody don't go in and help us."

"Well," he says, "with the family I got, I'd like to help you, but I can't." He said, "If I give any of mine away, *we* won't make it." He said, "I've got a big family of kids, me and my wife."

And he said, "Pardon me," and went on.

And the next [man] told him the same thing. . . . But when Jack left, was walking on, he run and overtook Jack and patted him on the right shoulder, and Jack turned around to see him, and he, he said, "Son, I happened to think after you left, that they have a fellow *way* on yonder with a *big*, beautiful log cabin." And he said, "It's up on a rise, in a pretty, black farming land, and it's right on the other side of a cold-water creek." And he said, "He used to run a mill, grist mill down that creek. But," he says, "it's shut down, and I ain't heared it run in a good while." And said, "You go on, and see him, he might let you start that mill up. And you can get some eating for you and your mother."

And so he went on through the big forest and hit the top end of that cold-water creek, and when he come through, out of the forest, up on the rise end of that ridge, from the creek—pretty land, cleared up—was that big log cabin. And he walked up and *hollered*, "*Hello. Hello.*"

And the fellow come out, and he said, "*Goll.* . . . Why be you here?"

He said, "Me and my mother is about up agin it without anything to eat, and we ain't a-going to make it." And said, "The second fellow told me you used to run a grist mill down the creek, and if I come on, that you might let me start it up and make us some vittles or food."

And he said, "*Hush! Hush! Hush, son! Hush!*" He said, "I don't want to think of that mill." He says, "I've hired *fifty men* that stays with the bunk, and stays in the millhouse." Said, "I've hired fifty, and I quit it, shut it down," said, "when I hired up the fifty, and each man was dead in the millhouse next morning." And he said, "Me, and my neighbors a-helping, got tired of digging graves. [Laughter]

"And back, the last ones, I hope to dig in my country, of the six-feet graves, the hole six feet deep and . . . with a homemade coffin. Six feet deep. And we'd hit rock and have to chop that . . . out with a old ax and, God, it took work." [Laughter]

And so Jack kept on—he said, "Let's go and look at the mill."

He said, "I *told* you, I don't want to see you." And directly he says, "Well, I reckon I'll walk down the creek and let you look at it."

And they walked down there. And the millhouse was [made] out of logs, notched and fixed out of logs, and a big water wheel, and the watergate, the water flume into the wheel. And Jack got in there. And up around the . . . wall of the log millhouse was twelve windows, square windows. (See, they didn't know what a glass light was, nor nothing, for a long time there we didn't, people, as they come through.) And he looked up around them twelve windows, the biggest one around the top, down to the least one, as they changed. And then [from] the least one up to the biggest window of twelve, a dozen square windows to let the dust out of the grinding of the meal.

And Jack looked and he said, "Let me run it, please?"

He said, "Son," said, "You're young and got a life to live." And said, "If you run this mill, you'll be dead here in the morning." And said, "You're young."

"Well," Jack said, "I'm going to starve to death anyhow. What does it make any difference?" [Laughter]

"*Young.*"

Said, "I'm going to starve to death young. What does it—"

"Why," he said, "that'd be right. Well," he says, "I reckon I'll let you run it."

They got word out that the mill had started, and he went back up to his log cabin and got Jack a frying pan and some meal to make him some ashcakes, and some meat to fry. And to get his eating, his supper on the fireplace, breakfast or dinner on the fireplace. It was in the morning about nine o'clock, and Jack ground a while, and ground.

And that evening he went in, to fix him a bite to eat, he was a-getting hungry. And he . . . went to start a fire, in the mudrock fireplace to get his eatin' fixed, and he heared a voice, out to the hitching [post]. "*Whoa! Whoa! Whoa!*"

And he looked out, and out there at the hitching [post] was a blond-headed fellow about five-something tall and had a, a donkey with a little poke of corn on it, and a scissor-tail coat on (that they used to wear, men—it hung down to here, and cut open, what they called, behind, a scissor-tail coat, that the men wore).

And so Jack just quit and didn't start his fire, went out, and said, "*Hello,* stranger." And Jack had done went and turned the watergate off, where he had ground. It had done given out nearly. He said, "*Ah,* I live so far that everytime I come to the mill here, the mill man's always shut down for night. And I don't get my corn ground, my poke of corn."

Jack looked at him. He said, "You'll get it ground with me, if I have to *crawl* back up the creek to turn the water on and grind your poke of corn, and go turn it back off." And Jack went, turned it on, and ground his poke of corn.

And before he left, he said, "Son, you're in a witch gang. *Witch gang.*" And he said, "Here." He said, "Them men didn't help me a-grind my corn and I didn't help them." And he said, "You ground my corn, and young," and said,

"Here's a silver sword. And that's all that'll have any effect on a witch person, is silver."

And so Jack took it and thanked him. And he left on his donkey, and his poke of corn ground.

And Jack went back in to the fireplace and got his fire a-going, and the fire blazed, and it was bright, [whispering] and all at once, it come dark so fast, just darkness shot up. Wasn't natural darkness: just shot up dark. And the darkness put out the firelight shining in the millhouse. And Jack said, "*Goll-l. Bedad.* What a dreary—what a dreary-feeling place I've got in." Then about that time, the darkness left, and he put his ashcakes in to bake, and was a-frying his meat . . . in the steel pan. And he turned his head around up at them twelve windows, and when he looked, they was twelve black cats. The kitten in the little window, as it changed up to the next biggest kitten, up to the next biggest, till it was up to the big window, and then the big cat was in *it*. And so, when you went down from the big cat, it changed a-going around the windows down to the little kitten at the little window again, of twelve. And he said, "*God, bedad, gosh.* Bedad, I've come where they're a lot of black cats." [Laughter]

And so he was a-frying his meat, and that *big cat*, that was in the big square window, sudden, said, "*Sop Doll.*" Then directly, the big cat jumped down out of that window on the mill floor, millhouse floor, *ka-flump*, with its feet, and come up on the left of Jack, and got up about five, four or five feet of him, and said, "*Sop Doll!*" And Jack said, "You sop your doll [laughter] in my grease and meat, and I'll cut it off." And that cat come on up on the left of him, with its right paw, and he had the silver knife a-laying there, and that cat went into the pan with its right paw, and he come down with that silver knife. And when he went [back to cooking his meat], he looked in [the pan], and it was a woman's—lady's hand in it, cut off, with a gold ring on that finger.

And he said, "*Gosh! Bedad*, I thought I cut off a *cat's* paw. And I cut off a lady's hand." Said, "I cut off a cat's paw, I thought." And so he wrapped it up and laid it up on the millhouse fireboard.

The next morning, that fellow up at the big log cabin hollered in at his wife. Said, "*Honey*, get up and get me a little breakfast." Said, "I know that young lad's dead, and I got to get my neighbors; there'll be a grave today."

She says, "I'm sick." His wife said, "I'm sick."

Well, he got him a little breakfast himself, eat it, and went on down the creek, and a-walking. He got about halfway down, and he *heared the mill a-running*. And he said, "*Goll*, that lad's not dead." And he got on down to the millhouse, and he said, "Go cut that watergate off, Jack." Said, "You're the only one that's lived through here to tell what's *here.*"

Well, Jack went and cut the water off to talk to him.

And he said, "What happened here?"

He says, "Them windows was full . . . —up to the biggest one, down to the littlest one—of black cats." And said, "There come a man, that had me grind for him and give me a silver knife," and he said, "I cut a *cat's paw* off, and it's a woman's hand that's in the pan, and I've got it laying on the fireboard."

He said, "I ain't going to—I want to see it." He got it down, and he said, "Gosh! That was my *old lady's* hand." Said, "No wonder she is sick this morning [laughter], about getting me breakfast." Said, "I didn't know that I was married to a witch—lead witch."

And so Jack ground all of the men's, their grinding, their pokes of corn, and when he got done that second day, [the man] took that hand and went up, him and Jack, to his log cabin, and went in the room where his wife was at, and he asked for her right hand. He said, "Honey, I want to see your right hand." She'd stick out her left, out from under the covers.

He said, "I want to see your right hand"—the second time. She stick out her left. And the third time she stuck it out. The fourth time he watched, when she wasn't a-thinking, and he grabbed down under the cover and got her right arm, and her hand was off right there, and he says, "Do you want any of the—" (doctors that used to ride the horse with the medicine . . . bag on the saddle, out of the leather, to carry the medicine in). He said, "Do you want any of them, any of em to come doctor your hand?"

She says, "*No!*"

"Well," he says "is there any other women, women neighbors that you'd like, and the young, young daughters, to come help with your hand?"

And she called over eleven more names of them little kitten cats and all that she was a-training to be a witch. And so, they was in there with that witch talk— *dihdihdihdihdihdihdihdihdih*—like that, and you couldn't understand a word they said. [Laughter]

And, and so they got out, they got out, him and Jack, and them all in there together, of the twelve of all of em, [the ones] she was a-training, the ones next to her, and then the other ones that was nearly good as she was a witch, and on down to the twelve. Through the twelve. And so they got out of there, and them so excited in there, and set the corner of that log cabin afire, and said that beat any popping and cracking you ever heared, with that twelve witches . . . a-burning up.

Well, now *here* is what I was told in my mountain country, and they'd tell us a *lot* of the ghost stories—that was our entertaining—chills up our backbone of a night, and have to walk home. [Laughter] *Goll.* And, and so they'd tell them, of ghost stories and witch stories, and, and so we'd have to walk home. And scared. I'd be by myself. Of the witches. And so I've got Jack in. They burn em up and here's what they told, as I growed up, in the mountains, and all the others. How to be a witch. What to do to become a witch. . . .

Well, what they told, was kill twelve black cats, coal-black cats. Kill twelve coal-black cats, and then go [to] a miry hog pen, where a mother hog had pigs and get you a tit and suck that hog. . . . Nine days. In that pen. Then look at the sun what time you could stand it. And I'll say it'll make *something* out of you. [Laughter] I'll say, that hog'll make something out of you, and killing the twelve cats. That's what I was told, but I never did, I never try it, and I never did see nobody else try it. But that's what they told, and so that's the end of the "Sop Doll."

[Applause]

32. Mule Eggs

RAY HICKS
Watauga County, North Carolina
Recorded at the National
Storytelling Festival,
Jonesborough, Tennessee,
October 3, 1998

Though known primarily for his Jack Tales, Ray was a master of the tall tale as well. The brevity, humor, and relative accessibility of this tale made it an ideal vehicle for opening his hour-long featured performance at the 1998 National Storytelling Festival.

Hi, to all!
[Audience yells back, "Hi."]
. . . I've been sick several days. And I ain't a-feeling that good now, and I didn't think I was going to get to be with you all. And so, I told it in the other tent, but probably there's some here that didn't hear it. And I'm going to tell it over again—of a *mule egg.*

Now back, way back in Model T time (Model T Ford, Henry Ford), my father, Nathan Talbert Hicks, bought a used, used twenty-three model. Now, I

Ray Hicks performing a Jack Tale, 1976 National Storytelling Festival, Jonesboro, Tennessee. (Photo by Mimi Pickering, Appalshop)

was born in nineteen and twenty-two. August the twenty-nine. And so he bought the car used, . . . later on up, where I was . . . some older, you know.

And so they cleared—my grandfather cleared a lot of newground, at that time. Of all the community people. And that's the way they lived. The people lived then about in a *lot* of places, Tennessee, all the states, lived different with their food, a-raising it, [not] as it is in the years later now, with the food shipped in.

And so all of them baked pumpkins. They was a yellow pumpkin, the biggest, that growed about that big. And in the wintertime, if you could keep em from spoiling, . . . and not break that stem off, in the wintertime, when there's a big snow on the ground, you could bake them and put just a little sugar on it before you baked it in the oven of a . . . wood cookstove. And you talk about a flavor. *Gree. . . .* It's a little more watery than a tater pumpkin, but you could boil em down and make pumpkin butter, and it'd give a biscuit a college education when you eat it. [Laughter and applause; Ray laughs too.]

You'd give it a college education, a good baked biscuit. *Goll.* And so, [my father] and Mama, my mother, went to Boone and the other kids, just left me there, it was on a Saturday, . . . to sell them pumpkins. And so, he told me to sell em at a quarter apiece.

And so, there's a little old wagon road come down in to home (and the road that's there now's been fixed, a gravel road, with the state, or Watauga County). And I was there with the pumpkins, and I heared a motor, the way they run pretty rough, vibrating: a Model T Ford did that, and they haven't gotten em fixed too good yet [laughter].

And it's a-going *bum-bum-bum-bum-bum-bum-bum,* coming down that rough, rough road. It come on down, there's a Model T Ford car. A fellow got out of it, and he come down, and he says, "I've heared it advertised in this country somewhere, that they is somebody in this country sells *mule eggs.*"

Said I: "You hit the right place; [laughter] now this is where you get em at. That yellow, yellow mule egg. Yellow, whole mule eggs."

"Well," he said, "what's the price of em. . . ?"

"They's twenty-five cents apiece."

He says, "I've always wanted to raise me a team of mules. To farm with. But, but," he says, "I ain't never lucked out to get a hold of none yet."

"Well, . . . you can get em *now,* if it works out. You can buy you two."

So he bought two, and I asked him, "Now it's hard, you'll have to sit on em anyway, four or five weeks." [Laughter] "To hatch em. And are you married?"

He said, "Yeah, I'm married, to a loving wife."

"Well, you and her can take turn-about a-keeping em warm." [Laughter]

And he took two and went off and cranked his motor up, *bum-bum-bum-bum,* and left. And them weeks come up, and I was a-selling em again, if I could sell any, and here come that same car, making the racket of a motor down the little old road, and he got out, and it was *him.* And he come down, and I could see he maybe wasn't mad, but he wasn't a-feeling good. [Laughter]

And he said, "Son, them mule eggs wasn't no good." [Laughter] He said, he said, "They spoiled on us."

"Well, . . . did you'uns forget and go to sleep and forget and let em get cold?" [Laughter]

Said, "No. We thought we kept em warm, . . . and they *spoiled* on us." Said, "God, they stunk when I cracked em open."

"Oh, you hit two bad ones. [Laughter] But I'll sell you two more for half price. [Laughter] I'll sell you two more for a quarter, twelve cents and a half apiece."

And he took two, went out toward the road. And Mama . . . kept a black-berry briar patch out just from the house there, in a rich holler out from the house, near the apple trees we had, and plum trees, and pear trees, and some grapevines. And he got out there with them two—one under one arm, one under the other'n—and he dropped the right one out, and it rolled (it was a little steep) and it rolled. And the other'n went out from under his left arm. And there happened to be two bunny-rabbits sitting in there in their nest. And [the pumpkins] jumped both of em. Two bunny rabbits was a-setting in that thicket of a briar patch, amid all the grapevines and the apple tree. And here he went at em. And they look a little like a mule, baby mule. [Laughter]

And here he took after one, and the other one'd run out, and he'd take after it. And then maybe they run in the same way, and he run till his breath is gone, and come through with his tongue a-hanging out, kind of panting, *ah-ah-ah-ah*, that way, and he said, "Son," he said, "you can keep them mule eggs." He said, "If they run that dang fast that little," [laughter] said, "I'll never do nothing with em when they get grown, no how."

[Laughter and applause]

2

SARA CLEVELAND

IRISH AMERICAN TALES FROM BRANT LAKE, NEW YORK

Sara Cleveland is known as one of the country's most prolific folksingers, but her storytelling arts have gone largely unacknowledged. In some ways, it is easy to see how one could overlook her stories, for her musical repertoire, embracing more than 400 songs, was so extensive that she could sing for days on end without repeating herself. Among this vast cache of tunes were 189 that she labeled "old traditional songs"; these were passed down largely within her family tradition, and they reflect the family's Irish roots.

Born Sara Jane Creedon on January 1, 1905, in Hartford, New York, she was the youngest daughter of Gerald, an Irishman from Cork who had come to America in 1873. Sara's mother, Sarah Wiggins, was American-born, but both of Sarah's parents had been born in the north of Ireland. Sara Cleveland's songs and stories reflect the fact that the Old Country was never far from the family's thoughts. Banshees, fairies, and legendary Irish heroes inhabit the tales that follow.

Kenneth S. Goldstein, one of the twentieth century's greatest folksong collectors, met Sara in the 1960s, and set about recording all of her "old traditional songs." Goldstein also possessed a keen interest in folk narrative; he recorded all the tales that are presented here. Sara became a frequent visitor to the Goldstein house in Philadelphia; she often spent a week at a time with the Goldsteins, and she won the affection of the entire family. Kenneth Goldstein's daughter, folklorist Diane Goldstein, recalls that Sara was like a "third grandmother." Kenneth's wife, Rochelle, and Sara were both early risers, and they spent many predawn hours exchanging stories in the Goldstein home in Philadelphia. Rochelle recalls Sara as an absolutely straight talker, free, forthright, and unshakable

Sara Cleveland of Brant Lake, New York, teller of stories 33–46. (Photo by Sandy Paton, Folk-Legacy Records)

in her opinions, and as a farm woman who never left the farm behind, even during her frequent visits to the big city.

Rochelle once asked Sara's advice about a lilac bush in the Goldsteins' front yard that would not bloom. Sara immediately volunteered, "It needs cow manure." Arriving for her next visit, Sara opened the trunk to expose a pile of manure, which she then shoveled out of the car and spread around the lilac bush. She had driven her load of untreated and unpackaged waste more than 200 miles to perform this neighborly act. The next year, the lilac bore the most beautiful blooms, Rochelle remembers.

It is difficult to tell how many stories Sara knew and told, but it is certain that the extent of her recorded tale trove is much smaller than her song repertoire. Nevertheless, there is significant diversity in the fourteen tales that she shared

Folklorist Kenneth S. Goldstein in 1993. Goldstein worked closely with Sara Cleveland, and his work as a collector, record producer, teacher, and writer profoundly influenced the preservation and analysis of folk music and folk narrative. (Photo by Robin Hiteshew, © 1993)

with Kenneth Goldstein on the tape that he deposited with the American Folklife Center in 1970. Here, Sara narrates personal experience narratives embedded in childhood memories, family legends based on their American experience, other family legends set in Ireland, Irish belief tales of witches and fairies in which no family members appear, three fictional magic tales ("fairy tales"), and two jokes. The first five of the tales that follow are set in upstate New York. All of the remaining nine are set in Ireland.

A constant theme linking these diverse genres is the supernatural. American dreamers and fortunetellers predict death and kisses, Irish witches and fairies cast spells and steal children, magic tale heroes fly on eagles and talk to corpses. Even in the jokes, the devil moves mountains and lakes.

Many of the tales are marked by a tension between belief and disbelief. There are doubters in Sara's family: her father refuses to believe in the powers of a spiritualist (story 37). Sara herself comes to disbelieve the claim that Finn MacCool threw rocks across the ocean (story 33), and she laughs when confiding that she lacks her grandmother's powers to foretell death through dreams (story 36). Yet, at one time or another, Sara's mother, father, uncle, and grandmother expressed belief in the supernatural occurrences related in the family legends.

Sara rarely as much as hints at what she herself believes. She tells all of the tales in the same calm, measured voice, seldom emphasizing her words or giving any other vocal indications that the events she is describing are remarkable in any way. This proves to be a very effective storytelling style. By letting the plot speak for itself, Sara lets the listeners decide what to believe, what not to believe, and how to feel about the story.

33. Finn MacCool and the Rocks

SARA CLEVELAND
Brant Lake, New York
Recorded by Kenneth S. Goldstein,
1968

This tale illustrates in a very concrete way how much of Ireland Sara's family brought with them across the waters to New York. Finn MacCool (or MacCumhaill, in Irish) is a legendary warrior who has been the subject of tales since at least the seventh century. In Ireland, as in this brief tale, storytellers often attribute strange or seemingly out-of-place rock formations to Finn's feats of strength.

I had a sister, lived way up in the Adirondacks, and we used to take a mountain road up . . . over the mountain to go to my sister's home, and all along that dirt road up over the mountain, was great big rocks. And my mother used to tell me they were the rocks that Finn MacCool in Ireland used to put on his thumb and flip his thumb and send them way over here to this country. And that was how we got all our rocks, was that Finn MacCool flipped them and they came over here. At first I used to believe it, but when I got a little older I kind of doubted it.

34. Black Horses

SARA CLEVELAND
Brant Lake, New York
Recorded by Kenneth S.
Goldstein,
1968

My Muppy really did believe in dreams. She had a lot of dreams she would believe in. Anytime she would have a dream of a black horse, it meant death, and it always seemed to work for her.

Because she told me that one time her first husband, he . . . hadn't been sick, there'd been nothing wrong with him. But the night before, she had dreamed she stood in a window on this country road where they lived, and she could see all these horses and wagons going by and each one was pulled by a black horse. And she was standing in the window looking at them and telling her husband who was in each wagon. But the people in the wagons were all people that were dead, and she'd tell him, "This is Aunt So-and-so, and that's Uncle So-and-so," and that's this and that's that, while he was sitting there in the chair.

So when she woke up the next morning, and after breakfast, she was telling him all about this. There was nothing wrong with him, and he just laughed, you know, about her and her dreams. But that night at eight o'clock, he was dead. He'd had what they call acute indigestion. Course, she always thought afterward it was a heart attack.

But that was the first time she had ever dreamed of these black horses. But from then on in, any time she dreamt of a black horse, well, that was death to her. And if we would come home, she'd always tell us about these dreams she had. And it always seemed to work because anytime she dreamed of black horses, somebody in the family died.

Never worked for me that way. I could dream of all colors, [laughing] nothing ever happened with me. So I guess that gift didn't come on to me.

35. Telling Fortunes with Cards

SARA CLEVELAND
Brant Lake, New York
Recorded by Kenneth S.
Goldstein,
1968

My mother used to tell fortunes with cards. When I was a young kid around there, there was a colored lady named Mrs. Hazzard that lived down the corner near us, and she used to come up and tell my mother's fortune. And she taught my mother how to tell fortunes with the cards. Each card meant something or other, and she would tell Mama's fortune.

I remember when I was a little girl, one night she was sitting there telling my mother's fortune, and said to my mother, "There's a man coming to the house, and he's got a lot of packages in his hand. His arms are full of packages." And we just sat there watching her, you know, and listening, and all at once there was a noise at the door. And somebody opened the door, and here stood my brother. And he had both arms full of groceries. And it was him at the door and he had kicked the door so we would open it. And after that [laughing] I always believed in fortunes.

In the summertime, I used to take our horses—we had some saddle horses—and I used to take them to a children's camp over in Argyle. And this night I came home, and my mother was telling my fortune. And she was going through the cards and she says, "You're going to get a big surprise, because somebody is going to kiss you."

And I said, "Oh, he'll be the one that'll get the surprise." And that was that.

So I went back to camp, and it was the next night after all my work was done, and the kids were all through with their riding lessons. Why, I had taken one horse that had acted up a little that day. He just didn't want to do anything he should do. So I had taken him out to give him a little extra work.

And when I came back from around the lake, I came through the camp, down by the social hall. And there was one man that was part owner of this camp, and his name was [Sonny]. And he lived in New York. But he had had infantile paralysis when he was a child, and was crippled. Although he could walk and get around, he still was crippled up pretty bad.

So, when I came through with Big Red, why, the kids were all out there, petting the horse, and Sonny came along and was petting him, and he said, "Gee, Sara, I'd give anything in the world if I could ride a horse again." He said, "You know, I used to ride when I was young, but I'd give anything to ride a horse."

And I said, "Oh, you could ride him. Anybody could ride him. He's so gentle and good."

And he said, "Do you really think I could?"

And I said, "Why, sure you could." So I got off Big Red and we helped Sonny up on Big Red. And the horse went away with him and did everything Sonny wanted him to, came back, and just as nice as could be. Never did a wrong thing. So Sonny got off the horse, and he was so happy to think that he could ride that horse, he grabbed me quick and kissed me on the cheek.

And I thought, "Well, [laughing] that's one time Ma's fortune came true!" So when I got home the next time, I told Mom, "Well, that fortune came true." And I told her what happened. And you should have heard her laugh!

36. Spiritualism and Fortune Telling

SARA CLEVELAND
Brant Lake, New York
Recorded by Kenneth S. Goldstein,
1968

At the end of this tale, Sara's father expresses disbelief in the power of the spiritualist who has "shared" his own harrowing experience, even though at other times he readily asserts the truth of tales about other supernatural events that he did not experience (for example, in story 38, he swears that his uncle was visited by a banshee).

[M]y mother] used to believe in spiritualism. And there was a lady in Glens Falls when I was a kid, she used to go to. And this woman would go into a trance and tell things. And she had told my mother an *awful* lot of things. But, if my mother wasn't sure of something or other, she would go to this lady, and she would tell her fortune.

So one of my brothers ran away, and my mother didn't know where he was. He was about fourteen or fifteen. And no one knew anything about where he was at. So, the first time my mother went to this woman, someone had told her of her, and my mother went to her because this boy had ran away. So the lady went into a trance, and she told my mother why she had came there, and she said, "It's about a boy, a young boy, and you're worried about him and all." And she said, "You don't have to worry. He is all right. And you're going to get a letter from him. He is working somewhere near a big city. He lives on the outskirts of the city, but he goes from door to door in that city, in some kind of a cart. And he goes from house to house, but you're going to hear from him. He's all right and you're going to hear from him, and he's coming home soon."

So, my mother thanked her and paid her and came home and told what the woman had told her. Now, a few days later she got a letter from my brother. He was working outside of Troy for a dairyman. He was driving a horse and a wagon, delivering milk from door to door, through the city of Troy. And he came home right afterward, and *that* evidently came true.

My mother had gone to this same woman and she was telling my mother's fortune. And all at once she stopped and she threw her hands up and she kept gasping for breath, and like she was brushing something away from her face. And my mother said, "I thought she was having a fit."

And all at once, the woman came out of it and she said, "Oh, that was *awful*. That was *awful*." And she said, "That didn't happen to you."

My mother said, "No, I don't think that ever happened to me."

She said, "Well, that was a terrible thing. It was just as though someone had thrown a whole lot of sand in my face and I couldn't breathe."

And Mama laughed afterwards and came home and was telling about it. So, that was a Tuesday at around ten o'clock, when that happened. So, my father was working up in Corinth, and they were building roads in there, and he was working there. So he came home on Saturday night and he was telling my mother all that happened through the week, how she came near being a widow. He said that they were unloading sand in these big boxcars and they had sort of a trestle that went up, and they'd get the sand—they'd dump the boxcars and the sand would come down where they were making the road.

Well, he had a bunch of Italians working for him, and they were just over from the old country, and they couldn't understand too good. And, of course, my father being Irish, nobody could ever do anything to suit him anyway. So, they got the big boxcar up on the thing and *this* one, the gravel in it *stuck*. It didn't come down when they opened the boxcar. And the Italians were up there, trying to get it loose, but they didn't do it fast enough to suit my father. So he goes up and he takes a crow bar, and he's hitting around the edges of the boxcar, trying to get the gravel loose. So he gets inside the boxcar, on top of the gravel, and he's hitting around there, and just about the time he got that going, the gravel let loose, and down it came, and my father came right along down with it. And he was *buried* underneath it.

But all the Italians grabbed their shovels and they ran like the devil [laughing]. They went down and they dug him out. But he was almost dead when they dug him out. And it was just ten o'clock on a Tuesday morning when that happened.

That woman *knew* when that happened. Well, then Mama told him about the woman telling her all about it. And he said, "Well, it didn't happen to you, but it *did* happen to me. But I still don't believe in fortune tellers." [Laughs]

37. Pull, God Damn You, Pull!

SARA CLEVELAND
Brant Lake, New York
Recorded by Kenneth S.
Goldstein,
1968

My mother had an uncle who lived in West Fort Ann, which is on the east side of Lake George. It was better known [as] Hogtown years ago, the name of the little town. And this uncle lived in a house up on top of the hill. And the house was haunted, they *claimed*. Every time they'd sit down for supper, they'd hear a noise and it was just as though a barrel was rolling down the stairs. And it would hit the stair door, and that stair door would fly open, but there wouldn't be a thing there.

And this room that was haunted, the bedclothes would always be pulled off the bed in the middle of the night. So they had another cousin that lived in what they called the swamp out near Dunham's Basin, and he was a big devil anyway, he was always getting in mischief. So he went up to spend the weekend with them, and he slept in this room with the two boys that night.

So, when they got to bed, he was put to the back of the bed, over near the wall. So in the middle of the night the boy on the front said, "Hang on! It's pulling, it's pulling."

So they hung on, but about the time the bedclothes got pulled off Chris, he said, "Well, it's you. You're the one that's pulling the bedclothes off."

And the boy in the front of the bed said, "All right. You change places with me."

So Chris climbed over and changed places with the cousin on the front. So, pretty soon the bedclothes started being pulled off again. And they all said, "Hang on! Hang on!" So Chris was hanging on for dear life. But pretty soon those bedclothes were being pulled right off him.

So he hung on, and just about the time the bedclothes was coming off him, he said, "Pull, God damn you, pull!" About that time, they tore the bedclothes right straight in two [laughing]. But [whatever it was,] it never did pull the clothes off the bed again in that room.

38. The Kiln Is Burning

SARA CLEVELAND
Brant Lake, New York
Recorded by Kenneth S.
Goldstein,
1968

According to widespread Irish folk traditions still current, the cry of the banshee (Irish for "fairy woman") foretells death. The kiln to which the unseen spirit refers is a large oven for drying grain. Such ovens were commonly attached to the ends of Irish barns or farmhouses, so a burning kiln would spell disaster for the farmer.

This is a story my father used to tell, and he always swore it was true. He said that he had an uncle that lived in Ireland, and one night they were wakened with someone knocking on the door. And when the uncle called out "Who's there?" someone answered, "The kiln is burning!"

So the uncle rushed out and looked over, but there was no fire anywhere to be seen. So he went back to bed.

And after a while, a knock came on the door again, and he went to the door and hollered, "Who's there?"

And somebody hollered again, "The kiln is burning!" But when he opened the door there was nothing around, or nobody, and he couldn't see anything. So he went back to bed that time.

So the third time, the rap came to the door and wakened him and he went to the door and said, "Who's there?" again.

But they just simply said, "The kiln is burning!" So he rushed out again, but there was nothing around anywhere, so he went back to bed.

And in the morning the wife got up and she went to get breakfast, and when she got breakfast, she went to the bed to awaken him, but he was dead. And my father always swore it was a banshee that came there to warn him of death.

39. Baby's Gone

SARA CLEVELAND
Brant Lake, New York
Recorded by Kenneth S.
Goldstein,
1968

Unlike the playful and benevolent fairies that inhabit Disney cartoons, Renaissance fairs, and other expressions of American popular culture, the fairies of Irish tradition often behave in ways threatening to humans. One of their most frequent harmful acts is to steal human infants and replace them with "changelings," beings that possess the appearance, but not the nature, of mortals.

My mother used to tell us that her father would tell them a story about something that happened in Ireland. He said one night his mother and father were in the bed asleep and the mother woke up suddenly and reached over where the baby should be lying, and the baby was gone.

So she called to her husband, "Quick! Quick! The baby's gone!" So they jumped out of bed and lit a candle and they found the baby way over by the door. So they ran over, and picked the baby up and brought her over to the bed and looked her over and she was all right except she had a red mark on her side. And they always said that was where the fairies had grabbed her when they pulled her over to the door. And if they hadn't found her just then, that the fairies would have stolen her and they never would have seen her again. But she had that mark until the day she died.

40. The Witch and the Donkey

SARA CLEVELAND
Brant Lake, New York
Recorded by Kenneth S.
Goldstein,
1968

This haunting legend, set in Ireland, begins in a rather distant world and ends on a more personal note. Sara had never been to Ireland when she told this tale. Nevertheless, she inserts herself into the story as she is concluding it by saying that she never went back to look for the witch. This closing flourish adds power and immediacy to Sara's tale.

There was a farmer in Ireland who took his horse and cart and was going to market with a big load of green goods and stuff he had from his farm. And the old horse couldn't pull very good. He was pretty old, and there was a big load on the wagon, so the farmer walked along beside the horse because he felt so sorry for him.

So while he's going down the road he comes around a bend in the road, and he sees an old woman standing by the side of the road. So when he gets up to the old woman, she asks him if he would give her a ride into market. Well, the farmer said, "I'm awfully sorry, Mother, but my horse has such a load on the wagon he can hardly pull it. And I have to walk myself."

Well, the old woman was pretty angry, and she said to him, "Well, you won't get very far anyway." So they go on down the road. And she went toward an old shack over in the woods. So they come around a bend, and they come to a bridge across a little creek. And here the horse stops, he won't go any further. So the farmer tries coaxing him and pulling on him, but no avail. He just won't go across that bridge.

So the farmer finally gets mad and he gets a switch and he starts beating the horse, but *still* he won't move. So finally he gets real mad and he grabs a big club and he starts beating the horse real hard. And in doing so he knocked out one of the horse's eyes. Well, then he felt so bad to think he had hurt this horse that he dropped the club.

And all at once he remembered about the old woman telling him, "Well, you won't get very far anyway." So he goes back down the road to where he's seen her go back to this little shack in the woods. And he goes over to the shack and he raps on the door, but no one comes to the door. So he opens the door and he walks in. And over in the corner he sees a cot with some one on it all covered up, head and all. So he goes over to the cot and he pulls the covers down and here's the old woman lying on the cot. And she's all black and blue and bruised, and she has one eye out.

So he leaves the shack and he goes back to his horse and that time when he took a hold of the horse he walked right across the bridge and they went on to market.

So then next morning when he got up and went out to his horse, the horse had a new eye. He'd grown a new eye overnight. Far as the old woman's concerned, I don't know, because I never went back to find out whether she did or not.

41. The Lady and the Fairy

SARA CLEVELAND
Brant Lake, New York
Recorded by Kenneth S.
Goldstein,
1968

In this tale, Sara sides with a fairy that has brought harm upon a woman. In so doing, she is expressing the conviction, widespread in Ireland, that it is best not to meddle with the fairies unless absolutely necessary.

There was a lady in Ireland who went to the green grocer's to get some food. And while she was there she was walking around looking over the greens to see what she wanted. And all at once she noticed a little man with a red cap on his head and he had a basket on his arm. And he would go along and he'd take a little of this, put in the basket, and take a little of that and put it in the basket.

And she watched him for a while, and pretty soon she patted him on the head, and he squinted up at her and she said, "Little man, don't you know that's stealing?"

And he said to her, "Which eye do you see me with?"

And she said, "Why this one," pointing to her right eye.

And he went *puff* and blew her eye right out. Well, that should have taught her a lesson, because it wasn't her greens he was stealing, and I bet after that she minded her own business.

42. Little Red Night Cap

SARA CLEVELAND
Brant Lake, New York
Recorded by Kenneth S.
Goldstein,
1968

This märchen, or wonder tale, is Sara's longest recorded narrative, passed down to her from her mother, who was born in 1840. Sara's use of understated language adds considerable effect to her performance. Even when narrating extremely cruel acts (as when the old biddy jumps up and down joyfully after setting fire to her stepsons' home) or magical happenings (as when the blackthorn stick miraculously beats on Sean's enemies), Sara's voice maintains a steady, matter-of-fact tone. It may be significant that the villain of this tale resembles the vengeful fairy of "The Lady and the Fairy" (story 41). Both are small men who wear red caps.

There was a man who lived in Ireland and he had three sons. His wife died and he married another woman who was an old biddy. She hated the three boys and did everything she could to make life miserable for em. And she was always trying to get the old man to chase em away from home. But he wouldn't agree to that.

But one night she got him real drunk. She kept feeding him drinks until he was so drunk he finally agreed he'd do anything to shut her up.

So in the meantime the youngest son happened to be going by the window and he heard them talking and listened. So he went out to the little shack in back where they stayed, and he told the brothers that the woman wanted to get rid of them. She had told the old man that when . . . the boys got to sleep they would burn the shack down and that time they'd get rid of them for once and for all. So the boys decided they'd go out in the woods and watch. They didn't think the old man would agree to something like that, but they thought they'd be on the safe side and stay in the woods.

So they took what little food they had and they went out in the woods. And pretty soon out came the old woman. The old man, he'd got so drunk he passed out so she had to do the dirty work herself. So she set fire to the building and stood there watching it burn and was very happy, jumping up and down.

So, the boys felt pretty bad, to think their father would do something like that to them. And they decided they'd better go somewhere else, so they took off down the road. They hadn't gone down the road too far when they saw an old beggar along beside the road, and he asked them for some food.

Well, the two older ones told him that they didn't have only enough food for themselves and they couldn't give him any. But the youngest son, he felt sorry for the old beggar, so he gave him a part of what he had. And he told his brothers, "He's older than I am and he needs it a lot worse than I do." Well, the two older brothers didn't agree. They told him he was foolish to give away his food. They didn't have hardly any anyway. When he got hungry he could go without, if he was fool enough to give his food away. But Sean was the youngest boy's name, and he gave him the food anyway. And the two brothers went down the road.

So the old beggar gave Sean a blackthorn stick, and he told him it was a magic stick: that anytime he got in trouble, to say to the stick, "Arrogowan," and the stick would get up and fight for him. So Sean took the stick and thanked him and started down the road after his brothers. They looked back and they saw him coming, and one said to the other, "There, look at the poor fool. He's so weak now he can't stand up. He has to get a stick to help him walk and yet he'll give away his food." So they kept talking to him and making fun of him when he got up with them, but he never told him the black stick was supposed to be magic, and they kept on going.

So pretty soon they came to a town where everybody was weeping and crying and carrying on, and when they asked what was wrong, the people told them that the king's daughter had been stolen by Little Red Night Cap and if anyone could get her back the king would give them a big bunch of gold and the daughter for a bride.

Well, the two older boys thought the gold sounded pretty good but Sean, he thought, well, he wouldn't mind having a wife. So they decided that they would go down looking for the girl.

So the king gave them some food and he gave em a man to show em where Little Red Night Cap lived. So they went down the road, and by the time they got to where this cave was, with a big hole that went down in the ground, the man pointed out the cave to them and then he left. He didn't want no part of Little Red Night Cap.

Well, they go up to the cave, and the oldest brother, Pat, said that he was the oldest, that he would go down the hole first. So they took the food out of the basket and put a rope on the basket and they lowered him down this hole into the bottom of the cave. So he hadn't anymore than got down there and he decided he'd eat. So he's got his food all ready to eat and he just about sat down to eat when out popped a little man with a red cap on his head. And he said he wanted something to eat. Well, Pat told him he only had food enough for himself. So therefore the little man grabbed a club and started beating *him* up. And he beat him until Pat ran over to where the basket was and he tugged on the rope and the other brothers hauled him up. And he told them he'd had enough of that, *he* wasn't going down again.

So the next time, it was the second son's turn. His name was Dennis. So Dennis got in the basket and they lowered him down the hole with his food. So he got the food ready to eat and while he was starting to eat out popped the little man with the red cap on his head again. So he said he wanted some food. Well, he told him he only had enough to eat for himself. He didn't have any to give away. So the Little Red Night Cap picked up the club again and he started beating him up. So Dennis ran over to the basket and climbed in and tugged on the rope, and they pulled him up out of the hole, and *he* wouldn't go back.

So the third time it was Sean's turn. So Sean got in the basket with his food and they lowered him down the hole. So he hadn't any more than got ready to eat when in popped Little Red Night Cap again. And he said he wanted some food. So Sean said, "Well, there it is. Help yourself."

And he said, "No, I want you to wait on me."

And Sean said, "If you're hungry enough, you'll help yourself."

So Little Red Night Cap grabbed the club and started for Sean, but Sean had taken his blackthorn stick with him down the hole so he said to the stick, "Arragowan." So the stick up and he starts beating Little Red Night Cap. And it beat him so hard that Little Red Night Cap finally told him if he'd make the stick stop whipping him up, beating him all up like he was, he'd give him the king's daughter and all his gold and jewels also. So Sean finally let the stick give him a few more whacks and he told him to stop.

So he got the king's daughter and he got all the jewels and all the gold and then Little Red Night Cap took off. So Sean went over to where the basket was and he put all the gold and the jewels in the basket and he tugged on the rope and the two brothers hauled it up. So they sent the basket back down again, and then Sean put the girl in it and tugged on the rope and sent her up. So that time before the basket came down it took a little longer and Sean thought that was kind of funny. So when the basket came down that time, instead of getting into the basket himself, he took a big rock and put it in the basket and tugged on the rope and they pulled the basket back up. So they got it up just about halfway, and they cut the rope and down come basket, rock, and all.

So Sean said to himself, "Well, that's nice. That's a nice thing to do. Now how am I supposed to get out of here? What'll I do down here?" And he paces around and he's doing a lot of thinking. So, while, in the meantime, while he's doing all this worrying, down this big hole comes a great big bird.

And Sean said to the bird, "If you will fly me out of here on your back, I will give you all the food I have." Well, the bird was pretty weak but Sean gave him some food, and he got stronger, and Sean climbed on his back with a basket of food. And they started up the hole. Well, they got up quite a ways and Sean kept reaching around putting a piece of meat into the bird's mouth. And they almost got out, but just before they got to the end of it, they ran out of food. And the bird was getting weaker. So Sean took his knife and reached back, cut a slice off his backside, and reached around and stuck it in the bird's face. So that way they got out of the hole.

So Sean took his blackthorn stick and he started back towards the king's town where he lived, and the more he walked the madder he got. And he kept thinking all he'd do to those two brothers if he ever did catch up with them. So he finally came into the town and he was pretty mad by that time too, so the two brothers were there, strutting around and telling everyone how brave they were and of all the wonderful things they'd done, and how they had gotten rid of old Red Night Cap, and how they rescued the girl. And the girl, all she'd do was cry, and she wouldn't say she'd marry either one of them. She wouldn't pick between the two of them. So, all at once in the midst of their bragging, they look up and there's their brother Sean. So they said to him, "How did *you* get out?"

And Sean said, "I flew out. And you two had better start flying right now." So he said to the stick, "Arragowan," and the stick took right off after them. So the girl came over to Sean and said to her father, "This is the man that saved me, and I won't marry anyone else." So the king gave the girl to Sean and they were married.

And then Sean got thinking about how his father was, so he decided he better go home and see how the father was making out. So he went home, and the old man was feeling terribly bad to think that he had did such a thing. And the old woman had died in the meantime, so Sean took the father and the girl and went back to the king's palace, and the last I knew they were still there. And as for the brothers: don't know whether they ever did get away from that stick. The last I heard they were *still* running.

43. Old Graybeard

SARA CLEVELAND
Brant Lake, New York
Recorded by Kenneth S.
Goldstein,
1968

This tale, very similar in plot to "Little Red Night Cap" (story 42), represents one of the most popular tale types found in Ireland as well as in the English-Scottish-Irish traditions of the Appalachians. It is a close cousin to Kentuckian Jane Muncy Fugate's "Old Greasybeard" (story 79).

There was a woman who lived in Ireland and had three sons. She had very little money to buy food with, and the boys decided they would get out in the world and seek their fortune and see if they couldn't help her.

Well, much as she hated to see them go, she gave them her blessing and most of the food she had and they started out after bidding her goodbye.

They felt pretty bad as they went down the road, but after a while they came to a town where the people even felt worse. And when they asked some of the people what was the trouble, they said that Old Graybeard had stolen the King's daughter. And no one was able to get her back. But the one that could get her back, the King would give a lot of gold to, and he could also have the daughter for his bride. Well, the boys thought that might be a good way to get something, so they told the King if he would give them some food, they would go and see if they couldn't find the girl.

So the King told em they could have all the food they wanted. So the next morning they took the food and they started down the road. Pretty soon they came to a place where there was a big fair going on. And they stopped to see what was going on at the fair. There was a contest being held between three men. One was Mountain Shover, one was Tree Twister, and one was Rock Crusher. And the contest was to see who was the strongest man. So the boys decided they'd stop and see how the contest made out.

So Mountain Shover was the first one that came out to do his part in the contest. So he put his back against a big mountain and he shoved it right out of the way. So then Tree Twister came out, and he took hold of the big tree and he twisted it right out of the ground. So then it was Rock Crusher's turn. So he picked up a great big stone, and he crumbled it up in his fingers, and made sand out of it. So the judges couldn't decide who was the best, so they thought the best thing to do was divide the prize among the three of them, which they did.

So the boys thought they were pretty good men, so they went over and asked the men if they would go along with them. So the three men said, well, they'd go along with them as far as they were going. Maybe they could help them.

So they all started out. And it was a good thing the men went with the boys, because they hadn't gone too far till they came to a big mountain. And it was so high they couldn't get over it, and it was so big they couldn't get around it. So Mountain Shover put his back against the mountain and he shoved it right out of the way. So then they went on. And the first road they came to after that, Mountain Shover left them after the boys thanked him.

So they went on little further and pretty soon they came to a forest that was full of great big trees. And they were so thick that they couldn't get through them. So, Tree Twister said, "Well, I think I can handle this." So, he goes over where the trees were and he takes tree by tree and he twists them right out of the ground—and made a path right through for the boys. So when they got on to the next road, he went home and left them after the boys thanked him.

So they kept on going and pretty soon they got to where there was a place with great big rocks. The place had rocks all over, and they couldn't get through. So Rock Crusher said, "Well, I think I can fix this." So he takes the rocks one by one and he crumbles em up in his hands and makes sand out of them. So the boys walked right through on the nice path he made them. So they went on a ways further, and then they came to the road where he had to leave them. So he wished them luck, and they thanked him for all his help and they went on.

Well, they were getting lonesome by that time, after everybody had gone, so first thing they saw was a little shack over in the woods. So they decided they'd go over there and spend the night. So the oldest brother said he'd get supper for them and the other two boys could go out and get some wood for to have for the next day. So he starts getting the supper and he gets the supper all ready, and then he goes to the door to see if the brothers was coming with the wood. But while he was looking out the door for the brothers, a little old man with a gray beard popped into the room and he grabbed the supper and *he left*. So, when the boys came back with the wood and looked around there was no supper and they never did know what happened to it. But they all went to bed hungry that night.

So the next day the other brother, the second brother, said he would get the supper, and the other two could go get wood. So he got supper all ready, and while his back was turned, in popped the same little man with a gray beard and he stole the supper and then he left. So when the brothers come back, they all three of them went hungry that night too.

So the third night the youngest brother, he decided he'd get supper. So when he had supper all ready, in came the little man. And he was all set to grab the supper, but the boy grabbed him first and started beating him up. So after he'd beat him awhile, the little man told him if he'd only let him go and stop beating him, he'd give him the King's daughter. So after giving him a few more licks, the boy let him go.

And he took him out to where he had the girl hidden and gave her to the boy and then he took off as fast as his short legs could carry him. So when the other two brothers came back with the wood, they not only had supper but the girl was there too.

So they eat the supper and then the next morning all four of them took off and started back for the King's palace. And when they got back there, everybody was so happy to see the girl and the boys back that they had a big party for them. So then the girl and the youngest brother got married. And the two older brothers went back to get the mother and bring her back to where the rest of them were. And they all lived happily *ever* after and the last I knew, they were still there.

44. Shiver and Shake

SARA CLEVELAND
Brant Lake, New York
Recorded by Kenneth S. Goldstein,
1968

There was a woman lived in Ireland, and she had one son. And he wasn't very bright, but he was very brave. What he lacked in brains he had in brawn, because he *wasn't* afraid of anything. And when anyone would get frightened and say how they shivered and shook, he didn't know what they were talking about. And he *couldn't* shiver and shake. No matter what happened, he never could shiver and shake.

Well the king had a room in his castle. It was haunted. But if anyone could spend three nights in that room, the spell would be broken. And the king said if he could get someone that would break that spell, he would give them the daughter for a bride and he would also give them a lot of money.

So the mother decided, well, maybe Tim was brave enough to do that. So the king came to Tim and asked him if he would try it, and Tim said sure, he wasn't afraid of anything. So they went to the king's castle and they put Tim up in this room that was haunted and gave him some food.

So, Tim sits down to the table to eat. He could always eat. And while he was eating, the door rolled open and in rolled a coffin. And Tim said to himself, "I wonder what's in that box?" So he gets up and looks in the box and here's a skeleton. So Tim looks him over, and he said, "Gee, that guy looks hungry. Maybe he could eat some food too." So he takes the skeleton out of the box and he puts him in a chair and tries feeding him. Well, the skeleton didn't seem to be hungry, and he wouldn't eat. So that made Tim mad. He grabbed the skeleton and he threw him back in the box and he wheeled that out the door. And then he went back and ate his supper and went to bed.

So when he went down in the morning, they asked him, "What happened?"

And he told them what happened, and they said, "Well, weren't you scared? Didn't you shiver and shake?"

He said, "No, I didn't shiver and shake." So that was one night.

Well, the next night, he takes his food and he goes up to the room to see what he could do that night. And he sits down to the table to eat the food and in [rolls] the coffin again. So Tim goes over and looks at it. And he thought, "Well, Gee, maybe that guy is lonesome and wants somebody to talk to."

So, he takes the corpse out of the coffin again and he sits him in a chair and tries talking to him. Well, he talks till he's black in the face but the skeleton doesn't say a word back. So, Tim gets mad again and he throws him back in the coffin and he pushes it out the door, and that was that. So he went to bed.

Well, the next morning he gets up and goes downstairs and they want to know what happened that night, so he told them all that happened, and they said, "Well, weren't you scared? Didn't you shiver and shake?"

And he said, "No, I didn't shiver and shake." Well, that was two nights. He only had one more night.

So the third night he goes to the room again and he sits down and starts eating, and in rolls the same coffin with the same skeleton. So, Tim looks him over that time, and he thinks, "Well now, maybe that poor guy's cold." So he takes the skeleton out of the coffin and he puts him in bed with him and tries to warm him up. But skeletons don't warm up very good, so Tim gets him out of the bed and throws him back into the coffin and wheels him out the door. So that was the third night, and the *spell* was broken.

So when he went down that morning, they asked him what happened, and he told them. And they said, "And you didn't shiver and shake?"

He said, "No, I didn't shiver and shake."

But the spell was broken, so everything was fine.

So Tim and the king's daughter got married. And everything went on fine for a while. Only thing was she could never get him out of bed in the morning. She'd call and call and try to get him up, but that just didn't work. He wouldn't get up.

So one morning, she got good and mad, and she went out to the well in the yard, and she got a big pail of ice cold water out of that well. And she went in and she threw it on Tim and the bed, and he got out of bed in a hurry and you know what? *That time* he shivered and shook!

45. Rob Haww

SARA CLEVELAND
Brant Lake, New York
Recorded by Kenneth S.
Goldstein,
1968

There was a man in Ireland who was named Rob Haww, and he had a very big appetite. No matter how much he ate, he never seemed to get filled up. And every place he'd go, he'd eat everybody out of house and home.

So one day two men had an argument about it and said that they thought he could eat a whole cow. Well, one man said no one could eat a whole cow. So they made a bet that the one that lost the contest—or the one that lost to the other one—would *pay* for the cow. So, they got hold of Rob, and sure enough, he'd eat the cow, or he'd try anything once.

So they got to the place where the contest was to be held, and they cooked the cow and they thought it would be easier to feed it to him one piece at a time. So they brought it in a piece at a time and they gave it to him and he ate.

So pretty soon it just disappeared. So the one that lost said, "Well, I'll pay for that." So they went to Rob and told him the contest was over and he could go home.

And Rob said, "Why, I can't go home yet! I've got a whole cow to eat yet!"

46. One Thing the Devil Can't Do

SARA CLEVELAND
Brant Lake, New York
Recorded by Kenneth S.
Goldstein,
1968

There were three men in Ireland and they were walking down a country road. One was an Englishman, one was a Scotsman, and one was an Irishman. And as they were walking down the road, out of the bushes popped the devil. And he said to them, "Now I've got you! I'm going to whip you way to Hell."

Well the three men didn't want to go to Hell. So they tried to talk the devil out of it. Well, finally he said if they could tell him one thing he couldn't do in a minute, that he'd let them stay on earth.

So the Englishman, it was his turn first. And he looked over and he saw a great big mountain. So he said to the devil, "Make that mountain disappear in a minute." So the devil goes *whoosh*, and away went the mountain. And the devil goes *whoosh*, and away went the Englishman.

So then it was the Scotsman's turn. So he looked all around, and he saw a big lake over there. So he said to the devil, "Make that lake disappear in a minute." So the devil goes *whoosh*, and away went the lake. And the devil goes *whoosh*, and away went the Scotsman.

So then it was Pat's turn. So Pat looked all around, and all at once he looked at the devil and he let a big fart. And he said to the devil, "Catch that, paint it green and bottle it, all in a minute." And the devil could not do it. And you know, he had to let Pat go. And I'm darned glad there's one thing that the devil can't do.

3

J.D. SUGGS
ITINERANT MASTER

"I hear a story once and I never forget it," said J.D. Suggs, a remarkable African American narrator not known for boasting. We have every reason to take this modest man at his word, because Richard M. Dorson recorded 175 tales from Suggs in eight visits to his home.

J.D. Suggs, said Dorson, "proved the best storyteller I ever met." These words, coming from one of the country's most prolific fieldworkers, are rich praise indeed. Dorson had heard thousands of tales from an extraordinarily diverse and numerous group of oral artists. He recorded Ojibwe narrators performing Native American myths, French Americans passing on *loup-garou* (werewolf) legends, Maine fishermen crafting tall tales. He listened to hundreds of African American narrators. Sixty-nine accomplished storytellers contributed to *Negro Folktales in Michigan*, the first of Dorson's books to feature Suggs's tales. Yet, in Dorson's opinion, Suggs's extraordinary verbal talents overshadowed the arts of all the others.

When Dorson met Suggs in Calvin, Michigan, in March 1952, the storyteller had accumulated lifetimes' worth of experience. Born in Kosciusko, Mississippi, in 1887, Suggs was the son of country farmers. At the same time that he learned farmwork, he was absorbing a rich repertoire of locally told African American folktales. His family and neighbors exchanged numerous animal tales (including many featuring the exploits of the celebrated Brer Rabbit); jokes about John and Old Master (which portrayed the relationships between black and white, slave and master, sharecropper and landowner, with both trenchant humor and acute social commentary); belief tales about hoodoo and witches; and stories, some devout, some playfully irreverent, about God, the devil, and religion.

Suggs left the farm to become a prison guard, and began a dizzying series of

J.D. Suggs entertaining Richard Dorson, Calvin, Michigan, 1952. Watching from the window inside the Suggs home are Suggs's children Beatrice, Toka, and Wink. (Photo by George T. Kolehmainen of Gwinn, Michigan)

wanderings that eventually took him to thirty-nine states as well as overseas. His verbal, singing, and dancing talents earned him a role in the Rabbit Foot Minstrel Show, which toured not only in the South but also to places as distant as North Dakota. His athletic skills made him a player in the Sliding Delta professional baseball team. His patriotism led him to enlist in the army during World War I, and his unit was deployed in France. A series of other jobs—short-order cook, Mississippi River boatman, railroad brakeman—brought Suggs to Chicago, where he worked with his landlord brother renting apartments. In 1950, he left the big city to return to rural life. He settled in Calvin, Michigan, one of the rare northern farming towns in which blacks outnumbered whites. African Americans had been migrating to Calvin since before the Civil War, and when Suggs arrived, there were established social and cultural differences between the northern blacks and the more recent arrivals from the South. The northerners were more staid, businesslike, and prosperous; the southerners, though poorer, were more animated and more given to displays of traditional artistry: storytelling, singing, dance.

Not even his numerous extraordinary skills could gain Suggs financial security. He was one of the poorest of Calvin's poor southerners. He, his wife, and their ten children lived from hand to mouth shortly after moving to Michigan. By the time Dorson came to Calvin, looking for accomplished African American narrators, the family had found a house to live in, but, in the words of the neighbor who guided Dorson to their home, "they can use any help you give them."

At their first meeting, Suggs performed joyously for Dorson, and Dorson proved an avid listener: "We swapped yarns for two hours straight." They established a close and intense relationship based on their mutual love of story: "For whole days," wrote Dorson, "from morning till midnight, he dictated tales to me, or recited them into the tape recorder, faultlessly and with great gusto."

With this note, Dorson marks a significant difference between him and the other great American collectors of his era. Herbert Halpert, Alan Lomax, and other folklorists who preceded Dorson into the field relied heavily upon (often primitive) sound equipment to record more stories than they ever transcribed or published. Dorson, however, relied principally upon dictation and made relatively few sound recordings of his informants. Of the "nearly two hundred tales" that J.D. Suggs performed for him, only twenty-five can be found on the tapes that Dorson deposited with the American Folklife Center. Versions of all but one of these tales appear in written form in Dorson's books, but the Library of Congress taped performances differ significantly from those that appear in the books. The majority of the tales transcribed below have never previously appeared in print, and some of them differ so radically from the earlier published versions that they tell us a great deal about the protean flexibility of Suggs's art.

The AFC tapes demonstrate that Suggs was every bit the master performer that Dorson had claimed he was. He is an animated speaker who takes so much delight in telling his tales that his joy automatically becomes the listener's, too: "Whatever he described, he etched fully with myriad details and hues. He did not merely tell the story but acted it out and dressed it up with sounds, gestures, and tumbling words."

These recorded performances also intimate a bond of mutual respect, even affection between the African American master storyteller and the European American master academic. Dorson addresses the artist, "Mr. Suggs," and usually adds an admiring comment when Suggs has finished a tale. Suggs expresses glee when Dorson asks for certain favorite tales. The two men join together in evaluating the characters and analyzing the stories. When Suggs describes his major characters—Brother Rabbit, Brother Bear, and the slave Efan—he speaks as if they were living, breathing people; when Dorson responds, he describes the characters in much the same way.

The bond between Suggs and Dorson extended beyond the boundaries of their story-swapping sessions. Dorson sent Suggs a photo of the two men together, and Suggs carried the picture with him everywhere. In 1956, upon hearing that his favorite storyteller had recently passed away, Dorson wrote, "I learn with heartache of the death of Suggs." Twelve years later, Dorson dedicated his great collection, *American Negro Folktales*, "to the memory of James Douglas Suggs."

Nearly fifty years after Suggs's death and more than two decades after Dorson's, the children of the master storyteller continue to celebrate the friendship of the two men as a model of racial harmony. Suggs's love of storytelling and Dorson's skill in documentation inspired Suggs's daughter Martha Ann Suggs Spencer to collect and publish a number of family stories centered on black-white relationships: *Suggs Black Backtracks* (1995) presents the stories of twenty Suggs family members as well as Martha's recollections of her father. In 1994 Martha and her sister Toka Suggs Saunders established the Suggs Freedom Festival, which honors the family and its role in combating slavery and racism. They remember their father as a prophet who foresaw a world based on mutual love and understanding, and they view his relationship with Dorson as symbolic of that better life to come. Martha chose "Black and White Coming Together" as the motto of the Suggs Freedom Festival. The phrase is based on a visionary moment, years before Dorson's first visit, in which her father saw the afflictions of the past giving way to the rewards of the future. "One day when we were fishing," Martha writes in *Suggs Black Backtracks*, "my father told me things about his life as a young boy growing up in the Mississippi Delta. Slavery, black and white, was always the main subject. That particular day, we had to rush home, half-running. A storm was coming, and there was a hill we had to climb. Once up on the top of this hill, my father said, 'Look up at those clouds.' He pointed to the east, then to the west. He said, 'Those clouds are coming together. Sure as those clouds are coming together, black and white will come together. I might not live that long to see it. But remember what I tell you.' His words came true for me on June 3, 1994, at the Suggs Historical Site, which was established on that day, in Vandalia, Michigan, home of the Underground Railroad."

Today, the James Suggs Underground Railroad Museum stands near the spot where Suggs saw the clouds converge. Outside the museum stand two life-size silhouettes cut from metal: on the left, painted white, is the image of Richard

James Suggs Underground Railroad Museum and Historical Site, Vandalia, Michigan. Martha Ann Suggs Spencer (left) and Toka Suggs Saunders stand between two metal figures representing Richard Dorson (left) and J.D. Suggs. The sign reads, in part, "The last conversation of two friends, Professor Richard Dorson and James Suggs. Little did they know that they would never see each other again. Sculpture created from history book entitled Negro Folktales from Michigan.*" (Photo by Carl Lindahl)*

Dorson; on the right, painted black, the shape of James Douglas Suggs. The two metal men face each other, frozen in the same postures that they assume in the photo that Suggs carried in his pocket until the day he died.

Martha Suggs Spencer and Toka Suggs Saunders have read, repeatedly and carefully, the thousands of words that Dorson wrote about their father. They have very few corrections to offer. Most pointedly, they wish readers to know that the Suggs family never lived in a chicken shed, though one of their neighbors had told Dorson as much and Dorson had repeated the error in *Negro Folktales in Michigan* (1956). The overwhelming sentiment of the Suggs family toward Dorson is one of gratitude and respect. "Dorson kept our father alive for us; he saved those stories from dying, and that was a gift to everybody," said Martha. To underline her points, she produced a photocopy of her favorite passage from Dorson, written shortly after Suggs's death: "Professor Arthur Palmer Hudson . . . said that Suggs and William Faulkner should meet each other as the two greatest storytellers of northern Mississippi. It is consoling to know that the spirit and salt and kindly humor of Suggs will not completely vanish with his death."

47. How I Learned My Tales

J.D. SUGGS
Kosciusko, Mississippi, and
Calvin, Michigan
Recorded by Richard M. Dorson,
ca. 1952

When Dorson found J.D. Suggs in Michigan, the master narrator was in the process of re-creating the intimate rural lifestyle that had characterized his own childhood. Although Suggs had traveled to Europe as a soldier, to the American West as a baseball player, and through wide swaths of the country as a railroad employee, he wanted his children to experience the world much as he had as a boy in Mississippi when his father had first told him folktales.

Suggs's fourth child, Martha Suggs Spencer, wishes to preface her father's memories of childhood with her own childhood memories of her father, beginning with the family's travels from Bono, Arkansas (where Martha was born), to Michigan and focusing on Suggs's relationship with his children.

Martha was 4 years old in the spring of 1945, when the Suggses left Arkansas in search of a better life, particularly a place where the children could attend school, as there was no school available to them in Bono. At the train station, writes Martha, there was "hugging, kissing, crying, many tears. I cried because others were crying. This was the first time I saw my parents cry. Not known what the future hold for the poor Suggs family. I knew one thing for sure: father knew best.

"Arriving in Chicago, getting off the train, looking around, I was so thrilled: tall buildings, black and white people. In Arkansas, I'd seen only white people; we were the only black family where we lived.

"I began to yell out, 'Look at Superman!' (In Arkansas I used to listen to Superman on the radio.) My father said, 'That's not Superman; that's a nun.' It was still Superman to me.

"Our family stayed a short time in Chicago. My father did not like the fast life in the city. Finally, we were on our way to Michigan. What a beautiful country: in Arkansas I'd seen only goats and hogs, but here were large cornfields, peas, tomatoes. I asked my father if I could eat a Michigan tomato: they looked larger and redder than the ones in Arkansas. With a big smile he said yes.

"My father found a job in South Bend, Indiana, working construction. He helped build an addition to Memorial Hospital, Notre Dame University.

"A short time later, another child was born. My father named him Allen Dale. He was the cutest baby I had ever seen. I asked my mother if I could take care of him. She said yes. That is what I did. It was a great pleasure to take care of him. But then things went badly for the family. Doc Newsome came out to our home. Looking the baby over, I heard him speaking softly to my father. He said the baby would not live long. My father began to pray. As he prayed, I cried. I ran outside, looking into the sky. I tried repeating the things my dad was saying. Allen died that cold night, December 10, 1949. I did not understand about death. At Allen's funeral I was so small my father had to pick me up, so I could get the last look at Allen. He laid there so relaxed and calm. I ask my father would he even come back home. My father said, 'We will talk about it later.'

"Then one day I remember so well, there was a knock at the door. My father open the door. There stood a white man. He said his name was Richard Dorson and he was a professor Dorson. He was collecting stories. He asked my father if he knew any old folktales. My father begin to pop stories out like popcorn. He said, 'I know a million. I do not think that you can record all I know.' For the next two years, my father and Dorson recorded stories.

"I remember one late evening, Dorson and my father got back late from recording. My mother yell out to Dorson, 'Hey, Mister.' My father hurried her back into the house. The next recording session, my father told Dorson, people had told my mother that the two were not recording; they were chasing women.

"Late in 1953 our family moved to Niles, Michigan. A short time in Niles, my father began to get sick. I become closer to my father. Many of times he would tell me to go and get Roosevelt Washington to take him to Memorial Hospital. Coming home for the last time, my father call the family together and told them about his cancer. He said that he would not live much longer. He had this encounter with a spirit. One early morning before day, this black woman appeared to him in the hospital. She said, 'Get yourself ready. It is time to go.' My father, he got up and went to the restroom. He was washing up. He wanted to be clean going home. This white woman came into the room. She said, 'Mr. Suggs, why are you out of bed?' He said, 'This black woman that was in here told me to get up. It was time to go.' He said, 'I want to be clean going home.' This white woman's face turned a reddish color. She said, 'There are no black women working on this floor.'

"My father said this was a token of death.

"My mother did not read or write. I was the oldest at home so I was in charge of my father's funeral. At 14 years old I knew I had to grow up fast. I knew I had a job to do for the family.

"June 19, 1955: this day happened to be a Sunday. Going to the hospital to see my father that day, I had a funny feeling. As the family was riding toward the Cass County infirmary I put my head down. I cried softly.

"At the hospital the family gathered around my father's bed. I had to squeeze my way to my father's bedside. I had his first grandchild in my arms: Rosemary Gilliam. I placed the baby on the bed beside my father. I ask him how he felt. He had his hand on the baby. He smiled, dropped his hand. Then he was gone.

"I grab the baby and ran outside. I put the baby on the ground. I laid beside her. I cried. The baby was crying as loud as I was. Finally the family came out and helped us into the car.

"The days ahead was dark, gloomy. I knew that I had a big job ahead of me. I had promised my father that I would do all I could to keep the family together. I gained my strength and I did just that. People used to look at me and shake their heads, saying, 'How can a child that young do all of this work?' I was taught from a small child, if you do something, do it well. I feel now that I have completed my mission."

In the summer of 2003, when Martha wrote this account, six of Suggs's children—Tommie, James Jr., Allen Dale, Isiah ("Wink"), Delartic, and Beatrice—had died, but six others—Myrtle, Martha, Ethel, Mary, Trudy, and Toka—were still alive, along with forty-eight grandchildren, some eighty great-grandchildren, and 130 great-great-grandchildren. Suggs's widow, Sylvia, now 94 years old, was living in South Bend, Indiana.

Richard M. Dorson: Mr. Suggs, where did you learn most of your stories from?]

Well, I learned the most of em from my father. Well, see, we'd sit around the fireplace. We didn't have moving picture shows to go to like the people do now, you know. Well, my father, and lots of times just me . . . would tell these tales—and all we kids sat on the floor and listened to them—about haints and hoodoos and all like that. Well, see, we heared it so regular that we could memorize em, you know.

We didn't have anything to do but shooting our mouths. When the night come, you didn't have anything to do but just sit up and listen at the . . . tales.

[Richard M. Dorson: Where do you think your father learned the stories from?]

Well, he learned em from *his* father.

[Richard M. Dorson: That was on a plantation in the old days.]

On a plantation, that's correct. And the way they'd do, they would meet up, you know, and just have a big tale telling, you know. Just like, they'd meet at a dance, you know, and one would tell a tale, and after he tell, the regulars and all'd like to see who told the most.

48. Mr. Snake and the Farmer

J.D. SUGGS
Kosciusko, Mississippi, and
Calvin, Michigan
Recorded by Richard M. Dorson,
ca. 1952

Suggs was both a great entertainer and a serious moralist. He often ended his tales with pointed and well-explained lessons. At the end of this performance, he and collector Richard Dorson engage in a discussion of the tale's meaning.

Richard M. Dorson: Maybe you'll tell me a story or two, that you were telling me the other night. How about the one concerning the farmer and the snake?]

[Laughing] I tell you, that's a good one, that's a good one. It goes something like this. Well, you know, a snake, in the wintertime, he goes in the ground and he don't never wake up. When the cold weather gets bad, he never wakes up till the weather warms up.

So the farmer goes out, he's going to break his ground up at the end of February. So he plows up Mr. Snake. "Ain't that something? Here's Mr. Snake."

And Mr. Snake says, "Why I'm just so *cold*, I don't know what I'll do. I just practically froze this winter." He was so stiff, he couldn't move. Said, "Will you put me in your bosom, Mr. Farmer, and let me warm . . . up?"

The farmer says [laughing nervously], "No. Mr. Snake, you'll bite me." Said, "I know it."

"No, I wouldn't bite." Said, "Let me tell you, Mr. Farmer, I'm just *cold*. Don't you know I wouldn't bite you after you warmed me up?" . . .

Said, "No. . . . But you a *snake*."

Said, "Mr. Farmer, I won't bite you. Just warm me up, please. . . ."

Farmer take him up and unbutton his shirt, put him in his bosom. Oh, he's a *great* big snake. I think he must have been a rattlesnake. . . . And so he plowed along until about nine o'clock. He stopped his mules and unbuttons his bosom, and he pulled it out, like this, you know, and he looks down in there, says, "How you feel, Mr. Snake?"

He says [in a feeble, high-pitched voice], "Well, I feel a little better. I'm kind of warming up."

"Good, good." Says, "*Gitty-up!*" So he goes around and he plows till about ten thirty. Then, "*Whoa!*" Mules stop. He opens his bosom, and he looked down (just like I'm looking in my bosom now), and he says, "How you feel, Mr. Snake?"

He says [slightly stronger voice], "Well, I'm feeling pretty good. I'm warming up good."

He says, "Good, good. *Gitty-up!*" Mules started on up, and he plowed and he plowed till about eleven thirty. And so he could feel the snake kind of twisting, you know, and he just stopped, you know. Pulled his . . . shirt out and looks in his bosom again.

"How you feel, Mr. Snake?"

Says [strong voice], "Oh, I'm feeling a whole lot better. I'm warming up. You feel me moving?"

Said, "Yeah! I *thought* you was doing better."

"Yes, I'm feeling a whole *lot* better."

"Well," farmer says, "Well, I'll be out plowing awhile longer, and I'll quit and go to dinner, then I'm going to get my dinner and put him out at the end."

So he plowed till about fifteen minutes till twelve. He pulled out his shirt and he looked down there again. He said, "Well how are you, Mr. Snake?"

Says, "Oh, I'm warm. I'm just feeling good."

He says, "Good." Says, "Well, I'll go a round or two, and then when I get ready to go to dinner, I'll put you out at the end." So he plowed around, and when he got near about back, Snake didn't wait for him to open his shirt. He done stuck his head out, twitching away out between the shirt buttons, and looking at him in his face and licking out his tongue. Well, a snake's angry. Every time he see you and go to licking out his tongue, he's mad. And the farmer *knew* he's going to bite then.

He said, "Now, Mr. Snake." Said, "Now you told me you wouldn't bite me after I warmed you."

"Yeah. But you knowed that I's a *snake.*"

He said, "Yeah. [Laughing] But . . . don't do that, don't bite me. Please."

"You see, I'm a snake. I'm *supposed* to bite you."

He said, "Yeah. But you told me you wasn't going to bite me."

"Yeah, but you know I's a *snake* before. I'm supposed to bite you, and you know that." So he all went on [and bit] the farmer, right in the mouth. His face begin to swell, so he goes to the house, running. He didn't take time to take his mules out of there. Went in.

Wife says, "Well, what the matter?"

He said, "Well, Mr. Snake. I seen him out there in the field. I plowed him up, and he said he was so cold he was stiff. And if I would warm him up, he would not bite me." And said, "After I got him warm, he bit me in the face." And said, "Let me tell you one lesson. Don't care when you see a snake, don't never warm him, put him in your bosom, put him up, cause when he gets warm, he's sure going to bite you."

Then he laid down and died.

And that's why he left word with his wife, "Don't never fool with a snake."

[Richard M. Dorson: There's a real lesson in that story, isn't there?]

Real lesson there. That's correct. Well, you know we have people that way. Long as you got something he wants, he just gets right in your bosom, and soon as he get what he wants, then he's going to do you harm.

[Richard M. Dorson: I see.]

When you know that a fellow is a crook or a thief, a robber, don't care how he tell you how he done quit it, don't never put him in your bosom, for when he gets warm, first chance, he going to trip you.

[Richard M. Dorson: So there's something really to be understood in that story.]

Yes. Never put a snake in your bosom.

49. Buzzard Goes to Europe

J.D. SUGGS
Kosciusko, Mississippi, and
Calvin, Michigan
Recorded by Richard M. Dorson,
ca. 1952

There are many African American tales featuring a greedy, lazy buzzard, but this, according to collector Richard Dorson, is the only one set in Europe. Suggs himself served as a soldier in World War I, and this tale humorously reflects Suggs's firsthand experience with the horrors of battlefield carnage.

Richard M. Dorson: Now there's another one about how the buzzard wanted to go to Europe, if you could tell us that.]

Well, it started something like this. You know the World War, [nineteen] seventeen—you know, and the United States and Germany was fighting. Well, the buzzards heared that they wasn't burying em over there, you know. And so they all gets together, and he says, "Do you know one thing? They tell me they's not burying them over in Europe, in those countries. They's killing em so fast they're not burying em. So let's go over there."

So they all get down to sing, begin to sing. The old big buzzard say,

I'm going where the living don't bury the dead

The little bitty one, he say like this [singing in refrain]:

Lawdy, Lawdy, Lawdy, Lawdy, Lawd

The big one:

I'm a-going where the living don't bury the dead

So they all packs up, you know, in the air, and takes off, going to Europe. When he gets over there, they wasn't burying em, but they was *burning* em, you see. Well, they began to get hungry, you know, and the old buzzard sat down and began to get to think about back over here in America, you know, where he could get, something to eat every once in awhile, and he . . . commence to sing. Said [singing]:

I'm going where people throw away something sometimes

And the little one said,

Lawd, lawd, lawd, we going where the people throw away something some time

See, when they was over here, why he . . . didn't know he could have plenty to eat. When he got over there, they was . . . burning em up, you see, and he was still in worser shape.

That's the way the song was when he was over there.

50. Monkey Apes His Master

J.D. SUGGS
Kosciusko, Mississippi, and
Calvin, Michigan
Recorded by Richard M. Dorson,
ca. 1952

This brilliant tale of Mr. Jones, the engineer, and his diabolical pet, the monkey, combines three different episodes, linked together by the tale's central theme, imitation. In the first episode, the master throws a sheet over his head to assume the appearance of a "haint" (that is, a ghost). In the second episode, the monkey threatens his master's livelihood by hijacking a train. In the third and final episode, the master exacts a grim revenge; ironically, he is too close to the monkey to spare its life, even if he is too soft-hearted to strike the deathblow himself.

Richard M. Dorson: Now there was another very good one which I'd like to get from you again, the one about the monkey who imitated his master.]

Well, [Mr. Jones, the] engineer: he was the engineer, you know. So he gets him a monkey. He's a awful pet. So he learns the monkey lots of tricks, but [the monkey] never did any of em. But anyway, the monkey, he just went to doing everything, imitating everything that his master did.

So, [Mr. Jones] he went up, goes on down and he sees some boys coming home one night. Mr. Jones say, "Well, I'll just have some fun out of them boys." And there was a cemetery back there, so he just grabbed him a sheet and run out there and he laid down, you know. Well, he didn't know the monkey, the monkey was in the bed, you know, his little old monkey bed, in the same room. So the monkey grabbed him a towel. He lit out right behind Mr. Jones.

Well, Mr. Jones never looked back, you know, he just going after to scare the boys. He laid down, covered up in the sheet. The monkey run right behind him. He laid down and pulled his towel all around him, humped up like his master.

So here come two boys along. They're just talking. Said, "Look," he said, "I see a *haint*. A great, big haint."

The next boy says, "I see a little bitty haint, right behind the big haint."

That time, Mr. Jones looked back and he seen that little thing behind him. It was his monkey. But up he jump, you know, and light out running with the sheet, holding to it.

Then up jumped the monkey, right in behind him, with his little towel, with his towel behind *him*.

The boy said, "Look-y yonder, . . . behind the big haint is running . . . the little haint." Said, "*Run*, big haint, little haint'll catch you."

There go Mr. Jones, he run in the house. He's so scared he throwed his sheet off, and right in the bed he went. In go the monkey, he throws his towel and in his bed he went.

[Mr. Jones] laying there and wondering about that haint running him. Says, "I don't think I'll scare nobody else no more."

So the next night, the call boy come and call him out to take his engine out. So [Mr. Jones] gets up and puts on his overalls and gets his lunch, and he lights out down to the roundhouse. The monkey, he gets up right there behind him. [Mr. Jones] never looks back. And he crawls up in the cabin in there, and the monkey run out and got up on the turner, the coal turner, you know, watching him.

After a while, the conductor come out and said, "All aboard." Train starts: *Chuck-a chuck-a, chuck-a chuck-a, chuck-a chuck-a, chuck-a chuck-a.* And then the monkey's sitting watching, seeing how he handle that throttle, with his right hand there, laying out the window.

So they went about sixty miles or seventy, anyways, to the next station. They had to stop to get off, to see what they need. So the conductor, he crawls down, out of the caboose. He come on up. The engineer he crawled down, . . . he talked with him awhile while he's, you know, waiting for the orders—till the operator gets his orders ready.

So they's out there talking, the monkey *eased* down and got up over in the seat. Throwed his left hand over on the throttle, and . . . off it went. He pulled it. *Chuck-a chuck-a, chuck-a chucka-a.* And he just pulled it [breathlessly fast]: *Chuck-a chuck-a, chuck-a chucka-a, chuck-a chuck-a, chuck-a chucka-a.*

And they didn't know what was making it run. So that poor agent, he run out there, says, "*What's a matter?*"

He says, "The train's gone."

And the old monkey, he done laid his head out the window, you know, like that; left hand on the throttle, and the engineer said, "*That's my monkey*, got in the train and gone!"

He said, "Put out a telegram! Tell everything to side-track cause the monkey's on the main line" [laughing]. So that monkey run, and he run about *eighty* miles. See, he didn't have nobody behind [to feed the engine], so the steam all went down. Then the engine stopped.

So he gets another train, and they go to get Mr. Monkey, and they brought him back.

But he didn't want him no more, then. He didn't want to sell him. He thought too much of him to sell him, and he didn't want to give him away. He say, "I know what I'll do. I'm gonna make him kill his *own* self. He's imitating me, everything I do."

He goes in that night [to shave], made him a good lather up, you know, and got his glass [mirror]. He had a big mirror up on the wall. Well, he knowed the monkey couldn't stand up that far, so he put it down on the table, and when he got up, he just left his chair there. And so he lathers, and the monkey, he done hid over here in the corner, you know, watching. When he gets down, got through shaving, he take the back of the razor and draws it across his throat and walked on out.

Monkey he gets up there. He makes one or two strokes, you know, his face wasn't overly large, you know, but he didn't care whether he'd get any hair or not. And out he take the razor in the basin and he hit it, cut it across his artery and cut his throat. So he died, and that's the way the engineer got rid of his monkey.

He thought too much of him to sell him. And he thought too much to give him away, so, "I'll just make him kill himself."

51. Efan Outruns the Lord

J.D. SUGGS
Kosciusko, Mississippi, and
Calvin, Michigan
Recorded by Richard M. Dorson,
ca. 1952

An extensive African American joke tradition is devoted to tales of John, the wily slave, and his white owner, Master. When Suggs tells these tales, Efan takes on the role of the slave. Efan's wife, Dinah, and Jake, the plantation spy, are other stock characters found in several of the John and Old Master tales that Suggs told Dorson. In introducing the narrative, Suggs treats Efan as if he were a living, breathing man.

That Efan was a *awful* smart man.
[Richard M. Dorson: Efan was a pretty—]
He was a pretty smart fellow. He gets caught. Well, they *think* he gets caught, but he gets out of nearly everything.
[Richard M. Dorson: Well, the time that he wanted to go to heaven, though, he got caught, didn't he?]

No, he didn't. He *run* out of that one.

Well, you know, he wanted to go to heaven *so bad*. Said "Old Master." He get down a-praying. Says [singing],

"Oh, Lord. Old Master work me down here every day. He makes me work hard. He give me plenty of something to eat, but he don't let me go nowhere on Sunday night. And, Lord, I want you to come and take me to heaven."

So Jake, he's kind of prowling around. He crept around, you know, and he slip in there and find out everything.

He went back, said, "Old Master, you know Efan's down yonder praying for the Lord to come and get him and take him to heaven?"

"Say what? [I'm going down to meet him; I don't want nobody to see me going."]

[Efan] got down again: "Oh, Lord. I want you to come and get me. Carry me up to heaven where Old Master don't treat me so bad. He make me work hard all through the week. Then I have to hunt sometime; if he want a coon or possum, I got to go out and catch that for him."

So, Old Master's up in the pear tree. [Efan] didn't know he was up there, see? [The Lord] says, "Come down tomorrow night. I'm going to bring a chariot and carry you to heaven."

Efan says, "Okay, Lord, I'll be down here." Went on back home.

"Well, Dinah."

"What is it, Efan?"

"I'm leaving here tomorrow night."

"Oh, Efan, where you going?"

"Well, Lord says he's going to come get me."

"Well, Efan, you going to take me?"

"No, I can't take you along now. But I'll make arrangements. I'll come back and get you."

"Okay."

So he's down there the next night. He goes, "Well, Dinah, I'm going."

"Well, goodbye, Efan. Now don't forget me, Efan; you're going to come back and get me."

"Okay."

He got down there about nine o'clock as usual. Old Master was there and had a rope, let it down there, and had a big old white rag around it, you know, trying to make it look big, make it look like a chariot. And he say [singing], "Oh, Efan."

Efan got up there.

"Raise, raise up your head and stick it in the chariot."

Efan raised up and stuck his head in the rope. And so his master kept a-drawing him up.

Said [high, frantic voice], "Oh, no, no Lord. . . . It's choking me!"

So the master let him down a little lower, you see, so he could touch . . . the ground [with his feet]. He wanted him to get loose, you know.

Well, he got his head out, and yonder he go home. He says, "Dinah? You know, the Lord had me down there," said, "he liked to choke me to death. He liked to choke me to *death*." Says, "If he comes here after me, you tell him I ain't here."

So, "Okay, Efan."

Well, after awhile, here come Old Master, says [singing], "Oh, Efan."

He said [whispering], "Tell him I ain't here." He run up under the bed. "Tell the Lord I ain't here."

She said, "Efan not here, Lord."

Said, "Well, *you'll* do just as well, Dinah."

She said, "You better come out from under that bed, Efan, and tell the Lord to come get you. You better come out from under that bed."

Out from under the bed, there Efan come, out the back door. Old Master looked and see him and he came right after him.

And Dinah was running around. Said, "Oh, Lord, You can't catch Efan today. He's *barefooted*." Say, "You might as well quit now [laughing]. You can't catch Efan because he's *barefooted*." And she . . . thinks Efan could outrun the Lord, you know, because he was barefooted.

[Richard M. Dorson: So Efan got away again?]

He got away again.

52. Mr. Fox and Mr. Deer

J.D. SUGGS
Kosciusko, Mississippi, and
Calvin, Michigan
Recorded by Richard M. Dorson,
ca. 1952

In the following tale Suggs uses the term "electrocute" to signify "execute."

Richard M. Dorson: Oh, Mr. Suggs, someone was telling me about how the fox was guarding the deer and the deer got away. Remember that one?]

Oh, yeah. That's right. Well, the way that come about, Mister Fox and Mr. Deer, they raised a pea patch together. Mr. Deer, he wouldn't ever work. So he slipped down there and he'd *steal* peas. And he'd slip down and he'd steal.

So they caught him one night. So they built a *high* pen and carried him and put him in it after the carpenters had gone home. Punish him for it. Wanted to hang him.

So they put Mister Fox to watching the pen, and they's going off to getting ready to electrocute him, the next day. He was guarding.

So the [deer] he got to sitting over there and he begin to sing:

Shoo, Lally, shoo;
Shoo, Lally, shoo;
I do this in the wintertime,
I do this in the summertime,
Umh!

Brother Fox said, "Oo—ee! Where'd you learn that song at?"
"Here's where I learned it. Why, I been knowing that song."
"Lord, I've *never* heard nothing like that." Said, "Sing it again."
"No-o-o, I wouldn't sing that song for nothing."
"Won't you sing it for nothing?"
"Well, I would sing it if you'd throw down about four rails."
So off go the four rails.
He began to sing it again:

Shoo, Lally, shoo;
Shoo, Lally, shoo;
I do this in the wintertime,
I do this in the summertime,
Umh!

[Mr. Fox] said, "Lord, have mercy! I ain't *never* heard a song like that." He'd never heard nobody sing like that. Never did. "Sing it again."
"Oh, no. I couldn't be singing that song. I'm tired. I don't feel like it. Going to be electrocuted, and I just don't feel like singing at all. Well I—"
"What would you sing it for?"
"Well, I tell you. Throw me down twenty rails and I'll sing it for you."

Oh, Brother Fox he threw down the twenty rails, and he begin to sing it for him again:

Shoo, Lally, shoo;
Shoo, Lally, shoo;
I do this in the wintertime,
I do this in the summertime,
Umh!

"Lord, Lord, Lord, the more you sing, the better—"
"I wouldn't give nothing for that song."
Said, "Sing it again for me."
"Oh, no, I wouldn't do that. But if you throw down about twelve more rails, now I could get up close where I could put my head in your breast—now it really sounds *good* that way." Said, "You really think you heared something. You ain't heared nothing now."

Off go the . . . twelve rails. And after he walks up close, and when he got up there, he just leaped over and knocked the other ones down. . . . Sun was setting, and away he goes. He gets away.

So when they come, they electrocute the fox for letting Mr. Deer get away. [Richard M. Dorson: Well, that was a mighty good story, Mr. Suggs.]

53. Brother Rabbit Rides Brother Bear	J.D. SUGGS Kosciusko, Mississippi, and Calvin, Michigan Recorded by Richard M. Dorson, ca. 1952

[Richard M. Dorson: How bout the one where the rabbit makes the bear his riding horse?]

Oh [laughing], that was a funny one too.

Well, Brother Bear was courting a girl. And Brother Rabbit, he go—he have to go with him, and he didn't want Brer Rabbit to go. Cause Brer Rabbit was courting her too. He'd go back after [Brother Bear] leaves.

So he go up there with him, and so they let Brother Bear talk, and then he'd go back home, and then he'd slip back up there, and talk to the girl.

He said, "Did you know Brother Bear is my riding horse?"

She says, "Oh, no. Mister Bear couldn't be your riding horse."

"Why, sure he is. I'll prove it one of these days."

Went on one night. Went on, went on, went on.

So one night, here come Brother Bear along wanting Brother Rabbit to go back with him to the girl's house.

"No, I can't go."

"What's the trouble?"

Says, "I'm sick."

"And you can't go? Tonight's my marrying night."

"Yeah, but I can't go up there, even if it is your marrying night, I can't go."

"Will you go if I *carry* you?"

"Well, yeah—I don't know. I might."

"Brer Rabbit, now come on, I'll tote you up there, I'll tote you up there."

"Well, I don't feel like going. You know I never could ride without a bridle. You ain't never seen me ride without it."

"Why, no, I—well, that is right, I ain't never seen you ride without one."

Well, then Brother Rabbit gets his bridle and puts it on him. Says, "You know, I never could—how can I ride without a saddle? I've been having a saddle so long, I wouldn't know how to ride without it."

"Oh, that's all right," says, "here, I'll get you your saddle down. That's right. I ain't never seen you ride without a saddle."

So he gets his saddle. He said, "Now, listen; well, it ain't no—I don't need em, but it's custom for all cowboys. You know the long spurs I've got in there. I just want to put em on. I got so used to riding, I got to—"

"Well, I'll get em. That's all right." So he got em, and they were heading along, they rid, and they talked, talked, talked about first one thing and then the other, and so they get up there to the house. It was at night.

So, "Well, Get down, Brother Rabbit."

Says, "No! Go ahead on."

"Get down." He says, "I ain't going to carry you no . . . further."

So he popped them two spurs into him. Up to the doorstep he went, up to the porch. He said, "I told you . . . Brother Bear was my riding horse! I told you he was."

And so he rode Brother Bear on back home. So he got down off him. Then he went on back and told the girl. So she *kicked* Brother Bear. So he never could go see her no more.

[Richard M. Dorson: Well, it served him right.]

54. Brother Bear Meets Man

J.D. SUGGS
Kosciusko, Mississippi, and
Calvin, Michigan
Recorded by Richard M. Dorson,
ca. 1952

Richard M. Dorson: Mr. Suggs, did the animals ever meet the Man? Did they ever have an experience with the Man?]

Well, some of em have. All of em have. You take Brer Rabbit, he met Man directly, and most every time, the Rabbit always met Man, but Mr. Bear had never met man. [Laughs]

Brother Bear met Mr. Rabbit. Says, "Brother Rabbit," says, "I've heared people talking about Man. *Man*." Says, "I want to see Man."

Says, "Wait." Says, "Come on and follow me up the side of the road." Says, "Man'll be along. Some time, I reckon, he'll be along, I reckon."

[Brother Bear] got up there aside of the road, and he's standing, and he looked down the road and seen a little bitty boy a-coming. And he said to Brer Rabbit, says, "Is *that* Man yonder?"

Brer Rabbit peek. "No, that's *gonna be* a man."

[Brer Bear, sighing:] "Oh. Huh."

"Wait . . . Man'll be along, I reckon."

After awhile he looked, and he seen a old-looking—

[Suggs breaks into his description to impersonate Brother Bear:] "Hey, look, Brer Rabbit." Said, "Who's that yonder. That's Man?"

—this old, old man on a walking stick, yeah, [limping] along.

"No, that ain't him, Brother Bear. That be—*used to be* a man." Said, "Wait. Man'll be along, I reckon."

[Laughing] After a while, Brer Rabbit looked back out to the right and left of him.

"What do you see, Brer Rabbit?"

[Whispering] "Look, look, look."

Brother Bear looked around, and yonder come *Man*.

"Well, I'm going out to *see* Man." He went out and stood on his hind legs. And this young guy, about twenty-one, just *mean*. You know, a guy ain't afraid of nothing if he have a gun. So he throwed it down on him. Shot him. [Explosive sound:] *YOW*. Both barrels. So.

And Brother Rabbit, he done run off and left him there. Run off in the thicket, waiting off for him.

After a while, here come Brother Bear through the woods. Just flying around down there. . . .

"Brother Bear, did you see Man?"

"Yes, I seen Man." Said, "He lightening out one hand, and thundered out the other one. And look, he just filled me full of splinters all over."

So he knowed what Man was, and that's the end of it.

55. Brother Bear and Brother Deer Hold a Meeting

J.D. SUGGS
Kosciusko, Mississippi, and
Calvin, Michigan
Recorded by Richard M. Dorson,
ca. 1952

When telling animal tales, Suggs's narrative style often varies so radically from standard written English that readers may wonder if he grew up speaking a different language. In this tale, Suggs performs competently in both African American and standard English dialects. In the meeting of the animals, Brother Bear and Brother Deer speak with great formality. On the recording, Suggs portrays Brother Bear in a deep and pompous voice, appropriate for a preacher; Brother Bear's pleas for harmony sound as if they are being delivered from a pulpit.

Richard M. Dorson: Well, you know you were telling me that story about the rabbit and the dog at the meeting of all the animals.]

Oh, well, Mr. Bear he goes down, he and Mr. Deer. "Now, Mr. Deer," he says, "The way peoples is living here, we animals, we got to get together, all of us, and live as one. Now, you's a swift go-about. You go around and notify *all* animals to meet here at the hall tomorrow night."

So, Brother Deer, he run around and he told em all, so they all met at the hall. They made Brother Bear the moderator. So all of em set down in their seats, and Brother Rabbit, he's late getting in, and wasn't no seat nowhere but side of Mr. Hound Dog. So he sits down a-side of Mr. Hound Dog. Well, Mr. Hound Dog, was just full of fleas, and he just kicked and had the mange. You know, when a dog got the mange, it itches. And when he got fleas, they really eat him up too.

So they all sit down. So Mr. Bear, he gets up, says, "Now, ladies and gentlemen," says, "we here tonight, we wants to be as one." Says, "We got so that Mr. Rabbit—you take Mr. Rabbit there first. There's Mr. Dog, he'll bother him.

There's Mr. Owl, he'll bother him at night. Mr. Hawk, He'll catch him." He says, "*That's not right.* We got to live peaceful." And says, "There's Mr. Quail. The possum'll catch *him.*" And say, "We got to live peaceful. And there's Mr. Terrapin, he don't bother nobody." And says, "Mr. Deer, if he go through the woods, he'll jump over and kill every terrapin." And says, "We got to quit this."

And so at about that time, the Hound Dog, you know, the fleas commence biting him, and he reached over and went to scratch and Rabbit, *up* [claps] he jump and went to running around in the house, and had Mr. Bull Dog as a guard to keep everybody from going out.

So up jumped Mr. Deer. Says, "Mr., Mr. Moderator."

He says, "Mr. Deer."

"Now, Brother Rabbit, during the time of business—this is a *business* meeting. Every time you get in a good way of speaking, up he jump and go to running around." And says, "If I'm in order, whiles I'm on the floor, I'll motion that we'll fine Brother Rabbit five dollars."

Well, this was carried and seconded, and so they fined Brother Rabbit five dollars.

Said, "Now you have to sit down."

He goes back and he sit down beside of Mr. Hound Dog.

So he begin, Mr. Bear begin, with the discourse again. Says, "Now, ladies and gentlemen"—

About this time the fleas ate at Brother Hound Dog again, he went and reached out at a flea, and up go Mr. Rabbit again, *around* the house, *around* the house.

Mr. Moderator hits his gavel and says, "*Order! Order* in the house!" Says, "I'm tired of this disturbance. We've got to live as one." And says, "Brother Rabbit, you just keep jumping up here around this place."

Mr. Deer said, "Brother Moderator. So I've been a-thinking." Says, "Now this is the second time that Brother Rabbit—every time you get in a good way of your discourse, up he jump and go to run around and around. You can't do that. While I am on the floor, I'll motion that we'll fine him fifteen dollars."

It was carried and seconded, and so they fines him. Said, "Now, Mr. Rabbit, go and take your seat."

He goes back and he sit down.

Brother Bear gets up. "And now, ladies and gentlemen, I'll begin with my dis*course* now." Says, "We *got* to live in har*mo*-ny and peace. All of us live as one."

. . . And the fleas begin to bite Mr. Hound Dog, he reached down and commence to—*up* go Brer Rabbit, *round* the house, *round* the house. And after a while, he made for the door, the Bull Dog, the guard, he grabbed him and throwed him back in there.

And up Mr. Deer, said, "Mr. Rabbit! *Take* your seat. We can't *have* business this way. This is a business meeting."

Brother Rabbit sat down again.

Brother Deer said, "Brother Moderator," said Brother Deer, "now this is the third offense Brother Rabbit has done tonight." And says, "Whilst I'm on the floor, I'll motion we'll charge Brother Rabbit fifteen dollars." . . . And a Brother finally got up and says he'll second the motion.

Brother Bear says, "It's been moved and second that we'll fine Brother Rabbit . . . for his third offense, for running around in the time of a business meeting." And says, "Are you ready for the question?"

Up jumped Mr. Rabbit and says, "Not ready!"

Brother Bear, the moderator, says, "State your unreadiness, Brother Rabbit."

"Now the way I reckon is this." Says, "Now, Brother Bull Dog there," says, "you got to *move* him." Says, "The way he howls at people and throws em back in the hall," says, "somebody gonna get hurt."

And he knowed the bull dog, you know. . . . He aims to go outdoors. He's going to leave there, but the dog made him stay there.

So that was the cause he broke up the meeting, and the dogs never did come in harmony. They've been fighting. And the dogs have been running Brother Rabbit, and the hawks been catching him, and the weasels, they've been running, and they just never did get to meet in a business meeting again. So they never did call it. They just broke it up. They had no more meeting since.

56. The Devil's Daughter

J.D. SUGGS
Kosciusko, Mississippi, and
Calvin, Michigan
Recorded by Richard M. Dorson,
ca. 1952

Wonder tales (or fairy tales) are rare in African American oral tradition. One notable exception is the international tale known as "The Girl as Helper in the Hero's Flight," of which "The Devil's Daughter" is an example. It is a plot recorded repeatedly both from European Americans in the Appalachians and from African Americans in the South.

Though Suggs's tale is quite clearly a bald-faced fantasy, the narration does not begin with the typical "once upon a time," or with any other marker to inform the listener a fictional tale will follow. Even as the action develops, and as Suggs piles magical details on top of each other, he continues to present the forlorn, frightened man, the cocksure devil's daughter, and the devil himself as realistic characters, possessing clear motives and well-defined personalities.

Richard M. Dorson: You were telling me a very good story the other day about the devil's daughter, which you heard from your father. How does that one go?]

It's about a fellow going, hunting work, hunting a job. He was looking for work. It went something like this.

Well, see, in those days, way back, we didn't have shipping points for men, then, like we have now, to get a job. He just have to go out and get this job best way he can. Well, there's an old lady there, she was doing this smuggling, letting a few people know she had an eagle to carry em.

And so he went over to her, said, "I'm looking for a job. They tell me, over at Mr. Devil's you can get a good job."

She said, "Yes."

"So what are the expenses, for flying there?"

She said, "Well, that'll cost you four quarters of meat. Here's one, two, three—there're two hindquarters, and there're two forequarters. Now, if you can get that up, each time he hollers, you give him a piece, a quarter of that beef. And when you holler the last time," she says, "he'll land for you, all for nothing."

This fella, he goes out and he buys up four quarters of a beef. The old lady strapped it across the eagle's back and on his wing. He sat over him and catch him around the neck, you know.

Well he got going. Right about two thousand miles, the old eagle's squalled out, "WHAA-AA-AH!"

He reached back in his side and he reached him a beef, a quarter of beef. They're going on again, about the same distance, two thousand miles. "WHAA-AA-AH!" He reached on the left hand side, he got to make it balance, you know—there's two on one side and one on the other—and handed him another one. Keep going on. He go about the same distance, you know, he's making less time, about thirty-five minutes too—it was swifter than any plane we got now. Anyway, he hollered the next time. He got the next quarter. He handed it over to the eagle.

He was getting tired. He says, "I ain't got far to go now. I ain't got but one more quarter to hand him and I won't be long getting there. And it's getting late in the evening too." He wanted to get there before night, you know, so he could look around. He didn't know the place.

So the eagle squalled again and he reached and got the next quarter. He go, "WHAA-AA-AH!" After a time, he didn't holler no more, and he seen him commence spreading his wings, crooked, you know, like a bug. Did you ever see a bug go down? He crooked his wing and went, "VRMM-MM." That's like it sounded. So he crooked and he light down like a plane [right in front of a doorway]. He didn't go no further.

He got off. Said, "I'm looking for Mr. Devil."

[A girl opens the door.] She says, "Yeah?"

"Is he here?"

"Well, come on in." Said, "What do you want?"

"Your poppa," he said. "I want a job."

"So, I think he'll give you one. Well, he'll *give* you one." But she take a liking to him. Now that he got over there, she take a liking to him. Said, "He'll give you one, but let me tell you now. That eagle, after she put you down, she *gone*, you see. You can't get away. Whenever you get off her back, she's gone to where she came from. There's no way for you to leave. Then, if you can't do the devil's work, then he'll kill you."

She said, "Now, listen. Poppa'll be here directly in my opinion. It's too late to work. Don't you tell him no about nothing he tells you to do. You just say yes."

So he says, "Okay." He don't know she loved him, but *she* know.

So he goes on. After awhile, the devil comes in, about four thirty. He says, "Who is that there?"

His daughter says, "Why, it's a gentleman looking for work."

"Well, if he can do what I want him to do, he's hired. Now, at nine in the morning when you get up, I want you to go out yonder, clean out a thousand acres of land, burn all the brush, pile the logs, burn them up there, by noon."

He went out there next morning, he just a-firing . . . away with his ax. He's out there just, "Whack-a, whack-a, whack-a." Anyway, come eleven thirty.

Out come the daughter.

She says, "Ooh. That's all you got done?"

"Yeah," he says. "I know I can't do it."

"Well, I'll take care of it. Just hand me your ax." See, the little bushes was about like this, she called em a "tree." She says, "When I hit one size, I hit em all. You hit that bush, don't care how big the tree is, you can cut that one or even bigger. If I hit the other size, I hit em all. If one fall, they all fall."

And the whole thing fell.

"When I trim one limb, I trim em all."

When she trim one, the whole thing's trimmed.

"When I pile one, I pile em all."

"When I set fire to one, I set fire to em all. When one's burning, they're all burning."

She's setting em a-smoking.

Just went on till the old devil, he's ready in for dinner. He didn't make em work too much after dinner. You had to do it before dinner. He said, "Well, did you get it done?"

He said, "Yeah. . . ."

"Good job. Good job."

Now he's doing like that. He's a little too smart for him, you know. . . . Go get em hard.

He says, "Well, in the morning, what I want you to do is go out there, plow that land, and break it, plant it, and have it in roasting ears for dinner."

He knowed he couldn't do it. But the girl had told him to say yes—she don't care what he says.

So next day he went out there. Man, he plowed. He plowed. He plowed.

Eleven thirty comes. She come to bring him water every day. The old devil, he gone off somewhere. He going to be back by dinner, but he gone off to another job soon that morning.

So she come out.

She said, "I pick one furrow, I pick em all. I plow one furrow, I [plow em] all. When I come up one, I come up all together." All the field's plowed up.

Said, "When I hoe one row, I hoe it all." She hoed it all. She got it all hoed.

Said, "When I plants one grain, I plants it all." Planted one grain, and they're all planted.

Said, "Knee high! Waist high! Head high! Tassels! Shoots! Roasting ears!" And now all the rows were done.

He pulled the roasting ears and went in, and for dinner. And the devil came in.

"Son, did you get any corn?"

"Yes, sir. Yes, sir. I got it. I got roasting ears here for dinner."

Devil said, "Well." He didn't know what to do. He said, "Well, I'll see you in the morning." He aimed to kill him that night, you see.

But his daughter, she always knows his thoughts. So she slips out there with her sack, you know, when the devil's dozed off late that night.

So she come back to him, and said, "Now, listen. My Daddy's aiming to kill you tonight. Now listen. So let's get up and escape from here. He got two fast horses. He got a fast bull and a fast [horse], but before he wake up, we both can't go on the bull. We both can't go on the bull, so we'll just take the fast horse."

So they got up and they started riding out of there early that night. And so, about ten or eleven o'clock in the day, when the old man woke up and found out they were gone, they were out *way* yonder.

And she could look back. She could see him five or six hundred miles back. She said, "Oh-h-h, Look yonder. I see Daddy's coming. He's wearing them boots. He's bound to overtake us."

He said, "Lord? What we gonna do?"

She said, "I'll tell you what I'll do. I'll turn into a lake and be a duck. And you swim over, and you be a man shooting at me."

So when he come by, the devil was over there telling his boots, "Step, boot, step, five hundred miles." And every time he stepped, it'd be five hundred miles. So he sees the duck and the man shooting at it, and he passed by, so the devil passed on by.

After awhile he come back, he done wore them boots out. "Step, boots, step, hundred miles a step."

Now, he got to go plumb back home and get his bull. That was the fastest thing he got. He jumped three *thousand* miles a jump. Well, he had a long run, and he go back and come on. So here he come.

She looks back and seen him about eight thousand miles behind em. She says, "Look. Yonder come Daddy. And he's riding that bull." Says, "He's bound to overtake us. I know that."

He said, "Lord! What we gonna—" Oh, he was scared then. Sure enough.

And she said, "I'll tell you what to do. Just hand me a stone."

He handed her a stone. And she said, "When I plant one stone, I plant them all." Said, "Eight feet long! Eight feet high! Hundred feet wide! Fifty feet thick!"

And so that old devil's getting up there right quick and she's on the other side. And he was going yonder way and up across the other way, through the thicket. So the devil . . . and the bull couldn't jump it, and so he had to go back, and get a ax blade, you know, to cut the bushes, and so while they were going back, they got away.

And so the last I heard of em, they was married and living happy, in his country.

57. Where *Um-hum* Came From

J.D. SUGGS
Kosciusko, Mississippi, and
Calvin, Michigan
Recorded by Richard M. Dorson,
ca. 1952

African American storytelling is rich in origin stories, tales that explain how certain current phenomena came to be. Although the great majority of such narratives are not considered literally true, the narrator pretends to believe them. Here, Dorson plays along with Suggs; after the tale, Dorson states, "I didn't know that," seeming to accept the truth of the tale.

Richard M. Dorson: You were telling me a funny one about where the word *um-hum* came from.]

Oh [laughing], well that come from the devil. Well, he was going out, you know, and he called it getting souls. You know, he was getting em easy, you know. He'd grab one. Tell him a tale, why he'd just fall for it, same thing. He'd grab one, he'd just fill up his sack. And he kept it up until that fellow had a big sack of all he could carry on his back.

So he come along, and here come another big crowd. He grabbed—told the next fellow that tale. Then he had . . . a right hand full of em.

So he went on farther, and there was another big bunch. He told em a big tale, what he could do. He grabbed them. Now he had *both* hands full. He didn't know what to do then.

He was going on and seen another [bunch], probably about six . . . of em. He told *them* another big yarn about what power he had and what he could do. They just fell for him. . . . He didn't know what to do, and he wanted *them*. So he just stuffed them in his mouth, what he had in his right hand. And grabbed them others left standing out there, so he had his hands full, his bag full, all he could carry.

So he met the Lord, and the Lord said, "Mr. Satan," said, "you got a lot of souls." Said, "Do you want any more?"

He was afraid to open his mouth. He didn't want to *lose* none, you see. And he could have got them and taken them out of his mouth, and said, "Yes." But no, he didn't want to lose none. He said [imitating a man with his mouth so full he can't open it], "*Um-hum.*" Bowed his head. "*Um-hum.*" So that's where that word *um-hum* come—from the devil.

[Richard M. Dorson: Well, I never knew that.]

He was afraid to open his mouth. He didn't want to lose, he was so greedy that he wouldn't open his mouth and lose them. And instead of, "Yes, I'd like some more," he said, "*Um-hum.*" Well, people use that word today—*um-hum*—but they don't know where that word arised.

[Richard M. Dorson: It's just as well.]

58. Skin, Don't You Know Me?

J.D. SUGGS
Kosciusko, Mississippi, and
Calvin, Michigan
Recorded by Richard M. Dorson,
ca. 1952

In the previous two tales the devil is a fictional character, but in the following legend, the witch is a real person, one of Suggs's own neighbors. To many readers, Granny James's exploits will seem no more credible than those of Suggs's fictional devil, but Suggs makes a clear distinction. In responding to the tale, Dorson drops the playful suspension of disbelief with which he has spoken of Efan, Brer Rabbit, and Buzzard; rather, he can bring himself only to say that Suggs has told an interesting *story*.

Richard M. Dorson: Well, how bout that other story, that doesn't have any animals in it. It has to do with the witch, you know, the witch who got out of her skin?]

Oh, yeah. You know, used to, in the olden times, you know, there was *witches* used to go around, you know. And they could get out of their skin, and if you had any crack in [your house], they could ease in there and they'd ride you at night, you know, and they'd get on you and ride you. And if you had any jewelry or anything, they could carry that out.

So one fella come along, he says, says, "Now, that's terrible." Says, "I've lost a whole lots of jewelry," and said, "I can't *never* catch up with who done it."

So one gentlemen, he's coming in late one night (you know how some men stay out late at night) and he seen someone kept working up there. And he stopped. "I'm going to see what that is, that is out there."

[It was an old woman.] She begin to shed all her clothes, and she laid them down. Pull off her hat, she laid that down.

"I wonder what's happening."

And after a while, she got all of the things she had, off—got nude. And so, *now* what happened, you see, see the skin *worked* and after a while just *skin's* standing up there. And he walked up and touched it.

"And what's this all about?" The skin was damp.

And so he just stood there. He says, "Well, I do say. I'll *see* what it's all about."

So he eased down. He'd heard that if they put pepper and salt in a witch's hide—you get em, catch em, find out who it was. So he eased in there and he come back and he peppered and salt, peppered this hide, good. Pepper. Red pepper. You know, that's *hot.* [Laughs]

And after a while, the old lady, grandma, Granny James. She come out. She seen how the hide begin to shake, and after a while she get in there and she shake faster and faster. Get out and after a while she say, "Skin, don't you know me?" She walked around and jumped back in it and about burned up. "Skin, don't you know me?" And so she just kept it running. "Skin don't you know me?" So she couldn't get *in* there.

And so after a while she says, "If anybody'll wash that hide, hide, good, with salt and water—you know, table salt, and water—I'll give em all their jewelry back."

So this man goes, gets soap, water. He washes it good and greases it and make it slick, you know. And so she slipped in there, and that was Grandma James, the next neighbor. So that's who'd been stealing the jewelry.

[Richard M. Dorson: For heaven's sakes. That's quite a story.]

That's right.

59. The Great Watermelon

J.D. SUGGS
Kosciusko, Mississippi, and
Calvin, Michigan
Recorded by Richard M. Dorson,
ca. 1952

Suggs learned the lion's share of his tales as a boy from his father, but like any great narrator, he never stopped absorbing stories. He had lived in Calvin less than two years when he picked up this tall tale from a preacher in nearby Niles, Michigan. By the time he told the tale to Dorson, Suggs had made it thoroughly his own, even if he presented the narrative as a report from his neighbor rather than as his own personal experience.

Richard M. Dorson: Wasn't there another one that the preacher from Niles told you about the rich land down South?]

Oh, that was in Mississippi. He says he went out to plant him watermelons, and so he made up his hills and so he planted em, you know, and so when he got em all planted, and when he got up to the end, you know, he said, "Well," he said, "I guess I better put me a stick up here." And the watermelon, you know, had come in a packet, you know, and the [variety of] watermelon name on there, you know, "Tom Watson." Great big words, "Tom Watson," so he'd know exactly where Tom Watson at.

So he went out with his knife and he walks over to a tree well, I guess about thirty feet from him, he's going to cut him a stick and come back and stick this label on there, so he'd know where his Tom Watson was. So when he got to the tree, he looked down, there was something around his feet, and it tangled him around and throwed him down.

Down he fell flat. Before he could get up, said the vine had done covered him all up. He couldn't get loose at all. And he was laying on his stomach, and kind of looked over to his right and there was a *great* big old watermelon, great big one. The way he talk, it must have been about thirty-five or forty feet high, the way he talked. It done growed *that* fast.

So he just went to work on that watermelon, and he cut him a hole in it. And he crawled up in it, and he commenced eating. And he et there in that watermelon—that was in June. And frost down there [doesn't come] until fall until about the twenty or twenty-second of . . . October. And said, he stayed in that watermelon, et and slept out of that watermelon, until the frost come and killed the vine, and then he could crawl out, and he went home to his wife.

She didn't know *where* he was at. And he told her, there's where he had been, over in that big watermelon.

[Richard M. Dorson: That was a really big watermelon.]

That was a big watermelon. And it *growed* so fast, that was the thing. Well, he couldn't walk, and he didn't know it was the vine, and it up and tripped him.

60. Pull Me Up, Simon

J.D. SUGGS
Kosciusko, Mississippi, and
Calvin, Michigan
Recorded by Richard M. Dorson,
ca. 1952

Simon, he was a terrible fellow. He loved to fish on a Sunday. People would go up to him: "Simon, you better quit fishing."

"No. I fish Sundays."

So Simon goes out fishing. He dug him some worms and went on down there and he throws his hook off in the water. No sooner hits it—*pop*—a fish got line and all. Take it all, swallowed it.

[Fish] said [chanting]:

Pull me up, Simon.

Simon pulled him up.

Now put me on your string, Simon.

Simon put him on the string.

Now take me home, Simon.

Simon taking him home.

Now scrape me, Simon.

Simon taking all his scrapes [that is, "scales"] off.

Now gut me, Simon.

Simon taking all the insides out of him.

Now put on some grease, Simon.

Simon put on the grease.

Now put me on, Simon.

Simon put him on.

Now take me up, Simon.

Simon taking him up.

Now eat me up, Simon.

Simon ate him up.

Now swallow me, Simon.

Simon swallowed him.

Now lay down, Simon.

Simon laid down.

Now bust open, Simon.

So Simon bust open, and ever since then, kids don't get to go fishing on Sunday. Or they're going to be like Simon.

61. Brother Bill, the Wild Cowboy

J.D. SUGGS
Kosciusko, Mississippi, and Calvin, Michigan
Recorded by Richard M. Dorson, ca. 1952

Suggs heard this tall tale (told as true, as they usually are) in 1917 while visiting a friend in El Paso, Texas. The figure of Brother Bill, the black cowboy, had significant currency in African American tradition. Brother Bill's exploits closely shadow those of the better-known, white cowboy Pecos Bill, whose traditions thrived in the same West Texas region where Suggs heard this story told.

Oh, yeah. I was out there on a little visit. . . . [I had a friend] on a vacation down there and he had a brother that came down. And he was telling tales on his Brother Bill.

Said, "Do you know one thing? My Brother Bill was in town . . . yesterday."

"He was?"

Says, "Yeah, *man*. He come flying up the street there . . . riding a bobcat and had barbed wire for a bridle rein, had a live rattlesnake for a whip, and he run right up there to the drugstore, run in there to the pharmacist, told him to 'Give me a full glass of glycerin mixed with two sticks of dynamite.' He made it up, the pharmacist did.

"He drank it all right down.

"Walked out the door. Said, 'I'm a bad man.'

"He went down the street and killed twenty men. Come on back, and got on that bobcat."

And [that was] the last time he seen about Bill. He went out of town and he ain't heared of Brother Bill since then. But when he was leaving out of town, [Bill] was hollering back, "I'm a *bad* man."

4

JOSHUA ALLEY

DOWN-EAST TALES FROM JONESPORT, MAINE

Joshua Alley's stories represent some of the longest and oldest memories in the American Folklife Center collections. He vividly recalled the thoughts and pastimes that occupied him as a small child, growing up in the 1840s on a coastal island near Jonesport, Maine: "I remember when I used to sit in a chair like this, you see. . . . And I can remember getting into a chair and sitting down and seeing how nigh my feet would be to touch the floor. And keep at it to see if I growed any. I wanted to grow fast. I can remember rolling my pants way up as far as I could get em here and wade around in the little pond hole, and play with a little boat, little toy boat."

Alley also, it seems, remembered every story he heard, both fanciful fictions and historical accounts of the early days of settlement in his region, stories extending his memory back well into the eighteenth century. Born May 2, 1843, he was 91 on the July day in 1934 when linguist Marguerite Chapallaz first captured his voice on a giant, primitive sound machine. The storyteller and the interviewer were an unlikely match. Mlle. Chapallaz, an English citizen of Breton ancestry, was multi-national and multi-lingual, refined and highly educated. Mr. Alley was still living within a few miles of the island where he had been born, into a world of which few living souls had any recollection. When Chapallaz asked Alley about his schooling, suggesting that, back then, "you couldn't go to school as much . . . as [one] can now." Alley replied, "Oh, school. . . . No such a thing as a school where we lived, you know. We was down on an old desolate island."

Yet the enormous cultural differences between the two created no impediment, and Marguerite Chapallaz's professionalism, persistence, and obvious af-

Maine coastline near Baldridge estate as it appeared in 1931, when Joshua Alley was 87. (Library of Congress)

fection for Joshua Alley resulted in the creation of a remarkably rich and full record of his storytelling skills that has outlived him by nearly seventy years, and that will extend his memories hundreds of years into the future.

When Chapallaz happened upon Alley, she was working as an interviewer for the American Dialect Society. Her mission was to sound-record voices for linguistic research, and she was charged with engaging speakers long enough to capture the peculiarities of their accents, vocabulary, morphology, and syntax. She was working with a 200-pound aluminum-disk recorder that literally cut the record while the speaker was performing. Each side of each disk would record approximately four minutes of speech. It soon became apparent to Chapallaz that Joshua Alley had far more to say than could be contained on one disk, or even several disks. In fact, most of Alley's tales were too long to be recorded without interruption; the longest of them had to be interrupted eight times to allow Chapallaz and her co-worker R.L. Stone to turn over or change the disks. Nor was it long before Chappallaz realized that Joshua Alley's importance was not confined to the peculiarities of his dialect. The man was a living museum, a human repository of history, cultural information, and narrative traditions whose copious recollections begged to be recorded. Chapallaz visited Alley for a marathon session on July 6, 1934, during which they recorded fourteen disks. Not having come close to exhausting either Alley or his repertoire, she returned to Jonesport in December to spend six more days listening to him. She recorded many of his tales twice. Of the hundreds of persons from New England, the Mid-Atlantic, and the Southern Atlantic states whose voices were recorded by the American Dialectic Society, Joshua Alley contributed by far the most and the longest tales. His narratives and observations filled twenty-five and one-half aluminum disks, three times as many as the second-most-recorded speaker.

Joshua Alley deeply cared about both fiction and history, and he considered profoundly both the separate natures and the interdependence of the two. He told Marguerite Chapallaz, "I don't believe there ever was a story [that was] all true." A story "ain't all one kind of stuff." It is the storyteller's job to mingle just enough fact and just enough art to make it "stick together." After telling one story that he considered an obvious fiction, Alley emphasized that he knew it was fictional, but it was important for him to repeat it as it was told him: "I know that's wrong. But that's it: I heard it, I told it. That's the whole of that story." Nevertheless, his storyteller's art impelled him to add a flourish at the tale's end: "The last part of it, I put enough in it just to make it hold together, that's all."

When Chapallaz recorded Joshua Alley, the 91-year-old man was still working daily at a fish-cleaning and -packing concern run by his son. His world was still bounded by the sea. Just as, more than eighty-five years before, he had sailed wooden toy boats on his island pond, he was planning to carve a toy boat for a "little boy," perhaps his great-great-grandchild: "Now, I was looking around to get a little piece of wood, . . . a piece of pine, and make a little canoe for the little boy. I'm going to make him a canoe. I can make him a canoe, just like the ones the Indians used to have to paddle around in. I've made em; I can make em as nice as can be. Oh, yes. We used to make little boats and have sails on em and go down to the pond, us boys, play there. We had just so long to play. We didn't have so many hours give to us to play and then we'd have to go to work, helping the old man do something or other."

62. The Bear's Tale

JOSHUA ALLEY
Jonesport, Maine
Recorded by Marguerite
Chapallaz,
December 15, 1934

When Joshua Alley told this story to Marguerite Chapallaz, about eighty-five years had passed since he'd first heard it. By his estimation, in the intervening years, he had told it about a hundred times. Joshua classified his story in many ways. As often as he'd told it, he insisted that it wasn't his story, he didn't make it up. He believed that all stories, by nature, contained at least a touch of fiction. "I don't believe there ever was a story, all true. I don't think any man ever heard of one that was all true." But a good story, he continued, would have "truth enough in it to make it hold together, see? . . . If you are mixing up something, why, you can put stuff into that that you are mixing, something to make it stick together and hold together. It ain't all one kind of stuff. And that's the way of my story."

Maguerite Chapallaz recorded two complete performances of "The Bear's Tale" from Joshua Alley. Alley prefaced the second telling (which is not included in this book) with a description of how he had first heard the tale: "I told you a lie when you was here before, I suppose. . . . I didn't make it up, you know, myself. I got it all right from somebody else and I told it again, so I told you the lie of somebody else. No, it's a story. A story that was told to me when I was a little fella about so high. I always remembered it, though. . . . I always kept it in my memory so I could tell it to somebody else, and I have told it, I suppose, about a hundred times.

"There were a couple men walking way down across, way over town here, one night, on a winter's night, and me a-telling my story, and I told it to em. One said it was all right. The other said it was a great big lie, and I don't know but what it was. I ain't saying it's the truth. I don't tell it as the truth.

"When I was a little fellow, about so high, I lived down on the Head Harbor Island. . . . I was born, brought up down there, and there was an old fella come down there to buy some fish, of my father. I remember all these things. And he told the story, and it was a bitter cold day, and we sat outdoor. We walked down to the shore with him because he had paid his visit and bought the fish and was going to leave and said that he'd forgot to tell the old man, my father, this story before he left the house.

"So we sat down on the bank where the wind raked right on to us. Oh, a bitter cold day. And he told the story. And father learned it, hearing him tell it. And I set there as quiet as could be and never said a word.

"And when we got up to the house, my father says to me, 'You didn't learn that story, did you?'

"And I said, 'I think I did.'

" 'Well,' he says, 'Go ahead and tell it.'

"I told the story. Says he, 'You got it all right.'

"Now, I was but a little fellow about so high, but I've always remembered it."

At the end of the performance that follows, Alley presents another account of how he first heard "The Bear's Tale."

There was a widow woman and she had two daughters and a son. And she was poor and had to take in washings and mending and all such things as that she could get anything out of—to support em. And she kept at the boy to help her. He was old enough to help her, but he wouldn't. No, he wouldn't work a lick. But when he come from school, he'd take a newspaper out and read all he could in that. And she couldn't get no work out of him.

So he come from the school one day, and he took up a newspaper and he found where that they wanted a teacher, and he hove [threw] the paper down, and he said, "I want you to bundle my clothes up." He didn't have things to carry em around in the same as they have today. But they used to do em up in a big handkerchief and stick a stick through it and put it over their back. And go on.

And his mother says, "Where you going?"

"Why, I'm a-going to such a place to teach school."

And, "No," she says, "you can't do none of that, I don't believe."

He says, "Now, you put my clothes up. I'm going tomorrow morning."

So she put his little bundle of clothes up, and he got his breakfast and started on the road. And he traveled along until he got to the place . . . where the school was to be kept. And he inquired when he got there who to go see, and he come to the man that he wanted to see. And he says, "I'm the one that has charge of the school."

"Well," he says, "I come to see you and get a chance to teach the school."

"Now," he says, "you're small. And there's boys in that school are even larger than you are, and I don't think you can do that work. But never mind, you can try it."

"Well, now," he says, "where shall I go to get a boarding place?"

"Right with me. I board the teacher."

Well, then, he was right where he wanted to be. Well, he hauled up there, and in the morning he got his breakfast and went down to the schoolhouse. And the scholars come, and come in, and he taught, before noon, school all right. And went home to get his dinner. And . . . when he got ready to come back, these scholars all got all in a big platform in front of the door and stuck themselves up there solid.

Well, he come over to the schoolhouse: a sight to see em standing there, and he thought they were going to do him some mischief. And he walked along slow, to see if they'd move. And they didn't move. And he walked close to em, and they didn't move around none. So he went to the house. And he turned around and went back. And told the man he was done. He couldn't keep the school. He told him how he found the scholars and started to go down to the shore.

He was in a place where there was a sea-front bay, you know. Ships and one thing and another in there. And he walked down onto the wharf. And he saw a ship a-laying off there in particular. He noticed her, and she had a boat off her [being] rowed [by crewmen] toward the shore where he was.

So he stayed there. And they rowed in and landed, and the captain and mate got out and walked right up by him. Never paid no attention to him whatever. Well, the mate turned right around after walking by him, and walked right into this boy and says, "Would you like to go to sea?"

And he says, "Yes."

"Well," he says, "I'll hire you. Now," he says, "how long before you can be ready to go aboard the ship?"

"See, just as soon as I can get my little bundle of clothes."

"Well," he says, "you go ahead. We got to go uptown."

So the captain comes back and he says, "What did you do? Hire that boy?"

"Yes."

He says, "He won't be no use to us."

"Well," he says, "you don't know." He says, "He might be of some use. I hired him."

Well, he went up back to the boarding house and got his clothes and come down onto the wharf and stays there awhile, and by and by he sees the captain and mate coming and an *old* man, and a girl, and a bear. The girl leading a bear down. Well, he didn't like the looks of that.

And they got into the boat and went off to board the vessel, off to board the ship. Took the bear out and chained him on deck. Well, they got underway and went out, went to sea. And after being out a number of days to sea, the ship sprang a leak and they pumped all they could, and she was bound to fill up with water.

And there was a man aboard there by the name of Long Bill. And that is, they called him Long Bill, because he was a tall man. And he didn't like the boy. He liked the girl, but didn't like the boy.

And the girl liked the boy, and didn't like Long Bill. [Laughter]

Well. And the ship's leaking bad, and finally . . . the captain ordered the big boat. They had that big boat sitting on deck would hold lots of people, you know, and then they had a littler one . . . that big one only for use if they had to leave the ship, in case of a gale wind. Well, he ordered the big boat down and he, the captain called for this old man to get into the boat. The old man, being clumsy, well he made a stumble and hit his head and killed him, and he fell between the boat and the ship and sunk. That was this girl's father.

Well, then she went back to this boy and told what had happened and they, they called for the boy to come, they was all getting into the boat and wanted the boy to come, and he fell and stunted himself. He fell down on deck.

Well, they called the girl to get in and the girl said, "I ain't a-going. If the boy can't go, *I* ain't going. I'm going to stay with him."

"Well," they says, "all right," and they pulled off and left. Went off and left them on the ship.

The boy come to, and looked around and said, "They're all gone, are they?" And she said, "Yes."

"And now," he says, "I have a little boat left. And if we can manage to get away in her, we'll go. And now," he says, "you go into the cabin and pick up everything you want that you can find that you think can be of use to us and get what grub there is. And we'll get ready and I'll pick up the stuff round the deck." So he gathered up a sail and oars and found an old ax and he took that and put that into the boat. And she picked up a lot of stuff down in the cabin and they took this little boat and shoved her up to the rail of the vessel. So when that rail went under water they could shove out. He got her up there at the rail and the ship filled up with water and they shoved this little boat out over the rail.

Well, they set that, their little sail up, and started to go, and the bear parted [broke] his chain when the water got up around him.

[Marguerite Chapallaz: He what?]

The bear parted his chain. He was chained to it, on deck. And swum after the boat. And the boy took his ax to kill him, and the girl said, "Don't kill my bear. Take him into the boat."

He said, "I dasn't."

"Take him into the boat. He won't hurt nothing."

So the boy took the bear in, and he [the bear] went into the bow part of the boat and laid down like a dog. And they sailed on, all the rest of the day, and all night. In the morning, the bear get up and put his paws up on the side of the boat and begin to snuff [sniff] in a direction different from what they was a-steering.

He says, "I guess I'd better kill him," he says. "He's getting mad."

She says, "He ain't. You let him alone. He won't hurt nothing."

So, well, he snuffed for a while and then laid down again. And they sailed all that day, and the next night. And he get up again the next morning and done the same, the very same thing. Snuffed again. And he had some trouble with that bear.

"And I think he's snuffing for land. Smells land. And the way he's a-snuffing, I ain't a-going." Now, he says, "I got to shift my course the way the bear is snuffing." So he shifted his course and run the way the bear was snuffing. And when they finished that day up and that night, next morning he got up and snuffed again right ahead of the boat. There, you see, he snuffed the land.

So he steered on that day and that night; in the nighttime, he made land. And it was a beach, and a high head was raised up, a high clift of rocks on the end of the beach where he made in. And he started up the beach to see if he could see anything. And there was an awful sea going off that beach, so he dasn't land. And he saw a man on the beach and he hollered to him, and asked him how he come there.

He says, "I am Long Bill. We sailed and rode in here. And the sea took the boat and destroyed it and drowned everyone that was in the boat but just me. I'm alone here on this beach." And he says, "It's so rough you can't land."

So he sailed up the beach, to the further end of it and come to high mountainous rocks, ledges, and he couldn't land there. And he turned around and went back, down back. The place where he first come in. And there he found a hole made into that clift of rocks, and he told the girl, he said, "I'm going to see if this boat'll go in through there. Well, I'm going in through there," he says.

She says, "You can't get out again, from there."

"Yes I can." He put that boat, took the sail down, and let her go into that hole. She went right in through and come into a little pond, like. A little pool. Smooth a place as could be. And landed on a thatch bay.

[Marguerite Chapallaz: What's that?]

Where the thatch growed up. Kind of a grass, like. And jumped out, took his painter and hitched it, and the bear jumped out and took up the bank.

And when he chased the bear, when the bear stopped, he seen what he was doing. He was drinking water out of a boiling spring. He stopped. So he went and got a dish and lugged some water down to the girl after he drink what he wanted, and brought the girl up. And the bear, when he went back the last time, after water, the dish was small—he followed the bear and found the bear eating figs off of a fig tree. The bear was eating figs off this fig tree. So he gathered up some of them and took them down to the girl and told the girl that the bear had found a fig tree.

[Marguerite Chapallaz: It must have been a warm place.]

Oh, yeah. And plenty of figs. Well, but that's nice. So they, the next morning, they set out on over to look down on that beach, see what they would see. [Apparently, the boy, girl, and bear are now on high ground, at the top of a cliff overlooking a beach.] And there was this big old [man, Long Bill himself; they], thought they had seen him. And they took some figs over, and asked him if he had anything to eat, and he said "no." Couldn't get nothing there on that beach. And they hove him down some figs and said that they would feed him on figs, keep him alive. Well, he said that's first rate, so. . . .

And then they went back where the boat was, and they stayed down there awhile, but by and by they spied out a, what they called the roof of a house, way off a long ways, and they thought there was people living there, and so they took a good drink and started that they'd go on and see what it was.

And they traveled over and got there, and it was nothing but a tree, with a flat top to it, no tippy-top, flat. Looked like the roof of a house, a flat-roofed house. And the boy looked the tree over all around and he says, "Well. I'm going to make a house out of that tree."

And she says, "How you going to make a house out of that tree?"

"See, I'm going to cut it out—right in that bottom part, I'm going to come in and cut me a room in there."

So he went to work, and he worked day after day with his ax with that tree. Cut a door hole, and then worked in. When he got it done, he had a room eight feet square. In the butt of that tree. And so they moved in there. They didn't have much to move in but themselves. [Laughter]

But they went in there. And they had nothing to make a door out of. So they let the bear lay to the door, and watch for other animals might come out. And if it was an animal that would come there to bother em, why the bear'd tackle him, and then the man, the young man would take his ax, you know, and kill him.

Well, they forgot Long Bill. Working on his house, he forgot Long Bill. And he said to the girl, "We'll go see how Long Bill's getting along." They went over and carried over some figs, and he was all right. He was alive and ready for the figs. And he told em what he'd been doing. And he says, "Ain't there no way that you can get me up there where you are?"

Well, he said, "No, there ain't." Well, if there had been, he wouldn't have got him up there, because he would have took his girl away. That's the reason why. So, they let him stay down there.

"Well," he says, "I'll tell you what we'll do. We'll lug figs over here, so that you shan't starve to death. You can eat figs like we do." And so one day they went over to carry over some figs, and Long Bill was laying down on the beach. They asked him what the trouble was, and he said, "I tried to climb up there, over them cliffs of rocks, and I fell. And I guess I broke every bone in my body."

"Well," he says to the girl, "I've got to go down there where Long Bill is. Take care of him till he dies and bury him on that beach."

"Well," she says, "you mustn't go down, because if you go down there, you can't get back and I'll be alone up here."

So he went back to his boat and took his boat's painter off. And it wasn't long enough to reach down, as it was, so he unlaid the boat stringer and took it and he made three strands of it and tied em together and that would reach down. And he started to go down, and when he got pretty nigh down, that parted and he fell down the rest of the way onto the beach. But it didn't hurt him though. But there was his line up there, the biggest part of it. Well, he stayed there with Bill, until Bill died.

And she'd come over onto that cliff and talk with him all day. Then go over to her little house that he'd made there. Nights. Her and the bear.

And he buried Bill. So she'd go in there, and he had Bill buried. "Now," he says, "I'm going to come up where you are." So he took what line he had left and tied her up, tied a rock to her, and then he'd shin up and then he'd throw her around something to steady himself along until he got up where the rope was. And he shinned and he got about two thirds of the way up the clift and couldn't get no further. No way he could shinny any further up, but he could go around, one way or t'other, creep around, and he says (she's a-watching him), and he says, "I can't get no further up." Well, but he says, "I found a little hole here in the back, and I guess I'll crawl in there, that's a good place for us to stop. I'll crawl in there."

"Now," she says, "you crawl in there, and you won't get out again."

And he said, "Oh, yes, I will." So he crept into that hole and after he got in a ways, he made it bigger. And he crawled along, he crept over gravel, and he crept over water, through water, and he crept over old bones of beasts that had gone in there and died. And by and by he saw something that looked like two balls of fire ahead of him, shining. And he didn't like the looks of that. So he stopped crawling, and that kept coming towards him. And by and by it come up and rubbed up against him. And he put his hands out and felt him over and found it was a tame bear. So [the] bear turns around to go back the way he come, and he crept on after the bear, followed the bear right out within fifteen feet of where the girl was sitting on the land. She was surprised when he got right alongside of her. Then they went . . . over to the little house there that he'd made, and after awhile, so long a time, they had a girl born and—they had a boy, a boy. And the boy growed up, and so he could ride on the bear's back anywheres he wanted to. So he went away one day and when he come back, he brought some gold with him. And he didn't know what it was, but his father did. He showed it to his father, and his father said, "That's gold. No good to us, you know, if we're living here."

"Now," he says, "how much of it is there, do you suppose?"

"Well," the boy says, "Lots of it."

"Well," he says, "Let's go look." So they went over and looked, and there was a lot of it. And they gathered up lots of it.

Now he says, "That gold's no good to us. Here, we can't use it. . . ."

So . . . as he'd been crossing through the woods, he'd been hacking into trees, you know. And he found—there was pitch come out of the trees. And he took a rolled-up little ball one day and tossed it to the bear, and the bear'd catch anything in his mouth that he hove to him, so when he caught that roll of pitch, it stuck his jaws together. So he dug and dug around his jaws, you know, with his paws and at last he got em clear after awhile. He knew that stuff would stick clean to be solid. So he said to his girl, he says, "I've got to build a boat—our boat that we come in is old, she ain't safe to go to sea in. And I've got to build me one."

"Oh," she says, "How you going to build a boat?"

"Well, I'm going to build one."

So they had a girl born to em, and, uh, he went to work, and found a clay bank, and he modeled out his boat. . . .

And he went to the wood and he gathered leaves that was *three feet long*. And he took them out: take them out, and gather this pitch. And he put on a coat of pitch. And a coat of leaves. And that'd stick the leaves there, solid. And then a coat of leaves and a coat of pitch, until he got it thick as he wanted to make her. Then they turned her over, and got her down into the water, where she'd lay afloat. In case he wanted to use her to leave.

Well, he took his gold, and put it into the bottom of the hull and took these leaves and covered it over and cemented with that pitch so it was all solid, until he got that thick enough over the gold to hide the gold, so nobody wouldn't see it. Then he said he was ready to leave. He made him some square sails like topsails of a brig or a ship, you know, out of these leaves to stick up to help her along. And said he was going to go.

But now his wife says (we might as well call her his wife; of course, he's been living with her), she says, "I want to stay another night."

"Well," he says, "You can stay another night."

So she stayed that night, and he turned out in the morning and "Now," he says, "are you ready to go?"

And . . . she said, "No."

She wants to stay another night. Well, he let her stay another night. So they stayed another night. Up in the morning, he prepares to go—well, she'd like to stay another night.

And now he says, "We can't stay no longer, we're going. Got to go." So they got into the boat, went out to where they came in through that hole with the other boat, and she was too, a little too wide to go through. There were bunches, bunches [of] rock stuck out and would stop her from going out through.

So he took a hold of his ax and broke them off. And then that made room so she got on through. Got outside and got his square sails up and let her go.

Well, he sailed on . . . and spied out a ship. And he made a signal on his boat, thinking that them on board the ship might see it and come to help him.

And they saw it, and come down where he was. Wanted to know if he wanted any help, and he said yes, he did. He'd like to be carried in.

And he says, "If you'll take me back where I come from, I'll pay you well for it. . . ."

Well, he run alongside the ship. And he took em, he took em and hoisted the boat up and set her right on deck. Go north. And he was going right exactly where this fellow lived. So he carried him in, and he turned and trade the captain for taking him, took some of that gold and took it to the bank, exchanged it, paid him for his passage in, and then he looked around to see if he could find his mother.

He went to a store and inquired for his mother. And the clerk, one clerk says, "There was a woman lived here by that name, but," he says, "I don't know where she is now."

And the other one spoke up and he said, "She's dead."

"Why," he says, "my mother's dead, I can't help her now."

And he asks about his sisters, and they both married well off, and now he says, "My gold ain't going to do them no good."

So he bought as good a place as he could buy there in the village. And moved into it. And, by and by, the children would be all the time telling in the morning when they turned out they wanted to go home. Wanted to go home. And by and by one of em is taken sick, the boy, taken sick and died. Well, he had him put into a casket and sealed it up. The girl was taken sick and she died. So he put her in a casket and sealed it up tight. His wife was taken sick and *she* died. And so he had her done the same, put her in a casket. Then he went and bought a ship and filled her up with goods—all he wanted to put into her, anyway, and told this captain that if he'd carry him back where he come from, why, he'd give him the ship, and what he didn't want of goods that was in it.

Well, he says he'd do it. So he took him and the tame bear and the two children and his wife and carried em all back there. And landed em there, and he give the ship to the captain and goods what he didn't take ashore and he didn't need—and that's, I left em that way.

[Marguerite Chapallaz: Wonderful. Could you tell us how you came to know that story?]

All right. How I come by it. There was a man come by at my father's house when I was a little fellow, small boy, and he stopped on down—he was going to buy some fish, the old man, and he bought em and got em into his boat and Father wanted him to stay till after dinner, so he stopped by till after dinner—but I don't know the man's name now. And he knowed this story and was going to tell it to my father, but forgot it until he got down to the shore to go away. And now . . . he says, "Mr. Alley, I had a story to tell you, but I forgot it, till I got down here"—and it was kind of a cold, bitter-cold day, wind northwest, and Father says, "I don't suppose it's as long as that, you know," and he says, "Well, tell it to me. I'm in my short sleeves, but," he says, "tell it to me, I'll try and stand the cold." He told the story then, and he stayed and I stayed.

And that man told that story on that cold day, and I listened to it and learned it from that man.

63. Man Warren Beal and the Indians

JOSHUA ALLEY
Jonesport, Maine
Recorded by Marguerite
Chapallaz,
December 13, 1934

When Joshua Alley was growing up, there was still a substantial Native American presence near Jonesport. The stories passed down from earlier generations emphasized the negative relations between the Indians and the relatively recent arrivals. But by the time Joshua Alley reached adulthood, relationships tended to be much more positive. At one point, linguist Marguerite Chapallaz asked him, "You never have any trouble with them now, do you?" Alley responded, "Oh, no. No. They're all right now. They're all right. . . . I had the last trouble with em of anybody that I know of. They made up with me, you know. . . . Why, I had one of them boarding the vessels I went in. After that, they was just nice a man as you could want. Just as nice to me. They'd do anything for you in the world."

Chapallaz then asked if the Indians had "died out" in the Jonesport area. Alley answered, "Oh, yeah. Well, they thought the white people was taking a little too much advantage of em, you know. They taking their lands away from em, and they considered the land here their own. When the whites come here, they made their minds up that [the Indians] had no business here. They was here, and the others ought to leave.

"But when they very first started, when the whites come, they were all right. They treated [the whites] right. They thought they was angels. But they found out they weren't. [Laughter] Found out they weren't angels, and then they got mad."

A man by the name of Man Warren Beal, . . . he come from England. He weighed three hundred and sixty pounds. He was a little fellow, you see [laughing]. And his brother only weighed ninety pounds. He was a little fellow, he was. But the old big fellow, oh, he was stout as an ox. And he settled up here on what they call Beal's Island. My grandfather Alley, he come here, settled on Great Wass Island. . . . His old house and barn stands there today. But Man Warren Beal's, his is gone. But my grandfather's is there. Nice, good building.

And . . . then they would come and settle along here on this shore, over here, but a good ways apart. . . . It was all green groves of woods all along the shore here and solid full of Indians. And they was bad eggs. They'd kill you if they got a chance. Break into the house. They come round with what they called a battering ram, they called it. It was this club of wood. Big, heavy club of wood. Your door is shut, and they'd take it up and punch the door, try to punch the door down to get in. Or break the window in. But [the settlers] had that closed up solid and barred across, and across the door. And they come, one time, to one of these houses—now, I don't know which one now—but they come to one of em. And the woman (they had fireplaces, you know; they didn't have no stove), and the woman heard one of em going down under the house, and there was a trap-hatch door that they used to go down to what they called then the cellar.

Well, they got in there, under the house, and come up. And there was a crack, quite a big crack open by this cellar door, some way, and she heard this Indian coming along, and she put her tongs (that she had to handle the wood) in the fireplace, and got em real hot, just *red* hot, you know, and she took em, went along to this crack that he was looking up through, he wanted to see in the room. And she snapped em on to his nose.

Well, she hung on, you know. And he—screeching and screaming and jumping and springing to get away—tore his nose off where he burned it so bad. [Laughter]

Well, he took to the woods, you know, and the other ones run to the woods, and he after em, screeching and screaming. . . . [That] broke it all up, you know. They didn't do any more for the night. They're clear of em, for the night. And then they ran off into the woods and in a few days, why, they was back again, for another battle.

But that's the way they kept em out of the houses. But when they could break in, they would. And skunk you.

And then, as they got more used to the whites, you know, they weren't quite so bad. They'd come out of the woods, and went and talked to em. But it seemed they couldn't give up their ugliness. And this Mr. Beal, the big man I told you about, come from England, he had one of these tobacco boats I was telling you about. Well, he used to go down to . . . what they call Head Harbor Island now, and went into a cove there and put [his boat] up against a square rock over there, a ledge, and went around the island setting traps, to catch mink, and any kind of thing they could get, you know, that they could sell the fur from. . . . And they killed birds, lived on birds, you know, and picked the feathers off, for to sell the feathers, get fifty cents a pound for the feathers. Well, there was . . . plenty Indians, down around there. So [Man Warren Beal's party], after leaving this cove there, they went down into what they called Head Harbor, and went ashore there and set all the traps overnight.

There was a man with Man Warren Beal by the name of Wallis. *He* come from England. And they had the two boys with them. Well, the two boys wanted to go ashore in the morning, and get the traps cause they was going home in the morning. Get the traps and get what there was in the traps and go home. The Indians found out they had set the traps there, and that made em mad again. So they watched, and when these two boys come ashore, they killed em on the beach. [Man Warren Beal and Wallis] couldn't get ashore. . . . And it was because the boys had the boats, little boats.

Well, then this [Indian chief] Pirot I told you about, the head man, he swung off and got hold of the rudder of the little vessel, and wanted to hang it so they couldn't steer her, and then they could get aboard, the whole gang of em, and kill the two men. Didn't like Man Warren Beal, he was too big a man to stay around there. Wanted to get rid of him.

And [Beal] heard him foul the rudder. And he crept along after the gaff and he hooked the gaff right up under his jaw in here, and was going to haul him up so to kill him. Try to beat his brains out. But [Pirot] reached up in the middle of the gaff handle and unhooked his jaw . . . and he got clear.

Well, they, from the shore, they begin to fire their arrows off, toward the vessel, try to do some damage that way, but it was too far for em. They couldn't do no harm. And they got underway and got out and went home.

64. Wrestling the Chief

JOSHUA ALLEY
Jonesport, Maine
Recorded by Marguerite
Chapallaz,
December 13, 1934

Here Joshua Alley continues his tale of the rivalry between English settler Man Warren Beal and the Indian chief Pirot.

Then after a short time Pirot wanted to go up and have a wrestle with this big man. And picked the day. Wanted to pick a place to wrestle, and the old man, Man Warren, told him, about some place on the flat of a ledge, with a little moss growed over it, and [they could] wrestle on that. So the old man got ready and waited, and the time rolled round, and [Pirot] says he ain't coming. . . . Finally, the old Indian come up, wanted to know if he was ready to wrestle. Well, Man Warren Beal says, "I'm ready, yes."

He come up and wanted to know if he would wrestle him, and he told him yes. And he had no clothes on. Well, the old man put his hands onto him and found he was greased. He'd greased himself—and no clothes. Nothing for the old man to hold on to. Made him mad. And he being big, stout, and strong, he put his hands onto him and he sunk his fingers right through his skin and right into his flesh and . . . everywhere his fingers went, the blood come.

And the Indian screeched and hollered, told him to slack up, it was killing him. And the old man says, "I'll tear you all to pieces." He was mad, you know. And let him go.

And [Pirot] says, "We no more wrestle. We no more wrestle. We make up." And he let him go. So I guess that's all I can put in on that.

[Marguerite Chapallaz: So what happened after that? Were they more friendly? . . .]

Yeah. Oh, yes, because he got the head one. He cooked that old fellow, you know. And he was the head man of the Indian tribe. All of the rest had to do just what he said to do, they had to do it. . . . He was the head. He had charge over em all. Because he was a big man. He was a big Indian. Very big one.

Now, old Mr. Sawyer . . . built a new vessel, and it had three masts, and he named it Pirot, after the old Indian.

[Laughter]

I don't think I'd name anything for an Indian after he'd been so ugly.

[Marguerite Chapallaz: You never have any trouble with them now, do you?]

Oh, no. No. They're all right now.

65. Chute's Wedge Trick

JOSHUA ALLEY
Jonesport, Maine
Recorded by Marguerite Chapallaz,
December 15, 1934

The central figure of this legend, the lone survivor of an Indian raid who seems to live only for vengeance, is a common subject of frontier folktales. Joshua Alley's Chute bears a close resemblance to the hero of Roby Hicks's tale "Hooray for Old Sloosha!" (story 25)

Finally the whites overpowered [the Indians] and drove em, and that made em mad and they hung right to their ugliness then and, breaking on the nighttime, they'd take you, after dark. And they killed quite a lot. Quite a lot of the whites, they killed. And scalped em and all—and massacred em in almost every way. And some, when they couldn't get into the house, they'd set the house afire. Burn you up in it. Well, they kept on that way, and they couldn't do nothing with em and at last the Indians said they'd make peace. They'd come around with a pipe, called a peace pipe, smoke the peace pipe—that was all right. If you could smoke it, you were all right, they wouldn't bother you no more. But the ones that didn't smoke the peace pipe had to look out for themselves.

And [the whites] would see em out in the hay, the bushes—a-looking out, a-peeking out, just before dark. They were watching for em all the time. And . . . the Indians was watching for the whites, to see what time to attack the houses. And after it got just so dark, just at the time of evening, they'd hear em around the house, with these clubs of wood, trying to break the doors in, you know. Break in to get into the house to kill the people in the house.

Well, they was two or three of the settlers that settled close together, and when they thought they was coming, a good lot of them Indians, they would all leave then, go to one house, so to be together, and . . . there'd be a show then. If there was just one family to fight these Indians, you know, why they wouldn't stand no show at all. And so [the Indians would] start the house afire. They couldn't get in, so they start the house afire, and then they try to kill [the whites] when they come out [of the burning house].

[One time, the attacking Indians did not suspect that all the settlers were in one house.] But when they come out, there were so many of em—that they only just fired one shot at the Indians, and they run. Took into the woods, a-hollerin. Drove em off. . . .

Spring come. And when it come on warm weather, why then, [the Indians] kind of slacked up, and kind of made up with the white people, and the white people told em that they wouldn't hurt nor harm em if they'd just keep quiet about it.

Well, they had killed—gone in one house and killed all the—everyone in the house but one boy, during the winter. One boy was saved out of the whole family. The mother and father and all his brothers and sisters were killed by the Indians. And he had hid away in some part of the house and saved himself. So after the Indians went away, he told the neighbors on em. He said, "If I live to grow up, I'm going to be up square with the Indians. I'm going to kill as many Indians as they killed of the white people. And I ain't a-going to give up."

So they called him "Chute"—this boy. And he growed up. And he was out on a marsh, mowing hay—he was out on this marsh, mowing, and this stream ran right up through that marsh where he was—and he carried his gun wherever he went. So he carried his gun in the marsh and laid it around. And the Indians, they come out of the woods and see him on that marsh. One of em swung across through the stream and got that gun, and he sung out, he says, "Now," he says, "I'll shoot you with your own gun."

Chute looked, now he had his gun. He took his ax and he run toward the Indian. And the Indian didn't know what to do. See him coming right at him and he didn't know what to do. Whether to fire or run, or what to do. When he got near enough, he ripped him right across his guts, cut his guts right out, killed the Indian right there before he had the chance to fire the gun. Well, he had him. And the rest of em across in the woods was watching all it, and they all ran into the woods, they thought he was an awful man. That Chute was. So they took back into the woods.

And one time he was a-splitting a log, Chute was, and he had some wedges in the log to split it open, and he was driving them wedges. He hit one and he'd work on it till he split the log.

And the Indians surrounded him there. Well, when he looked around and found he was surrounded with Indians, they asked him what he was doing [with] that log. He says, "Splitting of it." Now, he says, "If you'll sit down there, and take your hands, some on one side of the log, and some on the other, and pull, help me split it."

Well, they laughed, you know, and got their hands in there, in that crack where he cracked it open and began to lay back and pull. And he was going to drive the wedges. Well, when they got a-pulling, he begin to knock wedges out. And he got all the wedges out, that log come out, that log come back together, and he got every Indian hung by the hands. And then he turned to and killed every one of em.

66. Dodging the Wolves

JOSHUA ALLEY
Jonesport, Maine
Recorded by Marguerite
Chapallaz,
December 13, 1934

There was wolves here. Wolf's an awful bad animal, you know. And, why, there was what the Indians call "Indian Devils" here.

[Marguerite Chapallaz: What's that?]

Well, it's a beast, short-legged beast. Terrible ugly. And . . . the Indians was scared of them. The Indians called them Indian Devils.

237

[Marguerite Chapallaz: Do you get them now?]

Well, once in a while there's one. There was one that tackled one of our men over at Addison and like to have killed him before they got him clear from him. They watch their chance and come up right behind you and jump right in betwixt the two shoulders, behind here, you see, you couldn't get at him. And his long claws stuck into you. Why, he ripped the clothes off of that man, tore his flesh to pieces, would have killed him in a very short time, but there was another man there that happened to get him off of him. Got him off. Else he'd a killed him. . . .

There was two young fellows that lived up here, on what we call Snare Creek. And they went with their father to go and take the oxen and go in the morning to get a load of hay. And they had to go to Addison . . . just below Columbia, down the river.

Well, they're two boys now. Well, we'll call em two young men. I guess that'd be best. No, they weren't little boys. They took a yoke of oxen and started after hay in the morning. They got over there, to Addison, and the oxen are slow to get around with.

And they had two pitchforks, three-tine forks. So they got over there and got the hay loaded on, and then the man that had the hay wanted em to stay and have something to eat so they wouldn't be hungry, going back. And that took em later than they ought to have stayed. And when they drove up and got into what they call the Five Mile Woods, they's coming into the woods there . . . and these wolves come out and surrounded the hay rack that the hay was in.

The older boy told the other one, the younger one, to take one side of the rack and he the other and not allow the wolves on to it, because if they did get up on there, they'd kill em both. And put, turned them forks into them. [Turned, drove] them forks at em to keep em off. Turn em off. And them two boys pitched them wolves. . . .

And they fought them wolves till they went through the Five Mile Woods and come out through the woods. Then the wolves went off, dropped off into the woods and followed along down through the woods, fast as the oxen went along.

So when they got a chance they'd . . . attack them again. Well, the oxen kept on going as fast as they could and [that wore] the oxen out. . . . Come up that hill there. . . . One of the oxen laid down. Tired out and beat and laid down low. . . .

Well, then, there was a man, where this ox laid down, [who] owned a yoke of younger ox. He told the boys to unhook them oxen and get em into his barn, take his young oxen and put em . . . onto the load of hay and on to home. And then in the evening they got their oxen up, the tired one up, and got em into the barn. And took the other man's young cattle and put em on the load of hay. And them wolves chased them clean home. Clean home to their building, where they lived. They lived down on what they call Snare Creek. Well, they got their cattle off, unhooked off the tongue, and got them into the barn, and shut the barn door up solid and took into the house. . . .

Well, in the morning they turned out and the wolves were gone, and unloaded their hay and took that man's oxen, carried em back, and got their'n. Now . . . these boys told me that themselves, you see. So I know that's true. I know that's true, all right.

67. Open, Saysem

JOSHUA ALLEY
Jonesport, Maine
Recorded by Marguerite Chapallaz,
December 13, 1934

Alley learned this tale as the report of a true event. As he says at the end, he added some fictional touches, "just to make it hold together." Yet Alley's final words to Marguerite Chapallaz indicate that he doubts that the story is true. Folklorists would tend to follow Alley's instincts. Whether or not such an incident ever occurred in Maine, this story follows the plot of the ancient and famous international folktale "Ali Baba and the Forty Thieves" and even retains a version of Ali Baba's famous magical formula, "Open, Sesame."

Well, there was two sisters and they married brothers. One was pretty well-to-do and could get along just as he wanted to. But the other one, the other sister, her husband was very poor. Couldn't get along. Couldn't get nothing. Couldn't earn nothing. And so that's the way they lived, and the other one, who had a plenty, would ask him what's the reason why that he couldn't have as much as he did. Well, he didn't know. Finally, they would have to take corn in a bag and lug it a long way on their backs to a mill to have it ground into meal.

So this poor fellow, he took his corn, started to leave in the morning, one morning, and traveling along through a strip of woods, . . . he see a little building in the woods, and he thought he'd go up to it. And he went up to the building

239

and got up behind it, and he found there was men in there talking. And he wanted to find out what they was talking about. And he said he found they was . . . counting money. And he knew it was a robbers' concern. Robbing everybody passed through the woods.

Well, he lay there and listened to em, and by and by one says they found there was a woman in the lot though, and found out—one says, "We'll go down to the main road." Well, this one went out through the door, one did, and he said,

"Open, Saysem."

And the door opened. And they all passed out, and he says to the door,

"Shut, Saysem."

And the door shut behind them.

Well, they went down outside in the woods, and he watched em. They went outside. And he went around to the door, and he says,

"Open, Saysem."

The door opened. He never told it to shut. Pretty cunning. And he went in and he found the money. So he dumped the corn out of the bag that he had, and put in what money he could load in the bag, in the room of corn. And he started to walk back home again.

He got home and he wanted a measurer. He didn't want to count it. He thought he'd measure it. So he sent over to his brother's and to borrow his measure, because he had some money. Well, his wife was a cunning critter, so she took and greased the bottom of the measure inside to find out what he measured, because something would stick to that. Well, he measured his money, and after he measured his money, why, he didn't think nothing about the measure any more than measuring money—sent the measure back. She found a half a dollar stuck to the bottom of the measure. So when her husband come home, she said, "Oh, let's go to your brother and find out where he got his money from." . . .

Well, he says "Why?"

And she says, "Well, he's been measuring money in our measure, and I've got a half a dollar that was stuck to the bottom of the measure. I greased it."

"Well," he said, he guessed he just got some money. Never had none.

"Well," she said, "just go on and see. And ask him how he got it. He's got it."

And he asked his brother where he got his money from that he measured in that measuring cup.

"What made you think I measured money in that measure?"

"Why," he said, "My wife greased the bottom of it before she sent it away, and she found a half a dollar of silver stuck to the bottom of the measure. Well, we've caught you now."

So he says, "Well, I don't want to tell you."

He says, "You tell me."

He says, "I don't want to tell you."

So he went back and told his wife [that his brother] wouldn't tell him. She drove him back there. Well, when he went to come back, and asked him again, [his brother] said, "Now, look. If you should go there, you'd be killed. I don't want you to go."

He says, "You tell me where you got it, and how you got it, and I'll run the risk of getting killed."

Well, he told him. Told him just what to do, and how to go to work to find out. So, he started. Went over. Found the same place, and he listened as the other one did, and when they went out, heared what they had to say, and watched em out of sight down to the woods, and he went around the door and told the door to open:

"Open, saysem."

The door opened alright. And he told it to shut, and it shut him in there, trapped him there. So he put in what money he thought he could lug, in the bag and went to the door. Said everything he could think of, and couldn't open it. Cause he couldn't, didn't say the right thing, he couldn't open it. Well. He was there so long that they come back and caught him there. And he never come home.

Well, his wife went over . . . to his brother's and then asked him what did he suppose the reason was why he hadn't come back yet.

"See, I know the reason. See, he's dead. They killed him." And he says, "To prove it, I'll go." So he started, went over, and went up behind the building and listened to who was in there, and when they went out, he went round and told the door to open—

"Open, saysem"

—and the door open. He just went in, took a look—and there was one quarter of him hung in one corner of that building, and another quarter hung in another corner of the building. And so he was quartered up, and there was four corners, and he was in each corner, a quarter of him. Killed and hung up there.

So he come back and told her, said, "Your husband is killed. He's just where I thought he was. And he's quartered up and hung up, one quarter in each corner of the house." And he says, "That's what you got by being a mistrustful woman. You weren't satisfied. If I'd have gone with him, he'd have come back alive."

That's the whole of that for you. I—of course, the last part of it, I put enough in it just to make it hold together, that's all. But don't you see that door opening?

[Marguerite Chapallaz: Yes.]

I know that's wrong. But that's it: I heard it, I told it.

68. The Murderers

JOSHUA ALLEY
Jonesport, Maine
Recorded by Marguerite
Chapallaz,
December 14, 1934

The white man was going through the barrens as we call it. And all alone. And he's traveling along, he's going for a number of miles, and by and by, he come to a nigger, sitting up by a brook of water. And the Negro—he looked to see what he was doing, and he had a loaf of bread. And he had a sword, the Negro had. The white man didn't have a thing. And . . . he looked up and said to the white man, "Sit down here, alongside of me, and help me eat this bread."

Well, he took the sword and sliced off a chunk of bread and then the white man sat down alongside him and he began to eat it. But he didn't like . . . he didn't like being with the nigger, you know, he didn't know when he might kill him with that sword.

Well, then they ate their lunch, you know, and started on a-traveling again. The Negro told the white man to go along with him—he'd protect him. Well, they traveled on, and along just about midday afternoon, why, they saw a little building in the woods, and the Negro says, "Let's go up to it." Well, the white man didn't care much for going up for it, but the Negro says, "Come on; I can take care of you."

So they went up. And there's nobody in the building. But . . . they looked around, and there was baked beans in the oven, and . . . they had a pie there, I think.

And now, the Negro says to the white man, "Let's have some baked beans." So they helped themselves to the baked beans and ate some of the pie. And there was a fireplace that went up in the end of it, and a ladder to go up into the chamber over the fireplace. Well, after they got all the baked beans they wanted, ate all they wanted, the Negro says, "I'm going up to the chamber. Look around."

And he went up, and there's nobody up there. And they found the beds up there. Now, he says, "Come on. Let's have a nap." [Laughing] So the white man went up, and laid down.

Now the Negro . . . laid his sword right alongside of him. Now the Negro says, "The least noise you hear, if I'm asleep, you wake me up carefully."

Well, . . . he said he didn't know if the Negro went to sleep or not, but he heard em come in, and he judged it was a couple or three men, and there was a woman in the loft. And of course the woman went along and said, "Somebody has been into the pie, and ate all of the pie."

. . . She went to the bean pot, she says, "Somebody's been into the beans, and ate all the beans." One man made a jump and he says, "Damn him," he says, "if I find him, he'll get it." Made for the ladder.

Well, [the white traveler] woke the nigger, and said he didn't know there were three, but the Negro come up, you know, got up, and took the sword and drawed it. When his head come in sight over the top of the flooring, he struck it and took it right off. Cut it right off, and the head tumbled back into the fireplace, and down onto the floor. And then they started to get out. Went down that [ladder] again, and out of the building and started down the road.

They didn't travel a great ways further before they come to the village and went into the first place they come to and reported this place that they'd been there, and what they had done. And [the villagers] went there, and they found these people there, and found that they'd been there a long time, and concluded that they'd robbed lots of men in the road, and got the money that they had and killed em for it, they said. And they took these people and put em in prison. Don't know what's become of em after that, he said.

There was a song made about it. . . .

69. The Haunted Sloop

JOSHUA ALLEY
Jonesport, Maine
Recorded by Marguerite
Chapallaz,
December 1934

As Joshua Alley began this family legend of a haunted ship, he explained to his listeners what a sloop is: "It would be a vessel with one mast, and if she had two, she'd be a schooner. If she had three, she'd be a ship." As the story begins, Joshua's grandfather develops an interest in purchasing a certain boat that he sees anchored in the harbor at Rockland, Maine.

Well, she had one mast. She was a big sloop. Carry about thirty cords of wood. Call her a big sloop. Well, [Grandfather Alley] said he'd like to have her. And looked her over, and the captain on her said he didn't know but what she could be bought.

Well, he said that when he come up again, that he'd see the owner of her.

So when he went up the next trip, to Rockland, [Grandfather Alley asked about the sloop again. The captain answered,] "We ain't using her. We give up using her."

But he didn't tell him what for. After the old man [Grandfather Alley] saw her the first time—she was all right when he saw her the first time—but after that, they couldn't go in her. Things aboard wasn't so they could use her. So, they didn't tell anyone about it. Wanted to sell her.

So [Grandfather Alley] went up. He says, "I'll make you an offer for her when I come up my next trip." So when he went up the next trip, it was getting to be late, getting along toward the winter setting in, and he said he thought he'd ferry his captain up and a man to come down with the captain in her—he was going to buy her if he could buy her before [the weather turned rough].

Went up and unloaded the vessel and he went and saw the owner, and the owner told him what he would take for her. And then [Grandfather Alley] told him, he said, "No, I'll make you an offer of what I'll give you, and if you want to sell her, why I'll give you that much money. If you don't want to sell her, you can keep her, and I'll keep my money."

Well, he wanted to get rid of her cause she was no use to him. Nobody wouldn't go in her. So he made him his offer, and he says, "She's yours. She's yours. You give me that much money and I'll give you a bill of sale for that sloop."

"All right." So he has the man draw it up and he give him his money for the sloop. And had the sloop and docked her down where the other vessel was till he started to . . . make for home.

Well, they started out late so they left from Rockland, just going dark. They got out into the bay and it come on dark and the men aboard the other schooner saw a big fire right in the middle of her deck. Well, they didn't know what had happened, so they run over towards her and called the men, and spoke to em.

[The sloop wasn't burning, but whenever the crew of the other vessel looked over at the sloop, they'd be a fire there.]

Well, they come across Rockland Bay, come over into Fox Island, on down through Fox Island and down through Deer Island and kept on a-coming along, run down and run into a cove called Molly Cove, way down on the lower end of the island. This sloop was run in there, anchored off Molly Cove. They haul her in there for the winter—she'd be in there for the winter.

They left this man aboard that went up for to come down with that mast. He asked him if he wanted to go ashore and he said, "No." He says, "I'll stay aboard." So he stayed, and [the other man] took the boat and went ashore and left him no boat. If he wanted to get ashore, he couldn't get ashore then.

So . . . he went below, he did, and turned in. To go to sleep. And he heard a noise. And he looked all around the cabin and he didn't see nothing. Looked everything over. Didn't see nothing. As quick as he'd lay down, that noise'd start up. Then he'd get up and hunt. All around. When he a-hunting around the cabin, it seemed [the noise] was in the vessel's hold. Well, when he'd go into the hold, he'd call crawl through the door hole and go into the hold and look there, and it'd be in the cabin.

So he kept on hunting and finally the last he heard of it was in the cabin, so he got back into the cabin and turned in again. And he hadn't more than turned in before it'd be in the hold, that noise would, and then in the cabin, kept going place to place. And he couldn't sleep. So he got up, dressed himself, put a heavy overcoat on, went out on deck. And when he left the cabin, that noise was in the cabin. Not a thing to be seen.

Well, then he got out around deck and heard it in the hold. He didn't bother looking no more. First thing he knew, there was a man alongside of him. And they walked the deck, backwards and forth from that time till daylight in the morning. Be said if he'd had a boat to get away from her, he wouldn't have stayed, but he *had* to stay. So in the morning, daylight, there was a boat rowed down by, and he hailed the boat and hollered to him and asked him if he wouldn't take him, he says, into shore.

And he says, "Yes, I'll take you to shore. Of course I will."

Well, he says, "I have walked side by side," he says, "I suppose with the devil all night. I don't know," he says, "there was a man walked side by side with me all night long. . . . I was hunting for him, and I heard him moving around, making noise," and he says, "I walked from that time till this time side by side with him. But he went away just," he says, "before you come alongside."

Well, that's all. They didn't nobody believe it, you know. And they hauled this schooner, this sloop into this cove . . . for the winter . . . and she laid there on the beach.

And my father was along by her—he was chopping wood there—and he passed along by her one day, and he thought she weren't laying very good. . . . And he was there to pick fuel wood . . . firewood. . . . [Part of the story is missing. Apparently Joshua's father tells Grandfather Alley that the sloop is in bad shape.]

So [Grandfather Alley] says, "We'll go down and take that sloop. Take her from there. And carry her. Fix her up home onto the beach, front of the house." . . . So they carried her up from there.

Well, his wife turned out early in the morning to get breakfast for the men as that worked, you know, in the woods. And she see a man come from that sloop. (They had her sail and rigging in the barn. Keep them in there dry for the winter, you know.) And she'd see a man leave that sloop, come up over the beach, pass along by the house, go into the barn. And then he come out of the barn, after being in there for a while, and go down back to board the sloop. After he went aboard the sloop, she didn't see him no more.

So she kept watch for a number of mornings, bout till the time that man would go. Come out of the sloop, go up into the barn, stay a while, come out, and get aboard the sloop.

So one morning she spoke to her husband, and said, "I want you to turn out in the morning when I do."

"What for?"

"Well," she says, "I want to show you something. Something," she says, "going on here that I don't understand. And I want you to turn out."

"Well," he says, "call me. I'll get up."

Oh, she looked one morning to get up, that man was coming. Getting out of the sloop. Went down to the beach. She went and called him.

"Now," she says, "I want you to watch that man, see where he goes."

He walked right up by the house and into the barn. And he kept watch. Didn't see him anymore and after a while he come out of the barn, walked down by the house, and down on board the sloop.

"Well, now," he says, "I'm gonna watch him." So he kept watch. The next morning he done the same thing. He'd like to know what there *was* in that *barn* that that man wanted to go in there and look at. So he watched him two or three mornings, and then he says, "Well. I'm going to find out why that man wants to be in the barn." So he, he went to the barn, and he looked around in there. There was nothing in there he could see, only just the sail and rigging that belonged to the sloop, and he told his wife, he said, "I believe that's what's haunted, I believe that's why they wanted to sell her, get rid of her. I don't believe we can do anything with her." He said, "I watched that man come out and go inside the barn—and the sail and rigging's in that barn belongs on her—

then he'd go down and board the sloop. Now," he says, "She's a good vessel. I don't know what to do with her. She's too good to burn up, and we can't use her if she's haunted. Well," he says, "I knew of a fellow, I knew of a young man that was in that vessel. I knew his name and talked with him. Fine young man. Nice young man. And there was a big man aboard there that abused him while I was right there. And I don't know but he's killed him, and his body may be in that sloop."

[Marguerite Chapallaz: Yes.]

So he says, "I don't know what to do with her."

"Well," says she, "Why don't you set fire to her and burn her all up and get rid of her, to get her out of the way so there won't be nothing for him to come around by here."

"Now," he says, "I'll think of it." So he took a week and thought it over, and turned out one morning. He spoke to his wife, he says, "Mother?" (That's what they used to call them, you know. Their wives, they'd call em "Mother." A lot of em does it now, down here anyway.) He says, "I've made my mind up to go and set fire to that sloop. It's too bad. Good vessel. I supposed I'd bought a good vessel and I had, why, but something's wrong with her. Now I have to go burn her up."

So he went down and start the sloop to fire. . . . Fire went through the cabin floor. And the fire went out.

And after the fire was all done, was out, he went onboard her, looking around the bottom of her, inside, and he found a dead man. Small, small man. And he looked at him. The fire had burned him some, he said, but he says he knew it was the same man, the young man that he saw aboard of her, and this big man was abusing him when he was there.

So he went up and told his wife, and he says, "Well, I found a dead man aboard that vessel." And he says, "I knew him by the looks of him, he ain't burnt so far anyway." And, he says, "I'm going to take him, and I'm going to have a casket made to put him in, and I'm going to bury him in our burying yard. And I'm going to name him, because I knew the name of the young man, and I'm going to call him by name."

And he took the, took this man out, had the casket made, carried him to the graveyard, and buried him under the name of this man that he saw—Rolaver. And there never was nothing ever seen of him afterwards.

That was my old Grandfather Alley. . . . Now that sounded funny, but nevertheless, he said that was *true*. So, would he burn a good vessel up unless there was something wrong about her? Of course, he wouldn't do it—he wouldn't have paid that money out for a vessel just to burn it up. He wouldn't do that. He burned her up. There's no doubt of that.

[Marguerite Chapallaz: I suppose they didn't have insurance in those days?]

70. Groans, Gold, Dreams, and the Devil

JOSHUA ALLEY
Jonesport, Maine
Recorded by Marguerite Chapallaz,
December 16, 1934

There was a cove on the island where we lived, you know, and we had to go around, round the cove, in order to go to my uncle's house. And my brother would go quite often over there, and he got around this cove.

And this night he started and went, and took another way to go around. And it was kind of dark, and he thought them rocks—he wouldn't travel through [them], he might get hurt. And he got about halfway when he heard a noise, and it was a bad noise. A big groan. And he said that he thought, at first, it was somebody, but when it come to groan again, he said he knew was no live person couldn't groan like that. He thought someone was there trying to scare him at first.

And then he said it was the devil. Believed it's the devil. And he says, if the devil comes, why, he says, I have to preach at him. Oh, he weren't so scared, you know. Well, he got, he kept going and he kept going, towards home. And [something attacked him]. And at last . . . he was down, hove down on to the ground. Well, he got up, after awhile, he got up, and about the time he'd get onto his feet to walk along, he'd get thrown down again.

[Marguerite Chapallaz: Did he see anything?]

Never seen a thing. Just something take hold and throw him down. And he was a big, stout man. And said he didn't seem to be scared. . . . And he kept throwing him down, onto the ground, till he got him so weak he couldn't hardly walk. And he just [barely] got home. And he said he was all in. He couldn't have walked a hundred yards further, when he got to the house. And his wife bathed him and says that they had an awful time of it trying to get him to feel better before he went to bed—it was in the evening, you know. And at last he felt a little better and he laid down. But he said he always thought it was the devil that was out there.

Well, I wasn't scared to go in the night, as I said, and I used to go up and see the old man [his uncle], but I used to go around a different way. But this time, how I happened to go, there was a girl there that was sick, that didn't belong there. Her mother lived there, that had married my uncle. And she had come home to them, sick. Well, that was when my mother was alive, and she wanted to know if I was going there. [She didn't want me to go into the house, because the girl] might have some kind of a disease I might catch. "You stay out down there until someone comes out of the house, then you ask em how the girl is, and then come right home."

Well, I went over. And any other time, there's some of the boys would be along to see [the uncle's family], speak to em. But that night, I was the only one showed up. Well, I stayed there and stayed there. And then the old man himself come out, with his kittle to go to the barn and milk his cows. By then it was dark.

And I says to him, "How is the girl, the sick girl in the house?"

And he says, "Come on. Go up to the barn with me." Never told me nothing about the girl. If he told me how the girl was, I could have gone right home. Well, I says, "I want to know how the girl is."

[He talked about] something else, and then I'd ask him about the girl, and he put it off on something else. . . . "Well," I said, "I'm about to go home. I can't find out anything."

"Well," he said, "hold on a while." So I stayed a little longer. I stayed till he milked both cows. And he says, "The girl *ain't any better*." Then.

I made it straight right down across his [mowing] field. Went right down where my brother heard that noise. I went along not thinking of anything like that. And the first thing I heard was a *groan*. And I stopped, and turned round, and looked toward where I'd heard the groan.

And I heard no one. And I says, "Now, I'm a-going. You won't scare me by groaning." And I thought it was one of my brother-in-laws, there, come there to scare me. I didn't notice whether the tide was up or down. I had never thought of it.

And I got down towards the mudflats, where the tides would come in. Never thought nothing about the tide. And I kept edging off [and that thing, it] kept groaning. Right behind me.

At last, I swung around and [got near home]. If the tide'd been up, I would have gone right in the ocean [laughs]. . . . And I run down across the mudflats, stepped around a pond of water, and when I got almost to the house . . . one of my brothers was coming across the field where we lived, from the other way. He'd been . . . over at another house on the other side of the island.

And he hollered, he said, "What is the trouble, with you running like that?"

[My legs were weak], and I could just walk to the house.

Well, when I got to the house, he met me and he says, "Now what was the trouble? What did you run that way for?"

I told him. And I says, "There was somebody there. And I think it was [the man that] married my sister. . . . Tomorrow morning I'm going to tackle him. So in the morning, I went up. . . . I asked my sister where he was. He weren't in the house. And she told me that he was down at the [fish hut] where he was salting his fish. I went down and I said, "Well, you thought you was going to do something great last night, didn't you?"

Says, "What was that?"

"Well," I says, "what was you up in the head of that cove for, trying to scare me?"

"Up in the head of the cove? I ain't been up in the head of the cove. See, go to the house and ask my woman if I was out of the house for the evening, and if she tells you I was out, why, you can believe it. And if she tells you I wasn't out, believe it."

Well I went up back to the house again. I asked my sister if [her husband] was out for the evening, anywhere. She said, "No, [he was] there in the house all evening." She wanted to know why I wanted to know that for.

Said, I heard some groaning up there in the head of the cove last night, and I said, I never was scareder in *my* life. . . .

What do you suppose it was?

[Marguerite Chapallaz: I don't know.]

Now, [my brother-in-law], I thought it was him, but it wasn't. Because my sister wouldn't have lied to me.

[Marguerite Chapallaz: Now, it didn't knock you down?]

No, no. I supposed it was the same thing that my brother heard, *exactly*. And they always said there was money buried there. The old folks claimed that . . . there was a pot of money there. And I have dreamed myself of the money being there, twice in particular.

[Marguerite Chapallaz: Is that so?]

Many years from one dream to the other.

5

WILL "GILLIE" GILCHRIST

TALES OF INJUSTICE IN THE URBAN SOUTH

In 1944, the celebrated African American poet Sterling Brown prevailed upon his friend Benjamin A. Botkin to deposit a series of sound-recorded narratives in the Archive of American Folk Song. Botkin acknowledged the gift with a brief and striking note to his colleagues:

> Professor Sterling Brown of Howard University has offered us for duplication nine 12-inch recordings made several years ago by him and Lewis Jones of Fisk University. These consist of personal narratives by a Negro barber in Nashville, Tennessee and throw valuable light on Southern life and lore, especially as they involve race relations. . . .

The disks were submitted with no further documentation; the narrator was not even mentioned by name, although former AFC director Alan Jabbour recalls that Brown often spoke admiringly of these performances.

The tapes contain a few long and artfully crafted personal experience stories, all told in the same voice by a man who identifies himself only as "Gil," "Gilchrist," or, once, "Will Gilchrist," a man better known to his many friends and admirers as "Gillie."

In 1928, when Sterling Brown was in residence as a visiting professor at Fisk University in Nashville, Tennessee, he struck up an acquaintance with Gillie, and the two became fast friends. I have not yet found any information on Will Gilchrist among Sterling Brown's writings, but two of Brown's friends have published a few paragraphs about the man.

Ophelia Settle Egypt, who met Brown in Nashville in 1928, wrote that Sterling Brown

Sterling Brown, collector of Will Gilchrist's tales (stories 71–75). (Moorland Spingarn Research Center, Howard University)

was in tune with his students and they loved him. So did Gilly [*sic*], the neighborhood barber, whose talent as story teller and entertainer sometimes interfered with his skillful barbering. This happened once when he became so involved in his story telling that he cut off all of his favorite customer's hair.

The next morning when Sterling entered the classroom, the students rose silently and walked out. They failed to recognize the strange bald-headed man and they were not about to have him take their beloved teacher's place.

Fisk University professor Lewis W. Jones, who joined with Brown in collecting these tales, has this to add:

> Sterling's pre-occupation with folk culture led him to search out the local folk artists. . . . There was Gillie. Will Gilchrist had a barber shop on Jefferson Street at 18th Avenue. He was a story teller without peer. His commentaries on life and people were always related with a straight face. He never showed any emotion, however much his audience would crack up, laughing until their eyes watered. He and Sterling became friends and on Sterling's recommendations, other Fisk faculty members became Gillie's customers and audience.

The AFC recordings bear witness to Gillie's hold on his hearers; his speech is frequently punctuated by the laughter of his audience, but in contrast to Jones's characterization, Gillie himself often joins in the laughter during these performances.

The nine disks on deposit at the American Folklife Center contain five lengthy stories that are more or less complete, along with fragments of a few others. It is probable that both Sterling Brown and Lewis Jones were present for all these performances, along with a fairly large audience, indicated by laughter and occasional background conversation. Gillie's Jefferson Street barbershop may have been the site of the performances, as at one point (in a passage that is not transcribed here) Gillie directs a listener, "Tell him we're closed."

A depressingly consistent strain of injustice runs through all the tales: Gilchrist is victimized by a thief or a careless driver, but when he seeks help to rectify the situation, he suffers humiliation, financial loss, or, more often, both. His intelligence and education cannot serve him, and his considerable verbal talents and his pride and justified anger work only to his disadvantage.

The sound quality of the recordings is generally good, and Gillie speaks with such clarity and force that most of his speech is easy to transcribe, but the brilliant intonations of his delivery cannot be translated into print. Not once in these long litanies of loss and abuse does his voice show the slightest hint of bitterness or self-pity. To the contrary, Gillie speaks with good-humored vigor, often breaking into laughter at points in his stories where a reader might expect a shout or a sob. Only rarely does his voice carry an angry edge. The few flashes of overt anger occur when he vocalizes the words of the various cops who threaten him. As often as not these bursts are followed by laughter. Then Gillie reassumes his even tone.

71. Robbed—and Taken for a Thief

WILL GILCHRIST
Nashville, Tennessee
Recorded by Sterling Brown and
Lewis Jones,
before 1944

About 12 o'clock, I'd been in bed about an hour. And they kept hollering, and I was asleep. I don't know why I was sleeping so sound, but I finally heard em.

"There's somebody getting in your window."

They thought it was some of the kids that hang around the shop, see? So, I rushed in there and saw a man going out the window with the last food. And turned the light on, but I realized I was naked and the people were just coming out of the shows, so I had to put the lights back out again and went back in and put on my pants, and looked—and all the clothes was gone off the racks in there, and I woke up the other boy and we decided . . . after looking around awhile, we'd go down to the station house and report it. So I went down there and told the desk sergeant that the place had been robbed out there and wished he could do something about it.

He said, "Well, I guess it'll be about an hour before one of the cops on that beat, they'll come by there, and just tell him about it." And I said, in the meantime, I'd like to have something done about it now. If we could get a man out there right away, we might, kind of trace—look around and run him down or something.

He said, "You go on on back and we'll send a man out there."

So I went back to the shop and sit around, and in about an hour, sure enough, a couple of big cops came in. Seemed to have been drunk. Guy said,

"Well, I come out here, to see about the place being robbed. Who's the man running the place?"

I says, "I run it."

"All right," he say, "you know who robbed it?"

I say, "No, sir."

"Then why do you think I'd know? You don't know. You run the place, don't you? [Drunken voice:] How do you think I ought to know?"

"Well, I don't know."

Says, "How'd he get in here?"

"He come in the window there."

"Was the window nailed or—"

"No, sir, it wasn't."

"Well, I be damned. You just raised your window and said, 'Come on in, little burglar,' eh?"

[Laughs] "No, sir, it wasn't like that," I said.

"Well, we'll see what we can do. We'll do a little investigating." Says, "How long you been running this place? What'd you lose?"

I said, "I lost about seven suits, a lot of ladies' dresses, a couple of women's coats, and three overcoats."

"Uh, huh. Pretty good pile of stuff, it seems. I'm going look around the house here."

The guy went out about fifteen minutes and came back. Says, "Whose car is that outside there?"

I had a Hudson. "That's mine."

"Your car, eh?"

"Yes, sir."

"Whose tires are those under the house around there?"

I says, "They're mine too."

"Why you got those tires laying around the house? They look like they're practically new. What they doing laying up under the house there?"

I said, "It looks like they're pretty good, but they aren't so good," I said.

"What's wrong with em?"

I said, "Well, one of em, when you pump it up, it's a big knot comes out of the side."

"That's right, because I've had tires like that. That's sand grooves. . . . That's one of em. Now, what's wrong with them other three?"

I say, "Well," I says, "One of em has a lot of [holes] in it."

"That's two wrong. Now what's wrong with the others?"

And I told him, on down to one. He says, "Now one of them under there is brand new. What in the hell are you doing with that one under there?" [Audience laughter]

And I said, "Well, to tell the truth, see, I don't have any lock on my spare tire, so I just put that under there in order to take care of it. So that when I did need it I could get it. Somebody might steal it off my car."

He says, "What the hell? Now here you are. You won't leave the tire on the car, because it ain't got no lock on it, but you throw it up under the house where it ain't locked and anybody can get it anyway." Said, "What the hell did you do that for?"

I said, "I thought it was locked."

"You *thought?* That's two times I caught you in a lie tonight. You *thought* it was locked."

Well, I began to get kind of tired of answering these questions. . . .

"Can you prove that you really bought them tires?"

"Yeah, I got a receipt to show that I bought em."

He said, "Where did you buy em?"

"I bought em at Quick Tire Sale. It's on Broad Street."

The guy says, "Show me an itemized statement where you bought em."

So I got a receipt, and it said on there "paid cash for five tires"—

[Interviewer: You had to do that—in the night?]

Oh yeah.

[Interviewer: My god.]

He said, "Show me where you paid cash for five tires in an itemized statement."

But the receipt just said, "Paid cash for five tires, seventy-five dollars," and had it marked "paid."

So this guy said, "That don't mean nothing. . . . That ain't nothing. That could be *any* kind of receipt, see," he says. "I want a itemized statement, where it says 'five Jones tires, description, size,' and whatnot. You ain't got that?"

I says, "No."

"By god, you got to get it."

[Laughs] "But—best I can do tonight. I—ain't nowhere I can get it."

"Uh, huh. You—you—you kind of cagey, see?" Say, "You—"

Then I said—I, I got kind of tired of—

[Interviewer: Meanwhile, the man's gone with all your clothes.]

Yeah, my clothes are gone. And I'm worried to death about a [lot] of stuff, and sent for the law to come out, . . . and I told him, I say, "I sent for you to come out here, to see about my place being robbed and try to help me out, and you jumped on me," I say. I was kind of getting up on my dignity and, as an American citizen and all that, and [laughter], well, he made me forget that pretty soon, because that guy, he just rushed up on me with his club, said, "Well, god damn it, you black son of a bitch, you can answer my questions, can't you?"

. . . I thought right quick, and I said—well, I had a pistol in my pocket too. I said [to myself], well, the best thing I can do is [lay low]. The man is drunk and all. And I don't want to answer for something. Well, I see the whole damn thing in a nutshell.

Told his partner, he says, "Now the thing that's happened: this nigger has sold all them clothes and took the money and bought tires and this big automobile with it, and now he's hollering 'robbery' to cover up his damn crime. Let's go." . . . He told me, he says, "Now, listen, nigger, you get them damn clothes and put em up on that rack, or I'm going to run your ass in, you understand" [laughs]—and walked on out, like he done solved the whole situation [laughing].

Well, one thing I forgot to say in this thing, this guy asked me, he said, "Them your tires?"

I told him, "Yes." He says, "Where'd you get em?"

I said, "I bought em."

"I know damn well you bought em. I mean where in the hell did you get em at? [Laughs] Where'd you get em at, is what I want to know. Oh, hell. Don't go telling me."

So the boy's [apparently, one of the kids who hang around the shop] standing around. [The cop] says, "What in the hell you doing here, boy?"

He says, "I just came here."

He says, "Look, partner, he says he just *came* here. [Laughs] Well, you get out." Well, the guy was all—

[Interviewer: He was giving em all hell—]

And then after he give everybody plenty of hell, he ain't said nothing about my place being robbed. He just dusted off his hands and said, "Well, I see the whole thing. Now you boys is innocent, most of you. But this big nigger, say, he smart. He's just using you all as a tool, and he stoled all the clothes and sold em and bought himself a big automobile and tires and all and now he's hollering robbery to cover up his damn crime."

257

72. More Cop Trouble

WILL GILCHRIST
Nashville, Tennessee
Recorded by Sterling Brown and
Lewis Jones,
before 1944

Another thing, all traffic cops . . . in the South seem to be mad as hell. I don't know. Look like they've been mistreated or something [laughs]. Old man Green got me to take him to town not long ago. And he said he didn't want to walk much. Wanted me to park in front of the courthouse. He had to go up there and rescue a deed. So, I saw a lot of cars parked and one man came out from there, parked at the curb. And I waited and got in his space. It said "no parking" on the curb, all the way around the courthouse. It says that all the way around there. As soon as I was getting in there, I hadn't got in there good, a colored fella came up and said, "You better not park there." Says, "You not allowed to park there."

[Then a policeman accosts Gillie:] "What the goddamn hell you doing parking in this space here?"

I said, "Well, I see all [sorts of] cars parked here."

"You mean to tell me if you see a son of a bitch jump out of a window, you going to go and jump out too?"

"No, sir."

"What in the hell you telling me about the cars being parked here, and that's why you parked here?"

"Well, I thought it would be all right."

"Let me tell you one thing, nigger. You get that goddamn raggedy-ass car out of here before I whip the goddamn hell out of you. Well, I have more trouble out of niggers than I do any goddamn—*get out of here with that goddamn thing!*" [Laughs] And his club was just bouncing up and down in the air.

Well, I was nervous as hell and I couldn't get the car started, because I was afraid the man was going to jump in there, and raise hell with me, but I finally got it out though.

And there ain't nowhere around town you can park. Nowhere, see? I don't know. Those people that's parked there, they must just *stay* there all the time, because any time you go to town, . . . all the places that don't have a sign on it, "DON'T PARK HERE"—why, there's a car in there.

And I finally parked about three blocks away, and I came back waiting for Mr. Green to come out of the courthouse. Because I had to be there. He might come out and he don't see the car, he don't know where in the hell I am, see? So I stands around until he comes out, and then we walked on.

I tell Green about it. And he's a man that's worth—I know he owns a hundred houses at least, and he's got a big store, and all that. Probably he's got a lot of money. And he's a Christian man, he's a preacher too, see. He says . . . , "We ought to could do something about that, Brother Gilchrist. It's a sin and a shame the way they do colored people."

And we come out, and he bought me gas, a gallon of gas, for carrying him up there, see? [Laughing] And everything was all right. It's not difficult—why hell, I just closed up my shop to take him up there and everything.

73. Courtroom Trouble

WILL GILCHRIST
Nashville, Tennessee
Recorded by Sterling Brown and
Lewis Jones,
before 1944

Well, one day, I left the shop and . . . I picked up a bunch of Fisk [University] boys. They just wanted a ride. I was going downtown to take some clothes to the cleaners. Had a cleaning place in conjunction with the barbershop, just a small place. And coming on back, we'd gone downtown and coming on back, got as far as Twelfth. On the corner of Twelfth and Jackson, a fellow named Sanders had a storage place—he moved and stored his furniture. So he had his truck parked there. He'd done unloaded, I guess, and he seemed to been aimed to turn around. He was facing north, kind of northeast, and he was going to back into Jackson and go back . . . south, towards town. But the motor didn't seem to be running. If it was, the car didn't seem to be moving or anything, and I thought he was just standing there, so I started in, and just as I get in Jackson, the man starts to backing up on me. And I mean, he came fast, just crushed the side of the car with the tailgate, broke it all down.

The man driving came out, he says, "Well, it's my fault." Says, "I'm looking up Jackson. I didn't look [your] way. It's kind of crowded up there and I couldn't see so well." Says, "It's my fault, so you just go to Mr. Sanders, the man who owns this truck," and says, "it's insured, I'm sure," and says, "he'll pay you. You ain't got nothing to worry about. It's all our fault."

I felt all right, and I still have the boys in the car, and I goes over to Mr. Sanders's house, he lived on Monroe Street. He was watering flowers, and I went up there and told him that I'd had a wreck with his truck. And I gave him a note that the driver sent, and he says, "The son of a bitch! Is he blind?" Says, "He ought to know if he's backing up, he's in the wrong. Just backed into your truck, huh?"

"Yes, sir."

"Well, you ain't got nothing to worry about. I'll fix it. Take it to one of the nice places and get an estimate on it, and call me up this evening, and tell me how much it costs."

So I called him that evening and told him it cost a hundred and ten dollars, cause they had to put a whole new side on it. It crushed the wood and all that from the hood all the way back to the back end.

He said, "A hundred and ten dollars?"

"Yes, sir."

"Gilchrist, my driver claims that you was kind of at fault."

I say, "I don't see how he could say that. He was *backin'*. And you know if a man's backing up, he's always at fault."

"Well, that's what he says, and I tell you what you do. You come down here tomorrow, and I'll have the driver here and we'll talk it over."

I says, "All right."

So I went down to his house the next morning, as he had told me, but he wasn't there. His people told me to go over to the warehouse where the wreck happened, he was over there. So I went over there, and they told me that he was at his office up at the Capitol Boulevard. And I went to the Capitol Boulevard. He wasn't there.

I run around trying to find him, I guess, for about a month, and I finally give up the idea of ever getting anything out of the wreck, because I'd paid for it already. And I said I'd let it go, but I was talking to a lawyer one day that hadn't been in the business long, and I told him about the wreck, and he said, "Gill, you can't lose nothing. I'll take the case on percentage. Whatever you get out of it, just give me half of it." Says, "That guy, if he was backing, then he was in the wrong."

So I took the man up on it, and he sued for a hundred and ten dollars. And the time that I had lost, use of the car, and all that stuff. Trying to make up enough for me to get my hundred and ten, and he get a hundred and ten [laughing] through some other way, see. So we won the case in the magistrate's court. [Sanders] didn't even have any witnesses at all. But he—in place of paying it off, why he carried it to the circuit court, and they have a jury over there.

We get over to the circuit court, and he's got a lot of witnesses. Men that didn't know a damned thing about it, I'm sure, but they were there as witnesses, and it seems that the one who tells the biggest lie wins out in lawsuits. Has the most witnesses. So . . . when the trial came up, they got a jury that had one colored fellow on there.

And there was a lawyer there. He tells [the driver of the truck], practically, what to say. Their lawyer . . . says, "Now, you was on this truck on June the fifteenth when Gilchrist ran into it, and just go ahead and state in your own way just what happened. Say now, first of all, . . . the truck wasn't in motion, it was standing perfectly still, and you heard a noise—in your own way now, go ahead." [Laughs]

And this nigger say, "Well, sir, I was sitting in the truck and all of sudden," said, "I heard a noise: *Ba-lam, Ba-lam, Ba-lam, Ba-lam, Ba-lam.*"

"And just what happened? That's a point I want to state here to the jury." Says, "Where this warehouse is situated, there's a hill there, and it's so steep, so when you come in on the bottom floor, when you get up to the alley, you can step in the second story window." (And that was true, see? It actually was, at that time. It's torn down now.) "And Gilchrist was going at such a high rate of speed. Tell the jury how far he had to go before he could come under control, get his car under control."

He said, "Well, boss, I tell you the truth—I just imagine he went a hundred yards before he could stop."

This lawyer says, "No," says, "Now, that's a little far." Says, "Bout a hundred feet. Is that right?"

He said, "Yassuh, Yassuh. That's about, that's about right. About a hundred feet," he says.

And he asked the man how long he'd been working for Sanders, and he told him he'd been working for him about ten years, and he's the nicest man he's ever met, and he's a fine man. So he excused him.

[Interviewer: Well, he called him "a fine colored gentleman," didn't he?" . . . I mean this guy working for him. Didn't you tell me that he was this "fine colored gentleman," but *you* were this "big brother nigger" with—]

Yeah, oh, yeah. But I didn't know that this lawyer that Sanders had: I'd *had him* myself. I'd hired him twice before. And he knew me, and he knew all of my business [laughs], and it kind of frightened me at first.

When I got on the stand, he says to me, he says, "Well," says, "Your name's Will Gilchrist." Says, "What kind of business you in, Gilchrist."

I say, "I run a barbershop and a pressing shop."

"Is that all?"

I says, "Yes, sir."

"You sure that's all?"

I say, "Yes, that's all."

"Well, I want to ask you, isn't it a fact that you're a bootlegger?"

"No, sir. Not a bootlegger, no sir."

"Well, I want to ask you, . . . right after Fourth of July, didn't Hal Thomas jump out of your car with [some liquor] . . . and run down through Shankton Alley? Is that right?"

I says, "No, you have some part of it right." I says, "Hal used to drive for me. He wasn't a chauffeur, but he used to do a little taxi business and pick up a little extra money with the car, because notes was pretty high, and I just had him like that. And he was arrested with two pints of whiskey in my car, but he never did drive it no more after that, because I didn't want nobody driving my car that even had anything to do with liquor. He didn't drive it no more after that. No, sir."

"Well, I want to ask you that on September the first, the same year, didn't they arrest the same nigger for speeding and drunk? He passed Sixteenth Avenue making sixty-five miles an hour, and the cop followed him on up to your place, and arrested Hal, and they pulled a nigger named Dan Mitchell out of the back seat with a pint of whiskey in his pocket, and he was so drunk to where we couldn't let him out on bond till the next morning."

I said, "No, sir." Well, that was a fact, see? But I just didn't want to admit it [laughs], and I told him "no."

And he said, "What you sitting there and lying like that, Gilchrist? You know good and well it's true."

I said, "No, sir." I never did own up to that, see?

But this jury, they began to look at me kind of funny. When old man Sanders come to the stand, they asked him, says, "Mr. Sanders, how long you been in business?"

"I been in business fifty years."

"What kind of business you in?"

"I move furniture and store furniture and pack and crate furniture," and all like that.

"How many hours a day do you work?"

"Some days I work all twenty-four hours." Says, "Just like yesterday. I moved some people to Lebanon, and we didn't quit. We just kept on, all through the night."

"Not like Gilchrist, just carousing around," says, "*You*, you work, huh?"

Says, "Yes."

"Go ahead and tell the jury just what you know about this case, Mr. Sanders. Take your time." Says, "I know how it is. You're not used to courts and things. Your own way."

Sanders said, "Well, I was just standing in my yard watering flowers, and I saw a great big car coming up the street with all the side tore open, and I wondered what had happened. And it stopped at my curb. I was watering the flowers. I started to run, cause I'm kind of scared of niggers, especially when I see so many of em together drinking that way, but my wife had told me that I had to water these flowers, and I's afraid to leave. And I stood there, stood my ground, even though I was afraid." And says, "This here nigger, Gilchrist, he was drunker than the rest, he was driving, but he seemed to have been a likeable kind of fella, and I, I, I thought I could stay there and not run. . . . He walked up to me (and the rest of these boys, they were all drinking), said, 'Mr. Sanders,' says, 'I'm a little drunk and I just hit your truck. I run into your truck and tore it up a little.' Says, 'I'm very sorry, and I come over to see if you wouldn't not, don't have me arrested,' he says. 'I believe you're a good man.' And I really felt sorry for the nigger.

[Audience laughs.]

"I decided I wouldn't have him arrested, and in fact I told him, I say, You come back over here, and I'll see what I can do. I thought I might help him fix his car. I know he was unfortunate and all. But he never did come back no more, so I didn't know what happened, and it was the biggest surprise I ever had: six months later he sues me. And that's all I know."

And that [lawyer], when he was telling the jury, I mean when he was charging the jury—or making his last bid [laughs] or whatever they do, he says, "Now, gentlemen of the jury, I think you've heard all the evidence in the case, and you see conclusively that this Gilchrist is a notorious character, a bootlegger, just carousing up and down the street in a big Hudson Super Six, [shouting] *in a Hudson Super Six*, the finest car in America, and nobody's safe—life and limb— nobody. Your wife or anybody is liable to be murdered. Just drunk, carousing up and down the street, and here's an honorable gentleman, been in business fifty years, told you right there that he's been working all night long. He ain't got no fine car, he rides in his truck. He ain't got no passenger car. I want you gentlemen of the jury to come back out here with a verdict in his favor, because this man is a bootlegger and a carouser. Just a bunch of the good-time people, just going around, raising hell."

I'd have been willing to give up right then [laughing], but the jury went out and they come back with a hung jury, see.

74. More Courtroom Trouble

WILL GILCHRIST
Nashville, Tennessee
Recorded by Sterling Brown and
Lewis Jones,
before 1944

I had an accident, see. It was a white firm. The Empire Furniture Company, and they had a colored driver. That was that winter when it was so cold, it was cold as hell and snow, see. So, I was . . . coming west on Jefferson, and a guy came off of Eighth Avenue, into Jefferson, north, see, and turned west right in front of me. He went two doors beyond that and whirled right back, just beyond Tenth, that's a alley there. I don't know whether you ever noticed it or not. It's a little alley and nobody ever comes out of that damn thing. But I wasn't expecting him to do that, see? I'm going along very carefully, because . . . if he stops I can't keep from running into him, see?

After he come over there, I got over on this side of the track, but without warning or anything, . . . he just *whipped in* . . . and whipped right back through that little alley there, man, and I couldn't do nothing. I blowed the hell out of my horn and [cut over] and I missed everything but the tailgate, see.

Well this guy gets out. . . . And by that time, two white fellows that was down in the alley there had read a warrant to take the furniture, and that's what the truck was doing out there, see. Two deputies, they came up there and says . . . "the boy was in the wrong. He forgot to hold out his hands [to signal his turn]. Here's a card of Empire Furniture Company. Just call em up. They've got insurance on this van. It's all right."

But when I called up the Empire Furniture Company, they didn't want to pay it, see. They said, that the boy said he was in the right.

So I told Luby [Gilchrist's lawyer] about it. He said, "We'll sue em. We'll sue em, see."

They had a witness up there. They had this other fellow says he saw it off the streetcar. . . . They had two lawyers, two white lawyers. So he says, "Now go ahead and tell the court what you know about this accident."

This guy says, "Well, I'm standing on a streetcar at Ninth and Jefferson, and Gilchrist come by there . . . running real fast. That's the reason I noticed him, see?

"I said to myself, said, 'that nigger's going to have a accident.' So I sat there, the streetcar rolling along, and when we got up to Tenth Avenue," says, "What happened? Just the time we got at Tenth Avenue, I heard a noise, *Blam! Ba-lam, Ba-lam!* . . . I looked out and there's Gilchrist. And say, 'Um-hum, I knowed it.' "

So, then his lawyer's talking to him. . . . Then Luby got up. I said to myself, I say, the judge didn't seem to be listening to what the guy was saying, or anything. So [Luby] got up and walked like he was going to pass this fellow, and when he got right even with him, he wheeled around and he says, "Who hired you to come up here?" [Laughter]

That scared that guy, and he said, "That man, right over there." Say, "His lawyer told me if he won the case, he'd pay me."

[The Empire Furniture Company lawyer] got up and said, "I didn't promise you anything. I told you . . . that if you would come up here as a witness—cause he's a mechanic, judge, and he makes pretty good money—and he didn't naturally want to leave his place, but I told him that if he would come up, that the county always paid witnesses. He could claim his fees for coming up here. That's what I told him."

And Luby said, "Well, I tell you what. I don't think that matters anyway. I just brought it out . . . to show you that I'm not holding it against you."

He says, "I know, but people in the courtroom might get the wrong idea."

He said, "Well." Old Luby just turned around to the court and said, "Ladies and gentlemen in the court, I don't believe that lawyer Brown here tried to bribe this witness." He said, "Is that all right?"

He said, "Yeah." That [laughing] was all of that, you see?

[Luby] said, "Now listen, Sam. You seem to know Gill pretty good, sir. You say you saw Gilchrist running past."

He said, "The reason I noticed him is he's been going so fast."

He said, "How fast was he going?"

He said, "Going about thirty-five miles an hour."

He said, "Well, how fast was you going—I meant, how fast was the streetcar going?"

"I don't know how fast it was going,"

He says, "Well, you was on the car. How do you know how fast Gilchrist was going, and *you* on the car and you don't know how fast the car was going?"

He said, "What's this about? Have mercy!" . . .

"You don't have to tell for sure how much. Just approximately. Best you can guess."

He says, "Well, we were going about five miles an hour, that's what, just about five miles an hour—cause it was a cold day—and we wasn't ripping up and down the street, acting like fools like that."

"All right. Then what happened?"

"Well, we rode on. I was on the car. The car went on."

He said, "Well, what else happened?"

He says, "Well, we stopped at Tenth Avenue and took on passengers."

"Then what happened?"

"Nothing. About that time I heard that noise."

He said, "Now look, if I understand you: Gilchrist passes you at Ninth and Jefferson, making thirty-five miles an hour, and you on the streetcar, traveling five miles an hour. You stopped at Tenth and Jefferson and picked up a passenger. How far was that—where the wreck happened—beyond Tenth?"

He says, "I don't know exactly."

He says, "Just about how much. Just guess."

He says, "It's two houses and a grocer on the corner, and there's two houses there, between the place and the corner where he had the wreck."

He says, "Well, those [store]fronts'd be about twenty-five feet, so that's probably fifty feet from the corner. And you was right there when the wreck happened?"

"Yes, sir."

Well, that was a hell of a thing, see: if he was just traveling five miles an hour and me traveling thirty-five, and he gets there the time I do, see, and stops to pick up a passenger. But the jury's not paying that no damn attention, seemingly. At all, see.

And they won out, finally. The judge says that he believed that if it'd been him driving, he could have stopped. The damn judge, see, could have been a lawyer himself, I mean—

[Listener: Right.]

—just the way he talked. He says, "Now, lawyer" . . . the judge asked them, were they willing to let the case go as, you know, just the testimony of the witnesses. And Luby said yes. But the white lawyers and all said, "We want to argue a point of law."

"Okay."

So they read article ten and . . . section five and seven, and it said something about coming on the left-hand side of a streetcar being against the law.

Then Luby told em that law had been stricken off the books because of the streetcar tracks being on the wrong side of the street. You remember, he won a suit against the company about that himself. He's the cause of it being off [the books], you know.

Judge, said, "Yeah, that don't apply to Jefferson Street and Twelfth Avenue side." . . .

Old Luby just walked over there, and he didn't have a book of his own. He picked up their book. Didn't even ask em for it. He just picked it up. He said, "Now, you read paragraphs five and seven. I just want to read one little paragraph here says that—and it's the only paragraph that has anything to do with the accident. So you left that out. I'll read that for you," he said. And it said in this paragraph that nobody driving a . . . car, or any kind of vehicle, should ever turn to the left in the middle of a block. If you have business on that side of the street, go up to the corner and turn around and come back down on that side. See? Says, "That's all."

Judge thought about it a minute and said that he believed that we both was negligent. . . .

I said, "But, Judge. Look it here. If this guy . . . had knowed that he was even driving, there wouldn't have been an accident. But he forgot about it." I said, "See, when he started across the street, I blowed my horn, and if he'd a looked out there, or held out his hand and showed me where he was going, I'd have had a chance to do something, but even after he forgot and started, if he'd have been awake and heard the horn, he could have gone up that-a-way or else hurried across, see, and I would have missed him. Because I'm *trying* to miss him, but he don't know nothing about it. He was just coming across there as hurried as hell, just right in, just had the street blocked, see? And he was the most surprised man in the world when the car hit him. He didn't know nothing. Damn scared to death."

So, we carried it to the circuit court. [The judge] said that it was one's fault as much as the other and he couldn't give me a verdict, so we said we'll take it to the circuit court.

So we went to the circuit court. First thing [Luby] done when he got up there, why, he asked the same Negro that said he was on the streetcar. He said, "Did you get your money?"

He says, "What money?"

"You know, . . . you told me down there that the white gentleman promised to pay you?"

[Gilchrist imitates the dismissive laughter of the witness:] "I ain't told you nothing."

[There is a break in the recording during which, apparently, Gillie narrates a growing conflict between Luby, Gilchrist's black attorney, and the black witness testifying against Gilchrist. When the story resumes, the witness is apparently speaking to Luby.]

"You might look like black, but you don't talk black."

"Don't I look like black?"

He said, "Well, yeah, but you don't talk like black. [Deep mushmouth voice:] I'm [not going to take no] more of that nigger. . . . I'm tired of him messing with me," and just got [up] and started out.

So the judge told him, said, "Come back here, boy. Answer this man's question."

"Make him stop [messing] with me," he said. Well, he figured that, by him being a witness for a white firm, I guess, and [up against] a Negro lawyer, that he could just talk any way he wanted, see. Of course, they give us plenty of time, let our witnesses talk, and they recognized Luby's motion that he was out of order and different things, but he had his mind made up, evidently, before the damn thing started. And he asked the driver of the car, did he hold out his hand. Said, "Did you hold out your hand when you went in there?"

He said, "No, sir, I didn't, but I kicked the door." Said, "That's the sign we drivers have when we drive trucks—that we just kick the door open, see?" Said, "It's so cold I didn't hold out my hand," said, "but I kicked the door open and he, he ought to have knowed it. I just slowed around." Said, "He, he, he must have been going pretty fast, cause he sure would have seen that door open."

"But you didn't hold out your hand?"

"No, sir, I didn't hold out my hand. No."

And the next witness that came up, he said he was riding in the cab with this driver, see. I don't think he was, though. I didn't see nobody on the thing with him, but I couldn't tell anybody that, so he said, "You was in the cab with him, wasn't you?"

"Yes, sir."

"Did he hold out his hand when, when the car passed?"

"Yes, sir. He sure did."

He said, "How did he do it?" [Laughing] Old Luby said, "How'd he do it," he said. "Held his hand out like that?" He said, "How'd you know he did that?"

"He had it out that way when he got out of the car—out of the truck. He still had his hand out, like that."

"Cold—it was pretty cold out there, wasn't it?"

He said, "Yeah."

"And he still had his hand out like that?"

He said, "Yeah."

"Well, now, if he was holding his hand out, do you think he would have knowed it? He'd have knowed . . . , wouldn't he?"

"Sure, he knowed it. He knowed it. He held his hand out. He knowed it."

He said, "Well, he says he didn't hold his hand out. He's a damn liar, that's one thing that he sure knows. I know that."

Well, the last witness has been up and everything, and me and Luby settled back, figured where we'd done won a verdict. The judge sits there, turned a few pages. About five minutes went past. "Well," he says, "I just can't give him a verdict. I can't see to save my life how I could." Says, "I can't see why Gilchrist couldn't have stopped his car."

I said, "Now look, Judge." [Laughing] Me and Luby argued with him. He acted like he was the lawyer for the white firm, see. I said, "Look, Judge. See, ice is on the street about half an inch thick. It's, it's just plumb bad, see. And I'm traveling as slow as I can drive a car, around ten or fifteen miles an hour. And this man comes out Tenth Avenue, and just say that it's in my car, and he don't go but about two houses, then he whips right back across me without any warning at all."

He say, "I know, but a car can't whip without going [fast]. When you see a car turn this-a-way," he say, "it turns gradually."

I say, "Not this man. This man just whipped around there," I said. And I'm right about six feet behind him, over in another lane, see."

"And when he started across there," he say, "why didn't you go over that way?"

I say the best thing I could do if I go that-a-away and away from him, you see? Because he's going that way, but the best thing I could do is to pull away from him, which I did. And," I say, "I missed everything but his tailgate. But he didn't try. He didn't do nothing. See what I mean? The man don't know that he's even driving." I say, "You can see that, can't you, Judge?"

"I still can't see it."

That was it then. He called next case. "Next case! Next case!"

75. Cop, Courtroom, and Jail Trouble

WILL GILCHRIST
Nashville, Tennessee
Recorded by Sterling Brown and Lewis Jones,
before 1944

Yeah. See, I was barbering over at D.J.'s. . . . I was back around eleven thirty and parked the car in the back of the shop. Along about one o'clock a cop came and he says, "Do you own a car?"

I told him, "Yes."

He says, "What kind of car?"

I say, "It's a Nash."

He says, "Let's see it."

I went to the back, to the porch with him. He looked out where the car should be, but it wasn't there.

He says, "You *had* a car, but you ain't got no car now. How long you been in the bed?"

I said, "Sir, I came in about eleven thirty."

"Where have you been?"

I told him I'd been to D.J.'s.

So he says, "Where's the clothes you wore before—I mean that you had on when you went to bed?"

And I showed him my clothes, and he examined them.

"No. So now tell the truth, Gilchrist," he says. "Somebody stoled your car and robbed a grocery up in Hendersonville, Tennessee. And seems that they were trying to put the blame right on you, because they stoled another car in Gallatin. Went through Hendersonville, through Gallatin, and stoled another car and piled your car with groceries, and when the law jumped em, they jumped in the car they stole in Gallatin and made the getaway, and the people down there's got the license number and called up here, told em that to find out whose car it was and it was Gilchrist's car, see. And they thinks it was you that robbed the store. And the car that they made their getaway in was found right in front of your barbershop, right out front." (I'm living in the back of the barbershop.) Says, "Now you come down in the morning and make a detailed report of this. Tell the people about it, and everything'll be all right."

So I went down the next morning, me and the other boys that stay in the room, and made a report, and one of these deputies told me, he say, "Now, Gilchrist, I'll go down and get that car for you for five dollars."

. . . It ain't but seventeen miles from here to Hendersonville. I figure I can go down there on a gallon of gas. I don't need to be giving him five dollars for that, see. Said, "I wouldn't give you that much."

He says, "Well, you'll be sorry. If you go down there—see, you don't know these country deputies like I do. You go down there after that car, them birds liable to put you *under* the jail."

I said, "Well I'll risk it anyway."

So I got a friend of mine—I put him a couple of gallons in there, and we rode down there. He told me the man that was the constable there was named Henderson, so I asked around, I saw a bunch of people standing there, seemed that nothing had happened in this little town for years. The whole town was out, just examining the place where the robbery was committed, looking all around the ground there where flour had been strewn. So I asked did they know Mr. Henderson. They showed him to me, so I went down there, I says, "Is this Mr. Henderson?"

He look me over, he say, "Yes. Henderson."

I said, "I'd like to speak to you." Caught him off to the side there, and I says, "Mr. Henderson," I says, "I'm Gilchrist. My car was stolen last night, and it's down here," and I said, "the law in Nashville told me if I would come down here and bring papers to prove to you that I really owned the car, that you would turn it over to me and that if it was any doubt about it, that you could call Sheriff Bowman and would substantiate that I am all right."

He says, "I *don't doubt* it's your car. I believe that. But what I wants to know is where in the hell was *you* when the robbery was being committed?"

I say, "Oh, I was in the bed."

"*Says you.* You was in the bed, eh? Well, I tell you. I ain't going to give you the car. Not now, anyway. That's my evidence. I'm holding that. I may give it to you later."

I say, "Well, when?" I say, "See, I run a little barbershop and every time I come down here, I have to close up my place. Give me some idea, and I can know how to work on it."

He say, "I don't know. I may give it to you tomorrow, I may give it to you next day. I may not never give it to you. Just according to how I feel." And walked away. Wasn't nothing else I could do. I say, "It's a hell of a situation." Now, I don't know whether to come back, or when to come back. But I waited two or three days and went back. Before I went back, I went by the chief of police here, and asked him to write me out some kind of statement.

He say, "You don't need that, Gil."

I say, "I know, but—"

"You really don't need any letters off any kind." Says, "When you get down there, if he don't believe what you say, tell him to call me. Just tell him to call me, and I will explain it to him. Because I know you. I knowed your daddy. I worked with him at the news shop before I got on the police force." Said, "I don't believe you'd tell a lie about it." He says, "Those fellas are kind of funny, but he'll listen to reason."

So I went back down there. I called him up. He said, "Back again, huh? You know, I ought to have arrested you when you was down here the other day."

[Listener: Was this in court? Was he in court?]

No, he was standing outside. There was still a big crowd out there. He says, "I ain't going to give you that god damn car. Ain't no need you keep running down here, asking me about it. And another thing: I believe you was in that robbery anyway. I *know* you were."

Well, I got hot like I did about the other car. See, I said, "Now listen. I run a barbershop in Nashville and I've been in the same spot twenty years." I say, "I make more money in one day than the whole town makes down here in a week." I was lying flatly, but I told him that. And I thought maybe the guy would kind of hush up, but man, that made him mad. [Laughing] He run up on to me, man. A little bitty fella, . . . see? He ran up under me and had me in the air.

He said, "Why, you black bastard, you." Says, "I'll put you *under* the jail. I ought to bust you." He hit at me. And I had to kind of grab his hand. And there's nothing around there but white folks, see? So I say, "I beg your pardon. I didn't mean any harm." [Laughing] I had to calm down. I tried to leave, but he held me. He hollered over there to the man that run the grocery, he said, "You want me to arrest this nigger?"

"No, don't arrest him."

"Well, you get out of this god damn town. *Get on out* now. I mean that."

And I'm hot. I tells him, I said, "Well, I tell you one thing. If somebody got more authority than you have, then I'm going to see them." I say, "Cause you won't listen to reason." I say, "I'm going to Gallatin" (that's the county seat) "and see the sheriff of this damn place and take out a . . . warrant and get the car."

He says, "I don't give a damn where you go. I run—*I'm* the law in this town. And I don't give a damn where you go."

But I forgot to tell you, when I went and told him that the chief [in Nashville] told me to tell him to call up, and he would tell him I was all right, he said, "I don't give a damn about them. They would help you rob us down here." Says, "All of you all work in cahoots. . . . *I* run this place," and so he said the same thing about Gallatin. He said, "Go anywhere you want to. You ain't going to get shit till I get ready to give it to you. I'm the law here." (I thought he was just a deputy, but he was a constable, see.) So I jumped in the car, and I had four or five boys in there with me, and we go on down to Gallatin.

I went in there, and it was an election coming up for president at the time. They had placards there, they had a great big black poll where Negroes voted. . . . I forget who was running at that time, but I think it was Roosevelt and somebody that . . . was going to have Negroes on the board of education. . . .

They had pictures of Negroes and white men together on these posters and things. And [the men in the sheriff's office] was hollering about that. And was hollering "nigger!" just like we weren't in there. . . . You know what I mean? White people will say "nigger," but if a Negro comes in, they usually kind of quiet down on it, you see. But *they* act just like we wasn't there. They was hollering "nigger," and those guys—there was a wooden floor in there, and they spit tobacco juice on it, all over it, in the sheriff's office they had little niches around the wall where they keep their sticks, what they whittle on. They whittle there, all day. They whittle, just whittle.

[Laughs] I don't know what made them mad. They just cussing. And the shavings was on the floor about *this* high. And they commenced to hollering, talking about niggers, see? So I told this man, I say, "I came up here from Hendersonville. I got a car down there, and the deputy's holding it and says he's holding it for evidence. He won't give it to me, and I want it returned."

He says, "You the man that they suspect of that robbery down there, huh?"

I didn't know that. I says, "I don't see how they could. When the police came to my house I was in the bed. And I wasn't—I didn't have on no kind of clothes or nothing. I didn't have no time to do away with all that. And they were there ten minutes after they got the call, see? But they were [really worked up about me] in Hendersonville."

"Yeah. But the whole town—see, nothing like that's happened there in years. They might lynch you, man. . . . Better get your car and get away from there if you can." Said, "Now, the warrant. . . . Have you got three dollars for the warrant?"

I had two dollars and sixty cents.

He says, "Well, I trust you for the other forty cents. But now who are you going to get to go on your bond? Do you know anybody in Gallatin?"

I said, "No. I don't know anybody around here."

He said, "Well, I can tell you. I know a colored fellow that's got a lot of property. And he's a pretty nice fella. Runs a drug store here. . . . Go down there and see him. And if he'll sign it, why you'll get it."

And I went down there, and met this man. I told him my troubles.

He say, "But I can't afford to fool with that." Says, "You don't know how it is in a small town like this." Says, "I'm respected here. And they've got you accused of highway robbery, you know, and burglary, and all that kind of stuff," and he says, "I don't *know* you. You may be innocent, but I don't know nothing about it." And says, "If they're going to find you guilty, why, they'll find me guilty right along with you, because I, you know, signed your bond and things like that. And I couldn't live here no more." Says, "I've been here all my life and accumulated quite a bit of property and everything. And they respect me, but I have to stay in my place." That's what he said. Mr. Reynolds, I think. Dr. Reynolds was his name.

So I told him that I rented from Professor Harris [of Fisk University in Nashville].

He said, "You rent from Richard Harris?" Said, "I went to school with him." Says, "Anytime you're a friend of Richard's, you're a friend of mine." Says, "I don't know you, but," says, "you got an honest face. I'm gonna sign that bond." Said, "I'll do that."

And he came on back with me. Got his coat, and we went back to sign the bond. But when we got in there, the sheriff says, "You're a little too late." Says, "I just got a wire, a call from Henderson[ville]. The constable there says don't give you no bond for the car, that he's coming up here with a warrant for your arrest. They got you charged with housebreaking and larceny, speeding, and a whole lot of other stuff. Running away from the scene, . . . and I don't know what."

So, [Reynolds] says, "Well, Gilchrist, you realize I've gone as far as I can go. But it's gone this far. I just can't go no further." Says, "I'm afraid, see. It'll jeopardize me."

I said [very softly], "Okay." And he went on out. . . .

But in the meantime, one of these deputies winked at the other one. They didn't say nothing, but he caught the wink, and they both walked out. They went down and fetched my car. They found a rope and a bucket in there. And they wanted to arrest all the boys was in the car, but they didn't. So I told two of the fellas that came in the jail with me to go back and tell I.U. Green (runs a grocery now), that I was in trouble up there and to try to get me out on bond.

This guy take me right on over and throws me into jail, see? When we was walking on over there, he told me, says, "I told you I was loyal to you, Gilchrist." Says, "I really don't believe that you stole it. And yet you look just exactly like the man. If it wasn't you, it was your brother."

So I looked right at him.

Says, "If it wasn't you, it was your brother." Said, "We got to hold you until you do something." Said, "I started to arrest you the other day. I didn't want to arrest you. You looked like a good man. But," he said, "you tried to bust me, and I'm going to show you the law." Put me in jail.

And Green owns a lot of property. I figured I wouldn't be in there long.

He'd get him a nice car and be right down to get me, and I would probably go back through there and put my hand on my nose at this man, see [laughs].

[Meanwhile, the boys who had driven to Gallatin with Gilchrist went to Green] and asked for Mr. Green to go my bond. And Mr. Green told em, says, "Now, I would go Gilchrist's bond as quick as I would my brother. But I wouldn't go my brother's bond. I don't go nobody's bond. That's just against my rules. I love Brother Gilchrist [audience laughter]. He's wonderful. He's awful wonderful. But I just, I just don't do that." [Laughing] So they went up to Mr. Harris. He had never told me how much he loved me or anything; in fact, I thought he was kind of selfish.

And Harris got in his car and brought his daughter and all down there, to get me out. But I don't know that, see. When I get in jail, there's nobody in there but one man, and he's about half crazy. And I talked to him until the crew came in. All the rest of the men were out working. So they came in that night. They all stayed in one place. They had us in one big cell where they all stayed. In fact, in the back part of this cell was a bathtub.

And they had a bathtub back there. And there was a little water in it. And it was very dirty and it had some green stuff like moss or something on it. It's been in there, I guess, a long time. It smelled pretty bad and it was awful dirty in there. And you could see all kind of roaches and bedbugs and things. So I was standing just right out in the middle of this thing, all the time I was down there. I wouldn't touch nothing, because I didn't want to get nothing on me, and I was looking to get out of there any minute.

These fellas began to make fun of me, just from the time they came in. "Who's that in there? They's got a man in there." And this here fella that was there already said, "He's from Nashville." And they named me "Nashville," see? "What they got you for, Nashville?" and says, "I know how it is." Says, "Ain't a man in prison nowhere that's done nothing. It's all accusing him, see." Says, "You ain't guilty. But what they accuse you of, see? Just tell me that."

"Well, they say I'm the fella that robbed the grocery store."

"Oh, *that*. So they got you for that?" Said. "Damn, that's a hell of a thing. I heard this man on the chain gang today, talking about that, said they was right after him. So you the man, huh?" Said, "You ain't guilty, though. You'll get out."

And a white guy in the other side (I couldn't see him, but he was looking at me through a crack, I guess), he says [yelling], "Hey, Nashville!"

I said, "What?"

"Listen here," he says. "They can't hold you for that." Says, "You tell em that *I* said let you out." Says, "It's all right, just a-head on out." [Laughing] I was mad as hell.

The guys, they began to wash up, see? They washed back there with the water running. They didn't have a hole or nothing. They just let the water run into this tub. After they washed their hands and things, then they washed their pans. They had to wash their own pans, what they eat out of. They getting ready for supper, see. And the water's cold coming out of that thing, and they didn't have any soap. . . . And they didn't get half the trash out of the damn pan that was already in it. They washed it a little, and dried it on a coattail or something, and handed it out, and a man bring back the pan, full of food. They had all that stuff that's cooked up together, soup and different things in there.

They hand me one. I said, "I don't want nothing." One of these niggers said, "Listen. I done that when I first got in here. Just like you, I wouldn't eat a bite." And he said, "But, now, you *may not* eat tomorrow. You may not eat no breakfast, and you may not eat no supper. But I bet you, if you in here the *next* day, you'll be the first one to have one of them pans, and you'll like it." Said, "You'll really like it. But in the meantime," he said, "now, you get that, and give it to me. I'll eat your part until [laughing], until you can even eat this shit." See. Well I got it and gave it to him.

And they commence playing checkers.

But before that, they wanted to give me a little trial. A little kangaroo trial there. . . . They're going to have a kangaroo trial. Said, "Now, Gilchrist, we got you charged with robbing a grocery store and running away from the scene of an accident and whatnot. Guilty or not guilty?" Says, "Before you answer, we want you to know that if you're found guilty, we gonna give you fifty lashes or fifty cents."

I said, "Now, let me tell you one thing, boys. I've caught enough hell here today already. And I'm really innocent." I said, "But if either one of you start after me," I say, "you'll have *me* to kill." I said [laughing], "I don't want no shit out of none of you guys."

So the fella says, "Well, he has had a pretty hard time." Says, "Let's just don't try him." See, so they didn't try me in the kangaroo court. And they played checkers, and got at me all the time about me being all dressed up and nowhere to go, all that kind of stuff, and I was guilty but I wouldn't admit it. And I was gonna eat that slop tomorrow, see.

So it's getting pretty late, and I begin to get worried like hell. I was standing back there. . . . So, these boys, after they eat and everything, they played checkers. And just as happy as a bunch of larks, you know. Talking and laughing about everything that happened on the job, and about the boss, and all that and that. And I'm standing back there. My head's just going round and round.

Trial was set for next week. I wasn't taking no chances on getting a shyster lawyer, because I realized that I was in a fair spot of trouble. And I hired a good lawyer, the lawyer cost fifty dollars, because he said the better part of the fee would be spent down there. . . . And, in the meantime, . . . he got me another bond, signed. He says, "I know you'll be bound over, and we'll get that fixed before we go down there." So, I had to go . . . get another bond made and carry my witnesses with me. And we went down there.

And they had the trial in Hendersonville in the grocery store. There was no jail there. The jail's at Gallatin, being the county seat. . . . They tried me there where the crime was committed, and it seemed to be a holiday everywhere out in the country. Everyone was in town to see this trial. And they were sitting on lard barrels and meal barrels, and things like that. There wasn't any chairs in there. The magistrate was going to sleep. They had to wake him up to get him to get his verdict [laughing], that's the actual fact. . . .

The constable says, "Now, I've been watching this store for twelve years, and on the night of the robbery, I saw a car coming from Nashville—and any time I see a car, I don't forget it. And one of the main reasons I remembered it, it had one of the lights out. And I told my deputy, I said, 'Ah, I saw a car with a light out—it's a Nash.'

"So they went on towards Gallatin and in about an hour they comes back and they got a Ford coupe behind em. I say 'Yeah, here come that car back.'

" 'Boss, how you know it's the car?'

" 'Well, it had a light out, and it was a Nash, and it was the same car.' (And it stops right there.) 'And they're stopping right here.'

"Come to a stop right, right there. And we're across the street. 'I wonder what they think they'll do.' And they went around there and broke into the store. And commenced to filling up this truck." Says, "I could have killed them right there, but I thought I'd rather catch em red-handed. And I told my buddy, 'Now, we'll take surroundings on em: you go around that way and I'll go around this-a-way.' But when I got in the middle of the street a light from a car coming from Gallatin shined on me, and they spied me, and they lit out.

"And . . . this nigger here, Gilchrist," said, "I shot at him, and I missed him. [To Gilchrist:] But you better thank your stars: I never missed nothing before in my life. I'm a good shot." Said, "God must have been with you." Says, "I really aimed to kill you, but I missed you. And you better thank your stars."

And he says, "They jumped in the Ford coupe and got away. And we got his car, and found his name and [called] down there, . . . and found he was the man that owned the car. And the bootblack that works in his shop was one of the men that was with him. And he came up with him before, but he didn't bring him down here this time." Says, "I should have arrested him then. But . . . the bootblack's a little black nigger . . . and *he* [Gilchrist] was the man, he was the leader of the gang. There was three of em. But Gilchrist sure was the leader, and I missed him." And he says, "To show you that he was, we found the coupe right in front of his barbershop. Went down there, and the coupe was right parked in front of his shop. He got out of it and went to bed."

And [the constable] woke the magistrate up after they had all the testimony, and the magistrate says [slow, sleepy voice], "Well," says, "I don't believe that I could give a verdict in anybody's favor cause I believe the boy is telling the truth to some extent, but the constable . . . , he just *knows* it so well until I can't doubt what he says, and I just have to bind him over."

And they bound me over to criminal court. But when we got outside, the lawyer told me, he said, "Now, that's all of it." Says, "If they . . . turn you loose, you might bring a suit against him or something, but it'll never come up."

I say, "Can I get my car?"

He say, "Yeah, you can get your car now."

So he went over there and told the man, "Let me have the car."

And he said, "Well, we got a garage fee on it." Says, "It's been here now two weeks. Charge you about a dollar and a half a day, you know—[laughs] it's pretty hard to keep things like that in order." I didn't have quite enough money, and the guy that arrested me loaned me two dollars, see. And he came to Nashville later and got it.

But the car wouldn't run. I had to hire a mechanic to fix it. They'd been running the car, ever since it had been down there. Heh, heh.

6

JANE MUNCY FUGATE

HEALING TALES FOR A MOUNTAIN CHILD AND TROUBLED ADULTS

Jane Muncy Fugate (born Jane Muncy in 1938), one of the nation's finest traditional storytellers, has until recently also been one of the most elusive. For more than half a century folklorists knew Jane almost exclusively through a series of published tales. In the spring of 1949 folklorist Leonard Roberts visited an Appalachian mountain schoolhouse and asked the children to record their family's folktales on the first reel-to-reel tape recorder that anyone had seen in Leslie County, Kentucky. One by one they marched up to the mike, spoke their piece, and took their seats again to listen to the other kids. Most of the tellers demonstrated that however carefully they had listened to their family tales, they hadn't yet learned how to tell them. The one great exception was 11-year-old Jane Muncy, who spoke with precocious composure and style. Most of the children told one story, a few returned to the mike to tell a second, but Jane told five, crafted as carefully as any adult could. In 1955, they were published in Roberts's *South from Hell-fer-Sartin*, a landmark collection of Appalachian tales. Roberts ran into Jane again in 1955, when she was 17. She recorded six more tales for him at that time, and four of these later performances, including the title tale, were eventually published in *Old Greasybeard: Tales from the Cumberland Gap* (1969).

We got to know these tales long before we got to know Jane. Accompanying the printed stories were only two sentences attempting to explain who she was. Roberts wrote that Jane was an excellent narrator who lived with her grandmother and learned the stories from her.

Not knowing Jane didn't keep us from loving her stories. Thousands read the tales published in Roberts's books, and a tape recording of one of Jane's

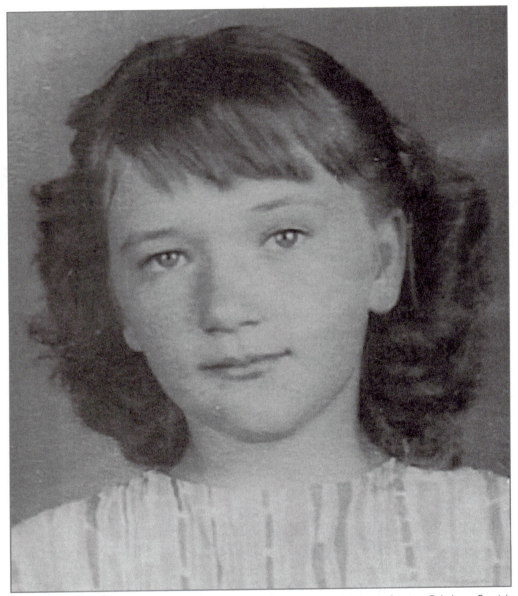

Jane Muncy at age 11 in 1949, when she first recorded folktales for Leonard Roberts. (Courtesy Bob Jason Fugate)

youthful performances ("Tailipoe," story 84) circulated among and captivated hundreds of folklore graduate students. Yet the stories kept begging us to imagine just how Jane had grown so wise so young. With no more than Roberts's few words as evidence, one folklorist wrote an essay on Jane Muncy's relationship with her grandmother.

In 1997, conducting fieldwork in eastern Kentucky and knowing that Jane would still be under 60 at that time, I went looking for her. It seemed to me that it would be easy enough to find her—until I discovered that Muncy is one of the most common surnames in Leslie County, Kentucky. After locating three different Jane Muncys, none of whom was the storyteller I sought, I traveled to Berea College on the western slopes of the Kentucky mountains, where the 1949 and 1955 tape recordings of Jane's folktales are housed. Listening to those tapes, I learned from Jane herself how I could find her. She introduced her telling of "Tailipoe," "My name is Janie Muncy, and I learned this story from my grandmother, Mrs. Sidney Farmer—that was her maiden name." That was the name I needed.

After a search long and strange enough to make a folktale in itself, I finally met Jane and her husband, Bob Fugate, in Melbourne, Florida, in June 2000. It was fitting that the name of Jane's grandmother led me to Jane, because, from the first moment I met Jane, she led me back to her grandmother. Decades after her death, Jane's grandmother was still alive in the Fugate home. The first photo I saw upon entering the house was a portrait of Sidney Farmer. The lavish and delicious supper served to me by Jane and Bob was the same Sunday supper that Jane's grandmother had made for Jane. And when we sat down to tape Jane's tales for the first time in forty-five years, Jane prefaced her performance with a detailed and loving reminiscence of her grandmother (story 76). To me, the tale of how Jane learned her tales is as compelling as the folktales themselves.

Jane's brilliant, resourceful, and headstrong grandmother was born in Leslie County in 1876. Sidney's mother, Rachel Wilson Farmer, was "of Scottish descent and quite, quite the stern taskmaster. Her father, whose name was Hiram, was very gentle, very loving, very permissive, and she, being the last child in her family, was doted on by her father a great deal. Her mother was always wanting her to do something constructive and stay around the house, and she told me that much of the time in the early years, she'd spent sort of running away from home to the nearest tall tree, where she would climb the tree with a book under her arm and spend time reading.

"When she grew to young adulthood—I would imagine in her late teens—the family arranged, as was the custom in those days, for her to marry . . . a man from a leading family in the community whose last name was Morgan. . . . This family had quite a bit of land and they were considered well-to-do, and as the Farmers were considered genteel, the two of them got together and arranged for their kids to get together. She married him. He was handsome, and I think she used the word 'rakish' to describe him. It turned out he was kind of a rake in a way, because . . . when they got together, according to her and other people's stories that I've heard, she was left alone a great deal while he was off with friends, and particularly gambling . . . while leaving her alone on their little farm that their families had given them, with a few chickens and a cow and a mule— part of the dowry. I guess one of the times when she was left alone, she decided, 'that's enough,' and she climbed aboard the mule and rode the mule back to her family's home and said, 'I'm here, and I'm not going back.'

"And it seems like an official divorce took place, which was unheard of in the early nineteen hundreds. She also told her family that she wanted to continue to be a teacher, as she wanted to before. She had been to the eighth grade. She'd studied art. She had been to an institute for teaching, and she wanted to teach. In those days, it was prohibitive for a teacher to be a divorced person. This would contaminate the minds of the people that she taught, so, so it was explained to her that she could not get a school, in the community, because of her divorced status. And so she said, 'Well, I will do the next thing. I will be a circuit-riding teacher.' And the circuit-riding teacher's job was to go to outlying communities, farm communities. The farmers in the area would gather up, and I guess it probably sometimes would be a whole family, a large group of children, and she would stay at a home and teach these kids, and then ride on and teach another group of kids, and on and on and on. . . .

"During one of these teaching periods, she went back to Berea College, where she attended the . . . educational institute. And it was there that she saw my grandfather William. He was a young man, very handsome, according to her, talking to a group of young women who were all tittering over him, and she said to her wagon mate that she came with, 'I'm going to go home with that fellow.' And she did. She ended up meeting with him during the institute, and they became friends and he took her home. And it wasn't long until they were seeing each other, and then they were married. . . . His parents didn't— . . . I don't think she was considered very favorably by them because of her divorced status, but she held her head high, and they had a home and they began to have children, and I think in the beginning they both taught. Granddaddy Will was quite talented. He could play the fiddle; he did so for dances. He could teach and preach, and did so for the Presbyterian Church. And he could, he could carpenter—he could build things, fine things and rugged things, and he did that too, and so between their teaching—which didn't pay very much—and his extra-curricular jobs . . . they made a living. And they had a family.

"I guess the family went okay. I have a feeling that maybe she was, like her mother, the head of her family, and he was, like her father, a very playful, kind of loving man. When my dad was in college, right during the Depression, Grandfather Will was working on a coal tipple and doing carpentry there and was hit in the head with a piece of slate and eventually died from the fractured skull and the brain damage that resulted. My grandmother carried on, had a boarding house, took in boarders, and continued to try to raise her children."

By 1942, when Jane came to live with her, Sidney Farmer Muncy had been a widow for twelve years and was herself a boarder in a house run by another widow in Kentucky. As Jane explains (in story 76), she was an emotional orphan when she arrived at her grandmother's house, and Grandmother Muncy used tales in a number of ways, as comforting, teaching, and morale-building devices to strengthen Jane. Those early narrative gifts gave Jane a sense of the healing power of stories that exerted a powerful shaping influence on her adult professional life: "The stories in Appalachia gave me a sense of healing for myself, and also gave me the idea that, 'Hey, there might be something in the story, the passed-down tale, that I could give to this person that would let them work for themself.'" Jane went on to earn a master's degree in social work and set to work at healing children, employing techniques not altogether different from those that her grandmother had used on her. She also treated adult drug and alcohol abusers and found that they, too, had things in common with her own childhood condition: "You cannot work with drug and alcohol populations without seeing people who have been wounded in their early childhood." During the Vietnam War, her work expanded to focus on adult males with post-traumatic stress disorder. Jane found that the healing lessons of her grandmother's stories could be translated fruitfully for all these diverse sufferers. Like her grandmother, she exploited the rich metaphoric potential of traditional tales to suggest, without explicitly stating, paths to wholeness for her patients. "In my healing, coming from a small, inadequate, undernourished, emotionally abandoned child to a woman that was seeking knowledge, trying to find out who I am, going into the field of psychology, looking at how I could help other people, I finally got on the notion of working with that part of the unconscious or subconscious mind, letting people know through metaphor what it is that they really need to know about themselves that I don't know in the first place. So they can take that information and do what they want with it, based on the stories that we tell."

Only one of Jane's early recordings ("Tailipoe," story 84) can be found in the collections of the Library of Congress. All the other stories published here were told by Jane during a three-day session in Florida in June 2000 and during two visits that she made to the University of Houston campus (March and

November 2001). In "How I Learned My Tales" (story 76), and in introducing "Merrywise" (story 77), she discusses her grandmother's healing techniques. In introducing "One-My-Darling" (story 78) and "The Tarnished Star" (story 83), Jane talks about how she uses tales with her patients.

76. How I Learned My Tales

JANE MUNCY FUGATE
Hyden, Kentucky, and Melbourne, Florida
Recorded by Carl Lindahl, Melbourne, Florida, June 3, 2000

My grandmother was Sidney Farmer Muncy. She was born Sidney Farmer. I think she was named from a . . . "drummer," who was a salesman who came through her community and his name was Sidney and so her family liked that name and they named her Sidney. She always kind of liked it too, and she liked the independence of just having one name, and didn't want anybody to shorten it, or abuse it in any way. That was her name, and she valued it. . . .

First time that I *remember* meeting her, I was about four, and my father and mother had lived in Pennsylvania. World War II had just started—the bombing of Pearl Harbor—and my father and mother were getting a divorce. And my father won custody and he wrote her a telegram. I saw the telegram when I was just a child, and the telegram said, "MOM, COME AND GET JANE I'M GOING IN / STOP." And so that she did. She got on a train and she rode on a train from Frankfurt, Kentucky, all the way to Pennsylvania—Philadelphia— to pick up little Jane.

And, she was a stranger to me, and I was basically a stranger to her. She was sixty-seven and, as far as she knew, I was going to be her charge for a long time, because the war had started, my dad was going in the Marines, and he was going to be far away, and she was going to have me on her own.

And she, she did just that. She told me many times that I was her salvation, that I kept her young. She slept with me. She cuddled me. She said I was terribly, terribly thin and small, and that she must revive me. She was surprised that I was living, as thin and small as I was, and she could carry me on one arm.

We made the train trip, and she took me into an apartment where she had been living with my Aunt Hope and said to the apartment lady (it was an adult apartment), "I *must* bring this child in, because she's practically an orphan." And whatever she said, she convinced the apartment owner that I could come there and I could live, as long as I was *quiet*. And that was fairly easy for me, and she saw to it that I kept busy with quiet activities like drawing and writing and listening to stories and listening to the radio with her, and mapping where her sons were as they traveled around the world in the various armed services. . . .

At the time that I met my grandmother—officially, in *my* mind—for the first time, when she came to get me, she had been a widow for many years. She had developed some sort of heart palpitations or flutterings that caused her to have some concern about her heart. She had Aunt Nora who was married with children of her own, and my grandmother had helped her raise some of those children. . . .

But our life together alone took on a pattern of creativity on her part to keep me occupied and quiet (naturally) and also teaching: teaching me how to read, teaching me how to listen to stories, and teaching me how to read the censored letters that came from my father and my Uncle Gill. Uncle Gill was a straightforward kind of guy, who liked to drink a lot, and he would write on and on and on and many times say things that were disclosing things the war effort people didn't want him to disclose. So his letters would be one or two sentences, and then a whole lot of cut-outs, and one or two sentences, and a whole lot of cut-outs—which was very frustrating to us, as we were trying to figure out where he was, because he couldn't tell us. My dad, however, was more cunning, and he would say things to her like, "Mom, you know that necklace that I sent to Jane? Well, that necklace came from Uncle Sol's store. Remember Uncle Sol? You can remember him, where he lived out on that little place all by himself."

And she would go get the map of Europe and the East, and she would say, "Ah, okay, it means he's on the Solomon Islands, it's an island all by itself, and that's the Sol he's talking about and they have shells." And so we, we had like a little war map and flags and his picture nearby. And he was my hero.

And *she* was my comfort. One of the things that she did for me for comfort was, I was allowed to sleep with her. I think in the beginning it was because she had a big bed, and not a little bed. But maybe not. I think families did sleep together a great deal in those years.

But the comforting thing we did at night was, we looked at the map one more time, we listened to the war news, we got into our nightgowns—I don't remember what *mine* looked like, but I remember hers was white and cotton and it had tiny bits of lace around the neck and around the sleeves. And then we wound up the clock. If we lived in a place that had a fireplace, we banked the fire, and we went to bed. But that wasn't the end of the day, because the end of the day usually involved her telling me at least a couple of stories that she'd heard as a child—and then drifting off to sleep. I would always drift off to sleep with my ear at her back, because I liked to hear her heart beat.

And then she would talk about *all* her ancestors: "and so-and-so had so-and-so and so-and-so and so-and-so, and then *they* had so-and-so and so-and-so and so-and-so." Kind of like reading the chapter of the Bible called Kings, when you just heard about who descended from whom and not much else about them.

So we were bedtime buddies and bedtime storytellers, and I would tell her a *favorite* story I wanted to hear, and she would usually tell that, and then she would tell me the favorite story she wanted to tell me, which I realize now as I'm older: they were not always folktales handed down from generation to generation, but sometimes found in fairytale books, sometimes found in the Arabian Nights stories. Sometimes they were stories about her family, things that actually happened in her family.

But it was a long tradition during that period—of about six years before I saw my father again. He was in the war until the war was over. At the end of the war he was wounded and sent to China to recoup and so he was over there for quite a long time before he actually came home, even though the war was over.

So that's how we, we got to the storytelling phase of our lives. And it continued. Even after Daddy came home. . . .

When I would ask for favorite stories, they would sometimes be the Jack Tales. The names of the people in her stories: they generally were about young men. And the names would be Tom, and Bill, and either Jack or—my *favorite* story was "Merrywise." And when I look at the name Merrywise, you know, he was not only the hero who was the youngest, but he was smarter than Tom and Bill. And could figure out things that they couldn't figure out. And so, the message to me was, you can be little, and you can be frail, and you can be the youngest, and you can be alone, but you can also be the smartest. And the Merrywise—"merry" meaning "happy"—you could be happy. You could be happy and you could be wise, and you can overcome. And so I thought of myself as that overcomer.

77. Merrywise

JANE MUNCY FUGATE
Hyden, Kentucky, and Melbourne, Florida
Recorded by Carl Lindahl in a folklore classroom,
University of Houston, Houston, Texas,
March 29, 2001

I will be sixty-four years old, and stories, or folktales, have been a part of my life for at least sixty of those years, a very important part of my life. I use stories in my work now. I'm a psychotherapist. I have a private practice. I work hospital work, adolescent units, drug and alcohol. I use stories to help my clients see themsel[ves] through the words that are about something else, or someone else. And for me it works.

I learned how to do that by having that apply in my own life. When I was four, I came to live with my grandmother, and she and I lived together, with various aunts and uncles coming in and out of our life. She told me stories, and in those days the stories were multi-purposeful. One of the purposes was to keep me occupied. Another purpose for the stories that we told were family gatherings, because the family were storytellers in general, and when we got together, we often sat around an open fireplace, or sat around some place that was cozy in the house, and, and told the stories that people remembered. Another purpose for the stories in those early days was to help us learn something. And I'll tell you one of the stories that, that I learned something about myself as a child, and I'll tell you another story that I've passed along to my children and often refer to them when I'm wanting to teach them something about themselves. My children are all grown. My oldest granddaughter graduated from Georgia Tech last year. So, there has been a couple of generations of stories since I learned the stories that I learned.

My grandmother was . . . an educated woman, a dynamic woman, a very caring woman, and a woman who had a lot to teach me, a little four-year-old who came to live with her. She said when I came to live with her that she could carry me on one arm. I had been probably a little malnourished and had what we now know in growth and development as failure to thrive syndrome. So she carried me around, and at night I slept with her. She would say, "Scoot up close next to my back, and I'll tell you a story." And

I would scoot up, either in the crook of her arm or next to her back, and listen as I got tired and eventually fell to sleep. So many times I learned what was coming next in her stories. Although . . . she could diversify, and go off on a little tangent from time to time, she also stuck pretty much to the same theme, and I found that as I got older, and there was something she wanted me to know in the story that was different than what she had told me earlier, I might hear a little different complexion of the person who was the hero—most of them were heroes, not heroines—but I would hear a little different complexion of the hero.

I became very acquainted with a little guy named Merrywise. Now Merrywise was an overcomer. I tell my clients there are two ways to be in the world. One way is to be a mastery person: you do everything right all the time. Things come easy. A mastery person doesn't know very well how to deal with failure. Or you can be a coping person. A coping person—and that's the way to be—a coping person has a tool kit and when they come to an obstacle in their road, they will take out something from the tool kit, and use it to chop through, go over, walk around, dig under the obstacle, and get to the other side.

Well, Merrywise was very much a coping kind of guy. He was the youngest in his family. He had two brothers, Tom and Bill. And while they were older and stronger and had more experience and people trusted them sometimes, it was always Merrywise, with his smallness and his cunning and his ability to craft his way through his world, that got them all out of a big jam. So I'd like to tell you now about Merrywise and his brothers as they left home and started out to seek their fortune.

You know, of course, being college students, that at some point you all will leave home and start off to seek your fortunes. Maybe you already have. It's an exciting time.

For Merrywise and his brothers, Bill and Tom, it happened after their parents—their father had died and their mother was old and sick, and she said, "Okay, boys, it's time for you to go out now and seek your fortune because I won't be here very long. And you two older boys need to go ahead and get started and Merrywise, you're *very* young, and I'd like you to stay with our neighbor lady. She's a very good person and she'll take care of you."

Well, Merrywise was also stubborn, and so Merrywise said, "No, I'm going." And they all said, "No, you can't." He said, "Yes, I can," and they started off to seek their fortune. Well, they walked and they walked and they walked and they walked up the mountains, down the valleys, through the hollows, and it was getting dark. And they were very tired and they were hungry. They hadn't taken anything to eat. And they found a house. And the house had a light coming from the inside as though there was a fire burning somewhere. Maybe a lantern. And so they said, "Should we knock on the door?"

And Merrywise said, "I will." So he *knocked* on the door. And the door opened. And there was a very *ugly* woman who answered the door. She had long, shaggy gray hair. She had a pimply face that had lumps all over in different places, and she had a long, skinny nose. And she was dressed in black. And so she opened the door, and Merrywise said, "Hi, Granny. We need a place to stay tonight."

And she said, "You *could be* my grandson. You could really be my grandson. Come in."

And he said, "My brothers are coming." And so the brothers came out from behind the bushes and they came in with him, and she saw Bill and Tom. And the old lady said [crafty voice], "Ah, yes. Come on in." Because one of the things she liked to do for hobby and entertainment was kill people. [Laughter]

And although she found Merrywise *very* charming and wanted [him] truly to be her grandson, she could see some hobbying entertainment coming from these other two. And so she fed them all meager food. And she said, "And now it's time to go to bed." And so she said to Bill and Tom, "I have two boys." And there were two pale-faced, kind of wimpy-looking little guys in the background, "and *they* sleep upstairs in the loft. And Bill and Tom, you go up, and you sleep in the loft with my two boys."

And Merrywise is watching all of this. And she says, "Merrywise, you sleep with me." Now "sleeping with" was a pretty good thing in those days, because it was cold in the cabin, and families had the family-bed kind of thing and people did sleep with people, and it seemed very natural that he would kind of sleep with her, because she was warm and, and—so he went and crawled into her bed, but he had that uneasy Merrywise feeling.

So she said to Bill and Tom, "Go up there and sleep with my two boys in the attic," and she went up with four caps. And two of the caps were red and two of the caps were white. And she said to her two boys, "You put on the two white caps," and she said to Bill and Tom, "You put on the red caps." And so they all got in their little respective beds, her two boys in one bed and Merrywise's brothers in the other bed, and it was time to go to sleep.

And pretty soon the old lady (she was a witch, you know) began to snore, and Merrywise was getting very relaxed, but he had that uneasy Merrywise feeling. And so he started to pretend like he was snoring. And she was snoring away. And in a little while her snoring stopped, and she scooted over to the edge of the bed, and put her little skinny legs over the edge of the bed, and she said [whispering, chanting voice], "I'll get up and whet my knife. I'll get up and whet my knife. I'll get up and whet my knife."

Well, his eyes got big and his ears started perking up, and he listened, but he lay very still. And she started to put on some kind of shoes to walk upstairs and had this knife and this whetting stone. And he said, "Ah, Granny, I'll go with you. I'll go with you."

And she said, "No, no. That's all right. You go on back to bed now. You go on back to bed."

. . . He said, "No, I don't wanna go. I want to go with you."

So she said, "Well, it's kind of cold out here. We'll, we'll both go back to sleep. Just go on back to sleep. Just go on back to sleep."

So he did, he cuddled under the covers and she put the covers up all around his face. He pretended he was asleep, and he pretended how to snore. We all know how to do that. And, sure enough, not too much longer, she got up and said it in a lower voice:

"I'll get up and whet my knife. I'll get up and whet my knife."

And he watched while she got up, and he said, "Granny! Granny! I'm going with you."

And she said, "No, no. Now. You're just waking up all the time here now. You've got to go back to sleep. Now watch me. I'm going back to sleep." And so she got back in bed again, and they went through the whole thing again. He acted like he was asleep. And she lay down and pretty soon her breathing got very regular, and she was drifting off, and he said, "Phew, my time has come."

And so he *scooted* out of the bed, very stealthfully in a Merrywise fashion. And up the stairs he went, very quietly, and he figured out that he better change caps on those two boys, and so he took the red caps off his brothers and put those on the sons of the wicked witch. And he took the white caps off of them, and he put those on his brothers, and he sneaked back downstairs as carefully as he could, and got into bed, and waited while he pretended to snore. Well, she kind of roused a little bit, and then she said again, in a much lower voice:

[Whispering] "I'll get up and whet my knife. I'll get up and whet my knife."

This time he continued to snore. And she did. She got up. She went up the stairs. Didn't hear a sound except, "Thud, thud." And she came back and got in bed.

Well, he figured that some dirty deed had gone on, but he still pretended to sleep, and pretty soon she was sawing logs. She was sleeping very hard. So Merrywise carefully got out of his side of the bed, and went up, and kicked his brothers, and, "Get out of that bed. Get out of that bed. You slept through something horrible. Look over there."

And there were her two sons with their heads chopped off. And he came back downstairs. And he and the brothers took off, as fast as they could leave, leaving that house, high and dry. But as they went through her yard and across her property, they picked up something for good luck, because we know, when we leave a bad place, we have to take a little something with us for good luck. And so Bill went through the hen house, and he grabs an egg, stuck it in his pocket. Tom passed a pile of rocks by the well. He grabbed a rock and stuck it in his pocket. Merrywise was going past a hickory tree, and he grabbed a hickory nut, and put that in his pocket. And *farewell to the place.* They took off down the road running as fast as they could.

Well, the wicked witch old lady slept until dawn and then she woke up. Merrywise was gone. She went upstairs. She saw what she had done, and *she was mad.* Mad enough to use a very important thing. She went to her cabinet and she took out her Seven-Mile-a-Step boots and she put them on. Now, these were magical boots, because when you walked in them, you took one step that went seven miles. And so she took off down her pathway and out of her property, going seven-mile-a-step, seven-mile-a-step, seven-mile-a-step, and it doesn't take many of those to catch three running boys.

And so, when she came up to them, Bill took out the rock in his pocket and he threw it down and a giant rock wall sprung up, too far to get around and too high to get over. She was on the other side of it, and they were running as fast as they could off in the distance. Now, she had another magical power, and that was, she could call for anything she wanted to call for. And so she started calling from the top of her voice and crying out, "Come, all you animals of the world and beat a hole in this rock! Come and beat a hole in this rock so I can get through it!"

And of course the animals in the world obeyed her, and they came and they started beating through the rock and beating through the rock, with their horns and their hooves, and it took a while, but eventually there was a hole and the old lady went through, Seven-Mile-a-Step boots and all. And she took off again: seven-mile-a-step, seven-mile-a-step, seven-mile-a-step, seven-mile-a-step—and the boys were running so fast but they couldn't outrun her. She almost caught them again.

And so Tom took out his egg and he threw it down on the ground and a giant lake of egg came up all around, too deep to get through and too wide to go around. And the witch lady was on the other side of the egg, and they were high-tailing it down the road as fast as they could go again.

Well, one thing I forgot to tell you: when witches go on trips like this, they always take their bag of gold. Now that bag of gold was right along with her as she was walking seven-mile-a-step, seven-mile-a-step. So she's holding on to the bag of gold and she uses that magical voice of hers, and she calls, "All the animals in the world, come! Come and rescue me quick! Come and drink up this lick—lake!" And so here came the animals of the world and they lapped and they lapped and they slurped and they slurped and they slurped, and they made a pathway right through the yellow egg. And she took her seven-mile-a-step boots, and she was really getting mad, and walked right through that pathway to the other side, going after those boys again. And she went seven-mile-a-step, seven-mile-a-step, seven-mile-a-step, seven-mile-a-step, seven-mile-a-step, and she caught them again.

Well, this time Merrywise was the only one that had his magical token left. And so he took his hickory nut out of his hand and threw it down on the ground and a hickory forest came up with tall, tall strong trees, and one particular strong tree. All the boys went up that tree. They were good tree climbers. They got up to the top of that tree, and they were looking down on this little old witch lady here. So she sat down her bag of gold and she took something from out of her pocket, and she opened it, and opened it, and opened it, and opened it again, and opened it again, until it was a giant bag, and she held it by the sides, and she said [cackling], "Ha, ha ha. Tom, jump down into my puddin-tuddin bag!" And Tom was looking down from the top of the hickory tree, and he went—sh-boom—right down into that puddin-tuddin bag. Merrywise was just shaking his head.

So she closed part of the bag up, and she says, "Bill! Jump down into my puddin-tuddin bag!" And Bill goes—pshoo-plink—right down into the bag. Right on top of his brother. And so she closed it up some more. And she opened it up and said, "Merrywise! Now you come down here into my puddin-tuddin bag!"

And he said, "No."

And she said, "I said come down here into this puddin-tuddin bag."

And he said, "I don't have to do what you say. I'm not coming down to the puddin-tuddin bag."

And she said, "I'm telling you one more time: come to the puddin-tuddin bag."

And he says, "No, Granny. I ain't coming."

And so she knotted up that bag, and she took up the tree after him. Well, he was very agile, and *he* came down. And she went up, and he came down. And she came down, and he went up, and this went on for a while, and she said, "My legs are tired. My knees are rusty. I'm old. I can't do this."

And when she said that, she was up at the top—up in the top of the tree. Well, he was aggravated at his silly brothers anyway, so he kicked em out that bag—opened the lid and he kicked them out of there. "Get out of there, brothers—quick. And take this bag of gold."

So he opens it up, and he says, "Granny! Come down into my puddin-tuddin bag!" And she went *pshoo* right down into the puddin-tuddin bag. Well, they quickly got some boulders, some big rocks, and they put em in there and they tied it tight and made another big knot in it, and they hauled it off, dragging it down to the creek, and threw it in the deep part of the creek where the sink hole is, and there it went way down, blub, blub, blub, blub, blub. And so Tom and Bill and Merrywise looked inside the bag of gold, and there was *all* the gold you could ever want in your entire life. And so they went on to the place where they could really spend their fortune and they met three beautiful women and got married and lived happy ever after.

78. One-My-Darling

JANE MUNCY FUGATE
Hyden, Kentucky, and Glendale, Arizona
Recorded by Carl Lindahl, Houston, Texas, November 10, 2001

Although no other version of "One-My-Darling" can be found in published collections of American folktales, this has been one of Jane's favorite tales for many years. Jane performs most of the tale in a haunting, near-whisper of a voice, and she sings the recurrent "One-My-Darling" chant in an equally haunting tone.

Jane has found "One-My-Darling" to be a particularly valuable tool in her psychology practice. "The story is about forgiveness, and I think, although it isn't said right out, it shows that this was a child for some reason, who was not loved and nurtured in her family of origin, who experienced trauma, and somehow made it out to a better place—through survivorship, but was able to forgive. I have a feeling about Esmerelda, that she would have forgiven, even if she had not met a handsome prince and even if she had not had a castle and maidservants—that forgiveness would have been a part of her life."

This performance was attended by ten people, most of whom were women specializing in psychological therapeutics or related forms of rehabilitation work. The audience response to the tale indicates a certain shock level; the listeners clearly expected a happier ending than the one Jane delivered.

I want to tell you a story that I have told in many women's groups . . . and very seldom do I have somebody who says to me, "That meant nothing," because most of the time it touches somewhere. It goes on . . . one of the themes I believe stories are helpful with . . . the theme of forgiveness. And so let me just start telling it.

In a cabin at the edge of a long group of mountains that were forested heavily with trees, there lived a woman and her four children. They were all daughters. The woman lived alone, raising her children.

In the forest, at the edge of the mountains, lived goblins and as you know, from your childhood, they like to eat people. And so this household . . . , like many of us who face danger, made plans, contingency plans, to survive. The woman had to go into the town, a little bit far away, and work. And so she left her children alone at home. Esmerelda, the heroine of our story, was the oldest, and it was her job to take care of the other three children while the mother was gone.

Now, because the goblins were well known to eat people, and to *relish* children—that was their dessert—the mother told her children, "*Do not* go out of the cabin while I'm gone. You can come to meet me and open the door *only* after you hear me come to the edge of our property and sing the following:

One-My-Darling, come to Mother,
Two-My-Darling, come to Mother,
Three-My-Darling, come to Mother—
Esmerelda, stay where you are."

Now, Esmerelda was used to this, and she took care of her sisters, the best she could, watching after them inside the cabin while the mother was gone to work. But there was one particular feisty, greedy, hungry goblin at the edge of the forest who had his eyes set on the children. He wanted them to eat. And so he watched diligently, learning what they did and how they did it, and one day, a few minutes before it was time for the mother to come home, he went to the edge of the clearing, and he said [gruff, parodic voice],

"One-My-Darling, come to Mother,
Two-My-Darling, come to Mother,
Three-My-Darling, come to Mother—
Esmerelda, stay where you are."

When the children started to run to the door and open it, Esmerelda said, "*No! No!*" and put herself against the door and, "*No!* You can't go! That isn't my mother."

And so after trying it again, and nobody came, [the goblin] gave up and stamped his foot, and went back to the woods—to wait.

And so within a few minutes, Mother came from the town where she'd been working, and said,

"One-My-Darling, come to Mother,
Two-My-Darling, come to Mother,
Three-My-Darling, come to Mother—
Esmerelda, stay where you are."

And so One, Two, and Three burst out the door and ran into their mother's arms, and she hugged them and kissed them and—"Oh, I missed you"—and walked with them back up the path to the house. Where they had a nice supper and a good evening . . . and enjoyed themselves.

Well, the goblin was crafty, and was not giving up on his favorite dessert dish . . . , and so he heard of a witch that might give him some ideas on how to handle this situation.

And he traveled . . . [into] the forest and sat down . . . , and he told her, "I want to make my voice sweeter. What is it that I need to do?"

And she told him how much he would have to pay her, of course, and she told him that she would make him—after he paid her this amount—a potion that would sweeten his voice, and he'd sound more like the mother.

And so, a few days later, she sent to him, and he went to get his potion, and drank it right away, and went to the edge of the forest—to wait.

When it became *almost* time for the mother to come home from her job in town, he hid behind a small bush at the edge of the clearing and said [in a rough voice, somewhat smoother than his last try],

"One-My-Darling, come to Mother,
Two-My-Darling, come to Mother,
Three-My-Darling, come to Mother—
Esmerelda, stay where you are."

And the children started to bound through the door and run to their mother, and Esmerelda *threw* herself against the cabin door, and said, "No! You cannot go. I cannot let you. That is not our mother. It is not our mother's voice."

And they were disgruntled, but they obeyed—their mother told them, "Always do what Esmerelda tells you—until you come to the door to meet me."

Well, again, the goblin gave up, and he went back to his goblin group, but he was, this time he was really mad, and really determined. So he went back to the witch in the forest, stamping holes in the ground as he walked. . . .

And he said to her, "I have been cheated. This potion did not make my voice sweet. Do you have power, or don't you have power?"

And she said, "Of course, I do."

And then he said, "Then I need to sound sweet."

And so she said, "Okay, I will add more ingredients and I will make you another potion, and here is what it will cost in gold, and come and see me in a few days."

Meanwhile, Mother went every day to work and came home every evening, and when she got to the edge of the clearing, she said

"One-My-Darling, come to Mother,
Two-My-Darling, come to Mother,
Three-My-Darling, come to Mother—
Esmerelda, stay where you are."

And Esmerelda stood back as the sisters ran through the door and received their mother's love, and got their hugs and their kisses. And they all walked joyfully back to the path, where Esmerelda usually did most of the dinner and cleaned, and they all had an enjoyable evening.

Well, the goblin visited the witch, and he got his second potion, and he drank it down thirstily. And so the following day when it was just about dark, with all that potion still inside of him, he went to the edge of the clearing and he said,

"One-My-Darling, come to Mother,
Two-My-Darling, come to Mother,
Three-My-Darling, come to Mother—
Esmerelda, stay where you are."

Listening very carefully, and thinking about what she had heard, Esmerelda said [whispering], "*No. No.* Don't go."

And the sisters said, "Yes, that *was* our mother. It was. It was."

And Esmerelda said, "No. It was not our mother. Stay where we are."

Well, *very* discouraged and *triple* angry, the goblin left and went back to his group. And a few minutes later, Mother came to the edge of the clearing, and said,

"One-My-Darling, come to Mother,
Two-My-Darling, come to Mother,
Three-My-Darling, come to Mother—
Esmerelda, stay where you are."

And the girls ran down the path, so joyous and glad to see their mother, bubbling over with things to talk about. Esmerelda cooked the dinner, cleaned— and they all had a joyous evening.

In a couple of days or so, the goblin went back to the witch to receive his *third* potion of magic voice softener. He paid a great deal of gold at the time, and he said, with his flashing red eyes, "This had better work."

And the witch said, "It *will*. It will."

And the next day came. And he drank half the potion the night before, and half the potion the morning of. He was loaded with potion. And ready to do his deed.

Mother was in town. It was time for her to come home. The children were waiting, and at the edge of the clearing, he said [in a voice much like the mother's]:

"One-My-Darling, come to Mother,
Two-My-Darling, come to Mother,

Three-My-Darling, come to Mother—
Esmerelda, stay where you are."

Esmerelda listened *very* carefully, because something was just a little bit off, but the girls were so sure they *burst* through the door and *ran* down the path just as he jumped out from behind the bush and gobbled them all up—smacking his lips, and eating them wholly and totally. There was nothing left but a greasy spot.

Esmerelda, having watched this, was in shock. She went back into the cabin and closed the door almost shut—letting just a flicker of light come in—and sat to wait for the mother.

So Mother came a little while later, and she said, from the edge of the clearing:

"One-My-Darling, come to Mother,
Two-My-Darling, come to Mother,
Three-My-Darling, come to Mother—
Esmerelda, stay where you are."

No children.

So, she thought, perhaps they were busy and they didn't hear her. And she said,

"One-My-Darling, come to Mother,
Two-My-Darling, come to Mother,
Three-My-Darling, come to Mother—
Esmerelda, stay where you are."

Silence. Nothing happened. And so she said a third time,

"One-My-Darling, come to Mother,"

[She saw the door was cracked open.]

"Two-My-Darling, come to Mother,
Three-My-Darling, come to Mother—
Esmerelda, Esmerelda?"

And Esmerelda left the cabin and walked sadly down the path, and together they went back into the cabin, and the mother heard the gruesome, awful, horrible, traumatic story. And she ran from the cabin, screaming, past the greasy spots that were her children. Her hair turned white instantly. Flushed, crazy, running with her arms in the air, off in the distance, disappearing.

Esmerelda settled back in a corner of the cabin, and only came out of the corner for a long time to eat, or get a drink of water. Very sad and lost.

Well, as happens in the tale, there was a handsome, eligible prince who lived in a place, two forests over, perhaps, who was riding through on a hunting excursion, and saw the cabin, and he said to his men, "Oh, ho! There's a cabin. Let's see who lives there."

When he went into the cabin and opened the door wide and the sun came in with all its generosity of light, *he saw* the most beautiful girl he had ever seen. Her hair hung in ringlets around her face, her eyes were sad and beautiful, and she was perfect in form.

He talked to her a bit—only just a bit—and then he fell madly in love with her, and asked her if she would come back to the kingdom and be his bride. She did. And in the new place, with someone who obviously loved her so much, she flourished. And their kingdom flourished. And he built her a beautiful castle with a walk around the top of her castle.

One day, her servants, who loved to be in her presence, said to her, "Queen Esmerelda? There's an old lady circling the edge of the castle. And she *seems* to be calling your name."

And Esmerelda said, "Well, I will go and look off the edge of my castle, and see." And when she did, she saw her mother, a much older version, hair hanging down in stringy fashion, with a face that looked as if it hadn't been washed, clothes tattered and torn, and her little voice was saying,

"One-My-Darling, come to Mother,
Two-My-Darling, come to Mother,
Three-My-Darling, come to Mother—
Esmerelda, where are you now?"

And so Esmerelda said to her maidservants, "Go and take her in. Feed her and wash her and clothe her, and see that she has all the comforts. Take care of her, and as much as possible, allow her to be—more happy."

[Listener: That's the way the story ends?]

Yes. [Laughter] What did you want to happen?

[Listener: I wanted her to find the goblin, sing, and have the children come out.]

Uh, uh. Life doesn't work that way—

[Listener: Sometimes in fairy tales it does.]

79. Old Greasybeard

JANE MUNCY FUGATE
Hyden, Kentucky, and Glendale, Arizona
Recorded by Carl Lindahl, Houston, Texas, November 8, 2001

Jane Muncy Fugate told "Old Greasybeard" in a unique context that demanded, and received, a wide range of her skills. She was addressing Carl Lindahl's senior-level folk narrative class at the University of Houston. Present were about twenty listeners, ranging more than 60 years in age, and Jane set herself the goal of making the story equally meaningful to all of them. The youngest listener, the 4-year-old son of a University of Houston graduate student, was directly facing Jane, who addressed her tale most specifically to him. Periodically, she asked him questions and made clarifications to make sure that he was following the story.

Jane's performance took place less than two months after the World Trade Center attacks of September 11, 2001. She saw this moment as an opportunity to portray the tale's villain, Old Greasybeard, in terms of a real-life character "who also has a long, gray, greasy beard," Osama bin Laden. She did not announce her intentions to her audience, but simply made a few crucial alterations in the way that she had typically told the story over the prior half century. As she explained a day after her telling, "I took the liberty of doing a little clandestine experiment last night. . . . Old Greasybeard . . . comes upon the three heroes in our story. He takes something that belongs to them. He goes back to his hole in the mountains . . . where three girls are kept. Now, I didn't change the story very much at all. The only slight changes that I made . . . were, I used the term 'routed out' [a phrase that U.S. president George W. Bush had been using frequently to describe the strategy for pursuing and capturing bin Laden and his al-Qaeda allies] and I used the phrase 'the girls were covered up' [to designate the birka that the Taliban required Afghan women to wear], and I think I used the phrase 'lifted the veil.' Now, in this whole story . . . that's about the only thing that I changed. But because these students had in their own subconscious . . . what is actually going on halfway around the world, they were able to incorporate that and see what happened." The story already contained a number of elements that resonated with the situation in Afghanistan: for example, "an eagle is called by Merrywise to come and save the central characters and, . . . and bring them out of the hole and bring them back to safety. I didn't make that up, but because it had all of these things that apply to them, it repeated in their own subconscious the story of what's happening. . . . That's what I find so interesting—that the story from then can be put in the context of now, and have meaning."

Jane's experiment worked: the students readily caught the references to current events and associated the villain with bin Laden and the heroes with the American effort to defeat the al-Qaeda and Taliban forces in Afghanistan.

As in all her performances, Jane geared her delivery to reach all her listeners. She simplified her diction and repeated certain crucial phrases to hold the attention of the child who was sitting directly in front of her, but she also fashioned her bin Laden metatext to engage the older listeners.

We would often sit at night around her fireplace and listen to the stories. And then I would cuddle up in my grandmother's lap and continue to listen as the adults continued to tell their stories. As I said, one of my *favorite* characters was Merrywise, and I'd like to tell you a Merrywise tale tonight.

[To the child in the audience:] Ready? You ready? Okay.

Well, Merrywise lived with his Mommy and his Poppy, and they lived in a mountain part of the country. And Merrywise had two brothers. The oldest brother's name was Tom, and the middle brother's name was Bill. And Merrywise was the youngest. He was the smallest. He was creative. He was cunning. He could figure out things because he was curious. Do you know what that means? It means you just can't wait to find out what's coming next. When you're curious you go look at things and you try to find out the answers.

So Merrywise was kind of his parents' baby . . . even though they were getting old (they had been older when they had these children). They called Bill and Tom and they said, "It's time for you boys to go out and seek your fortune—

Jane Muncy Fugate, age 63, in 2001, the year that she told most of her tales presented in this book. (Courtesy Bob Jason Fugate)

we're getting old and we can't take care of you. And when you've made enough money, when you've sought your fortune and you've found it, then I want you to come back and get Merrywise and take care of him too."

And Merrywise said, with his hands on his hips, "I want to go. I want to go seek my fortune."

And the Mommy and the Poppy said, "No, you're too little, you're too young. You can't go yet." And he raised such a fuss, such a big fuss that, when Bill and Tom had their knapsacks all ready, and they were ready to hit the road and seek their fortunes, Merrywise was going with them.

Well, guess where they were going? They were going through the mountains and the forests, and they were going out to find a place of their very own. And they were gonna do the things they knew how to do to make a life for themselves, and get their fortune.

Well, they did, with Merrywise in the knapsack, they took off, and they walked and they walked and they walked and they walked, and they finally found a place that was a clearing. And they cleared some more and they built a log cabin, and they were living there just as happy-ever-after as you could be, in their cabin. They even had a system. And the system that they had was this: that two of the boys would go out hunting, and the third guy would stay at home and he would clean a little bit and he would cook the supper and have it ready for them when they came home from their hunting trip.

Now it was getting wintertime, and lots of animals are stirring in the fall, so the hunting had been fairly good, so they had some deer meat, and some rabbit meat, and they had some squirrel meat, and they were eating pretty good. Taking turns about cooking, taking turns about taking care of themselves.

One day it was Merrywise and Bill's time to go out hunting, and Tom stayed home to cook the dinner. And so he was fixing around the house and working a little bit, and just about had the supper ready, and there was a knock at the door, and he said, "Come on in." And in through the door stuck this man's head. He was rather tall and he had a ten-gallon hat on, and it was greasy all around the brim. And he had a long greasy beard. And he said, "Hello." And he said, "I know you're Tom. And I've come to talk with you."

And Tom said, "Why, how did you know who I am?"

And he said, "Oh, I know all about you. I been studying you. I know all about you. I want to come in and talk with you for a while."

And so Tom said, "Okay. Come on in." And so the greasy-beard man came in and sat down in a split-bottom chair and leaned it up against the wall, and he began to talk with Tom about that part of the woods, and about where they lived, and . . . how they were eating—pleasant enough conversation, and almost time for the other two boys to come home from their hunting. And Tom said, " 'Scuse me, old man," he said. "I've got to go out to get some more kindling wood to put on the fire, because it's getting kind of cool, you know. And my brothers are going to be home any time now, and so, if you'll 'scuse me, I'm going out to the woodpile." So out he goes and he's chopping wood, getting it ready to bring in the house and put on the fire, and, and inside, the greasy-beard man has taken off his ten-gallon hat and dumped the squirrel meat and the fried potatoes and fried apples in his hat, and put that hat back on his head, and took off a-running.

Well, Tom saw that happen (the end of that), and he was amazed. And he went back in, and the brothers came home, and the brothers said, "Tom, we've been out hunting all day in this cold weather and, and here we come home looking for a hot supper. How come you don't have a hot supper on the stove?"

And Tom said, "Well, you won't believe what happened to me. This greasy-beard man, he came, he came to our house, and he sat back in that cane-bottomed chair—split-bottomed chair—and he said he wanted to talk to me. And I went out to get the kindling, and while I went out to get the kindling, he dumped his whole supper inside his hat and took off running with it. He even dumped the grease. Until I had to put this on. And I got some more rabbit meat here and I've got some potatoes, and it'll be a little while, but we'll get it ready."

So they sat around and they talked about that, and, and they sort of like, well, you know: "How did you let that happen?" And sort of cast a little blame his way. And so the next morning, the system was still working, and it was Tom's time to go hunting with Merrywise, and it was Bill's turn to stay home. And so Bill, he's fooling around. He's not quite the housekeeper that Tom is, but he's fooling around a little bit, doing this and that. And it comes time to get supper. And he's getting supper. It's getting cold and dark outside. And a knock on the door, and this head comes around the side of the door, and it's this greasy-beard old man with a ten-gallon hat on his head, and he says, "Hello, Bill. Can I come in and talk to you?"

And Bill said, "Oh, yeah, you can come in and talk to me. I been wanting to talk to you. Come in and sit down in the split-bottom chair."

So the old man did and leaned back and was basking in the fire, and Bill was cooking the supper, and it gets about time to add a little wood to the fire and Bill says to himself, "I'm going to make this real quick. This guy's not going to have any time to do anything, on *me*. But he says to the old man, "Old man,

I got to go outside and get some kindling, and I'm going to be real quick, and I'll be back, and the boys'll be home real soon for supper."

Well, it happens. Bill goes out. He's chopping the wood real fast, double time. He's getting ready to go back in the house just as he sees the greasy-beard man taking off his ten-gallon hat and dumping the whole full skillet (this night it was full of rabbit meat), and it was so delicious and it smelled so good, and they had fried potatoes and fried apples and biscuits. And the *whole thing* went into the ten-gallon hat, and it was gone.

Well, he just shook his head. He didn't know what to do. And sure enough, the boys came home, Tom and Merrywise. And this time they had a big discussion about it, and he said, [Tom] said, "Well, see I told you. You cast blame on me, and it wasn't my fault. You see, it happened again."

And Merrywise just sat there, and listened to the whole thing. Didn't say a whole lot, and then—so the boys said, "Okay, then, Merrywise. Tomorrow's your turn. You just see what you can do."

And he said, "Well, I think I can take care of it, boys. Just leave it to me. I think I can fix it."

And so the next morning it was starting to snow a little bit. It was very cold. And Bill and Tom go out hunting, and Merrywise goes to the smokehouse and gets some deer, and he's piddling around. It gets to be about lunch time, and he says, "Well, I think I better go do what I'm going to do."

So he goes out a little bit past the woodpile, and he finds a big log. And he splits that log, and puts a wedge in that log. And then he whistles and hums to himself, and goes back in the house, and he gets ready to begin to fix a good, hot supper for his tired, cold brothers coming home just waiting to eat.

Well, just about the time that the supper was almost ready, a knock came on the door. And he said, "Come in."

And old Mr. Greasybeard stuck his head inside the door again and said, "Hello, Merrywise."

And Merrywise said, "How did you know my name?"

And he said, "I know all about you. I been watching you from a distance. I know all about you: what time you do what you do, when you do it. I want to talk to you about what's going on in this part of the world, where you guys have set up here. I want to talk to you about that."

So he came in, and he sat by the stove in the split-bottom chair, and he leaned back, and they talked and talked, and it got time to add wood to the fire. And so Merrywise said, "Old man, would you step outside with me? I got to cut some kindling for the fire."

And old Mr. Greasybeard said, "No, I'm pretty comfortable. It's cold out there now, and it's starting to snow a lot, and I'm pretty comfortable in here. I'm going to sit right here, if you don't mind."

And Merrywise said, "Well, just go out with me for a minute. I've got something I want to show you."

And Mr. Greasybeard said, "Okay, just for a minute. And then I'm going to run in here and get warm—before I go on."

And so Merrywise said, "You can stay for supper if you want."

And he says, "No, I think I'll have to run along. But I'll go see just for a second. Then I'll come get warm."

So Merrywise steps outside, a little bit past the kindling pile. And Mr. Greasybeard steps outside right behind him. And he [Merrywise] says, "See right over there behind that log? Look over there behind that log. I want to show you that."

And Mr. Greasybeard—who had a long, greasy beard—looked over, and when he did, his beard worked right inside that log, and Merrywise—how cunning and smart he was, and what an engineer—kicked that log, and it closed shut really fast and closed up Mr. Greasybeard's beard right inside of that trap.

Well, Mr. Greasybeard was not used to being caught. And so he pulled and he yanked, and he yanked and he pulled, and pulled—and Merrywise just stood back and watched. And he pulled himself loose all right, but he pulled some of his hide off and some of the hair out of his beard, and he took off running through that snow just as hard as he could run.

Well, the boys came home. And Merrywise told them the story. "Mr. Greasybeard came today, and he, he tried to get our supper, but, boy, I got him. He got his beard caught in my trap, and . . . yanked—a good portion of his beard off. And he's run off. And look-y-there, there's blood spots in the snow from where he ran."

Well, the brothers gobbled down their supper real fast—cause, remember, it was cooking and it was ready—and they took out tracking while they could still see Mr. Greasybeard by the blood spots in the snow. Well, they tracked and tracked and tracked, and just as the moon was coming up really big and round— so that they could see—they found a hole. Well, Mr. Long-Greasybeard lived in a hole. He lived in the mountains, and back in a hole.

And these boys went to the edge of this deep hole, and they said, "Should we go down? It's dark down there."

And Tom said, "I'm going down."

And Bill said, "Well, I'm going down there and get him. He's not going to get my supper and get by with it."

And Merrywise said, "Well, if you boys are going, I guess I'll have to go with you, down into the mountains, into the hole. We'll have to rout him out. We'll have to flush him from his hole. And get Mr. Greasybeard."

And so Bill went down in the hole. And Tom went down in the hole. And there was Mr. Greasybeard, and he was waiting with a great big sharp crooked knife. And he said, "Now, boys, you've come on my land. And I don't like you coming to my part of the country. And so I'm going to have to kill you."

And so he takes after them with the knife, and just as he's going after Tom, Merrywise yanked him out of the way, and Old Greasybeard missed Tom. Didn't hit him. And then he starts after Bill with the sharp, jagged knife, and Merrywise pushed him real hard, and Bill fell over and the old man fell over, and he didn't get Bill either. And so Old Greasybeard came after Merrywise, and he was— "I'll get you. You're the one that's really causing all this trouble. I'll get you." And he started after Merrywise, . . . but he tripped over Bill's body in the bottom of the hole, and he fell, and fell on the knife—and that was the end of him.

Well, the boys got to searching around in this hole in the mountain part of the country, and they found that there was a lot of gold stored here and there in different places, and they also found that there was a room where three beautiful daughters sat, all covered up. They weren't allowed to come out from under their cover, and they weren't allowed to go anywhere, cause Old Greasybeard really had em stuck in that hole in the wall in the mountains, in the caves.

Well, right away, Tom lifted the cover of the oldest girl, and he said, "She's beautiful, and I want to take her home to be my wife." And so he asked her, and she said, "Yes."

And then Bill lifted the cover off the second girl, and said, "She's beautiful, and I want to take her home to be my wife." And she said, "Yes."

And Merrywise lifted the veil off the youngest and the prettiest and the sweetest of the girls, and he asked her if she would go home with him and be his wife, and she said, "Yes."

Now, getting in the hole was fairly easy, because they just sort of plunked down in it, but getting up out of it was not easy. And so the brothers tried to climb up out of the hole. Of course, Old Greasybeard knew that part of the country very well, and he could get away from anybody chasing him in that part of the country, and in his holes, in his caves. But these boys didn't quite know how to get out. They ended up standing on each other's shoulders. They did all kinds of things, and they weren't able to get out, and Merrywise—it's getting to be daylight by that time—and Merrywise said, "Ah. There's the mighty eagle. Well, I think I'll call upon the mighty eagle." And so he yelled up from the bottom of the cave, "Eagle, Eagle. If you'll come and take out my brother Tom, and his bride, I'll give you a big fat pig from my land when we get home."

And so—eagles like to eat big, fat pigs—and so he flew down and he took his brother Tom and his new bride and lifted them out of the hole. And as soon as they were up, it was getting more daylight and Merrywise called out, "Eagle, Eagle. Come back and get my brother Bill and his new bride. Lift him out of the hole, Mighty Eagle, and I will give you a big fat pig from my land when we get back."

And the eagle swooped down and picked up Bill and his bride and took em out of the hole, and carried them back to the land. And as the morning sun shone brightly and the snow was beginning to melt, and Merrywise said, "Mighty Eagle, come and help me in this land of all the caves and holes and bring me up out of this cave, and I'll give you a big, fat pig from my land when you get me up."

And, sure enough, the eagle flew down. He picked up Merrywise and his bride and they all went back to the homeplace. Back at the homeplace they helped each other build homes, and they got married, and—you know the ending—they lived happily ever after.

[Applause]

Does that remind you of anybody in the news today?

80. The King's Well

JANE MUNCY FUGATE
Hyden, Kentucky, and Glendale, Arizona
Recorded by Carl Lindahl, Houston, Texas, November 8, 2001

This is the third of the Merrywise stories in Jane Muncy Fugate's current repertoire. In this tale, as in the two others (stories 77 and 79), Merrywise and his two brothers end their adventures by getting married. Jane told this tale to the same audience that had just heard "Old Greasybeard." When she finished this performance, one of the listeners, noting that the three brothers had been married twice to new brides in the two tales, asked Jane, "Do you see the Merrywise stories happening to the same boy, in the same lifetime, or to the same character in different lifetimes?" Jane's answer: "Same character, but different situations, I guess sort of like a James Bond kind of thing, where you know he's James Bond, but one episode doesn't necessarily connect with the next one."

Listeners also asked why Jane's grandmother, a very strong willed woman with independent ideas, would choose a little boy as her most important folktale character, and why Jane would identify so strongly with Merrywise. Jane responded, "I think that [Merrywise] could do the things that you could not have a little heroine do—going off to seek her fortune and . . . fighting with people, all those things that nice little girls didn't do. But I did see me as Merrywise, and Merrywise had no limits."

Well, Merrywise is also the star of this story, and it starts kind of the same way: elderly parents, telling their sons to go out and seek their fortune. And the elderly parents thinking that Merrywise was too young to go, and Merrywise begging and kicking up a fuss, and saying, "I want to go."

This time Tom and Bill said, "Well, look, Merrywise, you're full of foolishness. You're always running off and doing something that distracts us from where we are and, and we really don't want you to go with us and drag us back. We need you to stay home until you're bigger."

And Merrywise said, "No. I'm big enough, and I want to go."

And so they started out. They finally gave in to him. He was very persistent; in addition to being cunning and creative, he was persistent, and so he ended up going with them.

Well, they journeyed and journeyed on throughout the morning, and it got time to sit down and have their lunch. And they were doing so, and they heard off in the distance, a chopping sound. *Chop, chop, thrash. Chop, chop, thrash.* Well, Merrywise, with his curiosity, said, "I wonder what that is?"

And the boys said, "Oh, no."

He said, "But I've got to go and see what that is."

And they said, "Okay, but we're not waiting along. And we don't like you going off in your tomfoolery ways. We want you to be here with us to go on our journey."

But off he goes, up the side of the hill, and when he gets up the side of the hill, pretty far off, he sees a strange and wondrous thing. There's a hatchet, an ax, all by itself, and the ax is chopping down trees. *Chop, chop,* and the tree falls, *thrash. Chop, chop, thrash.* Merrywise stands and watches that for a minute, and then he runs up, grabs the ax, takes the handle off, puts the ax part of the ax in his hip pocket, and starts back down the hill to where his brothers are finishing up their lunch. Well, when he got down to where the brothers were, they said, "Okay, Merrywise, what did you find?"

And he said, "Oh, nothing."

And they said, "What was making the noise?"

And he said, "Oh, just some trees falling."

And so they got up and got on their journey again, and they journeyed and journeyed and journeyed, and it got to be nighttime, and they were thirsty and tired and hungry and needed a cool place to rest, and sure enough they came to a beautiful pool, a pool of clear, crystal water. And it was coming from a waterfall, that was running down into the clear crystal water. And Merrywise said, "I wonder where that water comes from?"

And Tom said, "Oh, no, you don't, Merrywise. It's almost getting dark here, and we can't—you're not going off again on one of your tomfoolery things."

And Merrywise said, "Oh, I've got to. I've got to."

And so up the side of the mountain he goes, and down the side of the other mountain, and up and up another mountain, way up high, following the stream, the steady, beautiful, crystal-clear stream, as it runs through the rock. Well, when he got up to the mountain, he followed the stream to another place, and when he looked, there was a walnut. The walnut had a hole in it, and out of the hole in the walnut came this beautiful, crystal-clear water.

Well, being resourceful like he was, he picks some moss off a nearby tree, stuffed it into the hole in the walnut, put the walnut down in his shirt pocket, and he went back to where his brothers were camping down for the night. And they said, "Well, did you find out where the water comes from?"

And he said, "Oh, up and around the hill a piece."

And so the next day, the brothers got up and they journeyed and they journeyed and they journeyed and they journeyed, and the next day, and a few days went by, and they came to the king's territory. They knew it was the king's territory because it had a big sign, and right inside the sign that said, THE KING'S TERRITORY, was another big sign, and this sign said: THE KING'S WELLS ARE DRY. IF ANYONE CAN BRING WATER TO THE KING'S WELLS, HE CAN HAVE THE HAND OF THE BEAUTIFUL YOUNG PRINCESS IN MARRIAGE. And then, in smaller print: BUT IF YOU FAIL, YOU WILL HAVE TO GO TO THE CHOPPING BLOCK AND HAVE YOUR EARS LOPPED OFF.

Well, the boys puzzled about that for a while, and Tom said, "Hmm. I think I could probably do that. I'm pretty strong." And Bill said, "Well, I'm pretty persistent. I could probably do it. I keep on keeping on." And Merrywise didn't say much, but they continued to walk on into the king's territory and, sure enough, there was another sign. And it said about the same thing that the first sign said, with an emphasis on, YOUR EARS WILL BE LOPPED OFF, DON'T FORGET. [Laughter]

So, being adventurous as they were, and sort of needy, they went to the king's castle. And Tom said, "I'm gonna go tell the king I'll do it." So he went up to the king, and he said, "King, I, I want to take a chance and dig this well and bring some water to your kingdom, and I want the hand of your beautiful daughter, the princess, in marriage."

And the king said, "Well, let me warn you that if you try and do not succeed, you can lose your ears." . . .

And so Tom said, "Okay, that's all right. I'll try." And he did. He set about digging. And he dug and he dug and he dug and he dug and he dug. And he was very strong. Every shovel of dirt brought up more dirt, and it just was a big pile of dirt, but nothing in the hole.

Well, as the king had warned, he took Tom to the chopping block and chopped off his ears.

So, Bill said, "I think *I* can do it. I'm persistent. I don't give up. I keep on keeping digging. I just think Tom maybe didn't dig hard enough." And so, the next day, Bill went to the king and said, "King, I want to try to dig a hole and bring some water to your kingdom, and I would like to marry the beautiful young princess."

And the king warned him again, and said, "Well, now, you know that we will lop off your ears if you try and do not succeed."

And Bill said, "Yes, I know." And so he set about digging. And he dug and he dug and he dug and he *was* persistent. He dug and he dug and he dug, and he continued to dig, and he took only a few minutes to rest and to eat and he was back digging again. And you would be surprised how big the hole was— but no water.

Well, as the king had said, he took him to the chopping block and they chopped off his ears. So Merrywise said, "You know, boys. I think I can do this. I think I can do this."

And, and they said, "No, Merrywise don't do this."

And Merrywise said, "Yeah. I'm gonna try."

And so he went to the king and said, "King, I want to make a try at digging a new well for your kingdom, so that your people can all have water. And I want to marry your beautiful daughter, the princess. And so, I would like to try." And the king said, "Well, you're pretty small and pretty weak there. Your brothers couldn't do it. One was very strong and one was very persistent. I really hate to see a young guy like you lose your ears, but I need to tell you that if you do not succeed you will lose your ears."

And Merrywise said, "It's okay." And so he started to dig. He commenced to dig, and he dug and he dug and he dug and when he was down in the hole so deep that nobody could see him, he [whispering] slipped that walnut out of his pocket and put it down in the bottom of the hole. And he had to scurry like mad to get to the top, because the water kept coming right behind him, and the whole well was filled with beautiful crystal-clear running water. Oh, it was wonderful.

And the king was delighted. And Merry said, "Okay, I've come to marry the beautiful princess." Now the king, like fathers everywhere, sort of hated to let go of his youngest daughter, and *especially* to this puny, scraggly-looking mountain boy who didn't have anything to his name. And so he said, "Well, I'll tell you what. Here's the deal. I'll give you half my kingdom if you will not marry my daughter, you can have half my kingdom, half my riches, how's that?"

And Merrywise thought a minute and said, "Okay. That's good. So he got half the kingdom, and half the riches, and first thing he did was go back to his aging, sickly parents and build them a big fine home and put it full of big, fine things. And he stayed there with his parents for a while, but he got itchy feet. He wanted to adventure again. He wanted to go on another journey. And so he said to his mother and his father, he said, "You know, I think I better go back to the king's territory and see how my earless brothers are doing." [Laughter]

And so they said, "Okay, Merrywise, that's all right. You can go." And he took off, went back . . . journeyed and journeyed. Got back to the king's territory, which was smaller now, remember, because he had some of it himself. But when he got to the king's territory, there was a big sign. And it said, ATTENTION. THE GIANT HAS COME TO THE WOODS AND IS BOTHERING THE KING. AND THE KING WILL GIVE ANYONE HIS BEAUTIFUL YOUNG DAUGHTER'S HAND IN MARRIAGE WHO CAN RID HIM OF THE GIANT. And Merrywise read that. And down in smaller print it said, BUT IF YOU TRY AND YOU DO NOT SUCCEED, YOU WILL GO TO THE CHOPPING BLOCK AND YOUR HEAD WILL BE LOPPED OFF. Well, that was pretty ominous. So he went a little further, and there was another sign saying the same thing: AND REMEMBER, YOU COULD LOSE YOUR HEAD. So he ended up going to the king, and he said to the king, "King, I think I would like to rid you of the pesky giant, and I would like to marry your youngest daughter now. As you can see, I've got a little riches of my own, and I think it's time for me to settle down."

And the king said, "Well, I don't know. You know, you may have more money and you may look a little cleaner and better, but you still aren't very much bigger, and you're not as strong as your brothers. But, you know, if you want to *try*—but remember, you're gonna lose your *head* if this doesn't work."

And Merrywise said, "It's okay. I can do it." So he takes off for the part of the forest where the giant has been seen. Now the giant is—the way that he's really, really irritating the king is, he's cutting down all the trees in the forest and leaving all the forest lands just bare. And the king's kingdom is just getting to look like a desert. And so the giant is chopping down trees, bundling em up in bundles, carrying em off, day by day by day.

Well, Merrywise goes up to the giant. And he says, "Giant, what you doing there?"

And the giant says, "I'm chopping down trees and taking em back to my castle."

And Merrywise said, "How many trees did you chop today?"

The giant says, "I think I chopped about a hundred."

Merrywise says, "I think I can do a hundred in an hour."

And the giant says [low, slow, loud voice], "*You* could do a hundred in an hour? I don't think so."

And Merrywise said, "How about a contest?"

And the giant said, "How bout a contest. And you go over to that side of the mountain, and I'll go to this side of the mountain, and we'll see who can chop the most trees in an hour."

And so, sure enough, they split up, and you can guess what Merrywise does. He takes that axhead out of the back of his back pocket, he finds a nice strong stick that will make an ax handle, and he turns it loose. Meanwhile, the giant's over here cutting and thrashing and stacking and rolling, and Merrywise is standing back and watching the ax go *Chop chop, thrash, thrash. Chop, chop, thrash, thrash.* And so he walks over to where the giant is and says, "Come see what I've done."

And the giant could not believe what he saw. He shook his head and said, "Well, there's no doubt about it. You're the winner. Well, I'm gonna take my bundle and I'm just gonna go on home, and go out of here, and I probably won't be back from here and—but how would you like to go back with me, little man, and have supper?"

And Merrywise said, "Well I *am* right hungry. I'm feeling kind of puny, ready for my supper. I could do that." And so the giant gets to bundling up his trees, and he says, "I can carry this big bundle." And he stacks them all up and he starts draggin em.

And Merrywise says, "Wait, I'll help you." But instead, he's kind of riding along on the back of the brush of the trees. They get to the giant's castle, and the giant goes in, thinking to himself, "I'll feed this guy. He'll be asleep and I'll do away with him. That'll be the end of this pesky little guy in my life." So he puts on a giant feast. And he says, "I'm going to eat a hundred chickens. I'm going to eat a table full of biscuits. I'm going to eat a tub of cottage cheese. And I'm going to have another huge, big, deep tub full of milk."

And Merrywise says, "Well, that's kind of a light supper, but, okay, it'll do. Puny supper, but it'll do." So Merrywise positions himself near a window, and as the giant eats, Merrywise matches him plate for plate and pitches his on out the window. It comes time for bed, and the giant thinks that after such a huge meal, this little guy is going to sleep very soundly. And the giant says, "You sleep right here in this room, and I'll go over there and sleep in that room. And I'll see you in the morning." Merrywise went into his room and thought to himself, "Well, I think it might be wise for me to sleep under the bed. I think I'll trick the giant. And I'll sleep under the bed, not on top of the bed."

So he's sleeping under the bed, and hears—*screech*—his door open. And in comes the giant, in the middle of the night. And he has a huge, giant-sized bat with sharp nails sticking out all over the giant-sized bat.

Now Merrywise had taken one of the giant's pillows and put it in his place in the bed, covered it up, . . . so it looked like there was someone in the bed. And the giant takes to beating on that pillow, and beats it with his *sharp* bat with nails, and he beats it and he beats it and beats it and beats it. And finally he says [loud, giant voice], "That polished him off. Ho, ho, ho." And out he goes.

Well, Merrywise chuckled to himself so hard he could hardly get back to sleep. But morning came. And he came out to where the giant was sitting in his kitchen and he said, "I just want to ask you something, Mr. Giant. Do you have a lot of flies and gnats around this house?" He said, "I was sleeping last night. I was pretty tired, but sleeping a light bit restlessly, and the flies and the gnats kept lighting on me and bothering me all night long."

And the giant got up from the table and said, "This is too much for me. I'm out of here. I'm going to another kingdom to live. I can't share my kingdom with this guy. I'm out of here. Goodbye." And off he goes—never to be seen again. He was gone. Wicked giant. Gone.

So Merrywise went back to the king, and he said to the king, "Well, you haven't seen the giant around, have you?" And the king said, "No." And Merrywise said, "That's because he is gone and he will never come back again."

And the king said, "Well, not only do you now have some wealth, but you are very, very smart. And you know how to get things done. Big jobs. So not only am I going to give you my daughter's hand in marriage, but I am going to give you the other half of my kingdom." And so that's what happened. The king, to be polite, moved over into the giant's castle and lived there for the rest of his life. And Merrywise, to be polite—and also a very good brother—invited his brothers to come and stay with him. And found em some nice girls from the kingdom, that didn't mind having husbands with no ears [laughter], and they all lived happy ever after.

81. Rawhead and Bloodybones

JANE MUNCY FUGATE
Hyden, Kentucky, and Melbourne,
Florida
Recorded by Carl Lindahl,
Houston, Texas, March 29, 2001

About thirty University of Houston students attended this performance, and about half of them had previously heard a version recorded by Jane in 1949, when she was 11 years old.

I want to tell you one of the scary stories. And I've told this to my grandchildren, and *they're* scared about it. Now it doesn't seem very scary to me, but they thought it was. And it's called, it's called "Rawhead and Bloodybones."

Has anybody heard "Rawhead and Bloodybones" before? [Students throughout the classroom nod in response.] Okay. Well, you know that a central character is the young girl who lives in her home with her stepmother and her stepsister. And the father, as he often is in these stories, is away somewhere. He's either died or he's away somewhere. So this young beautiful, growing girl is living in a home with her wicked stepmother and her lazy, grouchy, wicked-thinking stepsister. And the stepmother is very disgruntled because all the attention goes to this beautiful young girl. We'll call her "Elsa." Now, Elsa has the admiration of everybody in the community and the stepmother's not too pleased with that. She wants *her* daughter to have that admiration, but, again, she's ugly and stupid and everything that a person shouldn't be, and so she doesn't have it. So the stepmother calls Elsa to her and says, "I need you to take this bucket and go to the end of the world. And I need you to bring back a bucket of water from the end of the world so that my daughter can have a drink of it and be well, from whatever's ailing her. And that's kind of an order: go ahead and do that."

So Elsa, without any qualms, packs herself a leftover morning biscuit and grabs an apple off the tree as she goes through the yard, and off she goes with the bucket to the end of the world.

And so she's going along and *along* and *along* and *along* walking toward the end of the world and it's time for lunch. So she sits down under a big tree to have her lunch. And up from behind the tree comes a small little man. He has a long beard and gray hair and is dressed very shabbily, and it looks like he hasn't eaten in a long time. And he says to her, "Would you share your lunch with me?"

And she says, "Well, of course I will. Have a seat." So he sits down and they have lunch together, and he's very happy with how things go. And she's happy. And the lunchtime ends, and she says, "Well, I must go now. I'm on my way to the end of the world to get a bucket of water." And so off she goes.

And so he sits there for a while and says, "Um, she is pretty. She is a beautiful girl. Why, she smells good. And she is very sweet. Um, what a nice girl." So he watches her go away, and she heads off toward the end of the world. And she walks and she walks and she walks and she walks and she walks. *Finally*, she reaches the end of the world and the water. And she goes to the end of the bank, puts her bucket in it, and she draws up her bucket and looks down in the bucket. And there's a Rawhead and Bloodybones. And she says, "What? What?"

And the Rawhead and Bloodybones says [in a whispery chant],

Wash me and dry me and lay me down easy.

And so she washes it, and she dries it off carefully, and she sits it up on the bank, in the sun, and it's basking there and feeling good. And so she takes her bucket and goes back to the water and draws the water. And there's another Rawhead and Bloodybones. And it says,

Wash me and dry me and lay me down easy.

And so she sits the bucket down and takes him up and washes him off and dries him very gently and puts him on the bank by the other one and goes back to get her bucket of water for her wicked stepsister. She dips the bucket down into the water and brings it up, and it's another one. And it says,

Wash me and dry me and lay me down easy.

And so she takes him out of the bucket very carefully and washes him and dries him and puts him over on the bank with the others, and she goes back. "Now I want to get my water to go home." And she dips in the water, and there's a *fourth* one. And he says,

Wash me and dry me and lay me down easy.

So she washes him and dries him and says, "Is this easy enough for you now? Let me put you here with your buddies." So they're all laying there in the afternoon sun, basking and enjoying themselves and—"Everybody all right?" And everybody says, "All right." So she gets the bucket and she starts back home at last.

And as she's walking through the woods, it's getting dark. She walks, and she walks and she walks and she walks. And she begins to get back to the edge of her town. She's walked a long way and many miles, *this time* carrying a bucket of water. And as she comes in to the town, people begin to smell this beautiful aroma. And they open up their windows and they say, "Ah. There she is. Look at her. She's so beautiful. And she smells so good."

But what they didn't know was, way back there on the bank, as she's getting ready to—I'm digressing here, and I'm picking it up, real fast—as she's getting ready to leave the bank, the one Rawhead and Bloodybones is looking after her, going down the road, and he says, "She smells so nice. You know, my wish for her is that she would smell like roses and everyone would wonder at how she smells."

"Um," they said, "that's a pretty good wish."

The second one said, "Well, I wish for her that she would be—well, she is already kind and loving and gentle—did you feel that touch?—that she would be the kindest and the lovingest and the gentlest of *all* the women in the world. And people would know it."

"Oh, yeah," they said, "that's a good one, that's a good one, that's a good one."

And the third one said, "And she is beautiful. And so my wish for her is that she would *only* increase in beauty. She would get more beautiful than ever, than ever, than ever. And all the people in the world would know it."

And the fourth one said, "Well, I wish for her, now, when she gets home, her hair would feel heavy. And she would take the comb to her hair. And when she took the comb to her hair, that out from the brush and the comb would fall diamonds and rubies and jewels and gold, in giant amounts."

"Oh," they said, "That's wonderful." "That's wonderful." "That's wonderful."

And now we pick her up again. She's coming in to the community and they've already begun to notice how good she smells and how beautiful she is, and they say, "We can just see the kindness on her face. Wow! What a person." And so she's walking on, and she's walking into her home, and her stepmother says, "*You're here?*" She never thought she'd make it. There were a lot of obstacles she thought would be in her way, but didn't happen.

And so the stepmother says [impatient, demanding voice], "Where's the water?"

And she said [gentle voice], "Here's the water, Stepmother."

So Elsa gives the water. And the stepmother takes it, gives it to her daughter. And she's mumbling and grumbling cause she surely thought that was the last she would have seen of this girl.

So Elsa says. "My head feels *so* heavy. I just feel as though I need to brush my hair. Oh, Stepmother, could you help me, please? If I put my head in your lap, could you, could you brush my hair? Could you comb it for me?"

And the stepmother says, "*No,* I *won't. Comb your own hair.* Brush your own hair. No!"

And so our young woman sits down to comb her hair, and when she does, out come the diamonds and the jewels and the gold, just in a big pile in the floor. All the riches you could imagine, at her feet. Well, the stepmother, who was not only cruel and unkind, but greedy, said, "You got *that* from going to the end of the world? Get up from there, daughter. Come on! I want you to go get a bucket, and *you* go to the end of the world and you, you come back here. Come on, let's be going, now."

And so the lazy stepsister got up and, "I don't wanna go. I'm hungry." And the stepmother said, "I'll make you some good food to eat." So she fried up a big fatback of bacon and she put some fried apples that had lots of cinnamon in em, and she put a potato that'd been sliced and fried up, and a big hunk of sausage, and she put it in this great big paper bag. And off went the stepsister, to the end of the world, grumbling and mumbling and complaining the whole way. And she walked pretty slowly. She didn't like carrying the lunch, and she didn't like carrying the bucket. But she came to a tree, and it looked like a shady place to have lunch. And so she sat down, and she spread it all out and was beginning to eat.

Now, she was kind of piggy, as well as mean and cruel and lazy and—so she started to eat, and from around the tree comes the little gray-haired man. A little, tiny elf-kind-of-guy, with hair hanging down all around him, and he was dirty and greasy-looking.

And she says, "What do *you* want?"

And he said, "I want to know if you would share your lunch with me."

And she said, "I will *not* share my lunch with you."

And he said, "But, I'm hungry."

"*No!* Go get your own lunch. Get out of here."

And so she ate everything she wanted and *threw* the rest away and started off with her bucket to the end of the world. And so she walked and walked and walked and walked and the sun was going down and that nice evening, afternoon-late sun was coming on, and she said [crabbed voice], "If I walk all night, I might get home, but I, I'm tired of this. I'm taking this bucket of water and going home and seeing about my own riches, and—"

She put the bucket in, and she looked down in it and said, "Ah! What is that?"

And it said,

Wash me and dry me and lay me down easy.

And she said, "No! I'm not gonna do that. Get out of here." And so she pushed it back down in the water, but the Rawhead and Bloodybones crawled up anyway on the side and sat there in the afternoon sun, sort of disgruntled-looking.

She put her bucket down in again and drew it up and there was another Rawhead and Bloodybones. And he said,

Wash me and dry me and lay me down easy.

And she said, " 'No!' I said. Get out of here!" And threw it back in again. And it had to struggle and strain and get itself back on the bank. And it did.

And so the third time she put her bucket in, and you know what happened. There was another Rawhead and Bloodybones. And he said,

Wash me and dry me and lay me down easy.

And she said, "I told your brother and your brother, I'm not doing it. Get out of here."

And so he got in the water, and got himself up on the bank, sitting there all disgruntled and unhappy-looking with the other two. And she said, "I better not get another one of those things this time!" And she put the bucket down in the water and drew up another Rawhead and Bloodybones. Sure as the world.

And he said,

Wash me and dry me and lay me down easy.

And she said, "I'm not gonna. Here!" And threw it, way out, and he had to struggle and struggle, coming from the water at the end of the world, up on the bank, and position himself up there with those three others.

Well, she put her bucket in. She got a bucket of muddy water, and she started to trudge on home: grumble, mumble, razzle, frazzle. Mumbling and complaining all the way, and as she left the area, Rawhead and Bloodybones Number One said, "She smelled bad. My wish for her is that she would stink the rest of her life and she would smell so bad, people couldn't stand to be around her."

And the second one said [hoarse, excited voice], "Yeah! Yeah! That's good. Yeah. Go!" And he said, "Well, she was ugly. And my wish for her is that she becomes more ugly than ever, and that her face is so ugly that people cannot ever stand to look at her and they have to hide their eyes from her, because her ugliness blinds them."

"Yeah. Yeah," they said. "Yeah. Good." [Laughter]

And so the third one said, "Well, I think she was mean, and I don't know how she could get *much* meaner, but, but I wish for her that her meanness just stands out, and just follows her everywhere she goes, and people *know* how mean she is."

"Ah, yeah." "Okay." "Okay."

And the fourth one says, "Well, hmm. My wish for her is that when she gets home, her hair would feel very heavy. And it would feel like it needed to be combed, and when she combs her hair, that out would come snakes and lizards and buzzards and snails and all the creepy things."

"Yeah," they said. They had a celebration.

And so she's walking back to home, after carrying the muddy water: grumble, mumble, mumble, grumble, grumble, grumble. And the little old man sees her go by, and she passes the tree where she was, and he says, "There she goes, and double to it."

So she's on her way. She gets to the edge of town, and all the people that had their windows opened, *closed* the windows and said, "Yo, this smells horrible. Something stinking is coming by. Yah. Look! Oh, no, don't look. It's too ugly. We can't stand it. It's awful." And then: "Oh, it's her. And she's so mean. Run. Get away. Don't go near her."

So there was a wide path. And the stepmother heard all the commotion and said, "Oh, she's coming, she's coming." Ran out to meet her. [Crone-like, quavering voice:] "Honey, come to me. Quick, I want to comb your hair." And sure enough, the stepmother sits down, and begins to comb her hair. And snakes come out and lizards and creepy things. And everything ugly falls out of her head and winds around her feet, and they go, "Ah!" And out they run way past the edge of town, gone in the gone-forever, never to be seen again.

But our heroine is still living there, and word gets around that she is the most beautiful, the best-smelling, and the sweetest—and also wealthy. Now who would want that kind of person? A handsome prince.

And so he's coming, riding through town. He rides through. He stops. He follows his nose. He's amazed at the beauty. And he takes her off with him. She becomes his queen, and they live happy ever after.

[One of the students notes a difference between Jane's 1949 performance and her 2001 performance: As a child, you didn't include the prince. She got to live happily ever after on her own with that money. . . . What do you think accounts for that difference—why the marriage?]

. . . That might have been kind of added in there as a happy ending because of all the exposure to stories with a happy ending. I still like stories that don't have a happy ending sometimes. But that one seemed like it needed one, and I think I got that from other relatives who told it, and it seems good now.

82. The Three Sillies

JANE MUNCY FUGATE
Hyden, Kentucky, and Glendale, Arizona
Recorded by Carl Lindahl, Houston, Texas, November 9, 2001

This is a favorite of Jane's grandchildren. According to Jane, "Supposedly it comes from Ireland. I don't know for sure. . . . 'The Three Sillies' became a cliché in our family. When somebody did something really, really dumb, one of us might say to that person, or she might often say to me, 'Do you also put your pants on the door?' "

This is the story about a young man who was going to marry into a family, and he liked the family very much. He'd been to dinner at their house. He had some good feelings about them all in general, but he hadn't spent a lot of time with them, and it was time to do that because the wedding was drawing close. So they were all sitting around the parlor and the father of the bride-to-be said, "Well, I think this calls for a great bottle of wine. And so, Daughter dear, would you please go down into the cellar and collect one of the best bottles of wine that we have there, and bring it up, and we'll all celebrate."

And so she said, "Certainly, Daddy dear." And she opened the cellar door and went down into the basement part of the house, the cellar part of the house, where the wine was kept in kegs and in bottles, and as she was reaching for some wine, she looked up on the wall, and there was a hatchet embedded in the wall. And she sat down on the wooden bench that was by the wine vat and began to cry. And she cried and cried and cried.

Meanwhile, upstairs all the people were sitting around, waiting for her to come back with this celebratory bottle of wine, and she didn't come. She didn't come. And so the father said, "Well, Big Brother, would you go down into the basement and look for your sister and see if you can hurry her on up here. We're waiting with our glasses ready."

So Big Brother goes to the cellar door and down the steps to the cellar and he sees right away his baby sister weeping her heart out on the bench. And he says, "Baby Sister, dear. What is wrong?"

And she says [sobbing], "I came to the basement and I saw the wine, but I also looked up and I saw *that hatchet*, embedded in the wall, and I said to myself, 'What if I marry, and we're here, and we have a child, and we send the child to the basement to get a bottle of wine, and the child comes down to the basement, and that hatchet falls out of the wall, and hits the head of our child and kills it?' "

And he says, "Oh, that's *terrible*." And he sits down beside her, and also starts to weep.

Time goes by. Father's still waiting, patting his foot. And he says, "Mother dear, I, I don't know what could be taking our children so long in the basement, but could you please go down to the cellar, and sort of hurry em up a little bit, so that we can enjoy our wine before it gets too dark out there." So the mother goes down, and the scenario is repeated all over again. She says, "Children—dear, what are you doing weeping?"

They said, "Well, there's a hatchet in the wall, and there *might* be children that come to the family, and they *may* come to the basement, and the hatchet *could* fall off on their heads and split their heads open and they would die, and *then* it would be awful."

And she says, "Oh, that is awful. It is terrible." And she says, "Scoot over." And she sits down beside them and begins to weep and cry and weep and cry.

Well, Father by this time was getting pretty restless, and he's pacing the floor. And so he says, "Excuse me, dear Son-in-Law-to-Be," and he goes downstairs to the cellar, and he sees his whole family before him weeping and crying, and they tell him the story about the hatchet in the wall, and how it could possibly split the head of one of his grandchildren. And he is overcome with anticipatory grief, and he sits down on the bench and begins to weep along with his nuclear family. It's the saddest thing.

Well, the bridegroom is—it is getting dark—and he's wondering what's happening to all these people who are going to the basement, and so he goes down the steps and he says, "What is going on here?" And they told him the story with [voice rising] *gestures* and with *emotion*, "*Some day*, you will marry our dear daughter and you will have children, and we will send the child to the basement, and the child will be reaching for a bottle of wine, and the hatchet will fall off the wall, split their head, and it will be dead, and we will all be devastated."

He can't believe it. He said, "Is *that* what this is all about," and they said, "Oh yes, isn't it terrible? Isn't it awful?" And they're holding each other, and slinging snot and crying beyond all belief. So he reaches up to the wall, and he takes the hatchet out of the piece of wood, and he says, "Let's put it on the floor." [Laughter] And then he said to them, "You are undoubtedly the silliest group of people I have ever seen in my life. You are beyond my understanding, and there is no way that I can marry into this family." And so they beg him because they love him. He's got a lot of attributes, including money [laughter] and security. And so they say, "No. No. Please give us a chance. Surely we're not the only people who have these silly notions."

And he said, "Well, okay. You're daughter is pretty nice, and I do kind of like so far what we *started* to have as a family, so we'll give it a chance. I was about to take a world tour before I fell in love with your daughter, and now I'm going to take that world tour. And I am going to find, if possible—and I don't even know if it's possible—three silly families, or three silly individuals as silly as you. And *if* I do—and I don't even know if it's possible—I don't think so.

If I do, I will come back, and I will have a gigantic wedding, and I will marry your daughter. And this will be a done deal."

And so they celebrate. They're very happy. They see him off. And off he goes, to think about this impending wedding, and to find people throughout the earth that are as silly as this family he was going to marry into. Well, the first place he goes is about a fourth of the way around the world. . . . [A little village where the houses] are imbedded in the mountainside, and the roofs are actually growing grass. And he hears from out of this house that he's going to stop by, he hears great groaning and moaning and grunting and carrying on. And he sticks his head inside the doorway and there's a man who has his cow by the harness, and he's trying to drag it up the chimley. And the wife and the children are pushing and helping and trying to get this cow up the chimley, and he says, "What are you doing?"

And they say, "There is grass on the roof, and our cow benefits from fresh grass. And so we're putting the cow up on the roof to eat the fresh grass." And he said, "Did it occur to you, you could step up the mountainside, walk up over to the thatched roof, pull up the fresh grass, and throw it down to the cow?"

"Ah, no," and so they did. And so he spent the night and he said, "Well, that's one." [Laughter]

And he went on around about another fourth of the world and he was traveling *quite* late that night, and the moon was out. It was a beautiful, shiny moon. And he was passing around the side of a lake. In the lake there was this great hunk of yellow, and the people in this community—particularly this one family that called themselves the Cheese family—were fishing with nets, trying to get this hunk of cheese from out of the lake. And they were throwing their nets and dragging them back, and throwing their nets and dragging them back. And nothing came back with the nets.

He said to them. "And what are you doing?"

And they said, "Well, you can see? See that cheese? We're the family here that provides cheese for the community, and it's a terrible job. We do not succeed, but we keep on trying because every once in a while this big hunk of cheese comes in the lake, and we're bound and determined that we're going to get it in."

And he said, "Did it ever occur to you that that's the reflection of the moon? And the reason that you don't see it all the time is because the moon is not that bright, and if you look at it, it's about the same size and color and proportion?"

And they said, "Oh, my! So that's why we can't get it in. Oh. Got to go back to using the cattle and goats, for the cheese."

So he said, "That's two." [Laughter]

And he goes around another fourth of the world, and he's getting ready to make his last leg of the journey home, saying to himself, "Gosh, I'm kind of missing out on that beautiful girl I was going to marry and her sorta-kinda nice, wacky family, but I've only found two, and I don't know. You know, I'm not gonna do very many stops between here and home, and I've really got to find this other family, and I don't, I don't think, I don't see any hope in it."

So he's staying in a small village where people often share rented rooms for the night, and so he goes into a village inn, and says to the innkeeper, "Do you have a room for the night? I'm getting ready to head to my home, and I'm very, very weary. I've been on a task that did not succeed."

The innkeeper said, "Well, you know, I do, but if you don't mind sharing with another person."

He said, "No, that's all right. I'll share with someone. That's fine."

So he goes to bed, and the other guest goes to bed, and just as the cock is beginning to crow, just as the sun barely gleams up over the mountains in the morning, he hears something weird in his room. *Dun-dum-da-da-dun-DUM. Dun-dum-da-da-dun-DUM. Dun-dum-da-da-da-dun-DUM.* And this goes on and on, and he gets one eye open, and he sees his roommate running across the room in the dimness of the light. And hitting against the door. And so he listens to it a little while longer, and it doesn't seem to be ending. And he said, "Excuse me, sir. What is it that you are doing?"

And his bedmate for the night said, "I'm putting on my pants."

And our hero says, "How are you putting on your pants?"

He said, "Well, I'm putting em on the only way my family ever puts on their pants. I hang them on a doorknob, I run from across the room, and *then I jump in them.*" [Laughter] And so he proceeds: *Dun-dum-da-da-dun-DUM,* hitting against the door and backing off.

And our hero said, "It must take you a long time to leave in the morning?"

He says, "Yes, it does. And that's why I have to get up very, very, very early to start putting my pants on." And so our bridegroom says, "I think that's three." [Laughter] And he goes home to his potential new family, and walks in their door and says, "Hello, I'm home. Let's get married. And live happy ever after."

83. The Tarnished Star

JANE MUNCY FUGATE
Hyden, Kentucky, and Glendale, Arizona
Recorded by Carl Lindahl, Houston, Texas, November 9, 2001

This is one of many tales that Jane learned from her aunt, Nora Lewis. As Jane recalls, "Aunt Nora was a great storyteller. . . . At Aunt Nora's house the dark would fall and the fire would be there, and we would sit around in rocking chairs. The little kids would come in and out of the shadows and sometimes we would at the end of the evening end up in our respective parents' laps, and listening to the stories, particularly if there was a scary one. And the scary ones would come toward the end of the day when they wanted us to come out of the shadows and get into the cuddling-down period. . . . And the fire would flicker, there was always looking in the fire. And for me toward the end of the evening there was that old familiar thing—of putting my ear on [my grandmother's] chest and listening to her heartbeat while I listened to the story. And that was a very bonding, bonding experience."

Jane told the following tale to a small group consisting primarily of women with professional experience in therapeutic counseling. She offered this version of "The Tarnished Star" as an example of her techniques in using folk narratives as tools in healing. At the tale's end, members of the group respond with their varied interpretations of its message.

Now, it's never been a good idea, I don't think, for anybody in the helping profession to say to the person that they're helping, "Here's what you got to do." Once in a while, when they're *so* broken, they may need some direction . . . , but most of the time it pays off to be subtle, and allow that person and all their internal resources to take the work and bubble it up from seemingly nowhere inside the individual and let them create their own mind's-eye version how to heal. Because self-healing is the very best kind of healing. It's less intrusive, it's longer-lasting. . . .

In my healing, coming from a small, inadequate, undernourished, emotionally abandoned child, to a woman that was seeking knowledge, trying to find out who I am, going into the field of psychology, looking at how I could help other people, I finally got on the notion of working with that part of the unconscious or subconscious mind, letting people know through metaphor what it is that they really need to know about themselves that I don't know in the first place. So they can take that information and do what they want with it, based on the stories that we tell.

Now, some of the stories that I've told my clients—and I have certainly worked with my share of little ones. And they like stories about people that sounded like themselves. Or like they like stories [about people] that sound like they want to be. And so it's easy to sit down and just be a bare-faced storyteller with a small child. And they will hop back out into the waiting room and they say to the parents, "When do I come back again?" Which you don't find with every client that you know. So that you see these changes begin subtly. Other stories are ones that *you* take as the client, . . . and *you* make of that story what you will, in *your* life.

Now let's pretend that you're a client who's come to me, and you say to me, "Okay, Jane, I'm recovering from alcohol, but I can't get it together as far as relationships. My relationships are falling apart. I meet a man, he's in the meetings, he's been in the twelve-step group for twelve years. I like him. He looks good. He's got everything I'd like to have. And then I *marry* him, and he's a jerk. And then I go and move in with him, after we've walked on the beach all night and said we love each other, and I find out that he's a jerk. And what is this? Why is this that I, that I, that I end up in these awful messes?"

And so I might say to her. "Well, I think I have the answer. I think you have a broken wheel. That somewhere in your mind about how to pick people, it got broken way back there in the early days. And you haven't fixed it yet." And most of the time they might scratch their head and say, "Well, I don't know exactly how that is. I thought I was getting it all together." And so, if you're my client, I'm going to tell you this story.

There was a woman who lived in a cabin, a little piece from the road. And she lived by herself, and she craved to be with somebody else. And this woman would, from time to time, walk down to the road, and look up the road to see if there was anything stirring there. And so this particular day, she did. She walked down to the dirt road [to see what was] coming from the mountains, and there was a cloud of dust. And she stared at it, and squinted her eyes, and she said to herself, "It *is*. It's *him*. It's really him."

And so she flies back as fast as her feet would take her, bursts through her cabin door, dives under her bed, where she has a cigar box that she's had for years. And she works her way through the dust kitties and brings out that cigar box, opens that cigar box, and inside she finds a tarnished old lonesome star. And so she takes out that star, and she shines it off on her sweater or on her coat, and she gets it all shined up, and she breathes on it, and spits on it, shines it up some more, and it gets shinier and shinier and finally it's *gleaming*, and she runs back as fast as her feet will take her again, to the edge of the road. And just as she does, he's walking up to her. And he's just strutting along, with all his maleness, coming down the road. And she's out stepping along in step with him. And within a few steps, she pins that tin star, that's gleaming in the sun, on his shoulder jacket.

And so, "Oh. You're the one. You're it. Oh." They're walking along together, and it doesn't take very long until he's just going to be himself. He burps and he farts and then he just sort of gets in with just being himself, and taking most of the road, and looking off in the distance and not paying a lot of attention to her.

She begins to think. "He's being bad to me." And they walk a little bit further and a little bit further, and he gets more obnoxious and does more of his same-self things, and she says, "He *deceived* me." Finally, the tin star, because he's swaggering so hard, falls right off his shoulder and into the dirt, and she picks up that tin star and gives him a piece of her mind and says, "How dare you act like you were something else, when you were always this, and you cheated me, and I'm the wrong person, and I'm leaving." And back she goes, dejectedly, to her cabin, gets that cigar box that's laying out on the table, puts the tin star back in the box, closes it, and puts it back under the bed.

Now if you're my client—

[Listener: I guess the thing that I get out of it. . . . Is that she was deceived by her desire to be with someone, . . . She doesn't see him, but just the emblem that she puts on him. The only way that she can recognize him is if he becomes the shiny star.]

[Second listener: She doesn't present herself to him. He's just a speck that she sees in the distance.]

Anybody notice anything else about that story?

[Third listener: She's just looking for a knight in shining armor.]

Another good metaphor. Anything else?

[Silence]

You think it's gonna happen again?

[Fourth listener: Oh, sure. Sure.]

So if you were my client, and you were listening to this story, you might come up with any or all of those things, and you might also say, "Well, she didn't even *know* him when she found him. She didn't even know him." And you might also say, "Am I in for this again?" And I might say, "Well, it could be, if nothing changes."

84. Tailipoe (1955)

JANE MUNCY
Hyden, Kentucky
Recorded by Leonard Roberts,
Hyden, Kentucky, April 1955

Of the eleven tales that the young Jane Muncy recorded for folklorist Leonard Roberts in 1949 and 1955, "Tailipoe" is the only performance available in the American Folklife Center. This recording was deposited by Kenneth S. Goldstein as part of a sampler he compiled from ten American, Caribbean, Irish, and Scottish narrators to illustrate the range and excellence of English-language storytelling traditions.

In this early performance, Jane speaks more quickly than in her adult recordings, and she alters her voice more pronouncedly when impersonating the hermit and the creature that stalks him.

My name is Janie Muncy. I'm seventeen years old. And I heard these stories from my grandmother, Mrs. Sidney Farmer—that's her maiden name.

[Leonard Roberts: And what story are you going to tell?]

"Tailipoe." Once upon a time, way back in the hills of Kentucky, there was a man that lived all by hisself. I guess now we'd call him a hermit. But then, people just—it was very natural for em to live out and hunt and get their own grub the way they could. So this man lived way back by hisself. And in the dusk of the evening, he was in his little log cabin sitting by the fire, and he happened to glance down, and through a *great, big* crack in the floor came a—the funniest critter he ever did see in his life. And it looked so funny, and it just looked at him, and it just growled. And so he grabbed up the hatchet that was sitting by the fire, and he says, "I'll fix you, you thing, you." So he hacked at it. And just as it went out the crack he cut its tail off.

Well, the tail looked so juicy and so good—and he hadn't been having very good hunting lately—so he fixed up a big pot over the fire and put the tail in it, and put water and salt and whatever he had in it, and made a great big soup off of the tail.

Well, that night he went to bed, and he was laying there resting, and just

Jane Muncy at age 17, in 1955, in Hyden, Kentucky. This was the year that she recorded her version of "Tailipoe" (story 84) for Leonard Roberts, and the year that she met her husband, Robert Fugate. (Courtesy of Bob Jason Fugate)

about to doze off to sleep, when all at once he heard something outside of his house [long, drawn out whisper]: "*Tailipoe, Tailipoe. I want my Tailipoe.*"

Well, he said, "Hyeh, hyeh, hyeh, dog. Come hyeh, dog." And the dog run in and . . . he opened the door, and the dog ran out, and he heard it go barking, barking down the hill, and he didn't hear the thing anymore.

So he went back to bed, and he was just about to doze off to sleep, and he heard something up, right outside his house: "*Tailipoe. I want my Tailipoe.*" So the man says, "Hyeh, hyeh, dog. Come hyeh, dog." And the dog raised up from the fireplace, and the man opened the door, and the dog ran out and chased the thing *way* down the hill. And he heard em going out of sight. So the man laid down, back again, and started to rest.

Well, as it was getting daylight, he'd forgotten his little matters and gone off to sleep and was dreaming real good dreams, and the day—the sun was coming over the hill, and he heard something open his door, and he heard something standing at the foot of his bed, and it says, "*Tailipoe. Tailipoe. I want my Tailipoe.*"

Well, he says, "Hyeh, dog. Hyeh. Come hyeh, dog." And the dog, that was pretty tired from running all night, raised up from the fireplace and chased the thing right out the door and down the hill. And he heard the dog howling and howling and barking and screaming. And he thought, "Well, upon my honor, that thing has et my dog up."

But he went back to bed, and it was just about to get daylight, and the birds were singing, and he was so tired, he laid down and went to sleep, which was unusual for a country person who usually gets up with the chickens. And he heard something come in his door, and it come to the foot of his bed. And it crawled up on his feet. And it came *up* to his chest. And it sit *right on his head.* And it says, "*Tailipoe. Tailipoe. I want my Tailipoe.*"

So he says, "Hyeh, dog. Hyeh, dog. Come hyeh, dog, and chase this thing off." But the dog didn't come. And he thought, "Oh, oh." And so it says, "*Tailipoe. I want my Tailipoe. I'm gonna git my Tailipoe.*"

And it jumped and tore the man all to pieces.

And so it says, way back there—I've heard people say that when you're on that side of the mountain and it's getting dark, or maybe daybreak, you can hear something say [in an eerie whisper], "*Tailipoe. Tailipoe.*"

85. Tailipoe (2001)

JANE MUNCY FUGATE
Hyden, Kentucky, and Glendale, Arizona
Recorded by Carl Lindahl, Houston, Texas, November 9, 2001

After this performance, Jane described "Tailipoe" as "a story that might be told around the fireplace to get the children to come a little closer, to come out of the shadows and come into the light of the fireplace and maybe up into somebody's lap, where they could cuddle down for the night and be either carried to bed or be sleepily just sort of hauled off to bed, because the fear was so great that they, that they wanted to be near the nurturing person. For me it was always my grandmother. . . . She always sat in a rocking chair, and I would sit in her lap, and again listen to her voice as it came through her chest, and that was very important for me."

Another story I'd like to tell you is a fanciful little story about a man who lived in the mountains. Who was one of those persons who went off to seek his fortune, found a place all his own, built himself a cabin with all the rustic stuff of a cabin nature, and proceeded to provide food and shelter for himself. He was kind of lonely, but he spent his day hunting and he spent his nights sitting by the fire carving or getting his guns ready to go hunting the next day, and was quite, quite content about them. One night he was sitting by the fireplace on a cold and winter night . . . cleaning his guns. Didn't have any bullets in em at that time, he was cleaning em. And *something* appeared in the cracks of the floor. And it sort of oozed and worked and wiggled its way up through the crack in the floor, until it appeared: this hairy monster with sharp teeth and spit coming out, and beady, sharp, flashing eyes.

Well, he was afraid, and he didn't have any bullets loaded in his gun at that point, but he did have something that always sat by the fireplace, which was his friendly ax. And so he grabbed his ax to chop at the thing just as it went down the crack in the floor from which it had come. Only, by the time it got through the crack in the floor, it didn't have its tail anymore.

He lopped off the tail.

Well, as I said, he was a hunter, and he was self-sufficient. He looked at that tail, and it had lots of meat on it. It was hairy, the way some tails are. But it had, it had meat, and you could see that it was a nice, clean cut, and so he said, "I think I'll just fix this tail in a pot of soup." And so he put it on the fireplace to cook, and it smelled delicious. And when it was all cooked, he had a delicious meal of tail soup. Well, that night, as he always did, he went to bed by himself. Nobody lived here with this man except himself and his big hound dog. And he called his hound dog "Hyeh-hyeh," because every time he called a dog, he called it, "Hyeh, hyeh, dog!"

The dog had seen the monster come from the crack in the floor, but didn't get there in time to do anything before the tail got lopped off, because he was all curled up in the corner enjoying the last moments of the day.

So the man and his dog went to sleep as they usually did. And were just snoozing down with a nice warm belly full of tail soup and he heard a sound come out around the mountain, from the other side of the pass. And he listened very carefully, and the dog was asleep. And the sound said [faint whisper], "*Tailipoe, I want my Tailipoe. Give me back my Tailipoe.*" And so he went to his door and opened his door and the wind flew in and he said. "Hyeh-hyeh! Come hyeh, dog! Hyeh-hyeh!" And the dog came out. And he says, "Sic him!" And the dog goes after the thing. And he hears screeching and hollering, and it's gone. And the dog comes back, scratches on the door, and they proceed to go to sleep.

Well, that day he got about his business, taking care of himself and hunting and fixing food and doing all the things he needed to do. And it came nighttime again and he went through his gun-cleaning ritual and everything was quiet, and it was time for bed, and just as he was getting ready for bed, snuggling down on his pillow, he heard, right outside his cabin door, "*Tailipoe, I want my Tailipoe. Give me back my Tailipoe.*" And so he says, "Come, Hyeh-hyeh," and gets the dog up, and he opens the door and he hears the dog barking and barking and running off through the woods. And no more disturbance from the creature that night.

Well, a night or two went by, and everything was fairly peaceful and he thought maybe the creature wanting his *Tailipoe* was gone for good, but sure enough, as he was snuggled down in his bed—and he'd banked his fire and put the coals up on his fire—there was a voice from inside his cabin, "*Tailipoe, I want my Tailipoe. Give me back my Tailipoe.*" And he called the dog, "Hyeh-hyeh! Git him, Hyeh-hyeh!" And the dog came running, the man opened the door, and the dog and the thing went outside and had the worst fight ever imaginable. The screaming and the screeching and the wild animal yelling and the fur flying, you never could see, but Hyeh-hyeh, the little dog, didn't come back.

So our hunter said, "Well, guess I better go to bed. I'll go out and look for him when it comes daylight." [Whispering] And in the night, as quiet as though it just appeared from nowhere, he heard, sitting on his chest, breathing on his face, "*Tailipoe, I want my Tailipoe. Give me back my Tailipoe.* [A screeching scream:] *KKKKCCCCKKKK!*"

And he knew no more.

[Long audience silence]

He didn't live happy ever after.

[Laughter and applause]

NOTES ON THE TALES

The following notes are comparative, designed to demonstrate the continuity and fluidity of American storytelling traditions by illustrating how the individual narratives in this collection resemble and vary from other American tales. The notes cite published performances by the same teller or other members of the teller's family, region, and ethnic group as well as from other groups and regions of the United States. Occasionally, the citations range farther afield to Africa, the Caribbean, Europe, Mexico, and South America in order to evaluate the parent traditions that fed the rich mix of American storytelling art.

In annotating these tales, I draw copiously on four major scholarly tools designed for comparative folktale research:

1. Antti Aarne and Stith Thompson's *Types of the Folktale* (1961), also called the Type Index, is a catalogue of the most common plots found internationally in oral fiction. This index assigns numbers to various "tale types" from various genres, including animal tales, märchen, jokes, and anecdotes. The notes below follow scholarly convention by citing internationally distributed Tale Types by the Aarne-Thompson, or "AT," number, followed by the title of the type. For example, Sam Harmon's tale "Stiff Dick" (story 7) is identified internationally as belonging to type AT 1640, *The Brave Tailor*.

2. Stith Thompson's *Motif-Index of Folk-Literature* (1955–1958) enumerates the various motifs found worldwide in märchen, legends, jokes, myths, tall tales, and other folk narrative forms. Thompson defined motif as "the smallest element in a tale having the power to persist in tradition" (1946: 415), and he saw motifs as falling generally into three categories: characters (e.g., G210, "Witch"; or B350, "Grateful animals"), "certain items in the background of the action" (e.g., D1521.1, "Seven-league boots"; or D1601.5, "Automatic cudgel"), or actions (e.g., H1320, "Quest for magic objects or animals"; or D672, "Obstacle flight. Fugitives throw objects behind them which magically become obstacles in pursuer's path"). According to Thompson, the great majority of motifs fell into the third category. Some of these action motifs might appear as episodes in tales otherwise dissimilar in plot. For example, motif K1611, "Substituted caps cause ogre to kill his own children," appears in three different tales in this collection (stories 77, 181, and 191) belonging to three different types (AT 315, AT 327, and AT 327+328, respectively). In all three tales, this particular episode unfolds more or less as described in Thompson's index: "The hero and heroine change places in bed with the ogre's children and put on them their caps so that the ogre is deceived." Thompson recognized that many motifs could in fact

335

stand on their own as independent tale types, and indeed the motif K1611, just described, is also classified as AT 1119, *The Ogre Kills His Own Children*. For those tales that have been assigned both a motif number and a tale type number, I have generally used the tale type number but not the motif number.

3. Ernest Baughman's *Type and Motif-Index of the Folktales of England and North America* (1966) employs the classification systems developed in the *Types of the Folktale* and the *Motif-Index*, but it greatly expands the latter to include many plots and story details not found in Thompson's work. In addition, Baughman provides as many examples as he has been able to find of the types and motifs that he lists, so that his work serves as a rough gauge for determining the relative popularity of the various tales. In my notes, I often cite the number of times a certain plot is reported in Baughman, but I generally do not list all the versions that he cites, for doing so would essentially duplicate Baughman's work; rather, I assume that interested readers will consult the Baughman index. I do, however, cite individual versions of tales published in 1960 and later, because Baughman's work does not. I also cite some important pre-1960 works that Baughman did not consult, works such as Arthur Huff Fauset's *Folklore from Nova Scotia* (1931) and Zora Neale Hurston's *Mules and Men* (1935).

4. Herbert Halpert and J.D.A. Widdowson's *Folktales of Newfoundland* (1996) constitutes not only a collection of tales but also the most thorough comparative references yet published on North American tales in the English language. This work presents 145 texts of tales told by Newfoundlanders, each followed by an exhaustive listing of archival and published texts from the New World and beyond. *Folktales of Newfoundland* often doubles or triples the number of references given earlier to the same tale by Baughman. When citing Halpert and Widdowson, as when I cite Baughman, I attempt, not to duplicate this massive body of research, but, rather, to build upon it.

The notes below also cite some of the more important studies of specific tale types. More important, they direct readers toward books and articles that have been published not only about the tales but also about the lives and traditions of the tellers and the folklorists who worked with them.

Certain tales, such as Will Gilchrist's (stories 71–75), based almost entirely on idiosyncratic personal experiences, receive little or no annotation. Other tales belong to widespread and popular traditions that require extensive treatment.

The Hicks-Harmon Family. Studies of the Hicks-Harmon family genealogy and history include James W. Thompson (1987); Hicks, Hicks, and Hicks (1991); Nicolaisen (1994); and Betty N. Smith (1997). Half of McCarthy's *Jack in Two Worlds* (1994) is devoted to studies and appreciations of the Hicks-Harmon family and individual narrators Ray Hicks, Frank Proffitt Jr., and Maud Long; see particularly the articles by Ellis, Lindahl, Nicolaisen, Oxford, and Sobol. The most-detailed published description of the folklife of the Hickses in the twentieth century is Robert Isbell's *The Last Chivaree* (1996), from which I have quoted Ray Hicks's remarks on the aspects of truth that he finds in the family tales (Isbell 1996: 30, 80).

The Jack Tales are discussed by Lindahl (1988; 1999; 2001), McCarthy (1994), McDermitt (1986), and Williams (1995), as well as in a special issue of the *North Carolina Folklore Journal* (1978). Reprints of the eighteenth-century "Jack the Giantkiller" (*The History of Jack and the Giants*, 1711) and "Jack and the Beanstalk" (*The Story of Jack Spriggins and the Enchanted Bean*, 1734) are found in Opie and Opie (1974: 58–82; 211–26).

Reverend Joseph Doddridge's account of storytelling in eighteenth-century Appalachia is quoted from Charles L. Perdue Jr. (1987: 97). Miles A. Ward's recollections of Council Harmon are from Richard Chase's introduction to *The Jack Tales* (1943: x).

Ray describes shelling beans to his grandfather's tales in Isbell (1996: 39); Daron Douglas's recollections come from an interview with Carl Lindahl, May 8, 1997. Austin Harmon's recollections of his grandfather, John Goulder Harmon, were recorded by Herbert Halpert for the Library of Congress (AFS 2879A, B).

The previously published Hick-Harmon performances from this section are Maud Long's "Jack and the Giants' New Ground" and "Jack and the Varmints" (both in Emrich 1972: 339–65), "The Heifer Hide" (transcribed by Ellis, McCarthy, Oxford, and Sobol in McCarthy 1994: 107–22), "Stiff Dick" (transcribed by Lindahl 2001: 1–6), and "Little Dicky Whigburn" (Emrich 1972: 390–93). The four tales previously issued on LPs are (Long 1955) "Jack and the Drill," "Jack and the Bull," "Jack and the Giants' New Ground," and "Jack and the Varmints."

Sam Harmon. The quotations from Sam Harmon are found on AFS recordings 2799A, 2799B, and 2901B1. On the latter record he makes the statement that his grandfather came from England when he was 4 years old; Nicolaisen (1994), Betty N. Smith (1997), James W. Thompson (1987), and Hicks, Hicks, and Hicks (1991) present strong evidence to dispute this assertion. Henry (1934; 1938: 19–23) and Niles (2000: 45) present brief treatments of Sam's life and family singing tradition, although these accounts do not mention the Jack Tales and they contain less information about the family than Sam and his son, Austin, told Herbert Halpert. Living conditions in Cades Cove during the time that Sam Harmon and his family lived there are described by many people in another AFC collection assembled in large part in the late 1930s by Joseph S. Hall (see, for example, AFS 10420A, cuts 76–77). Further documentation of the Cades Cove community can be found in the works of Dunn (1988) and Shields (1981). The American Folklife Center houses numerous songs and banjo pieces performed by Sam Harmon, including two commercially released versions of Child ballads: "Wild Boar," a version of Child no. 18 (Bronson 1960), and "Barbara Allen" (Child no. 84; Seeger 1964). The quotation from Richard Chase is found in Chase 1943: x.

1. *How I Bought and Stole My Wife* [AFS 2901B2–2903A1]. Polly's version of the tale appears in Mellinger E. Henry's *Folk-Songs from the Southern Highlands* (1938: 22–23).

2. *Telling Tales to My Grandkids* [AFS 2929A2, B1]. The special bond between grandfather and grandchild expressed in this tale is characteristic of the Harmon family. In spite of the fact that Sam listened endlessly to tales from his own grandfather and retold them endlessly to his grandchildren, Sam's son, Austin Harmon, learned very few songs from his father because he, like Sam, spent every moment he could afford listening to his own grandfather, John Goulder Harmon. Speaking of his father, Sam, and his grandfather John, Austin states, "I've learned the most from grandfather. I heard [my father] sing some, but it seems I was never interested in his singing like I was grandfather's, because we was always together, and no one else but us alone, out in the woods somewhere. I'd sit down and get so interested I never wanted him to quit" (AFS 2879B).

The tale that Sam tells to his grandchildren (motif K1082, "Ogres duped into fighting each other") is quite popular as an episode in American Jack Tales; see Roberts (1955: 4, 62a; 1969: nos. 32, 33); Halpert and Widdowson (1996: 4, 5, 6). The episode appears within many different types of giant tales, but it is almost certain that Sam drew his version from a tale that his cousin Jane Gentry called "Jack in the Giants' Newground," known to at least seven members of the family. See Chase 1943: no. 1; Long 1955: no. 1. Sam's relative Maud Long performs a long version of the tale in this book (story 14).

3. *The Great Pumpkin* [AFS 2928B-2929A]. The American Folklife Center notes label the tale "Raising Pumpkins," but earlier in the recording session (AFS 2928), Harmon himself says, "I call it 'The Great Pumpkin.' " Zora Neale Hurston (2001: 128) presents some close parallels from African American tradition. X1411.2, "Lies about large pumpkins." X1402.1*(ca), "Man plants seeds; the seeds come up immediately, and vine chases man across field." X1402.1*, "Lie: the fast-growing vine."

4. *Giant Mosquitoes* [AFS 2928A]. One of the commonest American tall tale themes. J.D. Suggs (narrator of stories 47–61 in this book) tells a related tale (AFS 10897) that is not transcribed here but does appear in a different form in Dorson 1956b: 176–77. Zora Neale Hurston recorded three related versions in the 1920s (2001: 128, 153–56). Halpert (1991) provides a lengthy discussion of giant mosquito tales in North American traditions, and McNeil (1989: 60–62, 158–59) provides six tales from the Ozarks with copious comparative notes. Motifs X1286.1.3, "Lie: the giant mosquito"; X1286.1.4.1, "Man hides under kettle to escape from mosquito; mosquito drills through [and flies] off with kettle."

5. *Jack, Tom, and Will* [AFS 2920B-2921B1]. Most other family members know this tale as "The Heifer Hide," and "it was repeatedly listed as a favorite by [Hicks-Harmon family member Maud] Long, her family, and her friends" (McCarthy 1994: 107). "The Heifer Hide" (or, more accurately, the final episodes of "The Heifer Hide") is the only one of her family tales that Maud Long's granddaughter Daron Douglas currently tells. Previously published Hicks-Harmon versions of "The Heifer Hide" come from Jane Hicks Gentry (Carter 1925: 343–46), Maud Long (two separate performances: Botkin 1949: 519–25; McCarthy 1994: 107–122), Marshall Ward (*North Carolina Folklore Journal* 26: 53–67), Ray Hicks (Hicks 1963), and, also in this volume, Daron Douglas (story 24). W.F.H. Nicolaisen analyzes three family members' performances of this tale ("Storytelling on Beech Mountain," in McCarthy 1994: 123–49; the narrators are Ray Hicks, Hattie Presnell, and Marshall Ward). Orville Hicks (1998) has recorded a version of this tale. Bill Ellis has published a transcription and thoughtful discussion of Maud Long's 1947 Library of Congress performances (McCarthy 1994: 93–122).

AT 1535, *The Rich and Poor Peasant*. The full-blown tale as told by the Hicks-Harmon family is relatively rare in U.S. tradition, though Hurston (2001: 98–101) has published a nearly identical tale collected from African American tradition in Eatonville, Florida. The final episode, in which Jack fools his brothers into taking his place in the sack, is one of the most popular plots in North America, often identified separately at AT 1737, *The Parson in the Sack to Heaven*. Halpert and Widdowson (1996) list nearly sixty performances from the United States; Lindahl, Owens, and Harvison (1997: no. 54) add another. In 1983, Michael Yates audio-recorded a version from Ethel Birchfield of Roan Mountain, Tennessee; that recording has recently been commericially released (Yates 2002a: track 23).

6. *The Marriage of the King's Daughter* [AFS 2922A2–2922B]. Harmon can be heard on the tape talking about the "nasty words" in this tale; the quotation "a little smutty" comes from Halpert's notes (1939: 60). Aside from Harmon's tale, no Appalachian version was attested before 1981, when folklorist Cheryl Oxford recorded "Jack in the Lion's Den" from Sam Harmon's distant relative Marshall Ward (see Oxford 1994: 70–92). "Jack in the Lion's Den" is transcribed and analyzed by Cheryl Oxford (McCarthy 1994: 56–92).

AT 559, *The Dungbeetle*. Aarne and Thompson list one Native American, one Caribbean, and sixteen French American versions; Baughman lists one version from England. There is a loud hum on the recording that makes the story particularly difficult to transcribe.

The scatological subject matter of this tale is no doubt the reason why it has been collected so seldom. In Marshall Ward's version, performed in front of children, the beetle becomes a June bug, and there are no references to plugging the anus of the princess's suitor. I feel reasonably confident that Ward's one recorded performance has been "cleaned up" for his child auditors. Nevertheless, there are other respects in which his telling differs enormously from Samuel Harmon's. Ward develops the first part of the tale at great length; Harmon, however, summarizes it very briefly, not even specifying the questions that the princess's suitors were posed. Also, Ward spends considerable time giving the tale a medieval cast, speaking about "European history" and "kings and dukes and things" (McCarthy 1994: 72); Harmon makes no such references.

7. *Stiff Dick* [AFS 2924B-2925A]. Chase (1943: no. 6), Maud Long (1955; see story 16 in this book), Ray Hicks (Oxford 1987: 267–83), and Orville Hicks (1998: no. 5) all call this tale "Jack and the Varmints," although Ray has also used the titles "Big Man Jack, Killed Seven at a Whack" (Ray Hicks 1963) and "The Unicorn and the Wild Boar" (story 29 in this volume). Jane Hicks Gentry (Carter 1925: 355–57; Betty N. Smith 1997: 106–7) called her version "Old Stiff Dick"; she is the only family teller who, like Sam, uses the obscene title for the hero, although Chase reported in 1943 that four of his sources for the tale used a rhyme that "had to be altered for printing" (1943: 192). Sound-recordings were made by Ray Hicks (1963) and Orville Hicks (1998).

AT 1640, *The Brave Tailor*. This is a very popular folktale plot in which the villains are usually giants, rather than a unicorn, a boar, and a lion. In spite of the fact that the Hicks-Harmon family repertoire is filled with giant tales, all family members tell this one with the three animals as Jack's adversaries. Halpert and Widdowson (1996) list twenty-eight published performances from the United States, including tales from the traditions of Native Americans (Penobscot, Taos, and Yaqui) and from Americans of Armenian (Michigan), French (Louisiana, Michigan, and Missouri), Italian (Michigan and West Virginia), Portuguese (Massachusetts), Russian (West Virginia), and Spanish (New Mexico) descent. Also see a French Creole version narrated by Cajun Julia Huval (Lindahl, Owens, and Harvison 1997: no. 189). There is an African American text in English from Louisiana (Fauset 1927, no. 6). All eleven published British American versions are from the Appalachians, including four from Kentucky (Roberts 1955: no. 62b; Roberts 1969: nos. 25, 32, and 33) and one from Virginia (Perdue 1987: no. 2). All of the Kentucky and Virginia tales feature giants, and most show more similarity to Maud Long's "Jack and the Giants' Newground" (story 14 in this book) than to "Stiff Dick." The theme of the "sham warrior" (motif K1951) often occurs in African American tales as well; see stories 152 and 170 in this book and their respective notes.

8. *The Mad King* [AFS 2925A2–2926A2]. AT 1000, *Bargain Not to Become Angry*; AT 1003, *Plowing*; AT 1004, *Hogs in the Mud, Sheep in the Air*. This brutal tale seems to be popular only where performed among workers who suffer equally brutal working conditions. In French Canada, for example, Luc Lacourcière lists thirty-two performances, collected primarily from migratory workers, peasant *(habitant)* farmers, and other exploited groups; Ó Súilleabháin and Christiansen list 116 Irish versions; the tale has also been collected from Gaelic-speaking Cape Breton Island in Nova Scotia (MacNeil and Shaw 1987: no. 11). Of the twenty published U.S. tellings cited in Halpert and Widdowson (1996), most are told in foreign languages within ethnic or immigrant communities, including southwestern Hispanics (4 versions), Louisiana Cajuns (3), Michigan Armenians (2), Massachusetts Portuguese (2). Except for a Chinese version told in English (in New York), all the remaining tales are from the British American tradition of Appalachia. Chase publishes a variant of this tale titled "Big Jack and Little Jack" (1943: no. 7) adapted from the tellings of Marshall Ward and Roby Hicks (teller of stories 25 and 26 in this volume); Ray Hicks (teller of stories 28–32 in this volume) called his version "Lucky and Unlucky Jack" (Kinkead 1988: 40–41).

9. *The Bean Tree* [AFS 2931B]. AT 328, *The Boy Steals the Giant's Treasure.* "Jack and the Beanstalk," to which this tale is related, may be the best-known tale in English-language story-book tradition. The earliest surviving printed version, published in England, goes back to 1734 (Opie and Opie 1974: 211–26), and it has been republished often in both England and the United States. Nevertheless, the tale has been reported relatively rarely in oral tradition (one exception is a Kentucky version collected by Roberts [1969: no. 18]). Sam's cousin Jane Gentry knew a version titled "Jack and the Beanstalk" (Carter 1925: 365–66; Betty N. Smith 1997: 120–21), which, unlike Sam's, has a happy ending for Jack, as he kills the giant and escapes. Jane's daughter Maud Long did not tell the tale to Duncan Emrich. If the beanstalk is relatively rare in American tradition, the tale type is not. There are many "horizontal" versions of the plot, in which female or male heroes (with names like Mutsmeg, Merrywise, and Nippy) travel over-land, rather than into the sky, to steal a giant's treasures. See, for example, Chase (1948: no. 4), Glassie (1964), and Roberts (1955: no. 11; 1969: nos. 17, 19, 32). A related tale is Jane Muncy Fugates's "Merrywise" (story 77 in this volume).

10. *Little Dicky Whigburn* [AFS 2798B–2799A1]. Previously transcribed in Emrich 1972: 390–93. My transcription differs from Emrich's in several particulars. The tale was also per-formed by Sam's first cousin Jane Gentry, although Jane's daughter Maud Long apparently did not tell it (Carter 1925: 366–68; Betty N. Smith 1997). This tale reached print long before the other Harmon performances. In fact, there was a version of it published by Mellinger E. Henry in 1938 (153–54), before Herbert Halpert recorded the version published here. The reason this tale received more and earlier attention than the Harmons' other stories is simple: the sung parts of "Little Dicky Whigburn" attracted the interest of the collectors, who were folksong specialists rather than narrative scholars. Henry, for example, transcribed only the sung parts of Samuel Harmon's performance and used his own words to summarize the prose portions of the tale.

In Henry's 1938 transcription, Dicky is searching for a bottle "of clear applesom," apparently a word that had no meaning for the Harmon family. Versions of the song recovered in New-foundland mention "Absalon" or "Absaloon" water. Earlier versions from England feature "Ep-som water," a reference to the curative power of Epsom salts, which are still used for medicinal purposes today (Halpert and Widdowson 1996: 702). Sam seems to vary the pronunciation of his name for this magic water, varying from "apthum," to "applelum," to "applesum."

AT 1360C, *Old Hildebrand.* Halpert and Widdowson list sixteen published U.S. variants of this tale, including four from the Appalachians, four English-language fragments collected by Halpert in New Jersey (see Halpert 1942a: 134–36), and five versions in French (from Louisiana and Missouri), two in Spanish (New Mexico), and one each in Greek and Portuguese, both collected in Massachusetts.

11. *Catskins* [AFS 2926A2–2927A1]. Sam Harmon's first cousin Jane Gentry told a version of Catskins similar to this (Carter 1925: 361–63; Betty N. Smith 1997: 118–19). Chase retells a version that he attributes to Hicks-Harmon family members Howard Ward and Marshall Ward of Watauga County; Chase also heard it from narrators in Kentucky and Virginia (Chase 1948: no. 11, plus notes, p. 236). AT 510B, *The Dress of Gold, of Silver, and of Stars*, a subtype of AT 510, *Cinderella and Cap o' Rushes.* Baughman (1966) lists eight additional American tellings, including five from Kentucky, one each from New York and Virginia, and a unique African American performance from Louisiana. In addition to those, Roberts has collected another Ken-tucky version (1969: no. 22), Chase presents a composite from Kentucky, Tennessee, and Virginia (1956: 31–35). Of the twelve catalogued U.S. versions, ten are Appalachian. Subtype 510B features a girl who leaves home, often after a conflict with her father; subtype 510A, popularized through the versions of Perrault, Grimm, and Disney, features the wicked stepmother and magical help from the mother's spirit or a fairy godmother. In the United States, 510B seems to be

considerably more popular among traditional narrators than 510A. Among the innumerable studies of the Cinderella tale in general, two major monographs (Cox 1893; Rooth 1951) study the worldwide distribution and plot variations, and Dundes (1988) has published a casebook in which many authors consider various performances and meanings of the tale.

12. *Old Black Dog* [AFS 2930B2–2931A1]. Sam's granddaughter Marietta Harmon, age 5, also tells a version of this tale, not transcribed here (AFS 2930B1). Marietta learned it from her sister Alberta.

Maud Long. The description of Dorland Institute is from Betty N. Smith 1997: 43, who also offers an admirably detailed description of life in Hot Springs when Maud was a child. Jane Douglas's remarks on her mother were recorded by Carl Lindahl, May 1997. Irving Bacheller is quoted in Emrich 1972: 339. Ellis (1994) offers a fine appreciation of Maud's role as a storyteller. In books that focus more on Maud's mother, Jane Gentry, than upon Maud herself, Painter (1987) describes Dorland Institute and other aspects of the environment in which Maud grew up.

13. *When My Mother Told Jack Tales* [AFS9159B]. Also transcribed in Emrich (1972: 340–41).

14. *Jack and the Giants' Newground* [AFS 9156A]. AT 1060, *Squeezing the (Supposed) Stone*; AT 1088, *Eating Contest*; K1082, "Ogres duped into fighting each other"; AT 1045, *Pulling the Lake Together*; AT 1063A, *Throwing Contest: Trickster Shouts*; G520, "Ogre deceived into self-injury." This performance was transcribed earlier by Duncan Emrich (1972: 341–57); Emrich's differs little from the present transcription. Maud Long's mother, Jane Gentry, told this story to Isabel Gordon Carter (1925: 351–54; Betty N. Smith 1997: 129–31); Carter gives the title, "Jack the Giant Killer." Richard Chase (1943: no. 1) drew upon the versions of four of Jane Gentry's relatives to create a tale much like Maud's and also titled "Jack and the Giants' Newground." In the most thorough accounting of this tale in North American tradition to date, Halpert and Widdowson (1996: no. 114) list thirty United States versions, including twelve from the Appalachians (of which one is Italian American, another Russian American, and the rest British American), five from the Spanish-language tradition of the American Southwest; four from Native American cultures (2 from Maine and 2 from the Southwest), four are from the French traditions of Michigan and Missouri. Like others, Halpert and Widdowson place this tale under the rubric of AT 1640, *The Brave Little Tailor*; however, without the telltale frame of "Seven with one blow" (see stories 7, 16, and 29 in this book), I find this attribution unjustified. In addition to the enormous list assembled by Halpert and Widdowson, add Reaver 1987: no. 9, a Florida fragment that includes types 1060 and 1063.

15. *Jack and the Drill* [AFS 9158A]. Jane Gentry titled this tale "The Enchanted Lady," and she ended the tale by explaining that "Jack killed the king and married his daughter and when I left there Jack uz rich" (Carter 1925: 330–31; Betty N. Smith 1997: 127–28). Maud's version, however, ends abruptly when the king cuts short Jack's song and asks Jack to cut off his head; in this respect, she follows Richard Chase's published version (1943: no. 10) more closely than her mother's. This tale, AT 570, *The Rabbit Herd*, is missing from the active repertoires of most members of the Hicks-Harmon family, possibly because its ending is confusing to many listeners, who don't understand why the king would want to have his own head cut off just to avoid hearing Jack sing some lies about the queen. Many versions of *The Rabbit Herd* are obscene: for example, in an Ozark version (Randolph 1976: no. 29), Jimmy, the hero, hopes to marry the king's daughter; the king will grant permission only if Jimmy will watch a rabbit for a week. Jimmy trains the rabbit to mind him. When the king, fearing that Jimmy will accomplish the task, sends in turn a female servant, the princess, and the queen to get the rabbit from him,

Jimmy demands sexual favors from each woman in return for his rabbit, but each time the woman leaves with the rabbit, Jimmy rings a bell and the rabbit escapes and returns to him. Finally, the king himself tries to wrest the rabbit from Jimmy, but Jimmy surrenders it only after the king has copulated with a donkey. In the final scene, the king will surrender his daughter only if Jimmy sings a bowl full. Jimmy sings "The first to come was the king's hired servant, / To steal away my skill; / I laid her down and honed her off. / Fill, Bowl, Fill!" When Jimmy gets to the verse mentioning the king's bestiality, the king cuts him off and gives him his daughter. It is likely that earlier versions of the Hicks-Harmon "Jack and the Drill" once possessed similarly obscene content. This tale is extremely rare in American tradition: In addition to Jane Gentry's and Maud Long's versions, and a recent performance by family member Orville Hicks (1990), there are only two other published versions of which I am aware: the Ozark version summarized above, and a second, "cleaned up" version told by the same Arkansas narrator in front of "mixed company" (Randolph 1952: 17–19, 185–86).

16. *Jack and the Varmints* [AFS 9161A, B]. AT 1640, *The Brave Tailor*. This tale, as transcribed by Duncan Emrich, was published in Emrich (1972: 357–65). Maud's relatives Samuel Harmon and Ray Hicks also tell versions of this story; see stories 7 and 29 in this book, and the notes to story 7 for a fuller discussion.

17. *Jack and the Bull* [AFS 9163]. AT 511A, *The Little Red Bull*. This tale, relatively common elsewhere in Appalachia, is, however, quite rare in the Hicks-Harmon family. Chase included a version in the *Jack Tales* (1943: no. 3), but he admits that he learned the tale from James Taylor Adams and four taletellers from Wise County, Virginia, none of whom was related to the Hickses and Harmons. Maud's telling, then, is almost certainly based on what she learned from Richard Chase. To my knowledge, only one other Hicks-Harmon family member has told a subsequently published version of this tale: Stanley Hicks (Oxford 1989). Among the other published Appalachian versions are Perdue (1987: nos. 3A–3E, collected from four taletellers; these tales were Chase's source), Glassie (1964), and Roberts (1955: nos. 20a–d). Jane Muncy, the teller of stories 76–85 in this volume, performed a version of "Jack and the Bull Stripe" (Roberts 1955: 20d) when she was 11 years old.

18. *Jack and the Doctor's Girl* [AFS 9158B]. AT 1525A, *The Master Thief*. Maud's relative Ray Hicks tells a related version (story 28 in this book), and Ray Hicks's brother-in-law Frank Proffitt Sr. told "Jack and the Old Rich Man," yet another version of the same type, from his father's storytelling tradition; Frank Proffitt Jr. has often told "Jack and the Old Rich Man" (see Lindahl 1994b). Lindahl discusses the Appalachian versions of the type (1988; 1994a: xxvii–xxxi).

19. *Jack and the Northwest Wind* [AFS 9151A]. Maud's mother Jane Gentry told a version of this tale (Carter 1925: 363–65); Richard Chase printed one version based on tellings by Marshall Ward and Ben Hicks, grandfather of Ray Hicks. Ray has also told the tale; one of his tellings is summarized by Isbell (1996: 80–89).

AT 563, *The Table, the Ass, and the Stick*. The general tale type is well known in the Appalachians and in Canada, and even more widely distributed in the Caribbean. The motif of the young boy in search of the wind is particularly popular in Scotland and other northern European cultures.

20. *Jack and One of His Hunting Trips* [AFS 9162B2]. AT 1890, *The Lucky Shot*; AT 1881, *Man Carried through the Air by Geese*; AT 1900, *How the Man Came out of the Tree Stump*; AT 1895, *Man Wading in Water Catches Many Fish in His Boots*. This tale is cognate to half of Richard Chase's "Jack and His Hunting Trips" (1943: no. 16). This is a tall tale rather than a märchen, and it does not seem to have been part of the family's Jack Tale repertoire before Chase

published his version. Nearly forty years later, in the 1980s, Ray Hicks told a similar version to Cheryl Oxford (Oxford 1987).

The motifs and themes wound together here by Maud Long are among the most popular in American folk tradition: one boy, alone in the woods, and short of ammunition, lucks his way into extraordinary prosperity. Halpert lists extensive parallels to most of these episodes (1942b; 1942c).

21. *Old Fire Dragaman* [AFS 9162A]. AT 301A, *Quest for a Vanished Princess.* One of the most popular of northern European folktales, with hundreds of Irish and Scandinavian variants, this tale is fairly well distributed in North America. It has enjoyed enormous popularity among Native American cultures along the Atlantic and Pacific coasts, as well as among French Canadians, where Lacourcière and Low identified 105 performances. A sizeable number of Mexican American versions have been collected in New Mexico, one by Arthur L. Campa (1947: 329–32), who contributed stories 156–159 to this book. Halpert and Widdowson (1996: no. 3) count seven Appalachian tellings, three from the Hicks-Harmon family (Carter 1925: 341–43; Chase 1943: no. 12; Chase 1955: 71–73). The other tales are Roberts 1955: no. 2; Roberts 1969: no. 11; Roberts 1974: no. 104; Campbell 1958: 78–82. Other Hicks-Harmon versions include Ray Hicks's audio (1963) and video performances (Hicks and Borrow 1997). Aside from the Appalachians and the Hispanic Southwest, the only regions reporting the tale are the Ozarks (Randolph 1952: 148–50; Randolph 1958: 17 [but this latter reference is debatable]) and upstate New York, where Sara Cleveland has told two distinctly different versions of the tale, both of which appear in this book (stories 42 and 43). The present volume contains not only Maud Long's performance and Sara Cleveland's two, but also a remarkable version by Jane Muncy Fugate (story 79).

22. *Love: A Riddle Tale* [AFS 9151B]. H543, "Death sentence escaped by propounding riddle." Duncan Emrich summarizes an analogous tale and offers the accompanying rhyme in *Folklore on the American Land* (1972: 173): "Once a man was in jail and was going to be hanged. They told him if he could make a riddle they couldn't guess, they'd set him free. He had a dog named Love, and he killed the dog and tanned its hide. From the hide he made a seat for his chair, a sole for his shoe, and a glove for his right hand. Then he gave this riddle: "On Love I sit, on Love I stand, / And Love I hold in my right hand."

23. *Jack and the Heifer Hide* [AFS 9155A]. See notes to story 5 in this book.

24. *Jack and the River* [AFC 2003/001]. Daron Douglas's truncation of this tale possesses many traditional precedents in American tradition, where the episode of the sack, the sheep, and the river is often told as an independent tale. AT 1535, *The Rich and Poor Peasant*, episode V. Halpert and Widdowson (1996: 804) find the tale so common that "there is obviously a need for an additional type number to designate the independent versions of AT 1535 (V)"; Aarne and Thompson (1961) did indeed assign this episode its own number—AT 1737, *The Parson in the Sack to Heaven*—but Halpert and Widdowson correctly point out that AT 1737, though parallel to episode IV of AT 1525, differs significantly from episode V of AT 1535. Halpert and Widdowson go on to list over seventy American tellings of the sack-substitution tale, including many from Appalachia, the African American South, the Hispanic Southwest, and the Caribbean. See, for example, Lindahl, Owens, and Harvison 1997: no. 5. The quotations from Daron's mother Jane come from an interview recorded by Carl Lindahl in May 1997.

25. *Hooray for Old Sloosha!* [AFS 15367A/15]. D1810.8, "Magic knowledge from dream"; Z356, "Unique survivor." The Warners' note says of this interview: "This is a real document." In this tale the son is the unique survivor and the boy's father the avenger. For a slightly different tale, in which the sole survivor is also the avenger, and in which the avenger dedicates his life to killing the Indians who killed his family, see story 65 in this book.

26. *Feathers in Her Hair* [AFS 15367]. K521, "Escape by disguise." Barden (1991: no. 70) prints a story, told in 1940 in Wise County, Virginia, in which a woman hides from Indian attackers by immersing herself in a barrel of feathers; in the Virginia tale, however, the woman does not emerge from the barrel of feathers to be mistaken for an Indian. In American oral tradition there are innumerable tales of narrow escapes from the Indians, but this is the only one I can identify in which the escapee succeeds by unintentionally disguising herself.

27. *The Yape* [AFS 15358A]. Tales of Bigfoot-like beings are relatively common in Appalachian tradition; see the note to story 104 in this collection. In addition to the narratives she recorded for the Warners, Buna Hicks contributed two tales to collector Sandy Paton in January 1962 (AFS 14206).

Ray Hicks. A detailed account of Ray's early life is found in Robert Isbell's *The Last Chivaree* (1996), which is the source for two of Ray's statements, quoted here, concerning what is and is not "true" in his stories (Isbell 1996: 32–33, 80; see also page 39 for other information summarized here); Isbell's book is my source for the tale of the fortune teller who predicted Ray's marriage to Rosa (1996: 113–15). Ray's words about learning stories from "Grandpa Andy" and Sam Ward were recorded by Frank A. Warner (AFS 13678). Barbara Freeman's account of Ray's first performance appears in Sobol 1999: 101. Other treatments of Ray's life and his tales include Oxford (1987), Jimmy Neil Smith (1988: 3–13), and Sobol (1994: 105–16, 133–35). Among the commercially released videos that feature Ray's life and artistry are Barret (1975) and Hadley and Hadley (2000). Available audio performances include Hicks (1963) and Hicks (1989).

28. *Jack and the Robbers* [AFS 15368]. This is the title given by Frank Warner to a tale known to Maud Long as "Jack and the Doctor's Daughter" (see story 18 in this book) and to Chase as "Jack and the Doctor's Girl" (1943: no. 13). AT 1525A, *The Master Thief.* Ray's relative Maud Long tells another version in this book: see story 18 in this book and the notes to story 18 for a discussion of its role in American tradition.

This tale should not be confused with Richard Chase's "Jack and the Robbers" (1943: no. 4), which is a version of *The Bremen Town Musicians* (AT 130).

29. *The Unicorn and the Wild Boar* [AFS 15368]. AT 1640, *The Brave Tailor.* For versions of the same plot as told by Samuel Harmon and Maud Long, see stories 7 and 16 in this book; see the note to story 7 for a discussion of the tale type.

30. *The Witch Woman on the Stone Mountain on the Tennessee Side* [AFC 2001/008]. This tale comes from the International Storytelling Collection. Ray recorded an incomplete version in 1951 for Frank A. and Anne Warner. A third version was recorded on the commercially released audio cassette *Jack Alive!* (Hicks 1989). Motifs G200, "Witch"; G284, "Witch as helper"; G286, "Initiation into witchcraft." The quote in the headnote that describes the crowd at the annual storytelling festival comes from an anonymous resident of Jonesborough who shared these thoughts with Carl Lindahl in May 2002.

31. *Grinding at the Mill* [AFC 2001/008]. Jane Gentry (Carter 1925: 354–55) and her daughter Maud Long (1947) both told versions of this tale; Maud's version was recorded by Duncan Emrich for the Library of Congress (AFS 9150B1, 9151A2). Although Ray Hicks tells this story as a fiction, he mentions at the end of his performance that many people believed in witches and were aware of rituals that could be practiced in order to obtain a witch's supernatural powers. The major motif of this tale is G275.12, "Witch in the form of an animal is injured or killed as a result of the injury to the animal; the witch's body suffers an injury identical to that of the animal"; Baughman introduced a more specific motif that exactly fits this tale: *G275.12(bcb), "Person cuts paw off cat; witch has hand missing"; see also G252, "Witch in form of cat"; H1417, "Fear test: night watch with magic cats."

32. *Mule Eggs* [AFC 2001/008]. AT 1319, *Pumpkin Sold as an Ass's Egg*. An audio-recorded version of this tale is found on Orville Hicks 1998: no. 3. Doc McConnell (teller of story 140 in this book) narrates a version in J.N. Smith 1988: 81–83. Richard Chase collected a version, not yet published, in the Appalachians ca. 1950 (AFS 8898B). Baughman records twelve U.S. versions spread about the country, with a substantial number of African American versions from the South.

Sara Cleveland. Biographical information is found in Kenneth Goldstein (1968) and Goldstein and Ben-Amos (1970); Kenneth Goldstein's wife, Rochelle (2003), and daughter Diane (1999) shared with me their memories of Sara, who was a close friend of the family. Many of Sara Cleveland's ballads and songs are preserved on an LP (Cleveland 1968, re-released as a cassette tape in 1997). Long after Sara's death, her family continues the tradition of singing her songs, as is evident on a recent CD (Cleveland Family 2002), on which Sara's grandchildren Colleen and James Cleveland sing, with instrumental accompaniment by grandson Curt Cleveland and his wife, Becky.

33. *Finn MacCool and the Rocks* [AFS 17020]. A901, "Topographical features caused by experiences of giant hero"; A977.1, "Giant responsible for certain stones"; F624.2.0.1, "Strong man throws enormous stone." For a millennium and more, Finn MacCool (rendered Fionn Mac Cumhaill and other related forms in Irish) has been the most popular of Ireland's mythological heroes. He appears in surviving literature earlier and survives much later and in many more stories than does Cu Chulainn, the famed hero of the Irish Ulster Cycle. Tales of Finn and his warrior band, the Fenians (or the Fianna), were widely told in Ireland and Highland Scotland in the nineteenth century, and there are many giant boulders in both locales that are said to have been flung to their current locations by the giant Finn. Sara Cleveland's tale represents the sort of place-name legend most commonly associated with Finn in Ireland and Scotland today. As Dáithí Ó hÓgáin writes, "Perhaps the most striking type of imagery concerning the Fianna in current lore is that which portrays them as having been giants, or at least as possessing colossal strength. . . . [T]his idea has proved to be the strongest survivor of all the lore. Many large rocks or boulders are still pointed out as having reached their present locations by way of being hurled as projectiles in a contest between Fionn Mac Cumhaill and a hostile giant. It is clear that in such cases we are dealing with ordinary aetiological giant-lore placed in the context of the Fenian tradition" (Almqvist, Ó Catháin and Ó Héalai 1987: 209–10). Ó hÓgáin goes on to explain that such tales have a very long history in Ireland and Scotland. Sara Cleveland's parents obviously brought with them to the New World their home-learned traditions of associating giant rocks with the great hero of their country of origin. On related Irish place-name legends, see Murphy 1953: xviii; on Fenian traditions in general, see Almqvist, Ó Caitháin and Ó Héalai 1987, and Ó hÓgáin 1988.

34. *Black Horses* [AFS 17020]. D1812.3.3.11, "Death of another revealed in dream." J157, "Wisdom (knowledge) from dream." Various indexes record beliefs similar in content if not always in meaning to that expressed here by Sara Cleveland; for example, Hand, Casetta, and Thederman (1981) list an Ohio belief that it is bad luck to dream of black horses, but also another belief that it is good luck to dream of them.

35. *Telling Fortunes with Cards* [AFS 17020]. D1810, "Magic knowledge."

36. *Spiritualism and Fortune Telling* [AFS 17020]. D1810.13, "Magic knowledge from the dead."

37. *Pull, God Damn You, Pull!* [AFS 17020]. E279.3, "Ghost pulls bedclothing from sleeper." A common motif, reported broadly from African American, European American, and Hispanic

communities throughout the United States. For an Arkansas variant, see McNeil 1985: no. 18; also Holzer (1983: 77–79).

38. *The Kiln Is Burning* [AFS 17020]. M301.6.1, "Banshees as portents of misfortune." On contemporary Irish beliefs in banshees, see Lysaght's excellent study (1986). Kilns figure as sites of supernatural activities in several Irish tales, such as the Wexford legend in which a kiln emits a ghostly light (Ó Muirithe and Nuttall 1999: 72). Although Sara's tale is set in rural Ireland, her son Bill and daughter-in-law Phyllis associated the kiln with the industrial landscape of modern America. As Phyllis explains, Sara "lived about a mile from the old kilns outside Hudson Falls, New York. I believe they did have fires there" (written communication from Phyllis Cleveland to Carl Lindahl, May 2003).

39. *Baby's Gone* [AFS 17020]. F321, "Fairy steals child from cradle." F321.1, "Changeling." Belief in changelings—i.e., supernatural beings substituted for humans—was widespread in Europe when the first colonists began their emigrations across the Atlantic. In the most common traditions, an infant or young child is abducted by fairies or elves, who leave one of their own in place of the child. Parents sometimes relied upon changeling beliefs to explain congenital birth defects and the extreme behavior of infants. It was relatively rare for the fairies to abduct an adult, although grown women were sometimes believed to be kidnapped, as in the famous 1895 Irish case of Bridget Cleary, the subject of two excellent recent treatments (Bourke 1999; Hoff and Yeats 2000; the Burke book contains a particularly valuable discussion of changeling beliefs). This story ends uncharacteristically happily, as the fairies are thwarted and the child remains with her family. The red mark on the child's side is the only token of the fairies' attempt at abducting her (F362.4, "Fairy causes mutilation (injury)"); cf. E542.1, "Ghostly fingers leave mark on person's body").

40. *The Witch and the Donkey* [AFS 17020]. G271.4.4, "Breaking spell on animal by bleeding or maiming animal." Baughman finds numerous parallels in the United States. Gardner (1937: 68–69) expands the number of references considerably.

41. *The Lady and the Fairy* [AFS 17020]. F361.3, "Fairies take revenge on person who spies on them"; cf. F451.2.7.1, "Dwarfs with red heads and red caps." Stories in which a fairy removes the eye of a prying human are quite common in Ireland. Because fairies tend to be invisible except in extraordinary circumstances, variants of this tale often explain how the mortal acquired the power to see the fairy in the first place. In some Irish versions (see, for example, O'Sullivan 1966: no. 24), the mortal woman has received her special powers of sight during a forced visit to the otherworld to serve as a midwife to the fairies. Although Thompson's motif index lists numerous Irish examples of this motif, Baughman was not able to locate a single example in the lore of North America.

42. *Little Red Night Cap* [AFS 17020]. AT 301A, *Search for a Vanished Princess*. F451.2.7.1, "Dwarfs with red heads and red caps"; F451.5.2, "Malevolent dwarf." This is one of the most popular tales in the present collection: see stories 21, 43, and 79 in this book and their respective notes. The sinister central figure of Sara Cleveland's tale comes right out of Irish folk tradition. The *Oxford English Dictionary* notes that the term "redcap" often serves as "the name of a sprite or goblin" (Halpert and Widdowson 1996: 28). A Newfoundland version of this tale features a similarly cruel being named Daddy Redcap (Halpert and Widdowson 1996: 20–26), previously published in Goldstein and Ben-Amos (1970: 45–51).

43. *Old Graybeard* [AFS 17020]. Yet another version of AT 301, though this is 301B, a subtype distinguished by the supernaturally strong helpers that appear in the opening scenes: motifs F601, "Extraordinary companions; a group of men with extraordinary powers travel together"; F6211, "Strong man: tree-puller. Can uproot all trees." After the strong men depart, the tale runs closely parallel to Jane Muncy Fugate's tale "Old Greasybeard," story 79 in this

volume. Instead of the telltale Irish red cap of the previous tale, the villain of this version possesses a beard as his distinguishing sign. As such, "Old Graybeard" shares traits with the villains of Appalachian tales who are noted for their offensive beards: for example, "Dirtybeard" (Roberts 1955: no. 2) and Jane Muncy Fugate's "Old Greasybeard"; see also Maud Long's tale "Old Fire Dragaman," story 21 in the present collection, previously published in Goldstein and Ben-Amos (1970: 53–57).

44. *Shiver and Shake* [AFS 17020]. AT 326, *The Youth Who Wanted to Learn What Fear Is.* Leonard Roberts identified this as "the most common and most richly varied [märchen tale] type that I have collected in the mountains" of eastern Kentucky. In the course of his dissertation fieldwork, he collected fourteen performances, four of which he published in his first book (1955: no. 9). It is important to note, however, that the majority of the Kentucky tales were told to him not as fantasy narratives but as legends, and they were purported to be true. In European American tradition, the most reliable rule of thumb for distinguishing märchen versions of this tale type from the legend versions is the ending: tales that end, as Sara Cleveland's does, with the hero's wife pouring cold water on him after their first night in bed almost always represent the märchen tradition. African American versions of the tale quite commonly end with a comic flourish as the brave man is finally frightened out of the house (see Botkin 1944: 710–11; Burrison 1991: 156–58; Dorson 1967: no. 192). For typical märchen versions, see the Grimm and Grimm (1987: no. 4). E281, "Ghosts haunt house"; H1411, "Fear test: staying in haunted house."

45. *Rob Haww* [AFS 17020]. This grotesque figure appears as a stock character in Scottish Traveller traditions. Storyteller Stanley Robertson states, "He got the name Rob Haa because he'd a great big stomach, a stickin-oot stomach. And Rob Haa means a gut-bag, ye ken, a glutton. But the man wisnae a glutton; it jist so happened he had a big stomach" (Robertson 1986: 204). Sara Cleveland's tradition obviously differs from that of the Traveller's in at least one particular: her Rob Haww is most certainly a glutton.

46. *One Thing the Devil Can't Do* [AFS 17020]. G303.16.19.3, "One is freed if he can set a task the devil cannot perform"; X621*, "Jokes about the Irish." In the mid-nineteenth century, the Irish immigrants to America were the subject of all sorts of stereotyping jokes (see Davies 1990: 153–63). These verbal caricatures became so widespread and ingrained in oral tradition that they remained popular in the African American and Appalachian culture into the mid-twentieth century (see Dorson 1967: nos. 241–44, for African American examples; Roberts 1955: nos. 40–55, for Appalachian examples). Sara Cleveland's joke is an Irishwoman's revenge, in which Pat outsmarts not only the Englishman and the Scotsman but also the devil himself. The basic plot has been found since medieval times in Europe. Baughman cites an American version in which the devil is stumped when a man belches and tells him to sew a button on the belch. For Irish jokes emphasizing a negative stereotype, see stories 173 and 174 in this collection.

J.D. Suggs. Dorson writes extensively on Suggs in several sources, presenting accounts of how the two met (1953; 1956a; 1956b: 4–7; 1967: 22–25), an appreciation of Suggs's repertoire (Dorson 1956a), and a brief biography of the narrator (Dorson 1967: 59–64). The Dorson quotations that appear in the first six paragraphs of the headnote are found in 1967: 23, 64; Dorson's words of sorrow on the death of Suggs are found in 1956b: 7; and Martha Suggs Spencer's favorite passage from Dorson appears in 1956a: 152. Martha's recollections of her father's vision appears in Spencer 1995: 110–11.

47. *How I Learned My Tales* [AFS 10897A]. Martha Suggs Spencer's account of her childhood with her father is condensed from an undated letter to Carl Lindahl, received in September 2003; some details of spelling and grammar have been standardized to aid the reader.

48. *Mr. Snake and the Farmer* [AFS 10897A]. AT 155, *Ungrateful Serpent Returned to Captivity*. A slightly different version is published by Dorson (1967: no. 22). In addition to this beautifully told tale, Dorson collected another in Michigan; he cites two others from the South, including a nineteenth-century version published by Joel Chandler Harris (1883: no. 46). More recently published versions include two texts from Louisiana: one in French (Ancelet 1994: no. 11) and one in English (Lindahl, Owens, and Harvison 1997: no. 206). The tale has a significant African distribution (Klipple 1938). Although popular in Europe and well distributed in Hispanic America (Robe 1973; Hansen 1957; Miller 1973: no. 64), the tale is not reported by Baughman in either Britain or in Anglo-America.

49. *Buzzard Goes to Europe* [AFS 10897B]. Although this brief tale has not been assigned a type or motif number, Dorson collected nine versions of it in Michigan and the South; he also identified three previous published versions (1967: nos. 27, 28). These tales are exclusively African American. In most tellings, the buzzard (or sometimes another bird) flies north and is disgusted by the lack of food or the poor food; in other versions, he flies south. Only in Suggs's version does the buzzard cross the ocean and visit Europe; only Suggs's is set during World War I.

50. *Monkey Apes His Master* [AFS 10897A]. AT 1676A, *Big 'Fraid and Little 'Fraid*, K585, "Fatal game: Shaving necks, dupe's head cut off." Dorson published a similar version of this tale from Suggs and titled it "Monkey Who Impitated [*sic*] His Master" (1967: no. 214). The type has been studied at length by John Minton (1993), who found it of particular significance for African American narrators. The tale is relatively rare among European Americans, but Jane Muncy (teller of stories 76–85 in this book) performed a version for Leonard Roberts when she was 11 years old. In addition to the thirty-six texts studied by Minton, Hartsfield (1987: no. 26) provides a Georgia text.

Suggs's version of the tale is quite complex, combining the ghost episode (AT 1676A) with the grisly barbershop scene (K585). As Minton's work demonstrates, African American narrators often combine these two types. Suggs links the two with a short scene in which the monkey hijacks a train. Dorson remarks that he has not been able to find a parallel for this short episode (1967: 349), but a recently published manuscript compiled by Zora Neale Hurston (2001: 227) contains a similar train-stealing monkey tale told by Louisiana-born Jerry Bennett.

51. *Efan Outruns the Lord* [AFS 10897B]. J217.0.1.1, "Trickster overhears man praying for death to take him; the trickster appears at man's house, usually in disguise, says he is God (or the devil). The man tells him to take his wife (or he runs away)." Zora Neale Hurston collected three similar tales; in addition to her version in *Mules and Men* (1935: 96–99), she left behind two posthumous texts, one featuring Tom and "his wife," and the second Ike and Dinah, from George Mills of Mobile, Alabama, and James Moseley of Eatonville, Florida (2001: 167–69). Brewer (1958: 7–9, 17–18) publishes two Texas versions, and Dance (1978: nos. 125, 383) includes a Virginia version performed in the 1970s.

The scene with which this tale opens, with John kneeling at the base of the praying tree, is a common episode in African American folktales (see, for example, Dorson 1967: no. 47).

52. *Mr. Fox and Mr. Deer* [AFS 10897B]. K606, "Escape by singing song." The Thompson *Motif-Index* lists an African and a Cape Verde Islands version as the only analogs to this tale. A similar Suggs telling was published by Dorson under the title "The Deer Escapes from the Fox" (1967: no. 15). This tale, Dorson writes, "gives a nice twist to Motif K622, 'Captive plays further and further from watchman and escapes.' " Unrecorded from European Americans, this plot is fairly common in the United States and in the Caribbean. In the great majority of cases, the captive trickster is a rabbit and not a deer.

53. *Brother Rabbit Rides Brother Bear* [AFS 10897B]. AT 72, *Rabbit Rides Fox a-Courting*; AT 4, *Carrying the Sham-Sick Trickster*; K1241, "Trickster rides dupe horseback." From the

earliest Uncle Remus book (Harris 1880: no. 6) to the present day, this tale has been particularly popular with African Americans. Its popularity no doubt derives from the fact that Brer Rabbit does not merely escape his more powerful opponent but, rather, converts the bully into a beast of burden. This turnabout represents a sweet compensation fantasy for people forced into sub-servient roles as slaves and sharecroppers. The story is especially common in the Caribbean, where Beckwith (1924: 235) reported it often and observed the Caribbean versions to be nearly identical to the U.S. versions; Abrahams (1985: 318) considers it "the most commonly heard Anansi story in the anglophonic West Indies." Not surprisingly, the Caribbean and southern versions possess African parallels, five of which were discovered by Klipple (1938). A related tale, collected in Arkansas, appears in Dorson (1967: no. 10).

54. *Brother Bear Meets Man* [AFS 10897B]. AT 157, *Learning to Fear Man.* This tale type, well known throughout the world, was seldom collected from African American narrators before Dorson published sixteen performances (1953). Dorson has remarked that the man who terrorizes the king of the beasts is sometimes characterized specifically as a black man. Nevertheless, some African Americans depict the man with the gun as a white man and treat this story much as they treat "Big 'Fraid" (story 50), as an expression of the unequal relations between whites and blacks in the South. For example, in Alfred Anderson's version of the tale (Lindahl, Owens, and Harvison 1997: no. 62), Brother Bear, the dupe who is shot by the cruel passerby, speaks with a stronger African American accent than the other characters, which has led some listeners to conclude that the trigger-happy shooter is meant to represent not merely "man" but more spe-cifically "white man." For the story's European tradition, see Lindahl 1984; for other African American examples, see Dorson 1967; Hurston 2001: 220–21, 240–42; Burrison 1991: 141–42.

55. *Brother Bear and Brother Deer Hold a Meeting* [AFS 10897A]. AT 62, *Peace among the Animals*; A2281, "Enmity between animals from original quarrel"; A2494.4.4, "Enmity between dog and rabbit"; B253, "Animals perform offices of church." I have not been able to find an exact parallel to this tale in American tradition, although Joel Chandler Harris published a distantly related tale explaining the enmity between dogs and rabbits (1883: no. 61). This ae-tiological account receives added color from its church setting. Here, Suggs taps a rich vein of lore. African American jokes on preachers and preaching are extraordinarily varied and numerous. J. Mason Brewer (1953) devoted an entire book to the subject, and the theme is assigned its own section in other collections (e.g., Dorson 1956b: 167–74; Dorson 1967: 363–72).

56. *The Devil's Daughter* [AFS 10897B]. AT 313A, *The Girl as Helper on the Hero's Flight.* Motifs D1521.1, "Seven-league boots"; and D672, "Obstacle flight. Fugitives throw objects behind them which magically become obstacles in pursuer's path." The only lengthy European-derived märchen in Suggs's repertoire, "The Devil's Daughter" is one of the few classic magic tales to have become a staple in African American tradition. Dorson collected four African American versions, including this one by Suggs, and listed copious variants (Dorson 1967: no. 142). Zora Neale Hurston collected at least three versions of the tale: one appears in *Mules and Men* (1935); the second and third, published posthumously, were performed by Louisiana-born Jerry Bennett and Floridian Julius Henry, the latter "about 14" years of age (2001: 48–51, 53–54). There are also dozens of other African variants that have been collected in the Caribbean (Parsons 1943: no. 172). Perhaps the major reason this, among all the European märchen brought to the United States, received such a warm welcome in the African American repertoire, is that it centers upon the adversarial relationship between a cruel landowner and a relatively powerless man who is repeatedly required to perform impossible feats of agricultural work. A slave or a sharecropper could readily identify with such a situation.

57. *Where* Um-hum *Came From* [AFS 10897A]. Hurston calls one version of this tale "How

the Devil Coined a Word" (1935: 204–5); she also collected a similar, but less elaborate version from Florida (2001: 60). Dorson collected six versions of this story; he did not publish the Suggs performance, but he does print one from a Mrs. John Grant (1967: no. 136).

58. *Skin, Don't You Know Me?* [AFS 10897B]. G229.1.1, "Witch who is out of skin is prevented from re-entering it when person salts or peppers skin." Baughman lists twelve occurrences of this motif, all but one from African American narrators and the great majority from the South. Dorson collected six versions from African Americans, including this version from Suggs (1967: 123). Dorson mentions two Caribbean versions (Parsons 1943: no. 163); see also Hurston 2001: 63–64. This tale is also an example of motif G249.7, "Witches go through keyholes," of which Baughman lists three English examples, but none from the United States.

59. *The Great Watermelon* [AFS 10897A]. X1411.1.1, "Lie: large watermelon."

60. *Pull Me Up, Simon* [AFS 10897B]. Q2236.3*, "Punishment for fishing on Sunday." Baughman identifies five versions on this general theme, including two tales very similar to the one told here by Suggs, which Baughman identified with the motif Q2236.3*I, "Fish caught on Sunday bursts man open." A similar version was published by Dorson ("Simon Fishing on Sunday"; 1967: no. 141), who added three more African versions. To Dorson's list add three African American versions from Georgia (Burrison 1991: 301–2, supplemented by two more in Burrison's notes) and a more distant analog from Hurston (2001: 210). The specific form taken by Suggs's narration, with its talking fish and bursting boy (usually named Simon), has been found almost exclusively in the African American South.

61. *Brother Bill, the Wild Cowboy* [AFS 10897B]. Dorson (1967: no. 220) detects a close relationship between Suggs's El Paso cowboy and Pecos Bill, the famous Anglo-American tall tale figure who became a star in American pulp journalism in 1923, following in the footsteps of Paul Bunyan. Dorson draws upon Suggs's account and two other African American tales featuring a bobcat-riding cowboy named Bill to suggest that there was indeed a substantial preexisting oral tradition behind the popular figure of Pecos Bill.

Joshua Alley. Marguerite Chapallaz describes her collecting experience on disk AFS 25592A. In 1956 folklorist Richard Dorson (collector of stories 47–61, 128, 188, 195, and 196 in this book) visited Jonesport, Maine, and environs and collected tales from Joshua Alley's nephews James and Frank and daughter-in-law Margaret, as well as from more distant relations; he describes his fieldwork and publishes many Alley family stories in several sources (notably Dorson 1957; Dorson 1964: 21–94). Stephanie Hall (1999) has written an appreciation of the American Dialect Society project and the work of Marguerite Chapallaz.

62. *The Bear's Tale* [AFS 25690A-25693A]. Marguerite Chapallaz recorded another, even longer version of the same tale from Joshua Alley on July 6, 1934 (AFS 25224A-25230A). Both performances are impressive; the version I chose to transcribe was the one with the better sound quality. I have found no close parallel to this remarkable narrative. Among the relevant motifs are L114.1, "Lazy hero"; B435.4, "Helpful bear"; and B562.1, "Animal shows man treasure."

63. *Man Warren Beal and the Indians* [AFS 25679A,B]. Marguerite Chapallaz recorded another version of the same tale from Joshua Alley on July 6, 1934 (AFS 25233A,B). The tale of the woman who evades the Indians by descending through the trap door has parallels under motif K515, "Escape by hiding."

64. *Wrestling the Chief* [AFS 25679B-25680A]. Marguerite Chapallaz recorded another version of the same tale from Joshua Alley on July 6, 1934 (AFS 25233B).

65. *Chute's Wedge Trick* [AFS 25694A,B]. Motif K551.29*, "Man asks captors to wait until he has split a log he is working on. He then asks them to pull the log apart by putting their hands in a crevice held open by a wedge. He then knocks the wedge out, catching their fingers

in the crevice." Some of the exploits that Alley attributed to Chute were also attached to stories about an early settler named Lazarus Rowe. On July 20, 1934, an American Dialect Society interviewer collected tales of Lazarus Row from William H. Meserve of Standish, Maine (AFS 25324). The same story is attached to settler Daniel Malcolm of Brunswick, Maine, and John Lovel of Washington, New Hampshire (Dorson 1946: 122). Outside New England, a Wise County, Virginia, story collected in 1940 attributes the wedge trick to Daniel Boone (Barden 1991: no. 78); among other frontier heroes claimed to have played the same trick is Tom Quick of New York State (Harold Thompson 1939: 51). Baughman lists additional variants from Missouri, New Jersey, and New York. The motif of the trickster who traps an antagonist's hand in a split log is widespread in both legends and oral fictions. In African American culture, there is a related fictional tale (AT 38, *Claw in Split Tree*) in which animals take on the roles of the pioneer and the Indians (see, for example, Harris 1883: no. 7); a motif that covers both the fictional and the legendary accounts is K1111, "Dupe puts hand (paws) into cleft of tree (wedge, vise)." Joshua Alley's tale also includes the motif of the sole survivor (Z356, "Unique survivor"; for a parallel to the sole survivor account, see story 25 in this book).

66. *Dodging the Wolves* [AFS 25680B-25681A]. Although naturalists have often pointed out that there is not one solidly documented case of a wolf gratuitously killing and eating a human being, tales of marauding wolves have been rife in many cultures for centuries. Tales of such narrow escapes abound in American lore. For a New England version in which the hero attacks by throwing fish behind him to divert the wolves, see Dorson 1949; for a Virginia example of a slave boy who plays a fiddle to escape them, see Barden (1991: no. 141).

67. *Open, Saysem* [AFS 25682]. AT 676, *Open Sesame*. Although this tale is well known from the literary tradition of the *Thousand and One Nights*, there is no record that any similarly localized versions exist in English-language oral traditions in the United States. Neither Aarne-Thompson (1961) nor Baughman (1966) lists a single English or Anglo-American version of this tale, although Fauset recorded a variant from an African American schoolboy in Nova Scotia (1931: no. 12). The tale is not rare elsewhere in the world, however; it is substantially reported in Ireland and the Caribbean, both regions that had significant influence on the story stock of coastal Maine. It has also been reported with some frequency among French and Spanish speakers in North America. There are several Spanish versions from Colorado and New Mexico (see, for example, Espinosa 1911: 424; Rael 1942: nos. 343–45). Alley's version runs closely parallel to the Grimms' "Simelei Mountain" (KHM 142). Both stories consist principally of the following motifs: N455.3, "Secret formula for opening treasure mountain overheard from robbers (Open Sesame)" (in Alley's version, however, the magic door opens a house and not a mountain); N475, "Secret name overheard by eavesdropper"; N471, "Foolish attempt of second man to overhear secrets—he is punished"; N476, "Secret wealth betrayed by money left in borrowed money scales." When Alley said that he added a bit to the end to make the tale stick together, he is probably referring to the I-told-you-so ending, in which the first brother blames his sister-in-law for her husband's death, because this is the major detail in which his tale differs from the Grimms' and other printed versions.

68. *The Murderers* [AFS 25685B]. K950, "Treacherous murder"; S110.5, "Murderer kills all who come to certain spot."

69. *The Haunted Sloop* [AFS 25721A-25723A]. E510, "Phantom sailors and travelers"; E334.2.1, "Ghost of murdered person haunts burial spot"; E412.3, "Dead without proper funeral rites cannot rest." Joshua Alley's tale runs closely parallel to a legend collected from Eban Walter Alley by Richard Dorson in 1956 (Dorson 1964: 36–38). I have not been able to determine how closely Joshua and Eban were related, but Eban was about thirty years younger than Joshua. Eban's tale begins, like Joshua's, as the narrator's grandfather purchases a haunted ship; in Eban's

tale, as in Joshua's, a man walking the deck is accompanied by a ghost, a body is later found on the ship, and the haunting ceases after the man has been buried on land. Differences between the two tales include the town in which the grandfather purchases the ship (in Eban's tale, Rockport, rather than Rockland, is the site), the sighting of a cat aboard the haunted ship (found in Eban's tale but not in Joshua's), and the burning of the haunted vessel (found in Joshua's tale but not in Eban's).

70. *Groans, Gold, Dreams, and the Devil* [AFS 25698A,B]. Cf. E547.1, "The dead groan"; G302.4.2, "Invisibility of demons"; G302.9.1, "Demons attack men"; N571, "Devil (demon) as guardian of treasure."

Will Gilchrist. Sterling Brown (1901–1989) was best known for his poetry (Brown 1980), but his work in incorporating forms of African American folk expression into his poems (Henderson 1980) and in articulating aspects of African American folk culture was substantial. He believed that both the academic and the nonacademic African American communities benefited from cultivating a mutual closeness (Camper 1997); in this sense, his relationship with Will Gilchrist was not unique but characteristic of his vision.

The scant documentation on Gilchrist includes Botkin's letter to Harold Spivacke of the Library of Congress Music Division, dated June 19, 1944, on file in the American Folklife Center; Ms. Egypt's comments (Black History Museum Committee 1976: 19); and Lewis Jones's observations (Black History Museum Committee 1976: 52).

71. *Robbed—and Taken for a Thief* [7602A,B].

72. *More Cop Trouble* [7604A,B].

73. *Courtroom Trouble* [AFS 7604B-7605B].

74. *More Courtroom Trouble* [7603A,B, 7607A].

75. *Cop, Courtroom, and Jail Trouble* [AFS 7607B-7609A, 7610A]. I have transcribed all of the tale currently available to researchers, but the B side of disk 7609 has never been recorded on a preservation tape; instead, in error, the engineers recorded side A twice. There is a significant break in the action between 7609A and 7610A; we can assume that this part of the narrative contains more details of Gilchrist's imprisonment and explains how he was released. In the text, an extra space on p. 277 indicates the spot at which the gap in the story occurs.

Jane Muncy Fugate. Jane's earliest recorded tales, made by Leonard Roberts, include a few narratives no longer in her repertoire. In 1949, at age 11, she recorded "Bully Bornes" (AT 425, *The Search for the Lost Husband*), which she now barely remembers, and "Jack and the Bull Stripe" (AT 511A, *The Little Red Bull*), which she no longer tells, though she remembers it vividly. In 1955, Leonard Roberts recorded from her two tales that he never published: "Foxy Loxy" and "The Hairy Man." It is my belief that Roberts omitted these tales from his published collections because he (correctly) considered them to be based on literary sources. Jane's family, however, did not discriminate between tales of literary origin and tales of oral origin; both were welcome parts of their story-sharing sessions. On Jane Muncy's family, life, and storytelling techniques, see Lindahl 2001: 82–89.

76. *How I Learned My Tales* [AFC 2003/001]. Before recording any of her tales, Jane shared these reminiscences about her grandmother, with the collector and her husband present.

77. *Merrywise* [AFC 2003/001]. AT 327B, *The Dwarf and the Giant*. K1611, "Substituted caps cause ogre to kill own children"; D1521.1, "Seven-league boots"; D2074, "Attracting by magic"; DD2074.1, "Animals magically called"; D2197, "Magic dominance over animals"; cf. K711.1, "Deception into magic bag which closes on prisoner"; and K711.4, "Witch tells boy to pass down some of fruit from tree, catches hold of him and puts him in her sack when he bends

Muncy Anderson (Lindahl 2001: 55–60), that diverge significantly from each other as well as from Jane's childhood performance.

Tales bearing plots close to that of "Rawhead and Bloodybones" are rife in Europe, Asia, and the New World; *The Kind and Unkind Girls*, as the type is titled, often appears in combination with the *Cinderella* story (AT 510). Yet Jane Muncy's version has a particular resonance with the tales of the British Isles. Many of the versions worldwide feature a girl falling down a well and finding a witch in a subterranean world; it is this witch who tests and rewards the protagonist and later tests and punishes the girl's stepsister. Typical English, Scottish, and Irish versions, however, feature a quest to draw water from a well at the world's end (motif H1371.1.1*) guarded by three severed heads that demand good treatment from the girls (E341.4*, "Heads of the well grateful for bath"). The head motif appears in English tradition at least as early as George Peele's play *The Old Wives Tale* (1595), which draws upon many märchen themes and plots; in one scene, as a girl appears at a well to draw water, a head floating in the well tells her, "Stroke me smooth and combe my head." By 1849, in a storybook tale titled "The Three Heads of the Well," a head floating in a well tells the girl, "Wash me, and comb me, and lay me down softly." Similarly, in Robert Chambers's *Popular Rhymes of Scotland* (1826), in a tale titled "The Wal at the Warld's End," the head requests, "Wash me, wash me, my bonnie May [i.e., Maid], and dry me wi' yer clean linen apron." Jane's tale seems to derive directly from British tradition.

Baughman identifies fifteen U.S. versions, including seven from Kentucky and two others from elsewhere in the Appalachians: one told by Jane Gentry, the mother of Maud Long (who tells stories 13–23 in this volume); the other is a composite cobbled together by Richard Chase from many sources, including members of the Hicks-Harmon family (tellers of stories 1–32 in this volume). Among the six remaining American versions are British American tellings from Arkansas, California, New York, and Texas, an Italian American tale from New York, and a Creole version from Louisiana. Since Baughman's index was printed, distant variants of AT 480 have surfaced from Florida (Reaver 1987: no. 12) and Louisiana (Lindahl, Owens, and Harvison 1997: no. 59). The Florida version was told by an African American from Louisiana; both these Louisiana versions may have Creole influence.

82. *The Three Sillies* [AFC 2003/001]. AT 1450, *Clever Elsie*; AT 1384, *The Husband Hunts Three Persons as Stupid as His Wife*; AT 1210, *Cow Is Taken to the Roof to Graze*; AT 1336, *Diving for Cheese*; AT 1286, *Jumping into the Breeches*. This is an extraordinarily popular and flexible folktale. The "Clever Elsie" frame, in which the fiancée is sent to the cellar to fetch liquor to celebrate a wedding agreement, but she scares away her future husband as a result of her foolish fears of future disasters, is very well known through the Brothers Grimm (1987: no. 34) and Joseph Jacobs (1893: no. 2). The fiancé's search for a woman as stupid as his intended often, but not always, follows this introduction; for example, the Grimm version omits the man's quest, and at the end of the Grimms' "Clever Elsie," the heroine disappears from the village unmarried. Those tales that feature the search for three stupid people, or "sillies," vary widely in the types of foolery they describe: other American versions of AT 1384 feature the fools who try to trap sunlight in a bag (AT 1245, as told by African Americans in South Carolina) or who carry a door up a tree in order to guard it (AT 1653A, told in Georgia). Jane's tale bears the same title as the enormously popular version published by Joseph Jacobs in 1893 and often subsequently reprinted. The two plots run closely parallel, with a few differences: in Jane's tale, the girl goes to the cellar for wine rather than Jacobs's beer, and in Jane's tale it is an ax rather than a mallet that gives rise to her fears. Yet in Jane's and Jacob's versions, the frustrated fiancé witnesses the same three silly acts: trying to graze a cow on a rooftop, mistaking the moon's reflection for cheese, and trying to jump into one's pants. Jane's version inverts the episodes of

the cheese and the pants. "The Three Sillies" seems to have been a popular name for this tale in the Appalachians: Leonard Roberts collected other versions with this title. The episodes of the cow and the pants are the two most popular foolish acts in American versions of this tale.

83. *The Tarnished Star* [AFC 2003/001]. I have not been able to identify any parallels for this tale, which Jane learned from her aunt Nora.

84. *Tailipoe (1955)* [AFS 17020, part of Kenneth S. Goldstein's folktale sampler]. AT 366, *The Man from the Gallows*. The performance was recorded in April 1955 by Leonard Roberts. Jane's version bears a close resemblance to an African American tale collected in West Virginia by John Harrington Cox (1934: 341–42) and reprinted in Benjamin Botkin's *Treasury of American Folklore* (1944: 679–80), a book that was the likely source for at least one other of the tales that Jane told Roberts in 1955. Jane's family had a second version of the tale; see the narrative told by Jane's aunt Glen Muncy Anderson (story 180 in this volume) as well as the notes to stories 85 and 179.

85. *Tailipoe (2001)* [AFC 2003/001]. AT 366, *The Man from the Gallows*. See the notes to stories 84, 179, and 180 in this volume.